Praise for Kay Showker's
CARIBBEAN PORTS OF CALL

"For both the first time cruiser as well as the aficionado, this book is perfect. It is absolutely indispensable to any person taking a cruise and can lend a totally added dimension to the cruise experience."

—Arthur Frommer, "Arthur Frommer's
Almanac of Travel," The Travel Channel

"Looking for a cruise to the Caribbean? *Caribbean Ports of Call* will help you narrow down which ships to choose among and which islands to visit. Besides descriptions of the crews, cuisine, entertainment, accommodations, and other facilities on the liners, there's plenty of information on what to do ashore, too."

—*Forbes*

"A must if you're heading that way."

—*USA Today*, Larry King's People Column

"Until now there has been no book especially for the cruise ship passenger in the Caribbean who must plan to get the most out of his all-too-brief time in port. . . . In fact, there's so much information here, that even non-cruisers will benefit by carrying along this unique guide."

—*Caribbean Travel and Life* magazine

"Great advice on how to make the most of your time in port."

—*New England Bride*

"The best single source of general information (on the Caribbean). . . . Useful in tailoring your specific interests to the ships and ports available."

—Colin Bessonette, *The Atlanta Journal*

"Filling a gap between the other cruise books and standard Caribbean guides, this one-of-a-kind title is tailored to cruise travelers with limited time to explore while their ship is in port."

—*New York Post*

CARIBBEAN PORTS OF CALL SERIES

CARIBBEAN PORTS OF CALL: NORTHERN AND NORTHEASTERN REGIONS

A Guide for Today's Cruise Passenger

Fourth Edition

KAY SHOWKER

A Voyager Book

The Globe Pequot Press

OLD SAYBROOK, CONNECTICUT

Cover Photo courtesy Fraink/Waterhouse/H. Armstrong Roberts
Cover design by Schwartzman Design
Text design by MaryAnn Dubé

Library of Congress Cataloging-in-Publication Data:

Showker, Kay.
    Caribbean ports of call. Northern and northeastern regions: a guide for today's cruise passenger / Kay Showker. — 4th. ed.
      p.   cm. — (Caribbean ports of call series)
    "A Voyager Book."
    Includes index.
    ISBN 0-7627-0124-2
    1. Caribbean Area — Guidebooks. 2. West Indies — Guidebooks. 3. Ocean travel — Guidebooks. I. Title. II. Title: Northern and northeastern regions. III. Series.
    F2165.S52   1997
    917.2904'52–DC21   97-30810
                                                                    CIP

Manufactured in the United States of America
Fourth Edition/First Printing

To my mother, who shares my enthusiasm
for the pleasures of cruising
and for the Caribbean
and who is a constant source of inspiration
to all who know her.

Contents

List of Maps

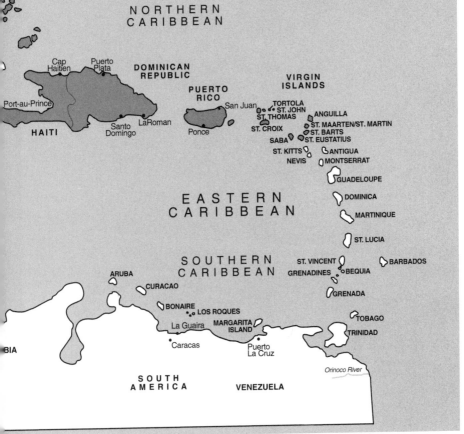

ATLANTIC
OCEAN

HAMAS

NORTHERN
CARIBBEAN

Cap
Haitien
Puerto
Plata
DOMINICAN
REPUBLIC
PUERTO
RICO
VIRGIN
ISLANDS

Port-au-Prince
San Juan
TORTOLA
ST. JOHN
ST. THOMAS
ANGUILLA
ST. CROIX
ST. MAARTEN/ST. MARTIN
ST. BARTS
ST. EUSTATIUS
SABA
HAITI
Santo
Domingo
LaRoman
Ponce

ST. KITTS
ANTIGUA
NEVIS
MONTSERRAT

GUADELOUPE

EASTERN
CARIBBEAN
DOMINICA

MARTINIQUE

ST. LUCIA

SOUTHERN
CARIBBEAN
ST. VINCENT
GRENADINES
BEQUIA
BARBADOS

ARUBA
GRENADA
CURACAO

BONAIRE
LOS ROQUES
La Guaira
MARGARITA
ISLAND
TOBAGO
TRINIDAD
BIA
Caracas
Puerto
La Cruz
Orinoco River

SOUTH
AMERICA
VENEZUELA

The Caribbean and The Bahamas Ports of Call

Basseterre, St. Kitts
Bequia, The Grenadines
*Bimini, The Bahamas
Bridgetown, Barbados
*Cap Haitien, Haiti
Castries, St. Lucia
Charlestown, Nevis
*Charlotte Amalie, St. Thomas, U.S. Virgin Islands
*Christiansted, St. Croix, U.S. Virgin Islands
*Cruz Bay, St. John, U.S. Virgin Islands
*Fort Bay, Saba
Fort-de-France, Martinique
*Frederiksted, St. Croix, U.S. Virgin Islands
*Freeport, Grand Bahama, Bahamas
Grand Cayman, Cayman Islands
*Great Guana Cay, Abaco, The Bahamas
*Gustavia, St. Barthélemy (St. Barts)
Iles des Saintes, French West Indies
*Jost Van Dyke, British Virgin Islands
Kingston, Jamaica
Kingstown, St. Vincent
Kralendijk, Bonaire
*Marigot, St. Martin
Mayreau, The Grenadines
Montego Bay, Jamaica
*Nassau, New Providence, Bahamas
*Philipsburg, Sint Maarten

Playa del Carmen (Cancun), Mexico
Plymouth, Montserrat
Pointe-à-Pitre, Guadeloupe
*Ponce, Puerto Rico
Port Antonio, Jamaica
Port-au-Prince, Haiti
Port-au-Spain, Trinidad
*Puerto Plata, Dominican Republic
Ocho Rios, Jamaica
Oranjestad, St. Eustatius
Oranjested, Aruba
Roseau, Dominica
St. George's, Grenada
St. Johns, Antigua
*Sandy Ground, Anguilla
*San Juan, Puerto Rico
San Miguel, Cozumel, Mexico
*Santo Domingo, Dominican Republic
Scarborough, Tobago
*Tortola, British Virgin Islands
*Virgin Gorda, British Virgin Islands
Willemstad, Curaçao

*These ports are covered in this volume; the balance appear in the companion volumes.

Every effort has been made to ensure the accuracy of the information in this book. But please bear in mind that prices (and exchange rates), schedules, etc., change constantly. Readers should always check with a cruise line regarding its ships and itineraries before making final plans.

PART I

CRUISING AND THE CARIBBEAN

THE UNBEATABLE COMBINATION

More than five million people are taking cruises each year and half of them are cruising in the waters of The Bahamas and the Caribbean. Proximity, prices, superb weather, and variety—of cultures, activity, scenery, sports and attractions—all are reasons that make the combination of cruising and the Caribbean a vacation choice that's hard to beat.

There are books about cruising that describe the ships in great detail and are useful in selecting one. However, these books give little or no attention to ports of call. Generally, once you are on board your ship heading for The Bahamas or the Caribbean, their value is marginal.

Likewise, a variety of guidebooks on The Bahamas and the Caribbean are available, but invariably, they assume you will arrive at a destination by plane and remain several days or longer on an island where you'll have plenty of time to explore the attractions. None is written for cruise passengers who spend only a few hours in port. Indeed, neither the standard cruise guide nor the typical Caribbean guidebook has the kind of information and detail cruise passengers need to help them plan and set priorities for their time in port. The series, *Caribbean Ports of Call* is intended to fill this gap. When it was first published in 1988, it was the first and has remained the only one of its kind. It has been designed both to help you plan your time in each port of call and to be taken along as a reference and guide in port.

Cruise passengers are as diverse a group as any set of travelers can be, and their interests and needs change, sometimes from port to port. Therefore, this book addresses a variety of those needs. For example, you may be sports-oriented— or more interested in history, art and culture. You may want only to stroll around and shop. There are people who will only venture beyond their cruise ship if they can take a tour and others who would not take an organized tour if it were offered to them free.

Many people who normally do not take tours will take one on their first visit to a new place to gain a quick, overall impression. The very newness of a place makes others want to be independent and explore on their own. Then, too, some ports lend themselves to organized touring; others are best seen by walking on one's own.

Some Caribbean ports such as San Juan are both a home base and a port of call for cruise ships. Passengers arrive by plane to board their ships and often come early or plan to stay a few days after their cruises when time is less of a constraint. They might want to plan both organized tours and independent travel.

To ensure that this book has the broadest possible application and can be used by many different kinds of cruise passengers, we have described the most frequently available shore excursions sold on board ships as well as provided specific information on how to see the port of call on your own. In any case the primary objective has been to help our readers organize and maximize their time in port to ensure they get the most out of a visit.

Caribbean Ports of Call appears in three volumes for practical reasons. We wanted each book to be portable; and we wanted the division of ports to reflect the pattern of Caribbean cruises.

This book, *Caribbean Ports of Call: Northern and Northeastern Region*, covers the ports of call on the itineraries of the majority of cruises that depart regularly from Florida to the Caribbean for lengths of one to seven days. The bulk of the cruises to The Bahamas are three- and four-day ones from Florida; those to the Caribbean are mostly seven-day cruises from Miami and Fort Lauderdale.

The companion book, *Caribbean Ports of Call: Eastern and Southern Region,* covers the ports of call for ships departing from San Juan to the Eastern and Southern Caribbean on seven-day or longer cruises and longer cruises departing from Florida and other ports that sail through the Eastern and Southern Caribbean en route to the Panama Canal.

Caribbean Ports of Call: Western Region covers the ports on itineraries that depart regularly from Florida to the Bahamas and Western Caribbean for two to seven days, as well as those that sail from Florida, Houston, New Orleans, and other ports for the Western Caribbean and Central America or en route to the Panama Canal.

The majority of Bahamas cruises last three or four days and depart from Miami, Ft. Lauderdale, and Port Canaveral in Florida. Some ships alternate their short Bahama cruises with those to the Western Caribbean.

As with my other books, I invite readers to send us their comments and suggestions on ways to improve the contents for future editions. Please let us hear from you. If we are able to use your ideas or information we will be happy to reward your effort with a copy of the next edition.

Kay Showker

HOW TO USE THIS GUIDE

Part One introduces you to the particular pleasures of the Caribbean, including its history and culture as well as its many attractions, and of cruising itself—the ideal way to become acquainted with the enjoyment of a vacation-at-sea. The section offers tips on traveling with children, cruising with your family, taking a cruise for your honeymoon and other special occasions.

Part Two provides basic advice to guide you in selecting and buying your cruise, with information on ways to save money on your cabin, no matter which ship you select. There are also suggestions on what you should know before you go, as you get ready for your trip.

Part Three has a detailed guide to each cruise line, designed to help you find the line and ship most likely to match your tastes and pocketbook. A convenient chart appears as an appendix at the back of this book, showing which cruise lines and ships stop at the various ports of call. The range of prices is indicated also.

Part Four covers the ports of call offered on the majority of Bahamas and Caribbean cruises. For easy reference, an alphabetical list of ports of call follows the Table of Contents.

PORTS OF CALL

All cruise lines would like you to take a cruise for the sake of the cruise, but they are the first to admit that most passengers select a cruise for its destinations. In the Caribbean, the destinations are as different as the American or British Virgin Islands, the French West Indies, and the Netherlands Antilles. Some are tropical and lush; others are sandy and arid. There are jungles, deserts, towering mountains, and low-lying islets. Together, the ports of a cruise itinerary provide a kaleidoscope of the region's history and cultures, scenery and sights, language and music.

Major port chapters include an introduction to the country with a general map, Fast Facts, Budget Planning, and the Author's Favorite Attractions. There is an introduction to the port and port profile with information on embarkation, facilities, location, accessibility, and local transportation. For those who prefer to tour with a group, there are descriptions of shore excursions offered by most cruise lines. For those who want to be on their own, each chapter has a walking tour with map, where appropriate, and descriptions of island attractions to see if one were to rent a car or hire a taxi.

Other major sections cover shopping, sports, dining, entertainment, cultural events, nightlife, and a list of holidays and festivals. We have tried to be consistent when at all practical in the presentation of information for each port of call. Nevertheless, each chapter has its own brief Table of Contents for convenience.

All ports, except those covered very briefly, open with "At a Glance," a generic list of attractions with ★ to ★★★★★ stars. The purpose is to give an instant picture of the port so you can judge how best to use your time. The stars are not used in the same sense as a restaurant critique; they are simply intended as a relatively objective guide to what the island has to offer; i.e., which of its attractions are comparatively the best. My personal list of Favorite Attractions could be used as a guide to tailor your own list of priorities.

A particularly difficult and frustrating aspect of writing this book has been trying to reconcile the enormous confusion and disparity in names of places, streets, historic buildings, and monuments throughout the Caribbean. Often, a particular street or building has had several names over its 200 or 300 years of history, and researchers in the past made no attempt to collate their information. In some places the local name and official name are not the same, so a street sign might use one name and a map another. More hours than we would like to recall have been spent poring over information and maps to ensure accuracy, and yet, there could still be mistakes. Please write us if you find any; we would be very grateful.

A cruise is the best and sometimes the only way to visit several Caribbean islands in one vacation. That's one of the main attractions of cruising. But if you don't plan you may come back thinking the islands are all alike. Using this book will enable you to have a balanced and varied itinerary by planning your activity in each port. In other words, if you were to spend all your time on a walking tour in Old San Juan, you might want to play golf or go diving in Nassau. If you plan to go shopping in St. Thomas because you have heard it's the best place, you should plan another activity as well because most people finish their shopping in an hour or two and then don't know what to do with themselves. A walking tour and shopping can easily be combined in Nassau, San Juan, St. Thomas, St. Croix, Antigua, Barbados, and Martinique.

Each port has a Budget Planning paragraph with tips on cost. Prices are not uniform in the Bahamas and the Caribbean. Generally, prices tend to be highest in the most popular places. You might sometimes have the feeling there's a "soak the tourist" attitude, but try to remember that a place such as Nassau must import almost all of its food and supplies. Since the islands cater mainly to Americans, costs are high because American tastes often cost a great deal to satisfy.

The islands depend on tourism. Local people want you to have a good impression of their islands so you will come back and bring your friends. They are on your side. On the other hand, don't blame them for your own gullibility or lack of planning. There are as many bad apples in New York or Miami as in San Juan or Nassau. This book gives you guidelines to help you avoid the bad ones. We hope you will use them and have a pleasant and memorable cruise.

THE PLEASURES OF THE CARIBBEAN

Sail away to the Caribbean and you will sail into a world that is foreign but familiar. It is an exotic world of vivid color and gentle trade winds. Paradise, the Caribbean is often called, and you will see why as your ship glides gently through aquamarine and sapphire waters to reach islands thick with jungle greenery down to their white sand shorelines.

The seas of The Bahamas and the Caribbean stretch across more than a million square miles from the coast of Florida to the coast of South America. The islands form an arc that cradles the Caribbean Sea and separates it from the Atlantic Ocean. The Caribbean region, known as the Eighth Continent of the World, contains tiny islands and islets, some no more than the peaks of long-submerged mountains; others are larger than fifteen states of the United States and have the geographic variety of a continent. The Caribbean has as many independent island-nations as there are countries in Europe, and they draw their heritage from the four corners of the globe.

LOCATING THE ISLANDS

On a map with the arm of the compass pointing north, the islands closest to the United States are known as the Greater Antilles; they include Cuba, the Caymans, Jamaica, Haiti, the Dominican Republic, and Puerto Rico. All but

Cuba are visited by cruise ships from U.S. ports and have daily, direct air service from New York, Miami, and other major U.S. cities.

The Bahamas and the British colony of the Turks and Caicos lie north of the Greater Antilles and generally southeast of Florida. They are entirely in the Atlantic Ocean, but because their tropical environment is so similar to that of the Caribbean, they are thought of as being part of the region. The Bahamas, but not the Turks and Caicos, are cruise stops; both have air service from the United States.

Farther along the compass to the Eastern Caribbean are the Lesser Antilles, the group starting with the Virgin Islands on the north and curving south to Grenada. The northern of these many small islands are known as the Leewards and comprise the United States and British Virgin Islands, Anguilla, St. Maarten, St. Barts, Saba, St. Eustatius, St. Kitts, Nevis, Antigua, Barbuda, Montserrat, and Guadeloupe. The south islands, called the Windwards, include Dominica, Martinique, St. Lucia, Barbados, St. Vincent and the Grenadines, and Grenada.

The Virgin Islands, St. Maarten, Antigua, Guadeloupe, Martinique, St. Lucia, Barbados, and Grenada are frequent cruise stops and have direct air service from the United States; the others can be reached by local airlines, and most are stops for small ships, particularly during the winter cruise season. In the south are Aruba, Bonaire, Curaçao, and Trinidad and Tobago, which lie off the coast of Venezuela. In the western Caribbean off the Yucatán Peninsula are Cancun and Cozumel, two islands belonging to Mexico.

Along the 2,000-mile Caribbean chain nature has been extravagant with its color, variety, and beauty. Verdant mountains rise from sun-bleached shores. Between the towering peaks and the sea, rivers and streams cascade over rocks and hillsides and disappear into mangrove swamps and deserts. Fields of flowers, trees with brilliant scarlet and magenta blossoms, and a multitude of birds and butterflies fill the landscape. The air, refreshed by quick tropical showers, is scented with spices and fruit.

And this is only nature's act above the ground. Below the sea is a wonderland of exotic fish in a setting often called the most beautiful in the world. Rainbows of brilliantly colored fish of every size and shape dart endlessly through the crystal waters to hide in caves and grottos, mingle between the swaying purple seafans, and burrow into boulders of coral and sponge.

Yet, what makes the Caribbean islands unique is not simply their beauty or geography but rather, the combination of this lovely and exotic scenery and the kaleidoscope of rich and diverse cultures. Like the vibrant landscape they reflect, the people and their cultures have evolved from a wide range of traditions, music, dance, art, architecture, and religions from around the world.

The intermingling of people and cultures has been so extensive that today it is hard to know a person's origin simply by looking at his or her face. And it happened so long ago that, more often than not, people do not know their roots. Some came from England, Spain, France, Ireland, Holland, Portugal, Sweden, and Africa; others from India, China, and the Mediterranean—all to be stirred into the greatest of the world's melting pots.

ENTER COLUMBUS

Before 1492 when Columbus sighted the New World, the lands of the Caribbean region were populated by Indian tribes. They included the Ciboneys who probably came from South America about 3,000 years ago. They were followed by the peaceful Tainos (known as the Arawaks, their more frequently used linguistic name) and the fierce Caribs who had been in the region about 600 years when Columbus arrived. It is from the latter group that the Caribbean Sea takes its name.

But in less than a century after Columbus's voyages, the native population had almost vanished because of war, disease, and enslavement. Their only survivors are a small group of the descendants of the Carib Indians on the island of Dominica. Our knowledge of the Indians is meager, but fortunately new research and excavations in Antigua, The Bahamas, Jamaica, Haiti, Puerto Rico, the Dominican Republic, and elsewhere are helping us gain a better understanding of them.

Columbus's discoveries brought waves of explorers, conquerors, settlers, merchant sailors, pirates, privateers, traders, and slavers from Europe, the Middle East, Africa, and Asia. For two centuries the West Indies, as the region came to be known, were a pawn in the battle for the New World which raged among the European nations. While they fought, they plundered the region's riches and searched for a route to the East. These were savage times, which disgraced even the noblest of aims.

By the dawn of the 18th century, Spain, England, France, Denmark, and Holland had sliced up the region, had planted their flags on various islands, and had begun to colonize their new territories. Gradually they replaced the decimated Indian population with African slaves to work the land that was to yield new fortunes in sugar, rum, cotton, and tobacco. After slavery was abolished in the British colonies in the 19th century (three decades before its abolition in the United States), the Africans were replaced by indentured laborers from Asia. They were in turn followed by waves of immigrants from the Mediterranean to the Americas in search of a better life.

Once entrenched in the Caribbean, the European governments began to make burdensome demands on their colonies. There many rebellions. Haiti's revolt was the only one to succeed in a complete break and led to the establishment of the first black republic in the Western Hemisphere two decades after the American Revolution.

Following abolition and the invention of the steam engine and cotton gin, the West Indies lost the base of their economy and soon became neglected outposts of European empires. With the end of the Spanish-American War, Spain gave up her holdings in the New World, and after World War II, Britain, France, and the Netherlands were forced to change their relationships with most of their colonies, granting them independence in most cases.

But the road to independence has been rough. The 1970s, with the oil crisis, inflation, and the world-wide recession, were particularly hard on these islands, which have few resources other than their people and natural beauty. Adding to their burdens, the troubled 1960s in the United States had sent shock waves of black power demands and rising expectations that were now washing ashore in the Caribbean. But from the experience a new Caribbean has taken shape.

CARIBBEAN CULTURE

Down through the centuries, the conquerors and settlers, the sailors and slaves, the merchants and workers, and the visitors and vacationers brought with them parts of their cultures—their church steeples, temples, brogues, high tea, high mass, masks, drums, colors, songs, dances, high-rises, and hamburgers. Out of this mélange has grown a new Caribbean as colorful, rich, and diverse as the landscape in which it flowers.

Although it might be difficult to single out an Anguillan or a Cruzan by sight, there is no mistaking the lilt of a Jamaican's voice when he speaks or a Trinidadian when he sings. Haitian art is instantly recognizable. The beguine began in Martinique; the merengue in the Dominican Republic. Calypso and steel bands were born in Trinidad, reggae in Jamaica, and salsa in Puerto Rico.

Reggae king Bob Marley, dancer/choreographer Rex Nettleford of Jamaica, and showman Geoffrey Holder of Trinidad are known to us as international stars, but throughout the Caribbean there is talent and creativity. Audiences around the world have enjoyed the artistry of the National Dance Theatre of Jamaica and the symphony orchestras of the Dominican Republic and Puerto Rico. Art galleries in Puerto Rico and Jamaica are filled with the works of local artists and sculptors that celebrate the joys and cry for the tragedies of the Caribbean experience. From Jamaica and Haiti to Martinique and Trinidad, bold jewelry and colorful fabrics have found their way onto the international stage of high fashion. Oscar de la Renta is Dominican.

The best time to see the evidence of the Caribbean's creative energy is during Carnival. Trinidad's Carnival is the best known; it rivals Rio's in spectacle and makes Mardi Gras in New Orleans pale by comparison. Trinidad's festival is held at the traditional pre-Lenten time, but Carnival in the Caribbean often developed from local events and is held at different times of the year. For example, Crop-Over in Barbados in July stems from the celebration of the harvest, and Antigua's Carnival in August started as a welcome to the British monarch during her visit in the 1960s.

Caribbean architecture, like its art, is a composite

of world cultures. English churches and Spanish cathedrals stand alongside warm-weather adaptations of Dutch farmhouses and French manors. The center of new Santo Domingo with its striking modern architecture is juxtaposed with the oldest colonial city in the New World. Victorian gingerbread mansions are pauses in the tango of brightly painted houses in the towns and villages of Haiti. Minarets and steeples pierce the sky of Trinidad; the oldest synagogue in the Western Hemisphere is a Curaçao landmark.

A NEW CUISINE

Caribbean cuisine, too, is a cornucopia of tastes from the four corners of the globe—a unique blend that evolved over the centuries and combines nature's bounty with the richness of the region's culinary heritage. The Spaniards not only discovered the New World, they found a continent of exotic fruits and vegetables Europeans had never seen: avocado, cassava, maize, peppers, papaya, chocolate, and potatoes, to name a few. From the natives, the Spaniards learned how to use the new ingredients and eventually adapted them for their own cooking; many became basic elements in classic Spanish and French cuisine. Others who arrived in the Caribbean added their specialties as well: the Danes, Dutch, Portuguese, English, Africans, Chinese, Indians, Greeks, Turks, Indonesians, and Arabs—all made their contributions.

Out of this potpourri evolved a Creole or West Indian cuisine eaten by the local people. It includes such standards as Cuban and Puerto Rican black bean soup, Jamaican pepperpot, St. Kitts goat water or mutton stew, Grenadian callaloo, and Guadeloupan fish cakes or accra. But until recently, outsiders had little opportunity to sample native dishes because only a handful of small hotels and guest houses served them.

Now that has changed. Following independence, a new generation of hotels and restaurant chefs has been developing a new and sophisticated Caribbean cuisine. Their creativity is being encouraged by their restaurant and hotel associations, which stage annual competitions judged by international food critics. The new cuisine has

resulted in such wonderful creations as Cold Papaya Bisque, Crab and Callaloo Soup, Breadfruit Vichyssoise, Flying Fish in Crust, Lobster Calypso, Fricassee of Red Snapper, Breadfruit Soufflé, Callaloo Quiche, Chicken Creole with Mango, Banana Lime Tart, Avocado Ice Cream, and Soursop Chiffon Pie, to name a few.

The starting point in the making of Caribbean cuisine is the market; a cultural potpourri where Africa meets the Caribbean and mixes with the Orient. Mountains of mango, melon, and banana and pyramids of papaya, pineapple, and pomegranate are stacked next to the plantain, okra, dasheen, coconut, cassava, cloves, coffee, and cinnamon. All are sold alongside piles of clothes and shoes to be haggled over by the townfolk and villagers. Visitors, too, frequently join the mélange because there is no better place than a market to take in the Caribbean kaleidoscope.

A WEALTH OF ACTIVITY

Against the Caribbean's rich and varied geographic and cultural landscape, visitors will find a cornucopia of sports and recreational facilities, entertainment, sight-seeing, and shopping possibilities.

For sports, the Caribbean has few rivals. Across its million square miles, sailing is suited for any type of boat from Sailfish to ocean yachts. Antigua, the Virgin Islands, St. Vincent, and Grenada are noted for superb anchorage and specialize in charters. Many yachtsmen consider the stretch south from St. Vincent through the Grenadines the finest sailing water in the world.

Snorkeling and scuba diving are excellent throughout the warm and exceptionally clear waters of the region. And while divers wander through the magnificent reefs and look for sunken treasures, nonswimmers need not miss the excitement. They can see it from the comfort of a glass-bottom boat, recreational submarines, or underwater observatories. The excursions have proven so popular they are quickly becoming part of the cruise agenda.

Golf is at its greatest on championship layouts created by the most famous names in golf course design. The Bahamas and Puerto Rico each offer a dozen championship courses; Jamaica has six of them. And they have the added attraction of the Caribbean's beautiful and colorful landscape decorating the greens. Many cruise lines have special programs that incorporate golf into their cruises, and most can make arrangements for their passengers to play golf at most ports of call.

You can also play tennis, squash, or polo and fish in the ocean or in mountain streams. There's horseback riding, jogging, hiking, biking, surfing, jet skiing, kayaking, windsurfing, waterskiing, parasailing, rafting, and rowing.

If you are less athletic or simply want to enjoy nature and the outdoors, there are miles-long, powdery sand beaches where you can stretch out for the day with no more company than a couple of birds. You can spend the morning gathering shells, have a picnic by a secluded cove, stroll along bougainvillea-decorated lanes, or wander along mountainsides overlooking deep green valleys and sapphire seas.

Throughout the region there are national parks, bird sanctuaries, mountain trails, and panoramas of magnificent scenery. Visitors can have a close-up look at a rain forest, drive into the crater of a volcano, bike over rolling meadows, hike through deep ravines, and explore some caves along the way.

DIVERSITY OF DESTINATIONS

No two Caribbean islands are alike; each has a personality, distinctive geographic features, and special charm with which it beguiles its admirers. Some are tiny idyllic hideaways far from the beaten path with names familiar only to mapmakers and yachtsmen. Others are big in size or seem big because of their strong character and regional influence; while others are big on action with gambling, shopping, and sophisticated dining and nightlife. Some islands have enough sports activity and entertainment to keep you busy every hour of the day; others test your ability to enjoy simple pleasures. Few islands fit neatly into only one category; most have features that contrast and overlap. One of the great advantages of a cruise is the chance to visit several destina-

tions at a time and sample some of this variety.

A visit to any Caribbean island is a visit to a foreign country—including those such as Puerto Rico and the U.S. Virgin Islands, which are under the American flag. You can have a Dutch treat in St. Maarten, order lunch in French in Martinique, and pick up some golf tips in Spanish in Puerto Rico. You will be able to count francs in Guadeloupe, pesos in the Dominican Republic, and gilders in Curaçao; and add to your kids' stamp collections from such offbeat places as Antigua, Dominica, Saba, and Grenada.

At the same time that you experience the new sights and sounds, enjoy the new cultures and cuisine, you have the security of knowing that English is used and understood throughout the islands. You can also count on having the amenities we Americans take for granted. The Caribbean is the best of both worlds—the exotic flavor of a foreign land in surroundings that are as familiar as home.

The Caribbean is a learning experience, too. The region is rich in historic monuments, old forts, plantation homes, sugar mills, churches and synagogues that have been beautifully restored and put to contemporary use as art galleries, boutiques, cafes, restaurants, inns, and museums. They help bring the region's history to life. Amateur archaeologists can start with the Indian petroglyphs on St. John and pick up a handful of ancient flintstones on Antigua, while history buffs walk the ramparts of El Morro in Puerto Rico. In Old San Juan in Puerto Rico or Nelson's Dockyard in Antigua, they can walk through the colonial history of the New World.

The oldest church of the Western Hemisphere is in Santo Domingo. It held the tomb of Christopher Columbus until 1992, when the memorial monument was moved to the Columbus Lighthouse as part of the Columbus Quincentennial commemoration. A park on Curaçao has a statue of Peter Stuyvesant, the island's governor before he made his name in New York. The statue of Lord Nelson dominates Trafalgar Square in Barbados; Napoleon's Josephine graces La Savane in her birthplace of Martinique. All are reminders of the span and complexity of the Caribbean's history.

THE NEW CARIBBEAN

Learning about its history is also a way to help understand the region today. It is bound to Europe by history, language, and culture; to Africa or Latin America by sentiment and emotion; and to the United States by economic and strategic necessity. So far, the islands have shown they have the ability to survive on their own, but their problems have certainly not disappeared. For some, they have worsened.

The brightest prospect on the horizon is tourism. Already tourist dollars pay for schools, roads, hospitals, and many other necessities. Tourism has limits, however. Too much can destroy the very elements that make the Caribbean so attractive.

Finally, a word about the people and pace of Paradise. Life in the Caribbean is leisurely. It is easy for Americans to become impatient with the slow pace of things, but remember, if you can, it's precisely the unhurried atmosphere you have come to enjoy. Americans often misinterpret the islanders' shyness and conservative nature toward strangers as unfriendliness. But after traveling from one end of the Caribbean to the other for two decades, I know from experience that the people of the Caribbean are as friendly as their music and as warm as their sunshine. They have wit, talent, dignity, and grace. They are generous and kind and will go out of their way to be helpful if you meet them with respect and greet them with a genuine smile.

I love the Caribbean. Its pleasures are like magic. I recognize the elements that create the magic, although I don't quite know what makes it happen. Yet, the experience is so delightful that I am happy to let the mystery remain.

THE PLEASURES OF CRUISING

People take cruises for various reasons. Some people are looking for fun, companionship, excitement, and romance—whether it's the romance of the sea or romance at sea. A cruise offers a change of pace and relaxation, new faces, new places and a foreign environment. It is a different kind of holiday. Indeed, a cruise is so completely unlike other holiday experiences, it is difficult for those who have never taken one to imagine its pleasures or realize its true built-in value.

But to understand cruising today, let's step back a moment to consider the changes in the nature of steamship travel that have helped to create today's cruising. Prior to the 1960s, most ships sailed between New York and Europe; Caribbean cruising was limited to the winter season, mainly because ships were not air-conditioned then. With the advent of the jet, which all but sank transatlantic passenger steamship travel, many ships shifted to the Caribbean in search of new markets.

Once the ships had taken up their new home ports, the pressure was on the cruise lines to get passengers from big centers in the northern United States to southern warm-weather ports with a minimum of difficulty. And this led to the birth of air/sea packages—the most value-packed holiday on the market today.

In other words, the steamship companies whose very existence was threatened by the advent of the jet in the early 1960s came to realize by the 1970s that the airlines were their best friends. Savings in fuel and the elimination of travel to and from northern ports in inclement weather were boons. At the same time the cruise companies broadened their appeal by changing the old image of cruising from that of a pleasure only for the rich and idle to a new one that would attract people from all walks of life.

CHANGING LIFESTYLES

Traditional steamship travel had three separate classes, but by the 1960s in the climate of America's growing affluence, class distinctions had become outmoded. Cruise lines were happy to acknowledge the change. By eliminating the facilities required to maintain separate classes, they had additional space for recreational facilities and entertainment. Thus, cruise ships became floating resorts, especially for warm-weather cruising.

In the past, people saved all their lives to make a single trip; the ultimate dream was a trip around the world by ship. Today, the stress of modern life and the pressures of work and urban living have made it desirable—even necessary—to get away often, if only for a few days. Shorter, less expensive cruises have not only enabled more people to take cruises, but to take them more often.

Speedier modes of transportation combined with greater affluence have made the short break the norm, especially for city dwellers. And nothing could be more ideal for the short, recuperative break than a cruise. No matter what your job or profession, a cruise offers a more complete break from the workaday world than almost anything you can do. The expanse of sea and open sky brings a freedom and an awareness of space that can be totally therapeutic.

Besides fitting in with national vacation trends, the popularization of cruise holidays has no doubt been helped by popular television programs such as "The Love Boat" and by satisfied customers who are spreading the word. Surveys show that cruising has upward of an 80-percent satisfaction rate, a record few other vacation alternatives can match.

Convenience and Hassle-Free Travel

A cruise ship is no farther away than the nearest airport. When cruise lines began combining air transportation with the cruise and selling them as one product—an air/sea package—they not only made the trip more economical, but also easier and more convenient for vacationers even from Salt Lake City or Detroit, who had never before dreamed of taking a cruise. The cruise lines, consequently, have found thousands of new customers.

Assembling all the parts of a vacation in advance has made possible a hassle-free holiday from the moment the passenger's travel begins. The air/sea combination is merely an extension of what the ship offers: namely, accommodations, meals, recreation, entertainment, sports, sight-seeing, and transportation from port to port.

Once you have checked in at the airport in your hometown, you won't have to bother with your luggage again. It will be waiting in your cabin. You will be brought from the airport by motor coach to the ship that awaits you at your port of embarkation without having to tote bags or pay extra for the transfer or give tips.

The ease and comfort with which you can visit places that are hard to reach on your own are part of cruising's great attractions. Almost any place in the Caribbean can be reached by plane but if you tried visiting Nassau, St. Thomas, St. Maarten, and Martinique in a week, you would spend most of your vacation in airports! Indeed, the more complex the travel—the more changes of hotels, trains, buses, and planes that a similar itinerary by land requires—the more attractive travel by ship can be. Your ship is not only your transportation, it is also your hotel. And that's where you gain the ultimate convenience—you pack and unpack only once. In my book, that's a real vacation!

The True Escape

Cruising is the ultimate escape. For a few days you can turn off your worries and live out your fantasies. There are no phones ringing, no television blaring, no computers blinking. Without even working at it, you relax. The pure air, the gentle movement of the ship gliding through the water and the unhurried rhythm of shipboard life provide an instant antidote to the pollution, noise, and pressures of city life.

Because people travel to escape does not mean they seek isolation. On the contrary, meeting new people is part of the fun of travel and there is no better or easier place to do this than on ship. You feel the friendly atmosphere as soon as you start up the gangplank where the smiling staff welcomes you aboard, eager to serve you and see you enjoy yourself. You meet people from all over the country and from other parts of the world in an atmosphere of camaraderie. Yet, if you really do not like to socialize, you can stand aside. Or, if you are shy about meeting people, the ship's staff has dozens of clever ways to make it easy.

ON-BOARD ACTIVITIES

A cruise is what a vacation should be—fun! In fact, there are more ways to have fun on a cruise than there are hours in the day to enjoy them all. People often have the false notion they will become bored on a cruise, but there's little chance of boredom if one takes advantage of all that is available.

For active people, there is swimming, fitness classes, yoga, deck tennis, ping pong, workout gyms, and exercise and dance classes. On some ships, on-board sports and fitness programs are combined with organized activities in port for snorkeling, scuba diving, sailing, windsurfing, tennis, golf, and fishing. Or you can simply head for a beach and do any of these activities on your own.

With lavish meals so much a part of the cruise experience, it might seem incongruous for lines to spend millions on elaborate facilities and fitness programs to turn their floating resorts into floating health spas. But once again, it is the cruise lines' response to changing lifestyles. Many have added new light dishes to their menus and marked off parts of their dining rooms and lounges for nonsmokers.

Those who like to learn are kept busy too. Ships frequently have instructors and tournaments for bridge, backgammon, chess, language, arts and crafts, wine tasting, cooking, and computers, to name a few. These enrichment programs, as the cruise lines call them, vary a great deal from ship to ship and cruise to cruise. Some ships build a cruise around a special theme such as bridge, mystery, or photography; others offer annual cruises featuring classical music or jazz festivals-at-sea. Bingo is alive and well on all ships, and so are other competitive games, along with casinos and slot machines. Many ships have video game rooms or computer rooms and computer classes.

Movies—new releases and old favorites—are shown daily in the ship's theater or on closed-circuit television in your cabin. The same film is scheduled twice or more and at different times so that everyone has a chance to see it. The theater is also used for such special events as concerts by visiting artists, fashion shows, or Broadway-style shows. And if this array of activity is still not enough, there's the visit to the bridge, the engine room, and the kitchens.

Every evening before you go to bed, a schedule of the next day's activities is slipped under your door. You can take in all of it, pick and choose, or ignore the lot of it.

A MOVEABLE FEAST

Cruising has given new meaning to "A Moveable Feast." The feasting starts with morning coffee and tea for the early birds and breakfast in the dining room or on one of the parlor decks. Mid-morning bouillon, afternoon tea, and the midnight buffet are cruise traditions. These snacks are provided in addition, of course, to lunch by the pool and the regular lunch and dinner served in the dining room. There, every day at every meal, the menu has three, four, or more selections for each course and a half-dozen courses for each meal. The ships also cater to special dietary requirements and can provide salt-free, diabetic, vegetarian, or kosher meals.

Of course, every line believes it offers the best cuisine on the high seas, and all work hard to distinguish themselves. Ships catering to Americans offer international menus that include familiar American dishes at every meal as well as ethnic choices that reflect the vessel's ownership or the makeup of the crew.

But dining on a cruise is a much more important part of the cruise experience than simply eating a meal. In addition to sampling specialties and new dishes, you have the chance to get to know your traveling companions in a relaxed and congenial atmosphere and to enjoy the best and most gracious part of shipboard service. Dining room staffs often have the training and polish found in the finest European hotels and restaurants; they take great pride in their work. The food, the wine, the music, the dances, the language, the people—all give a ship its personality and ambience and make a cruise a special kind of holiday.

Nightlife is another attraction on a cruise. Cruise lines go out of their way to provide a variety of entertainment for different age groups and interests. Almost all cruise ships have nightclubs and discotheques, and most in the Caribbean have casinos. Many of the larger ships offer fullscale Broadway- and Las Vegas-style shows. Best of all, they're there to enjoy only one or two decks away.

Each night when the ship is not in port, there is a different theme: ladies' night, the Captain's dinner, and at least one masquerade party. Kids particularly enjoy the masquerade, and most are ingenious about making something out of nothing. They get help with their costumes from the cruise staff, and so can you.

CRUISING WITH CHILDREN

A cruise is one of the best possible vacations for families with children. There is no end to a child's fascination with a ship. It is a totally new experience with an environment different from anything they have known at home. It's also an education. The crews—many of whom are away from their own children—are wonderful with young passengers. There are always baby-sitters around, and you are never far from the children when you want to spend time on your own.

Once strictly adult territory, some cruise ships are so well equipped for children, they could be called floating camps. Trained youth counselors, often teachers and counselors on holiday or leave from their regular jobs, plan and supervise shipboard activities geared to specific age groups. Some ships have year-round counselors; others provide them during summer and other traditional vacation periods.

During the first day at sea, the counselors meet with parents and their children to review the week's activities and answer questions about facilities. Each morning a printed schedule especially for children is slipped under their door with the program for the day. Pre-teens are kept busy with pool parties, arts and crafts projects, movies, masquerades, scavenger hunts, and special entertainment such as magic shows, sports tournaments on deck, "Coketails," ice cream parties, and talent shows.

Teenagers are likely to shun structured activities, and many prefer to be on their own. But the ship helps them get acquainted with a party. There are also pizza, hamburger, and disco parties to help ensure the shy ones don't miss out on the fun. Some ships give the teenagers exclusive use of the disco while the adults are at cocktails or dinner. Dance contests, sports tournaments, fitness classes, foreign-language lessons, and theatrical productions are some of the other activities.

Shows with magicians, puppets, dancers, and singers are big hits with kids as much as with their parents. And of course, there is children's favorite pastime—eating. Four servings of ice cream and three of pie, if they want them. A cruise might be the one time in your life you will hear your children say, "I can't eat any more."

Children often get their own tours of the bridge and even get to meet the captain. They see the radar, navigational charts, and equipment and often learn more about the ship and how it operates than many adults do. They learn about travel etiquette and different foods, experience new kinds of service, and learn how to socialize in new environments. They might also learn how to snorkel, count in francs or pesos, and meet people of faraway lands.

In port, the family can take the ship's organized tours or explore on its own. Counselors on some ships plan shore excursions especially for the youngsters. One of the great advantages of a cruise is its room for flexibility. If one member of the family does not want to go on a tour, it need not cause a family crisis. The ship is in full operation even when it is in port; one never need worry about being left alone.

FAMILY REUNIONS

Cruises are not only great for families with children but those with grandchildren too. And they are ideal for family reunions, especially for families scattered around the country who find it hard to gather in one place—and do all that cooking! A cruise gives all members of the family equal time to spend with their favorite aunts, uncles, and cousins. Thanks to a ship's wide range of activity, there's always plenty to do, regardless of the participant's age. By sailing together, family members across the country can take advantage of the free air plans and group rates. Your travel agent can piece the parts together for you. All you need to do is agree on the cruise and the date.

IDEAL HONEYMOON

A cruise is what a honeymoon should be—romantic, relaxing, glamorous, different, and fun. It is a fairytale come true. And it has the ingredients for a perfect honeymoon: privacy when you want it, attention when you need it; sports, music, dancing and entertainment to share, sight-seeing to enjoy. The atmosphere is a happy one. Honeymooners need not have a worry in the world. Everything is at their fingertips including breakfast in bed. There are no big decisions to make, no travel hassles to face.

A cruise offers them total flexibility in making plans. No matter what the wedding date, they will be able to find a cruise. And thanks to the all-inclusive nature of a cruise, a couple can know in advance the cost of the honeymoon and plan accordingly.

A travel agent can also arrange for the honeymooners' extras that most ships offer. These might include champagne on the first night, flowers in the cabin, a wedding cake, an album for honeymoon photos, and a reception by the captain. Almost all ships have tables for two and cabins with double beds, which a travel agent can request at the time the reservations are made.

Contrary to common belief, ship captains cannot perform marriages aboard ship unless they are state-licensed. Some ships have a ceremony during the cruise for reaffirmation of vows and couples are given certificates as a remembrance. Some ships also double as a wedding chapel in their home port. The cruise line will provide a notary to conduct the wedding ceremony or you can bring your own clergyman aboard to officiate. The ceremony can be simple or lavish and can be followed by a reception. Some couples have been known to take their wedding parties with them on their cruises!

PART II

SELECTING A CRUISE

SELECTING A CARIBBEAN CRUISE

With so many cruises going to so many different places, selecting one can be difficult. My suggestion is to start your planning at a travel agency. About 95 percent of all cruises are purchased through travel agents. It will not cost more than buying a cruise directly from a cruise line, and it will save you time.

USING A TRAVEL AGENT

A good travel agency stocks the brochures of the leading cruise lines; these show prices and details on the ship's itineraries and facilities. An *experienced agent* will help you understand the language of a cruise brochure, read a deck plan, and make reservations. The agent will help you make comparisons and guide you to the selection of a ship and an itinerary to match your interests. Your agent can book your dining room table, handle a particular request such as for an anniversary party or a special diet, and make special arrangements for honeymooners. Agents also know about packages and discounts that can help you save money.

In recent years, with the boom in cruising, there has been a rapid growth in travel agencies that sell only cruises. Such specialized agencies are more likely than general agencies, which sell all the products of travel, to have staffs with firsthand knowledge of many ships and can give you advice on which cabin to choose, the quality of the cuisine and entertainment, and the activities available. In short, an agent should be able to give you a profile of the ship, its crew and its personality. If not, you should go to another agency.

THE BUILT-IN VALUE OF A CRUISE VACATION

Of all the attractions of cruising, none is more important than value. For one price you get transportation, accommodations, meals, entertainment, use of all facilities, and a host of recreational activity. The only items not included are tips, drinks, a few personal services such as hairdressers, sometimes port tax, and shore excursions. There are no hidden costs.

Dollar for dollar, it's hard to beat a cruise for value. To make an accurate assessment of how the cost of a cruise compares with other types of holidays, be sure to compare similar elements. A holiday at sea should be compared with a holiday at a luxury resort, because the quality of service, food, and entertainment on most cruises is available only at posh resorts.

The average price of a one-week Caribbean cruise is about $200 to $250 per day and including all the ingredients previously described; shorter three- and four-day Bahamas cruises are lower, ranging from $130 to $150 per day.

Stretching Your Budget

Air/sea packages provide cruise passengers further measurable savings in airfare. Because cruise lines transport so many passengers to and from their departure cities on a regular basis, they can buy air transportation in volume at low group rates and offer it as "free air." There is no loss in the quality of air service and since, more often than not, the air travel is on regularly scheduled flights, cruise passengers have flexibility in making their travel plans. The packages also provide savings on baggage handling, two-way transfers from the airport to the ship, and other features.

Air/sea combinations are available in two forms: an all-in-one package combining a cruise and air transportation in one price; or a second type in which the cruise is priced separately and an air supplement is added on to the cruise price, or a credit for air transportation from one's hometown to the ship's nearest departure port is offered. The amount of the supplement or credit varies from one cruise line to another. But, usually, the supplement is slightly more the farther away from the departure port you live and is always listed in the cruise line's brochure. Still, the total cost is generally less to you than if the cruise and air transportation were purchased separately. The details are spelled out in the cruise line's brochure. Ask your travel agent to explain how the package works as it can be confusing.

Although air/sea packages save you money, it goes without saying that some definitely represent larger savings than others, depending on the cruise line, the cruise, and the time of year. Every line's policy is different and policies vary not only from line to line, but even from cruise to cruise on any specific ship. The introduction of many new cruise lines and cruise ships, particularly in the Caribbean, has created a buyer's market. It won't last forever, but while the cruise lines wait for demand to catch up with supply, there are real bargains available. As always, it pays to shop around.

SELECTING A SHIP

The ship and the cruise line's reputation are other considerations in making your selection. Not only do ships differ; so do their passengers. You are more likely to enjoy a cruise with people who are seeking a similar type of holiday and with whom you share a community of interests and activities. A good travel agent who specializes in selling cruises is aware of the differences and should be able to steer you to a ship that's right for you. But before you visit an agent or begin to cull the colorful and enticing brochures, here are some tips on the items affecting cost that can help you in making a selection.

SELECTING A CABIN

The largest single item in the cost of a cruise is the cabin, also known as a stateroom. The cost of a cabin varies greatly and is determined by its size and location. Generally, the cabins on the top deck are the largest and most expensive; the prices drop and the cabins narrow on each deck down from the top. (Elevators and stairs provide access between decks.) But the most expensive cabins are not necessarily the best. There are other factors to consider.

Almost all cabins on cruise ships have private bathrooms, but the size and fittings vary and affect cost. For example, cabins with full bathtubs are more expensive than those with showers only. Greater standardization of cabins is a feature of most new cruise ships.

Outside cabins are more costly than inside ones, although on new ships 75 percent or more of the cabins are outside ones. There is a common misconception that inside cabins are to be avoided. It dates back to the days before air-conditioning when an outside cabin above the water line was desirable because the porthole was used for ventilation. Cruise ships today are climate-controlled and an inside cabin is as comfortable as an outside one. What's more, on a Caribbean cruise particularly, you will spend very little time in your cabin; it is mainly a place to sleep and change clothes. An inside cabin often provides genuine savings and is definitely worth investigating for those on a limited budget.

For the most stable ride, the deck at water level or below has less roll (side to side motion) and the cabins in the center of the ship have the least pitch (back and forth motion). But these cabins also cost more than those in the front (fore) or the back (aft) of the ship. Fore (or the bow) has less motion and is therefore preferable to aft (or the stern) where sometimes there is vibration from the ship's engines.

A ship's deck plan shows the exact location of each cabin and its fittings. It does not give the dimensions of the cabin, but one can have a reasonable estimate since beds are standard single size—about 3 x 6 feet. Some ships have double beds, or twin beds that can be converted to doubles on request. The latter facility is becoming a standard feature on new ships.

Some ships have single cabins; otherwise, a passenger booking a cabin alone pays a rate that is one and a half times the price per person for two sharing a cabin. A few ships offer special single rates on certain cruises or reserve a few cabins for single occupancy at the same rate as the per person rate on a shared basis plus a small supplement. Your travel agent should be able to give you specific information about singles rates.

OTHER COST FACTORS

As might be expected, rates for the winter season in the Caribbean are higher than in the spring, summer, or fall. Cruises over Christmas, New Year's, and other major holidays are usually the year's most expensive, but often, real bargains are to be found on cruises immediately before or after a holiday season when demand drops and lines are eager to stimulate business.

The length of the cruise bears directly on its cost. Cruises of one or two weeks average $200–$250 per person per day, but very short ones, such as the one- to four-day cruises between Florida and the Bahamas, run as low as $130–$150 per person per day during high season. These prices drop by one-third or more during off-peak periods and special promotions.

The cost also varies depending on the ship's itinerary. For example, it is more economical for a line to operate a set schedule of the same ports throughout the year, such as the ships departing weekly from Florida to the Caribbean, than it is to change itineraries every few weeks. The latter tend to be the most expensive cruises.

Family Rates

If you are planning a family cruise, look for cruise lines that actively promote family travel and offer special rates for children or for third and fourth persons in a cabin. It means a bit of crowding but can yield big savings. Family rates vary from one cruise line to another. As a rule of thumb, children sharing a cabin with two paying adults get discounts of 50 percent or more of the minimum fare. Qualifying ages vary, too, with a child usually defined as 2 to 12, and sometimes up to 17 years. Some lines have teen fares, while at certain times of the year others have free or special rates for the third or fourth person sharing a cabin with two full-fare adults, regardless of age. Most lines permit infants under 2 years to travel free of charge.

CRUISE DISCOUNTS

To publicize a new ship or itinerary, to attract families, younger passengers, new passengers, singles and a diversity of people, and to maintain their positions in a highly competitive market, cruise lines offer special promotions, discounts, incentives, and standby fares. Some low fares are available year-round but may be limited to a certain number of cabins on each sailing; others are seasonal or may apply to specific cruises.

You can take advantage of fare discounts in two ways. If you book early, you can benefit from early bird discounts, which often are as much as 40 to 50 percent off brochure prices, and of course, you can be sure you have the cruise you want. On the other hand, if you are in a position to be flexible, you can wait to catch the last minute "fire sales."

Cruise lines do not advertise the fact, but you can sometimes negotiate the lowest price on the day of sailing. To take advantage of this situation, you need to have maximum flexibility. This year, particularly, is a time to look for bargains because the recent introduction of so many new ships and new cruise lines has stiffened competition.

And remember, when you are buying a cruise, you will have already paid for *all* your accommodations, *all* meals (three meals a day is only the beginning; most ships have seven or more food services daily), *all* entertainment, and *all* recreational facilities aboard ship, and, if you buy a package, round-trip airfare to the ship's departure port, baggage handling and transfers. It is this all-inclusive aspect of a cruise that makes it such a great value—a particularly significant advantage for families with children and those who need to know in advance the true cost of a vacation.

SELECTING SHORE EXCURSIONS

Sight-seeing tours, called shore excursions by the cruise lines, are available for an additional cost at every port of call in the Caribbean. A pamphlet on the shore excursions offered by the cruise line is usually included in the literature you receive prior to sailing.

A few lines encourage travel agents to sell their shore excursions in advance; most do not. Rather, you buy them on board ship either from the purser, cruise director, or tour office. Most people seem to prefer buying them on board since, frequently, their interests and plans change once the cruise is underway.

A word of caution: When I first wrote this book, in 1987, I found that there was very little difference between the cruise ships' prices for tours and those of local tour companies, if you were staying in a hotel. However, during the past few years, the situation has changed so dramatically that I feel I must alert readers to the change. In their need to keep their cruise prices down in the face of intense competition and rampant discounting, many cruise lines have come to regard shore excursions (as well as ancillary services such as shipboard shopping, bars, and spa facilities) as profit centers; some are selling their tours at exorbitant prices.

In a preliminary survey, I found some prices jacked up 30 to 50 percent; some are even double the prices you would pay on shore. To help you in your selection and to gauge fair prices, each port of call in this book contains a description of the main shore excursions offered by the majority of cruise lines, as well as some that you must arrange on your own, and the approximate price of each excursion when you buy it directly from a tour company on shore. The prices were accurate at press time but, of course, they are not guaranteed.

Since tours vary from vendor to vendor and cruise ship to cruise ship, it is difficult to generalize. Therefore, when you check prices, it is important that you compare like items and, when necessary, factor in such additional costs as transportation from the pier to the vendor's office or starting point.

The information and prices given here are intended as guidelines. Even if they change, the increase is not likely to be more than a dollar or two. If you come across shore excursion prices that appear to be high in comparison with those found in this book, please write to me and enclose a copy of the tours sold on your cruise, with their descriptions and their prices.

PORT TALKS

All ships offer what is known as a port talk—a brief description of the country or island and port where the ship will dock as well as shopping tips. The quality of these talks varies enormously, not only with the cruise line but also with the ship, and can depend on such wide-ranging considerations as the knowledge and skill of the cruise director to the policy of the cruise line as to the true purpose of the information.

You should be aware that cruise directors often receive commissions from local stores, even though they deny it. Hence, their vested interest could color their presentation and recommendations. A more recent practice involves the cruise lines themselves promoting certain stores with which they have exclusive promotional agreements. The port talks in these circumstances are intended to sell—shore excursions, certain shops—rather than inform.

There are three ways to avoid being misled. If a cruise line, a cruise director, a guide, or anyone else recommends one store to the exclusion of all others, that should alert you to shop around before buying. The recommended store may actually be the best place to buy—but it may not. Second, if you are planning to make sizable purchases of jewelry, cameras, or china, etc., check prices at home before you leave and bring a list of prices with you. Be sure, however, you are comparing like products. Finally, check the prices in shipboard shops, which are usually very competitive with those at ports of call.

Happily, because you have this book you do not need to rely on port talks for information, but if you do attend your ship's port talks and find that they have been more of a sales pitch than enlightenment for you, please write and let me know about your experience.

WHAT YOU SHOULD KNOW BEFORE YOU GO

LUGGAGE AND WARDROBE There are no limits on the amount of luggage you can bring on board ship, but most staterooms do not have much closet and storage space. More importantly, since you are likely to be flying to your departure port you need to be guided by airline regulations regarding excess baggage.

But not to worry. Life on a cruise, especially a Caribbean one, is casual. It is needless to be burdened with a lot of baggage; you will spend your days in sports clothes: slacks, shorts, T-shirts, bathing suits. Men usually are asked to wear a jacket at dinner. For women, cocktail dresses and dressy pants suits are appropriate.

The first and last nights of your cruise and the nights your ship is in port almost always call for informal dress. At least one night will be the captain's gala party where tuxedos for men and long dresses for women are requested but not mandatory. Another night is a masquerade party; it's entirely up to you whether or not to participate.

A gentleman who does not have a tuxedo should bring a basic dark suit and white shirt. Add a selection of slacks and sport shirts, one or two sports jackets, and at least two pairs of bathing trunks. Women will find nylon and similar synthetics are good to use on a cruise because they are easy to handle, but these fabrics can be hot under the tropical sun. It largely depends on your tolerance for synthetic fabrics in hot weather. Personally, I have found cottons and cotton blends to be the most comfortable. You will need two cocktail dresses for evening wear. A long dress for the captain's party is appropriate but not compulsory.

Lightweight mix-match ensembles with skirts, shirts, blouse or T-shirts, shorts, and slacks are practical. Colorful scarves are another way to change the look of an outfit. Add a sweater or stole for cool evening breezes and the ship's air-conditioning in the dining room and other rooms. Take along cosmetics and suntan lotion, but don't worry if you forget something. It will most likely be available in shipboard or portside duty-free shops.

Men and women should have sandals or rubber-soled shoes for walking on deck and a comfortable pair of walking shoes for sight-seeing. Sunglasses and a hat or sun visor for protection against the sun are essential. A tote bag comes in handy for carrying odds and ends; include several plastic bags for wet towels and bathing suits upon returning from a visit to an island beach. You might also want to keep camera equipment in plastic bags as protection against the salt air and water and sand. And don't forget to pack whatever sporting equipment and clothes you will need. If you plan to snorkel, scuba, or play tennis frequently, you can save a significant amount on rental fees by bringing your own gear.

DOCUMENTATION Requirements for vaccinations, visas, and so on, depend on the destinations of the ship and are detailed in the information you receive from the cruise lines. Among the Caribbean's many advantages is that no destination (except Cuba, which is not covered in this book) requires visas of U.S. citizens arriving as cruise passengers.

MEAL TIMES All but the most luxurious Caribbean cruise ships have two sittings for the main meals of the day. At the early sitting, breakfast is about 7 to 8 A.M.; lunch at noon to 1 P.M.; and dinner at 6:15 to 7:30 P.M. At the late sitting, breakfast is about 8 to 9 A.M.; lunch at 1:30 to 2:30 P.M.; and dinner at 8:15 to 9:30 P.M. If you are an early riser, you will probably be happy with the early sitting. If you are likely to close the disco every night, you might prefer the late one. Of course, you will not be confined to these meals as there's usually a buffet breakfast, lunch on deck, a midnight buffet, early-bird coffee, mid-morning bouillon, afternoon tea, and cocktail canapés.

REQUESTING A TABLE Your travel agent can request your table in advance, if, for example, you want a table for two or for your family. Some cruise lines will confirm your reservation in advance; others require you to sign up for your dining table with the maitre d'hotel soon after boarding your ship. In this day of computers, it's hard to understand why any cruise line would want to put a passenger through this unnecessary inconvenience, but some do.

ELECTRICAL APPLIANCES Cabins on almost all new ships are wired for the use of hairdryers but older ships are not. Instead, rooms with special outlets are provided. Few ships allow you to use electric irons in your cabin because of the potential fire hazard, but they do not object to the use of electric razors. Electric current is normally 115–120 volts—but not always—and plugs are the two-prong, American-type ones. Check with your cruise line for specific information.

LAUNDRY AND DRY CLEANING All ships have either laundry service for your personal clothing (for which there is an extra charge) or coin-operated laundry rooms. Only a very few have dry cleaning facilities. In the Caribbean, this is not an important consideration since the clothes required are cotton or cotton blends and should be easy to wash.

HAIRDRESSING Almost all Caribbean cruise ships have hairdressers for both men and women. Prices are comparable to those at deluxe resorts.

RELIGIOUS SERVICES All ships hold interdenominational services; many also have a daily Catholic mass. Services will be conducted by the captain or a clergyman. At ports of call you will be welcome to attend local services.

MEDICAL NEEDS All cruise ships are required by law to have at least one doctor, nurse, and infirmary or mini-hospital. Doctor visits and medicine are extra costs.

Seasickness First-time cruise passengers probably worry more about becoming seasick than about any other aspect of cruising. Certainly they worry more than they should, particularly on a Caribbean cruise where the sea is calm almost year-round. Ships today have stabilizers, which steady them in all but the roughest seas. But if you are still worried, there are several types of nonprescription medicines such as Dramamine and Bonine that help to guard against motion sickness. Buy some to bring along—you may not need it but having it with you is comforting. Also, the ship's doctor can provide you with Dramamine and other medication that will be immediately effective, should you need it.

Sea Bands are a fairly new product for seasickness prevention. They are a pair of elasticized wristbands, each with a small plastic disk that, based on the principle of acupuncture, applies pressure on the inside wrist. I use Sea Bands and have given them to friends to use and can attest to their effectiveness. They are particularly useful for people who have difficulty taking medication. Sea Bands are found in drug, toiletry, and health care stores and can be ordered from Travel Accessories, P.O. Box 391162, Solon, Ohio 44139. Tel. 216–248–8432. They even make sequined covers in a dozen colors to wear over the bands for evening.

There are two important things to remember about seasickness: Don't dwell on your fear. Even the best sailors and frequent cruisers need a day to get their "sea legs." If you should happen to get a queasy feeling, take some medicine immediately. The worst mistake you can make is to play the hero, thinking it will go away. When you deal with the symptoms immediately, relief is fast, and you are seldom likely to be sick. If you wait, the queasy feeling will linger and you run a much greater risk of being sick.

Caution Against the Caribbean Sun: You should be extra careful about the sun in the tropics. It is much stronger than the sun to which most people are accustomed. Do not stay in the direct sun for long stretches at a time, and use a sunscreen at all times. Nothing can spoil a vacation faster than a sunburn.

SHIPBOARD SHOPS There's always a shop for essentials you might have forgotten or that can't wait until the next port of call. Many ships—particularly the new ones—have elaborate shops competitive with stores at ports of call. It's another reason to pack lightly, since you are almost sure to buy gifts and souvenirs during the cruise.

TIPPING Tipping is a matter of a great deal of discussion but much less agreement. How much do you tip in a restaurant or a hotel? Normally, the tip should be about $3 per person per day for each of your cabin stewards and dining room waiters. On some ships, particularly those with Greek crews, the custom is to contribute to the ship's common kitty in the belief that those behind the scenes such as kitchen staffs should share in the bounty. On some ships, dining room staffs also pool their tips. The cruise director, as part of his advice-giving session at the end of the cruise, usually explains the ship's policy and offers minimum guidelines about tipping. Tipping guidelines are often printed in literature your cruise line sends in advance of your cruise. Celebrity Cruises and Fantasy Cruises include the information in their cruise brochures, enabling potential passengers to factor the expense into their budget even before booking a cruise.

TELEPHONE CALLS—SHIP-TO-SHORE AND SHORE-TO-SHIP Most of the new ships have telephones in cabins with direct international dialing capability and fax facilities in their offices. Be warned, however, that the service is very expensive—about $15 per minute.

If anyone at home or in your office needs to reach you in an emergency, they can telephone your ship directly. Those calling from the continental United States would dial the international access code 011, followed by 874 (the ocean area code for the Caribbean), followed by the seven-digit telephone number of your ship. Someone calling from Puerto Rico should dial 128 and ask for the long distance operator.

Instructions on how to make such calls, how to reach the ship, or who to notify in case of an emergency are usually included in the information sent to you by your cruise line along with your tickets and luggage tags. If not, your travel agent can obtain the information. You should have this information before you leave home.

PART III

CARIBBEAN CRUISE LINES AND THEIR SHIPS

A GUIDE

E very effort has been made to ensure the accuracy of the information on the cruise lines and their ships, their ports of call, and prices, but do keep in mind that cruise lines change their ships' itineraries often for a variety of reasons. Always check with the cruise line or with a travel agent before making plans. For specific information on the itineraries of ships cruising to the Eastern Caribbean, see charts at the end of this book.

AMERICAN CANADIAN CARIBBEAN LINE, 461 Water Street, Warren, RI 02885; 401–247–0955; 800–556–7450; fax 401–245–8303

Ships (Passengers): *Caribbean Prince* (83); *Grande-Carib* (100); *Mayan Prince* (90); *Niagara Prince* (84)

Departure ports: Various ports

Type of cruises: 12 days Panama Canal/San Blas; Central America; Virgin Islands; Trinidad/Orinoco/Tobago; and Aruba/Bonaire/Curaçao in winter

Life-style tips: Family-style dining; mature and experienced passengers; light adventure; no frills. Emphasis is on natural attraction and local culture

If you are looking for tranquility, informality, and conversation with fellow passengers instead of floor shows and casinos, American Canadian Caribbean Line offers low-key cruises around the Bahamas archipelago, Belize, the southwestern Caribbean, and Central America during the winter and early spring.

In 1964, founder Luther Blount designed his first small ship for cruising Canada's inland waterways.

By 1988, the line had expanded to the extent that it could add Caribbean to its name. In the intervening years, ACCL remained faithful to the concept that small, intimate ships with limited planned entertainment can be successful. The ships' innovative bow ramps and shallow drafts give passengers direct access to beaches, coves, and places that are inaccessible to larger ships.

ACCL's ships are popular with mature, well-traveled passengers who like hearty American menus and the informal atmosphere of family-style dining. It is an atmosphere for instant friendships and complete relaxation. The line's large number of repeaters would seem to indicate that passengers agree with its concept and appreciate the "in-close" facility the ships bring to the cruise experience.

CAPE CANAVERAL CRUISE LINES, 501 N. Wymore Road, Winter Park, FL 32789 409–975–5000; 800–910–SHIP

Ships (Passengers): *Dolphin IV* (692)

Departure ports: Port Canaveral

Type of cruises: 2 to 4 nights to the Bahamas

Life-style tip: Casual, informal for the budget-minded, first-time cruisers

The cruise line was launched in 1996 after acquiring *Dolphin IV* from Dolphin Cruise Line. The smallest ship in Bahamas service, the *Dolphin IV* has a cozy, friendly atmosphere that passengers seem to love and which is well suited for short cruises. The ship caters to budget-minded, first-time cruisers. It departs on informal two- to four-day cruises from Port Canaveral to the Bahamas and Key West.

Passenger facilities and cabins are on six decks. The Promenade Deck has the main public rooms: a lounge, showroom, library/video room, casino, disco, boutique, hair salon, video game room, children's playroom, pool, and lido dining area. Topside, the Sun Deck has large lounging areas aft.

The ship's twelve cabin categories range from inside ones with upper and lower berths to junior suites with sitting rooms and full baths. More than half the cabins are outside and most are furnished with twin beds, radio, and phone, but no television. Furnished in earth tones and pastels, the cabins are small but adequate for two people for short cruises. Inside cabins are often more spacious than outside ones. Most have minimal storage space; bathrooms have a small shower unit and a small shelf for toiletries.

The dining room, situated on a lower deck, as is typical of older ships, is cozy and nicely decorated in pastels. There are two seatings. Live piano music adds a nice touch to dinner. Self-service breakfast and lunch buffets are available in the Miramar Café and the outside lido area has a barbecue grill near the swimming pool.

CARNIVAL CRUISE LINES, 3655 N.W. 87th Avenue, Miami, FL 33178–2428; 305–599–2600; 800–327–7373; fax 305–599–8630

Ships (Passengers): *Carnival Destiny* (2,642); *Celebration* (1,486); *Ecstasy* (2,040); *Elation* (2,040); *Fantasy* (2,044); *Fascination* (2,040); *Holiday* (1,452); *Imagination* (2,044); *Inspiration* (2,044); *Jubilee* (1,486); *Paradise* (2,040); *Sensation* (2,040); *Tropicale* (1,022)
Departure ports: Miami, San Juan
Type of cruises: 7 days to Eastern, Southern, Western, and Northern Caribbean, and the Panama Canal
Life-style tip: The "Fun Ships," youthful, casual, action-filled; high value for money

When Kathie Lee Gifford flashes her pretty smile across your television screen and says, "Carnival, the most popular cruise line in the world," that's not simply advertising hype. It's true—and the story of how it got to that position is the stuff of legends.

In 1972 Florida-based cruise executive Ted Arison and an innovative Boston-based travel agency bought the *Empress of Canada*, which they renamed the *Mardi Gras* to start a cruise line that would stand the stodgy old steamship business on its ear. But alas, the *Mardi Gras* ran aground on her maiden cruise. After staring at losses three years in a row, Arison took full ownership of the company, assuming its $5 million

debt, buying its assets—i.e., the ship—for $1, and launched the "Fun Ships" concept that is Carnival's hallmark.

The idea was to get away from the class-conscious elitism that had long been associated with luxury liners and to fill the ship with so much action-packed fun that the ship itself would be the cruise experience. The line also aimed at lowering the average age of passengers by removing the formality associated with cruising and providing a wide selection of activity and entertainment to attract active young adults, young couples, honeymooners, and families with children at reasonable prices. In only a few months Carnival turned a profit and in the next two years added two more ships.

The line's next move was as surprising as it was bold. In 1978 when shipbuilding costs and fuel prices were skyrocketing—threatening the very future of vacations-at-sea, Carnival ordered a new ship, larger and more technologically advanced than any cruise ship in service. It changed the profile of ships and enhanced the "fun" aspects of cruises. But it was Carnival's next move that really set the trend of the eighties and beyond.

In 1982, less than ten years after its rocky start, Carnival ordered three "superliners," each carrying 1,800 passengers, with design and decor as far removed from the grand old luxury liner as could be imagined. Between 1985 and 1987, the three ships—*Holiday, Jubilee,* and *Celebration*—were put into service. The decor was so different, it was zany. The owners called it "a Disney World for adults." On the *Holiday,* the main promenade deck, called "Broadway," complete with boardwalk and a Times Square, runs double-width down only one side of the ship and is lined with bars, nightclubs, casinos, lounges, and disco with as much glitz and glitter as the neon on Broadway. At one end of the deck there's a marquee and an enormous theater spanning two decks where Broadway musical–style and Las Vegas cabaret–type shows are staged twice nightly.

In 1990, Carnival outdid itself with the *Fantasy,* the first of eight megaliners even more dazzling than the earlier superliners. A ship for the twenty-first century, the *Fantasy,* with its flashy decor and high-energy ambience, is something of a Las Vegas, Disneyland, and Starlight Express in one. The heart of the ship is an atrium, awash in lights, towering seven decks high. Here and in the entertainment areas, 15 miles of computerized lights are programmed to change color—constantly, but imperceptibly—from white and cool blue to hot red, altering the ambience with each change. The ships have full-fledged gyms and spas and so many entertainment and recreation outlets that you need more than one cruise to find them all. In December1996 *Carnival Destiny,* the world's largest cruise ship, made her debut.

Now headed by Arison's son, Micky, Carnival is directed by a young, energetic, and aggressive team that seems determined to entice *everybody*—single, married, families, children, retirees, disabled (on the new ships), first-time cruisers, repeat cruisers, people from the north, south, east, and west, and from all walks of life— to take a cruise. To that end, the cruises are priced aggressively and offer early bird and special rates for third and fourth persons in the cabin.

Do all these ideas work? You bet they do! By 1998 Carnival will have 13 cruise ships in service, carrying almost two million passengers a year. That's up from 80,000 passengers in its first year. In 1987 Carnival Cruise Lines went public, and the following year it began *Carnival Air Lines;* and purchased the long-established Holland America Line, which in turn owned Windstar Cruises. Later it acquired partial ownership in the Seabourn Cruise Line, with ultra-luxurious ships. Although these lines operate under their own banners, the combination makes Carnival one of the world's largest cruise lines and gives it enormous marketing clout across the widest possible spectrum. Recently, Carnival acquired ownership in Airtour, a large European tour company, as an avenue for expanding in Europe. And in 1997, in a joint venture, Carnival and Airtour bought Costa Cruises, Europe's largest cruise line.

CELEBRITY CRUISES,
5201 Blue Lagoon Drive, Miami, FL 33126; 305–262–6677; fax 800–437–5111

Ships (Passengers): *Century* (1,750); *Galaxy* (1,750); *Horizon* (1,354); *Mercury* (1,750); *Zenith* (1,374)
Departure ports: Ft. Lauderdale, San Juan
Type of cruises: 7, 10, 11 nights to the Bahamas and Northern Caribbean; Eastern and Western Caribbean; Bermuda
Life-style tip: Modestly deluxe cruises at moderate prices

In 1989, when John Chandris, the nephew of the founder of Chandris Cruises, announced the creation of a new deluxe mid-priced cruise line, he said the goal was "to bring more luxurious cruises to experienced travelers but still at affordable prices." He was met with a great deal of skepticism; "deluxe" and "mid-priced" seemed a contradiction in terms. But three years later, he had made believers out of all his doubters.

Not only did Celebrity Cruises accomplish what it set out to do, it did it better than anyone imagined and in record-breaking time. A Celebrity cruise is not only deluxe; it offers the best value for the money of any cruise line in its price category.

Celebrity was a completely new product with a new generation of ships designed for the 1990s. It defined the ideal size of a cruise ship and the appropriate layout, cabins, decor, and ambience for its market and set new standards of service and cuisine in its price category.

Celebrity's ships are not as glitzy as some of the new megaliners but they are spacious and have a similar array of entertainment and recreation. The once-standard one-lounge-for-all has been replaced with small, separate lounges, each with its own decor, ambience, and entertainment, and a variety of bars to give passengers a range of options. They have stunning, stylish decor that has brought back some of the glamour of cruising in bygone days but with a fresh, contemporary look.

From its inception, Celebrity Cruises aimed at creating superior cuisine as one way to distinguish itself. To achieve their goal, they engaged as their food consultant Michel Roux, the award-winning master French chef who operates two Michelin three-star restaurants and five other restaurants in England, a catering service, and other food enterprises. He spent six months developing the menus for Celebrity Cruises and working with the ships' chandlers and chefs.

Roux accomplished miracles and set a new standard for other cruise lines. The food is sophisticated but unpretentious; quality is more important than quantity, although there's no lack of quantity either. Using the best-quality products, Roux keeps the menus seasonal to the extent possible, changing them every three months. To make sure the cuisine stays at his demanding level, he sails on each ship several times during the year.

Celebrity was launched in 1990 with the brand-new *Horizon* and the *Meridian* (which was sold in early 1997). The stylish, elegant *Horizon* is classic and very contemporary at the same time. It has mostly outside staterooms equipped with closed-circuit television that carries daily programs of events, first-run movies, and world news. The ship has a piano bar, a nightclub, a duplex show lounge with state-of-the-art sound and lighting systems, a disco, a casino, and an observation lounge. There are shops, a sports and fitness center, two swimming pools, and three Jacuzzis. The *Zenith,* which lives up to its name in every way, followed in 1992 and is almost identical to the *Horizon.*

Celebrity received awards for its ships and its cuisine from the first year of operation. Now, in the suites, butler service is available. As a send-off on the last day of the cruise, all passengers may enjoy a classic high tea with white-glove service and classical music.

Also, in 1992 Celebrity teamed up with Overseas Shipholding Group, one of the world's largest bulk-shipping companies, to form a joint cruise company and launch three new megaliners known as the Century series—designed, the cruise line believes, for the twenty-first century. Among the innovations, Sony Corporation is providing the most advanced technology in entertainment and interactive services yet seen on cruise ships. The first ship, *Century,* made her debut in December 1996, followed by the *Galaxy* in November 1996 and the *Mercury* in 1997.

In 1997, Royal Caribbean Cruise Line bought Celebrity Cruises and will operate it as a seperate brand.

CLIPPER CRUISE LINE, 7711 Bonhomme Avenue, St. Louis, MO 63105; 314–727–2929; 800–325–0010; fax 314–727–6576

Ships (Passengers): *Clipper Adventurer* (122); *Nantucket Clipper* (102); *Yorktown*

Clipper (138)
Departure ports: St. Thomas, Grenada, Curaçao, Panama City
Type of cruises: 7 days to the Virgin Islands; 11 days to the Eastern and Southern Caribbean
Life-style tip: Small ships for nature-oriented travelers

Clipper Cruise Line is a special niche: nature-oriented cruises on comfortable small ships with pleasing interior decor, sailing to the little-known corners of the Caribbean and Central America in winter and other parts of North and South America during the other seasons. The ships' shallow drafts often enable them to sail into places where larger ships cannot go.

The ships carry Zodiacs that enable them to drop anchor frequently for passengers to enjoy a swim at secluded beaches, hike in a rain forest, or sail up a river to a remote village. Daily onboard seminars by a naturalist on the places to be visited are followed by discussions after the visit. The naturalist also acts as a guide for those who want to take nature walks and bird-watch.

The crew is American, mostly fresh out of college, and unfailingly polite and friendly. The itinerary is leisurely and so is the activity. Scuba diving, windsurfing, golf, or tennis can also be arranged, depending on the itinerary. Absent, but not missed by its passengers, are the casinos, pools, staged entertainment, and organized diversions of large ships. Both the ship and passenger complement are small enough that you get to know everyone aboard in the course of a week.

Clipper's ships have outside staterooms—most with large windows. Some are entered from the outside (as on river steamboats) rather than interior corridors. Cabins and lounges are nicely decorated with quality furnishings. Passengers dine at one seating on good American cuisine prepared by a staff headed by a chef from the prestigious Culinary Institute of America.

Clipper Cruise Line passengers are not bargain hunters or those looking for last-minute specials. Rather, they are mature and well-traveled.

In 1997, Clipper was acquired by INTRAV, a St. Louis–based, NASDAQ-traded travel company and added a third ship, *Clipper Adventurer,* which will begin sailing in 1998.

CLUB MEDITERRANEE, S.A.,
40 West 57th Street, New York, N.Y. 10019;
212–977–2100; 1-800–CLUB–MED;
fax 212–315–5392

Ships (Passengers): *Club Med I* (392);
Club Med II (392);
Departure port: Martinique
Type of cruises: 7 days to Eastern and
Southern Caribbean
Life-style tip: Casual and sports oriented

Club Med, a name synonomous with all-inclusive vacations and an easy life-style, took its popular formula to sea in 1990 with the introduction of the world's largest sailboat and geared it to upscale, sophisticated, and active vacationers. But theirs was no ordinary sailing ship.

Longer than two football fields, she is 610 feet long, and is rigged with five 164-foot masts. The $100-million ship was the last word in 21st century technology with seven computer-monitored sails. All 191 outside staterooms have a twin porthole and hand-rubbed mahogany cabinetwork. The spacious, 188 square-foot cabins are fitted with twin or king-sized beds. All cabins have private bath, closed circuit television, radio, safe, and minibar. A ship-to-shore phone is available in every cabin: It can also be used to order fresh towels and room service.

Guests are welcomed on the *Club Med I* with a fruit basket in their rooms. The ship has two restaurants: the Odyssey, located on the top deck, offers casual dining and has an outdoor veranda for breakfast and lucheon buffets; La Lousiane, on the deck directly below, is a more formal dining room with waiter service and a la carte menu. Complimentary wine and beer accompanies both luncheon and dinner and an extensive wine list is also available for an additional charge. Both restaurants have single unassigned seatings. Afternoon tea is served daily in the piano lounge with indoor and outdoor tables.

The ship has a fitness center with a panoramic view from the top deck, pine saunas and licensed massage therapists, tanning salon, two swimming pools, a discotheque, casino, twenty-four-hour room service and satellite telecommunications. Other facilities include a boutique, theater, hair

salon, and observation deck. Passangers can take aerobics, stretch, and other fitness classes.

In the stern, the ship carries water-sports equipment and has a special sports platform that unfolds into the sea from which passangers can sail, windsurf, scuba dive, water-ski, and snorkel. There are qualified instructors to teach the fine points. Scuba diving excursions, however, are reserved for certified divers who have their C-card.

During the winter season, *Club Med I* is based in Martinique from where she sails on five alternating itineraries that visit almost all the islands of the Eastern and Southern Caribbean from the U.S. and British Virgin Islands on the north to Los Roques, off the coast of Venezuela, on the south. In April 1997, *Club Med I* was purchased by Windstar Cruises, whose owning company is Carnival Cruise Lines. The ship will leave the Club Med fleet in March 1998 at the end of her winter Caribbean season. She will be renamed, *Wind Surf,* and start her new life with Windstar Cruises in May 1998. Meanwhile, Windstar is negotiating for the purchase of *Club Med II*, which has a different group of owners and sails in the South Pacific.

COSTA CRUISE LINES, World Trade
Center, 80 S.W. 8th Street, Miami, FL
33130-3097; 305–358–7325

Ships (Passengers): *CostaRomantica* (1300);
CostaVictoria (1,950)
Departure ports: Miami, San Juan
Type of cruises: 7 days to Western, Northern, Eastern, and Southern Caribbean
Life-style tip: More European atmosphere and service than similar mass-market ships

"Cruising Italian Style" has long been Costa Cruise Lines' stock in trade, with a fun and friendly atmosphere created by its Italian staff and largely Italian crew. The emphasis is on good Italian food, which means pasta, pizza, and espresso (there are other kinds of cuisine, too); European-style service, particularly in the dining room; and, not to forget the Italians' ancestry, a toga party, which is usually a hilarious affair, one night of the cruise.

The Genoa-based company of the Costa family has been in the shipping business for more than 100 years and in the passenger business for more than 50 years. Costa began offering one-week Caribbean cruises from Miami in 1959; it was the first to offer an air/sea program, introduced in the late 1960s.

Costa launched the 1990s with one of the newest fleets in the Caribbean. Each ship introduced interesting new features in its design, combining classic qualities with modern features and boasting unusually large cabins for their price category. Among the ships' nicest features are canvas-covered outdoor cafes and pizzerias serving pizza throughout the day without additional charge.

Serena Cay (Catalina Island) is Costa's "private" island off the southeast coast of the Dominican Republic featured on Eastern Caribbean cruises. The island is near the sprawling resort of Casa de Campo, which has, among its many facilities, two of the best golf courses in the Caribbean, a tennis village, horseback riding, and polo.

Costa's ships have fitness centers and spas (most services are extra), along with a health and fitness program to suit individual needs. Costa's shore excursions, which tend to be expensive, stress outdoor activities.

In 1996, the line's largest ship, *CostaVictoria,* made her Caribbean debut in November, sailing weekly from Miami and alternating between the Western and Eastern Caribbean. In 1997, Costa was bought jointly by Carnival Cruise Line and Airtour, one of Europe's largest tour companies.

CRYSTAL CRUISES, 2121 Avenue of the Stars, Suite 200, Los Angeles, CA 90067; 310–785–9300, 800–446–6645; fax 310–785–3891

Ships (Passengers): *Crystal Harmony* (960); *Crystal Symphony* (960)
Departure ports: Worldwide
Type of cruises: 10- to 17-day transcanal
Life-style tips: Ultra luxury for sophisticated travelers

The launching of Crystal Cruises in 1989 was one of the most anticipated in the cruising world. The new cruise line had begun spreading the word two years before its first ship had seen the water, and its owners spared no expense to ensure that the sleek *Crystal Harmony* would live up to its advance billing. Its goal was to create luxury cruises that would return elegance and personalized service to cruising and be designed for an upscale mass market at deluxe prices.

The *Crystal Harmony* exceded expectations. Indeed, it has been so well received by passengers and by its competition that it has become the ship by which others in its class—or trying to be in its class—are measured. But for my money, the Crystal sisters are in a class all their own.

Crystal Symphony is essentially a copy of the *Crystal Harmony,* with some refinements and new features; for example, there will be no inside staterooms. The ships are magnificent, with exquisite attention to detail. The food is excellent and the service superb, with the staff at every level smiling and gracious and always willing to go the extra mile.

Built in Japan by Mitsubishi Heavy Industries, these are spacious ships for experienced travelers with sophisticated life-styles. The luxury is evident from the moment you step on either ship. The atrium lobby, the ship's focus, is accented with greenery and hand-cut glass sculptures. The piano bar features—what else?—a crystal piano.

Staterooms have sitting areas, minibars, spacious closets, and such amenities as hairdryers, plush robes, VCRs, and 24-hour hookup with CNN and ESPN; more than half have verandas. The ships' penthouses have Jacuzzis and butler service. Facilities include spa and fitness centers and full promenade decks for jogging. The indoor/outdoor swimming pools have swim-up bars and lap pools with adjacent whirlpools. The casinos are the first "Caesars Palace at Sea."

The ships' most innovative feature is the choice of two dinner restaurants—Japanese or Asian and Italian—at no extra cost. These restaurants are in addition to standard meal service in the main dining room and 24-hour room service.

In 1996, Crystal Cruises introduced low single supplement rates, ranging from only 10–15 percent more than the per-person, double-occupancy rate for a cabin in Category A through E, which includes deluxe cabins with verandas.

CUNARD, 555 Fifth Avenue, New York, NY 10017; 212–880–7500; 800–221–4770 (outside New York)

Ships (Passengers): *Sea Goddess I* (116); *Sea Goddess II* (116); *Queen Elizabeth 2* (1,810);

Royal Viking Sun (740); *Vistafjord* (736)
Departure ports: Ft. Lauderdale, San Juan, St. Thomas, and Barbados
Type of cruises: 7 to 16 days for ships in Caribbean and transcanal on seasonal schedules
Life-style tip: Deluxe with a British touch, catering to affluent travelers

Cruise lines spend billions annually on promotion, but according to some tests, the only ship that the man-on-the-street can recall by name, unaided, is the *QE2*. That's perhaps not surprising when one considers that she is heir to a family of transatlantic liners reaching back over a century and a half and the only ship still on regular transatlantic service, from April to December.

The *Queens* have set the standard of elegance at sea in times of peace and served their country with distinction in times of war. Today, the *Queen*, which recently had a multi-million dollar makeover, sets the tone for Cunard. To many, she is the ultimate cruise experience. The *QE2* is a city-at-sea, dwarfing most other ships. She is proud, elegant, formal, and as British as—well, yes—the queen. The *QE2* isn't seen often in the Caribbean as her winters are taken mostly with an annual cruise around the world.

The other ships are important to the Cunard mix. The spacious and graceful *Vistafjord*, which has long epitomized luxury cruising, maintains the ambience of traditional cruising. Her Caribbean schedule is seasonal. The top-rated *Royal Viking Sun*, which Cunard bought in 1994, cruises the world, as do the ultra-deluxe *Sea Goddess* twins, built expressly to offer the most exclusive, elegant cruises in the world.

Their cabins, decor, itineraries, and cuisine were all planned to meet the expectations of a select group of very affluent people, offering highly personalized service and an unregimented ambience. The dining room has open seating and there is full meal service in staterooms around the clock. The ships have a stern platform that can be lowered to the level of the sea, enabling passengers to snorkel, swim, and enjoy other water sports from the boat. One of the twins sails on one-week itineraries of the Eastern Caribbean and longer transcanal ones.

Even though Cunard is one of the oldest lines

afloat, it has been very much an innovator, responding to today's changing life-styles with gusto and recognizing the impact of the electronic revolution on people's lives—including their holidays. The *QE2* was the first ship to have a full-fledged spa at sea, a computer learning center, and satellite-delivered world news.

DISNEY CRUISE LINE, 210 Celebration Place, Suite 400, Celebration, FL 34747-4600; 407–939–3727; fax 407–939–3750

Ships (Passengers): *Disney Magic* (1,760); *Disney Wonder* (1,760)
Departure port: Port Canaveral
Type of cruises: 3- and 4-day cruises combined with Disney World vacations
Life-style tip: Family-oriented but designed for all ages

Disney Cruise Line is scheduled to be launched in April 1998, with its first ship, *Disney Magic*, followed by a sister ship, *Disney Wonder*, in November. Both ships will have classic exteriors reminiscent of the great transatlantic ocean liners of the past, but inside they will be up-to-the-minute in fun and entertainment for people of all ages.

The line plans to combine a three- or four-day stay at a Walt Disney World Resort with a three- or four-day cruise aboard ship, sailing round-trip from Port Canaveral. The itinerary will include a daylong stop at Disney's own private island.

In addition to catering to families, passengers will find services, activities, and programs designed specifically for adults without children, as well as for honeymooners and seniors. For example, the ship will offer themed restaurants as well as an adults-only alternative restaurant, swimming pool, and night club.

Disney promises that nightly entertainment will be "unlike any other in the cruise industry" and will feature top Disney-produced shows with Broadway-quality entertainers, cabaret, and an adult-oriented lecture and enrichment program.

The children's programs are expected to be the most extensive in the industry with the largest children-dedicated space and age-specific activities and a large number of counselors. The ship will have a separate pool, lounge, teen club, and game arcade for older kids.

Disney Magic will sport spacious suites and cabins with 73 percent outside and almost half with small verandas.

DOLPHIN CRUISE LINE,
901 South America Way, Miami, FL
33132; 305–358–2111; 800–222–1003

Ships (Passengers): *IslandBreeze* (1,146);
OceanBreeze (772); *SeaBreeze* (840)
Departure ports: Miami, Montego Bay, Santo
Domingo
Type of cruises: 7-day cruise to Eastern and
Western Caribbean, Panama, Costa Rica
Life-style tip: Friendly, comfortable for all
ages, and economical

Dolphin Cruise Line made major changes in
1995, selling the *Dolphin IV,* dropping Aruba as a
home port for the *OceanBreeze,* and acquiring
Carnival Cruises' *Festivale,* which it renamed
IslandBreeze.

In early 1997 Dolphin was acquired by Cruise
Holdings, Inc., a private investment company that
operates several other cruise lines. (It also
acquired majority interest in Seawind Cruise Line
at the same time.) In late 1997 the lines
IslandBreeze will introduce innovative, alternating Eastern and Western Caribbean cruises that
depart Santo Domingo on Sundays.

During the winter season, *IslandBreeze* sails
weekly from Montego Bay to Panama with a partial transit of the canal; during summer she sails
from New York. The *SeaBreeze* continues on
cruises that alternate weekly between the
Western and Eastern Caribbean. The cruises can
be combined into a two-week cruise at a special
price.

When Dolphin Cruise Line started out in 1984,
it had a hard time going up against the giants of
Bahamas cruises, but affordable one-week packages, combining a three- or four-day cruise with
visits to Disney World/EPCOT or Miami helped it
succeed. Early bird discounts and special low
rates for children and third and fourth persons in
a cabin also helped.

Dolphin cruises are family-oriented. The
SeaBreeze has 32 cabins with adjoining doors,
especially for families; the *OceanBreeze* has cabins with Pullman beds and a children's playroom.
The ships have youth counselors on board seasonally to plan and supervise children's activities.
For active adults the ships have diving and snorkeling programs, as well as golf and tennis with

instruction on board and play in port. Dolphin's
sister line is Majesty Cruise Line, which caters to
a more upscale traveler than Dolphin.

HOLLAND AMERICA LINE,
300 Elliott Avenue West, Seattle,
WA 98119;
206–281–3535; 800–426–0327

Ships (Passengers): *Maasdam* (1,266);
Nieuw Amsterdam (1,214); *Noordam* (1,214);
Rotterdam VI(1,075); *Ryndam* (1,266);
Statendam (1,266); *Veendam* (1,266);
Westerdam (1,476)
Departure ports: Ft. Lauderdale, Tampa, New
York, New Orleans
Type of cruises: 7 days to Western and Eastern
Caribbean; 10 days to Southern Caribbean, and
10 to 23 days to Panama Canal
Life-style tip: Classic but contemporary

Begun in 1873 as a transatlantic shipping company between Rotterdam and the Americas,
Holland America Line stems from one of the oldest
steamship companies in the world. Through the
years and two wars her ships became an important
part of maritime history, particularly significant as
the westward passage of immigrants to America.
The line also owns Westours, the Seattle-based tour
company that pioneered tours and cruises to
Alaska five decades ago; and it acquired the
unusual Windstar Cruises in 1988. The following
year the entire group was purchased by Carnival
Cruise Lines, but all operate as separate entities.

Holland America now has one of the newest
fleets in cruising, having added four magnificent,
brand-new ships in three years: *Statendam,*
Maasdam, Ryndam, and *Veendam.* They combine the Old World with the New in decor and
ambience and boast million-dollar art and
antique collections reflecting Holland's association with trade and exploration in the Americas
and the Orient. Their Dutch officers and
Indonesian and Filipino crews are another
reminder of Holland's historical ties to Asia.

The ships have the space and elegance for the
long cruises of two weeks or more for which they
were designed. They feature a three-level atrium
lobby with a large fountain, an elegant two-level
dining room, small lounges and bars, disco,

casino, a large state-of-the-art spa, a sliding-glass dome for the swimming pool, spacious cabins, and premium amenities. All suites and 120 deluxe cabins have private verandas, whirlpool baths, minibars, and VCRs. There are bathtubs in all outside cabins (485 cabins out of 633 total—an unusually high percentage).

The *Westerdam,* bought from Home Lines in 1988, was given a $60 million stretch job to increase her capacity. She combines the style and refinement of great ocean liners with state-of-the art facilities and fits well into Holland America's fleet.

The *Nieuw Amsterdam* and *Noordam* are reflective of today's cruise ships, although they were thought revolutionary when they were inaugurated in the early 1980s. Each ship has a square stern that increased its open deck space by 20 percent over traditional design, providing additional room for recreational and entertainment facilities. There are two outdoor heated swimming pools, fully equipped gym and spa, sauna, massage, and whirlpool. Stateroom doors are opened with a coded card rather than a key; movies, nightclub entertainment, and other events can be viewed on television in the cabins. Many of these features, dazzling when they were introduced, have become standard on new ships.

Holland America's *Rotterdam,* launched in 1959, will be replaced in 1997 by the *Rotterdam VI.* It has the feel of a grand transatlantic liner with rich interiors, cozy bars, and big public rooms. When the ship is not on a long cruise in distant parts of the world, she sails from Ft. Lauderdale to the Caribbean.

Life aboard the ships of Holland America proceeds at a leisurely pace. Traditionally the line has attracted mature, experienced travelers and families. During the winter, all the fleet sails on Caribbean and Panama Canal cruises, some departing from Tampa, a port Holland America helped to develop for cruise ships, and New Orleans to the Western Caribbean and the Panama Canal; others leave from Ft. Lauderdale.

NORWEGIAN CRUISE LINE,
95 Merrick Way, Coral Gables, FL 33134;
305–447–9660; 800–327–7030

Ships (Passengers): *Norwegian Dream* (1,754); *Leeward* (950); *Norway* (2,022); *Norwegian Crown* (1,000); *Norwegian Dynasty* (800); *Norwegian Majesty* (1,056); *Norwegian Sea* (1,540); *Norwegian Star* (1,198); Norwegian Sea (1,540) *Norwegian Wind* (1,754)

Departure ports: Miami, Ft. Lauderdale, New York, San Juan, Los Angeles, Houston

Type of cruises: 3, 4, and 7 days to the Bahamas; Northern, Eastern, and Western Caribbean; Bermuda; Mexican Riviera

Life-style tip: Mainstream of modern cruising

Norwegian Cruise Line was started in 1966 by Knut Kloster, whose family has been in the steamship business in Scandinavia since 1906. Kloster is credited with launching modern cruising when he introduced the *Sunward* on year-round three- and four-day cruises from Miami to the Bahamas, thus creating the first mass-market packaging of cruises.

By 1971, Kloster had added three new ships and pioneered weekly cruises to Jamaica and other Caribbean destinations. He introduced a day-at-the-beach feature in the Caymans and bought a Bahamian island to add a day-on-a-private-island to the line's Bahamas cruises. The idea has since been adopted by most cruise lines sailing the Bahamas and Caribbean.

Yet, in its history loaded with "firsts," nothing caused as much excitement as the entry of the *Norway* in 1980. After buying her as the *France* for $18 million, NCL spent $100 million to transform her from the great ocean liner she had been to the trendsetting Caribbean cruise ship she became.

With space for 2,000 passengers, the *Norway* was the largest passenger ship afloat. Her size enabled NCL to create a completely new environment on board with restaurants, bars, and lounges of great diversity, shopping malls with "sidewalk" cafes, full Broadway shows and Las Vegas revues in its enormous theatre, full casino, and sports and entertainment facilities that can keep an active passenger in motion almost around the clock. Such innovations are now standard on all large ships.

The *Norway* was readied for the 1990s in a two-stage $65 million renovation that added a 4,000-square-foot health and fitness center, a jogging track, luxury staterooms, and two glass-enclosed decks. But the most spectacular addition was the Roman spa, covering 6,000 square feet and equipped with eight massage rooms, four herbal-therapy baths—cruising's first—and a gym. Spa services are not included in the cruise price; packages are available. Additional renovations in 1996 restored some of her original art deco features.

NCL added a fleet of new ships, beginning in 1988 with the debut of the *Seaward*, recently renamed *Norwegian Sea*, taking the line in a new direction. Each ship carries 1,200 to 1,400 passengers, going against the trend of larger ships but giving the line flexibility. These mid-range ships are aimed at upscale passengers who want the facilities of a superliner but prefer the more intimate feeling of smaller ships. Among their innovations, *Norwegian Dream* and her sister ship, *Norwegian Wind*, have four small dining rooms instead of the traditional one or two large ones. The concept gets away from the mega-dining room, and their multitiered design enables passengers to enjoy extensive views through panoramic windows. One of the sun decks is also tiered, getting away from the long lineup of deck chairs.

The *Norwegian Dream* was the first ship to have a sports bar and grill with multiple television screens featuring live broadcasts of ESPN and the NBA and NFL, which are now standard for all the fleet. Standard cabins have a separate sitting area; 75 percent are outside facing. In 1995 the line added the *Leeward*; it, too, has many of the NCL standard features.

NCL, which blankets the Caribbean, is known for its entertainment—some of the best in the business, ranging from comedy clubs and cabaret stars to Broadway shows. Although it did not originate water sports programs for passengers, the line has developed them further than most, offering instruction while the ships are at sea and in-water experience at ports of call. Year-round the ships have sports and fitness programs and theme cruises for golf, tennis, baseball, running, and others. NCL also has an extensive youth and children's program. In 1997 NCL expanded to South America and Europe and moved the *Norwegian Star* to her new base in Houston.

In 1984, Kloster Cruise Ltd., NCL's parent company, bought the prestigious Royal Viking Line,

and in 1990, it acquired Royal Cruise Line. The moves turned out to be bad ones, saddling the company with mountains of debt and forcing it to sell RVL in 1994 and to close RCL in 1996. RCL's popular *Royal Odyssey* joined the NCL fleet as the *Norwegian Crown;* along with the *Royal Odyssey*, now the *Norwegian Star* whose capacity was increased by adding third and fourth berths to two hundred cabins. Then in a surprising move in early 1997, NCL acquired Majesty Cruise Lines, adding her two ships, *Crown Majesty* (renamed *Norweigian Dynasty*) and *Royal Majesty* (renamed *Norwegian Majesty*). Also in early 1998, *Norwegian Dream* and *Norwegian Wind* will be "stretched" by adding 130-feet mid-sections to each.

PREMIER CRUISE LINES, 400 Challenger Road, Cape Canaveral, FL 32920; 407–783–5061

Ship (Passengers): *Star/Ship Atlantic* (1,600)
Departure port: Port Canaveral
Type of cruises: 3 and 4 days to the Bahamas combined with visits to Walt Disney World
Life-style tip: Fun for the whole family

Premier Cruise Lines is another of cruising's success stories—this time, almost overnight. Its success was all the more phenomenal because there was no shortage of pundits who told its founders that their brainchild wouldn't work.

Critics cited the poor facilities in Port Canaveral, an insufficient local population to support year-round cruises, the great distance from Port Canaveral to Nassau, and other reasons. On the other hand, the founders saw Walt Disney World—the nation's biggest tourist attraction—and the Kennedy Space Center, whose visitors were an enormous untapped reservoir of potential cruise passengers.

Premier Cruise Lines was formed in 1983 by Bruce Nierenberg, a brilliant maverick of cruise marketing who has left his imprint on several cruise lines, and Bjornar Hermansen, a financial and administrative whiz with whom Nierenberg had worked at another line. With the backing of the Dial Corporation, they bought a ship to use on short excursions between Port Canaveral and the Bahamas. Then they packaged Premier's three- and four-night cruises with special airfares, three nights of "free" deluxe accommodations in Orlando, three days of admission to the Disney theme parks, and a free tour of Spaceport U.S.A. at the Kennedy Space Center, plus the use of a rental car with unlimited mileage for a week, and priced the packages so reasonably that potential passengers couldn't refuse.

Eager to live up to the "star" billing it designated for itself with its Star/Ship name, it painted the ship's hulls bright red with orange and yellow trim (whoever heard of such a thing!) and hired an experienced staff. Known as the Big Red Boat, the result was a comfortable ship with nice decor and cabins for families—some for up to five persons—with amenities such as bath items found in deluxe hotels.

For the kids, there is a full-time staff of youth counselors that runs the "Junior Cruise Club," which has its own recreational center with day and night activities for the under-17 set. There is a computer learning center with PCs and CD-ROMs that are both educational and entertaining. The teen center has new state-of-the-art video, light, and audio equipment for teen dances and karaoke.

For those who want to stay in shape, there's the SeaSport fitness program, which combines the use of a gym full of Universal gear, aerobics class, jogging track, and a variety of sports activities during the day at the beach on Salt Cay, an uninhabited island in the Bahamas. For night owls, in addition to the entertainment, there are a casino, theater with first-run movies, video arcade, lounges, cabaret, piano bar, and disco. And for honeymooners, there are champagne in the room and double beds. Premier's Golf Academy provides instruction and swing analysis through video equipment and an onboard pro. Golfing with the pro at one of the courses in Nassau and Port Lucaya is also available.

After almost a decade as the "Official Cruise Line of Walt Disney World," which had generated a great deal of publicity, the Dial Corporation terminated the Disney agreement and the Big Red Boat brought on Looney Tunes under a licensing agreement with Warner Brothers Consumer Products. The Looney Tunes bunch—Bugs Bunny, Sylvester, Tweety, and friends—take a prominent onboard role.

In early 1997, Dial Corporation sold the cruise line to Cruise Holdings, which also owns Dolphin Cruises and Seawind Cruises.

**PRINCESS CRUISES
10100 Santa Monica Boulevard,
Los Angeles, CA 90067;
310–553–1770; 800–LOVE–BOAT**

Ships (Passengers): *Crown Princess* (1,590);
Dawn Princess (1,950); *Grand Princess* (2.600); *Island Princess* (640); *Pacific Princess* (640); *Regal Princess* (1,590); *Royal Princess* (1,200); *Sea Princess* (1,950); *Sky Princess* (1,200); *Sun Princess* (1,950)
Departure ports: Ft. Lauderdale, San Juan, Acapulco, Los Angeles
Type of cruises: 7 to 10 days, combining Western, Eastern, Southern Caribbean, and Panama Canal
Life-style tip: Casually stylish and modestly affluent

Princess Cruises, a West Coast pioneer begun in 1965, is credited with helping to create the relaxed and casual atmosphere that typifies life on board today's cruises. For one thing, one of its ships, the *Pacific Princess,* is the ship used in the popular television series *The Love Boat.* It's impossible to calculate, but that show probably did more to popularize modern cruising than all other cruise publicity combined. It was certainly a factor in dispelling cruising's elitist image and enabling people who might have never considered a cruise holiday to identify with it.

In 1988, Princess acquired the Los Angeles-based Sitmar Cruises, another innovative and well-established pioneer of West Coast cruising, creating one of the world's largest cruise companies and more than doubling Princess's capacity in one stroke.

The pride of the Princess fleet—its flagship, and one of the most stylish, elegant ships of the 1980s—is the *Royal Princess,* which was christened by the Princess of Wales. When she made her debut in 1983, the ship set new standards in passenger comfort with all outside cabins and refrigerators, televisions, and bathrooms fitted with tub as well as shower in every cabin category. The decor throughout is warm, inviting, and comfortable, and always with a touch of class. All suites, deluxe cabins, and some of those in lesser categories have private outside balconies—a first for cruising.

After a debut in Europe, the *Crown Princess* was officially christened by actress Sophia Loren in New York in 1990 during Princess Cruises' twenty-fifth anniversary. Very different in profile from other ships, the *Crown Princess* was designed by Renzo

Piano, the architect of the Pompidou Center in Paris. Her sleek lines were inspired by the shape of a dolphin. The top of the head holds "The Dome," the forward observation and entertainment area, and the casino. The spacious ship has large cabins and a high percentage of them have verandas. Its twin, *Regal Princess*, was launched in 1991. The *Island Princess* and *Pacific Princess* are identical twins, more casual than their sisters.

Princess's latest venture—*Sun Princess,* dubbed a "Super Love Boat"—is the line's largest vessel. Designed by Njal Eide, the architect of the elegant *Royal Princess*, the ship is the most beautiful large ship afloat with exquisite interiors of the finest Italian workmanship. It introduced many new features, including two atrium lobbies and two main show lounges, a true theater-at-sea, and a restaurant offering 24-hour dining. About 70 percent of the outside cabins have verandas. *Sun's* identical twin, *Dawn Princess*, debuted in May 1997 and sails on Eastern and Southern cruises from San Juan in winter.

In recent years, Princess has had one of the strongest presences in the Caribbean in the winter season. The line has a private beach, Princess Cays (on south Eleuthera in the Bahamas), where the ships call. Newly expanded and upgraded, the facility has just about every water sport a passenger could want; nature trails with guided walks; games; kiosks for local crafts; and a large dining pavilion where passengers are served lunch.

Princess caters to a modestly affluent clientele from 35 years of age plus, with a median age of 50 to 55. It is very aggressive with promotional fares and seasonal savings.

Princess's British sister, P&O Lines, is seen in the Caribbean during winter as their ships make their annual round-the-world voyages. Catering mostly to an established British clientele, they are gaining American fans as they become better known, especially for their new ship *Oriana*, and for the *Adriana*, formerly Princess's *Star Princess*.

RADISSON SEVEN SEAS CRUISES
600 Corporate Drive, No. 410,
Ft. Lauderdale, FL 33334;
305–776–6123; 800–477–7500;
800–333–3333; fax 305–772–3763

Ships (Passengers): *Bremen*(164); *Paul Gauguin* (320); *Hanseatic* (188); *Radisson Diamond* (354); *Song of Flower* (180)
Departure ports: San Juan and worldwide ports seasonally
Type of Cruises: 3 to 14 days; transcanal, Eastern Caribbean, Europe, Asia
Life-style tip: Luxury for affluent travelers

"Futuristic" and "revolutionary" were some of the words used to describe the semi-submersible *Radisson Diamond*, one of the decade's most innovative ships, when it made its debut in 1992. Well, it is certainly novel. Viewed from the front, it looks more like a UFO than a cruise ship.

Measuring 420 feet in length and 103 in width and sitting high in the water, the SSC *Radisson Diamond* is the largest twin-hull cruise ship ever constructed; it marked the first time the design technology called SWATH (small waterplace area twin hull) was applied to a luxury ship of this nature. The design is intended to provide greater stability than that of a single-hull ship of similar size. Speedboats and water-skiers have been known to race through the space between the hulls, under the underbelly.

Diamond Cruises, a joint venture of Finnish, Japanese, and U.S. interests, formed a partnership with Radisson Hotels International to market the ship. In 1995, Radisson Diamond joined with Seven Sea Cruises to form a new company, Radisson Seven Seas.

The focus of the *Diamond* is a five-story atrium with glass-enclosed elevators and a grand staircase. The cabins, most with private balconies, are large, luxurious, and very comfortable. They are fitted with minibars, televisions, VCRs, and full baths with tubs. Perhaps because of its spaciousness and design, the ship has more the look and feel of a hotel than of a ship.

The dining room and its cuisine are, without doubt, the ship's most outstanding features. The dining room, one of the prettiest at sea, is decorated in exquisite silks and other fine fabrics in soft blues, beige, gray, and gold draped from the floor-to-ceiling windows and covering the handsome dining chairs. The room functions like a restaurant, with passengers dining at their convenience. And they dine leisurely on cuisine that is truly gourmet and some of the finest at sea. Table service is rendered by female rather than male waiters—an unusual case for cruise ships. The waitresses are exceedingly pleasant and efficient. The bar has women attendants as well. The ship has a no-tipping policy.

On the top deck the Grill, with a more informal atmosphere, offers breakfast and in the evening becomes an Italian specialty restaurant with superb cuisine. It's probably the ship's most popular feature.

The *Diamond* has a spa and fitness center with a gym, saunas, and a jogging track; and at the stern there is a hydraulically operated floating marina with equipment for water sports. The ship has good facilities for meetings at sea, with three boardrooms, a large meeting room that can be subdivided into six small rooms, and business-related services such as in-house publishing and teleconference facilities, fax machines, a broadcast center, and secretarial services.

Sailing from its Caribbean home port of San Juan in the winter, the *Diamond* has a series of imaginative itineraries of 3 to 14 days, including Panama Canal itineraries. The deluxe *Song of Flower* cruises in Europe and Asia; *Hanseatic,* a deluxe adventure ship, sails on unusual, ever-changing itineraries from pole to pole; *Bremen,* a deluxe exploration ship sails on various itineraries from Europe to Antarctica; and *Paul Gauguin* cruises in French Polynesia.

REGAL CRUISES, 4199 34th Street, Suite B103, St. Petersburg, FL 33711; 813–867–1300; 800–270–SAIL

Ship/Passengers: *Regal Empress* (902)
Departure ports: Port Manatee, New York and South American ports seasonally
Type of Cruises: 3 to 14 days; Bahamas, Western Caribbean, transcanal
Life-style tip: Casual, informal for budget travelers

Regal Empress, built in 1953, was the *Olympia* of Greek Line and later became the *Caribe 1* of Commodore Cruises. The handsome ship was refurbished in 1993, when it was taken over by the owner of Liberty Travel to sail on short, budget-priced cruises from Port Manatee to the Western Caribbean in winter, New York to New England in summer, and a round-South America cruise in late fall, which the

line expects to make an annual event.

The ship's interior reflects the changes made by her various owners over the years, although some public rooms show the ship's quality when she was built. Particularly outstanding is the dining room, which has fine decorative woods, etched-glass, and some of the original murals.

The food—steak, lobster, and other similar choices sure to be crowd pleasers—is quite good for the budget price. The main show room offers nightly entertainment, and there are other lounges, a bar and dance floor, a casino, and a rather unusual disco created in the former theater.

Regal Empress has an enclosed promenade deck, typical of older ships; an outdoor swimming pool, two whirlpools, gym, beauty salon, boutique, small playroom, and a paneled library with glass-front bookcases and comfortable reading chairs. The ship has as many inside cabins as outside ones in a very wide variety of configurations. Bathrooms are small with shower only. Only suites have television. Passengers get their money's worth, but make no mistake, this lady has seen better days.

Regal Empress has a 14-day fall cruise from New York to her base at Port Manatee in Tampa Bay with a partial transit of the Panama Canal. Ports of call include Nassau, Montego Bay, San Blas Islands, Panama Canal, Puerto Limón (Costa Rica), San Andres (Colombia), and Cozumel. The cruise can also be broken into five-night segments.

ROYAL CARIBBEAN INTERNATIONAL, 1050 Caribbean Way, Miami, FL 33132; 305–539–6573; 800–327–6700

Ships (Passengers): *Enchantment of the Seas* (1,950); *Grandeur of the Seas* (1,950); *Legend of the Seas* (1,808); *Majesty of the Seas* (2,354); *Monarch of the Seas* (2,354); *Nordic Empress* (1,606); *Rhapsody of the Seas* (2,000); *Song of America* (1,414); *Sovereign of the Seas* (2,276); *Splendor of the Seas* (1,800); *Sun Viking* (714); *Viking Serenade* (1,514); *Vision of the Seas* (1,800)
Departure ports: Miami, San Juan, New York
Type of cruises: 3 to 10 days to the Bahamas and Western, Eastern, and Southern Caribbean
Life-style tip: Active, wholesome ambience

Royal Caribbean Cruise Line, launched in the early 1970s, was the first line to build a fleet of ships designed specially for year-round Caribbean cruising. The ships were established as top-of-the-line so quickly that within five years RCCL needed more capacity and did so by "stretching" two of the vessels. They were literally cut in half and prefabricated mid-sections were inserted. Although the method had been used on cargo and other vessels, RCCL's work was the first for cruise ships.

For the 1980s it added superliners with unique design features, and in 1988 it got a headstart on the 1990s with the *Sovereign of the Seas,* the first of the new generation of megaliners and the largest cruise ship afloat at the time. Few ships in history have received so much attention.

The *Sovereign,* RCCL's flagship, is three football fields in length but, miraculously, she does not seem gigantic to passengers on board because of her superb design. A dramatic midship atrium spanning five decks and featuring glass-walled elevators was a "first" for cruise ships and was quickly copied in most new ships. The atrium functions similarly to the lobby of a hotel and provides a friendly focal point for the ship. The atrium also separates the forward section of the ship, which contains all of the cabins, from the aft, where all public rooms, dining, entertainment, sports, and recreation facilities reside—a revolutionary design borrowed from *Song of America.* The arrangement has a double advantage: quieter sleeping areas and shorter walking distances from one location to another in the public area.

It would be impossible for even the most active passenger to participate in all the daily activities offered on the *Sovereign.* Fitness folks have a third-mile outside deck encircling the vessel and one of the best-equipped health clubs at sea, complete with ballet bars, sophisticated computerized exercise equipment, and a high-energy staff to put them through their paces. The sports deck has twin pools and a basketball court.

For those with something less strenuous in mind, there are small, sophisticated lounges for drinks, dancing, and cabaret entertainment. Enrichment programs run the gamut from napkin folding to wine tasting. The library resembles a sedate English club, with its wood paneling and leather chairs. Two feature films run daily in twin cinemas; the shopping boulevard has a sidewalk cafe; the show lounge, a multitiered theater with unobstructed views, runs two different Las Vegas-style revues and variety shows.

Somewhere there's music to suit every mood, from big band, steel band, Latin, country, rock, or strolling violins to classical concerts. The Schooner is a lively piano bar; Music Man has entertainers from blues to country; and the disco projects holograms on the mirrored walls and music videos around the dance floor. Casino Royale offers blackjack, 216 slot machines, and American roulette. The chic Champagne Bar is a quiet corner where 50 people clink flutes and scoop caviar.

Sovereign's twins, *Monarch of the Seas* and *Majesty of the Seas,* arrived in 1991 and 1992, with only a few changes, such as family suites for up to six people. When RCCL merged with Admiral Cruises in 1988, it acquired *Viking Serenade,* which it rebuilt, and for the first time, RCCL entered the short cruise market which had been Admiral's strength.

Designed as they are for Caribbean cruising, the ships have acres of open sun decks and large pools. The line offers low-fat, low-calorie fare and has a ShipShape program on all ships in the fleet. It is often combined with sports in port. Golf Ahoy! enables passengers to play golf at courses throughout the Caribbean. RCCL is the official cruise line of the Professional Golfer's Association of America.

All the ships have bright, cheerful Scandinavian decor, enhanced by Scandinavian art. The themes used throughout the fleet relate to hit musicals and operas. The officers are Norwegian, and the hotel and entertainment staff are a mini–United Nations. The cabins are compact—in fact, they are small, but given RCCL's success, it would seem not to matter; they are also functional and spotless. A top-deck lounge cantilevered from the funnel provides fabulous views from 12 stories above the sea. These lounges are RCCL's signature.

RCCL blankets the Caribbean year-round. It has cruises year-round on the West Coast and Mexico, and in Alaska and Europe in the summer. In 1995, the line added Asia. CocoCay, a small island in the Bahamas inherited from Admiral Cruises, is used for the ships' day at the beach. Labadee, RCCL's private resort on the north coast of Haiti, was created in 1987 and is very popular.

RCCL's enormous success results from its smooth and consistent operation, often winning

"Ship(s) of the Year" and "Cruise Line of the Year" awards. Founded in 1969 as a partnership of three prominent Norwegian shipping companies, RCCL went public in April 1993. Not content to rest on its laurels, however, RCCL is adding a new group of 1,800 to 2,000 passenger ships.

The first ship, *Legend of the Seas*, built in France at the same shipyard that constructed RCCL's three megaliners, was launched in 1995, introducing the first miniature golf course at sea and a spectacular "solarium"—an indoor/outdoor swimming, sunning, and fitness facility. Its sister ships, *Splendor* and *Grandeur*, arrived in 1996, *Rhapsody* and *Enchantment* arrived in 1997, and others are slated for 1998.

RCCL caters to a moderately upscale market and enjoys a high repeat business. The atmosphere is friendly and casual, and the activities are so varied that there is something for everyone at almost every hour of the day. All RCCL ships have programs for children and teenagers, because the line believes that a happy kid on a cruise now will still be a customer in 2020.

With the arrival of the new ships, RCCL is making significant and innovative changes: *Nordic Empress* moves to San Juan for the winter, sailing on 3/4-night cruises to St. Thomas, St. Maarten, and St. Croix—a first. *Sovereign* sails on Bahamas cruises from Miami, the largest cruise ship to sail the route.

In 1997, RCCL bought Celebrity Cruises and plans to operate it as a seperate brand.

ROYAL OLYMPIC LINE, 1 Rockefeller Plaza, Suite 315, New York, NY 10020; 212–397–6400; 800–872–6400

Ships (Passengers): *Stella Solaris* (620); *Odysseus* (400)
Departure ports: Ft. Lauderdale, Miami, Galveston, and Manaus, Brazil
Type of cruises: 10 to 14 days, Western, Eastern, and Southern Caribbean combined with South America and the Amazon or Panama Canal during winter
Life-style tip: Low-key deluxe cruises for an upscale market to off-the-beaten-track destinations

In August 1995, Sun Line merged with Piraeus-based Epirotiki Cruise Line to form a new company, Royal Olympic Cruises. The new line operates a fleet of ten cruise ships under two brands distinguished by the colors of the Greek flag: the "blue" ships of Sun Line are more traditional and upscale and include the *Stella Solaris, Stella Oceanis,* and Epirotiki's *Odysseus*. Three "white" ships of Epirotiki, the *Triton, Orpheus,* and *Olympic,* offer more casual cruises. The four other ships, are managed by Royal Olympic, primarily on charter. At the present time, only the *Stella Solaris,* which recently has been completely renovated, sails in the Caribbean; other members of the fleet cruise mainly in South America in winter or the Greek Isles and Eastern Mediterranean year-round.

Sun Line Cruises has been a pioneer and innovator of Caribbean cruises, being the first to combine the small islands of the Eastern Caribbean with a cruise up the Orinoco River in Venezuela; to extend an Eastern Caribbean cruise to the Amazon River; and to combine the Amazon and Panama Canal in one cruise. While it was not the first cruise line to go to Rio for Carnival, it was one of the few to combine the annual event with the Eastern Caribbean.

One of Sun Line's most popular cruises is timed for the spring equinox at Chichén Itzá in the Yucatán. Frequently, as in the case of the Yucatán and Amazon voyages, Sun Line engages experts to lecture on the cruise's destinations.

Sun Line was started in the mid-1950s by a well-respected Greek family whose patriarch, the late Ch. A. Keusseoglou, had already made his mark as head of Home Lines. At Sun Line, Keusseoglou introduced some of the first ships designed specifically for cruising that eliminated class distinction on board and provided large, sunny public rooms and outdoor areas for relaxation and deck sports.

And while many cruise lines are adding bigger and bigger ships, Sun Line's ships remain small and intimate. The size of the staff in relation to the number of passengers is high. The ships and their staffs are Greek. Many of the personnel have had 20 years of uninterrupted service with Sun Line.

Sun Line specializes in long cruises, but most itineraries can be taken in one week segments.

The combination of unusual itineraries, private club-like atmosphere, and members-of-the-family crew gives the ships special appeal to sophisticated and experienced travelers. Sun Line's passengers in the Caribbean winter season are affluent and tend to be age 45 and older. Often 50 percent are repeaters, an unusually strong testimonial for the line. Sun Line offers spa cuisine on its menus, and for its high percentage of single women passengers, it has a host program.

**SEABOURN CRUISE LINE,
55 Francisco Street, San Francisco, CA 94133; 415–391–7444; 800–929–9595; 800–527–0999 (Canada)**

Ships (Passengers): *Seabourn Legend* (214); *Seabourn Pride* (214); *Seabourn Spirit* (214)
Departure ports: Ft. Lauderdale, Barbados, Aruba, San Juan, Antigua
Type of cruises: 5 to 14 days in Eastern and Southern Caribbean and Panama Canal in winter; worldwide schedules year-round
Life-style tip: The ultimate luxury cruise

When Seabourn was formed in 1987, it set out to create the world's most deluxe cruises on the most elegant, luxurious ships afloat. To guide its debut it engaged Warren Titus, whose stewardship of Royal Viking Lines helped to set top-quality standards for the entire cruise industry. Despite very high per diem rates, Seabourn quickly won enough fans to add a second ship. In 1996, following Royal Cruise Line's demise, Seabourn acquired the former *Queen Odyssey,* which it rechristened the *Seabourn Legend* in July 1996 in New York.

The ships and cruises were designed with a certain type of person in mind—one who normally stays in the best rooms at a luxury hotel and books a deluxe suite on a luxury liner. The staterooms are luxuriously appointed in soft, warm colors and have television with CNN, VCRs, pre-stocked bars, refrigerators, walk-in closets, and large marble bathrooms with tub and shower. Each has a roomy sitting area beside a large picture window with electrically manipulated shades and outside cleaning mechanisms.

Passengers dine on gourmet cuisine served on Royal Doulton china and have open seating. They may also dine from the restaurant menu in their suites, and there is a 24-hour room service menu with a wide selection and a choice wine list.

Seabourn's ships have sleek profiles that resemble the most modern of yachts. A water sports platform at the stern has a "cage" that can be lowered into the water for passengers to swim in the open sea without fear. The ships carry windsurfers, snorkeling and dive equipment, and two high-speed boats. The ships' itineraries take them to all parts of the world, but at least one spends some of the winter in the Caribbean. On selected cruises Seabourn offers a low singles fare of 110 to 125 percent, rather than the standard 150 percent, and offers substantial discounts to repeaters, including free cruises after 140 days of sailing with Seabourn.

Seabourn is a privately held company; 75 percent is owned by its founder, Atle Brynestad, a Norwegian industrialist, and 25 percent is owned by Carnival Cruise Lines.

**SEAWIND CRUISE LINE
Bay Point Office Tower, 4770 Biscayne Boulevard, No. 700, Miami FL 33137; 305–573–3222; 800–258–8006; fax 305–576–1060**

Ship (Passengers): *Seawind Crown* (624)
Departure port: Aruba
Type of cruises: 7 days for Southern Caribbean
Life-style tip: Mainstream cruising at moderate prices

Launched in 1992, the Seawind was the first cruise line to use Aruba as its home port from which to provide weekly sails to the uncrowded ports of the Southern Caribbean, a refreshing alternative to the more traveled Caribbean routes. The cruises are designed for passengers who prefer to travel at an unhurried pace. They have been called a second-timer's cruise because of the nature of the ship and its itineraries.

Seawind Cruise Lines was originally owned by First Ocean Steamship Company, a complex partnership between Nordisk, a large Swedish travel comglomerate, and Waybell, a firm owned by George Potamianos, whose family owns the Epirotiki Line. Together the two own Panama-based Trans World Cruises, which in turn owned the Seawind Crown. In early 1997, Cruise

Holdings, a private investment group that had been an investor in *Seawind,* obtained majority control of the cruise line at the same time it acquired Dolphin Cruise Line. The *Seawind Crown* (the former *Vasco de Gama*) is a spacious ship, combining old-world elegance with contemporary features such as refrigerators, televisions, and hairdryers in every cabin. It was given a $40 million overhaul in 1988, and in 1994 more cabins were added. The attractive decor is mellowed by the fine wood paneling and trim found on older ships. The ship has shops, a casino, and a variety of of small lounges.

The ship sails on 7-day itineraries from Aruba, departing on Sundays to Curaçao, Caracas, Barbados, and St. Lucia, making full-day stops at each port. Both cruises have 2 full days at sea. The line also offers a "SEA-Aruba Cruise Resort Vacation" package for a pre- or post-cruise stay in Aruba.

SILVERSEA CRUISES, 110 East Broward Boulevard, Ft. Lauderdale, FL 33301; 800–321–0165
Ships (Passengers): *Silver Cloud* (306); *Silver Wind* (306)
Departure ports: Nassau, Ft. Lauderdale, Barbados
Type of cruises: Caribbean, seasonally
Life-style tip: Ultra-luxurious surroundings in a relaxing, friendly—not stuffy—atmosphere

Silversea Cruises was launched in late 1994 with the luxurious all-suite *Silver Cloud* designed by Oslo-based Petter Yran and Bjorn Storbraaten, the architects of the *Sea Goddess* and *Seabourn* ships. Her twin, *Silver Wind,* made her debut the following year.

The Silversea ships mirror Seabourn's in many ways but carry 306 passengers (100 more than Seabourn's), and 107 of the Silversea's 155 suites have verandas (Seabourn's suites do not).

Silversea's large suites, averaging 300 square feet, have a spacious sitting area, walk-in closet, fully stocked bar, hairdryer, TV with VCR, direct-dial telephone, and marble-floored bathroom with tub. Passengers are welcomed to their staterooms with fresh flowers, a bottle of champagne, a basket of fruit replenished daily, personalized stationery,

and plush terry robes for use during their cruise.

There is open seating in the dining room and 24-hour room service. The ship has a tiered show lounge spanning two decks, with a nightclub at the upper level, plus a casino, a spa, and a library.

The ships sail in Asia, Africa, and Europe most of the year, but at least one is in the Caribbean for transcanal, Central, and South American itineraries in winter. The co-owners of the line are passenger and shipping veterans Francesco Lefebvre of Rome and the Vlasov Group of Monaco, who were once partners in Sitmar Cruises. Silversea sails under the Italian flag with Italian officers and a European staff.

STAR CLIPPER, INC., 2833 Bird Avenue, Miami, Florida 33133–4504; 800–442–0551; fax 305–442–1611
Ships (Passengers): *Star Clipper* (180); *Star Flyer* (180)
Departure ports: Antigua, St. Maarten
Type of cruises: 7 and 14 days on alternating itineraries in the Eastern Caribbean
Life-style tip: For active travelers looking for the romance of sailing to out-of-the-way places

Star Clipper is the brainchild of Swedish shipping entrepreneur, Mikael Krafft, whose passions for sailing and building yachts and his love of the Clipper Ship (which he says is one of America's greatest inventions) led him to create a cruise line with Clipper ships. Launched in 1991 the cruises are priced to fit between the budget-conscious niche of Windjammer Barefoot Cruises and the pricey voyages of Windstar Cruises and other lines with yachtlike ships.

Star Clipper is truly distinctive. Its newly built tallships—each accommodating 180 passengers in 90 staterooms—are direct descendants of the fast, sleek clipper ships that ruled the seas during the mid 1800s. Built in Belgium the vessels are 357 feet long with four masts and square-rigged sails on the forward mast—a Barguentine configuration—with a total of 17 sails (36,000 square feet of sail area). They are manned, not computerized and capable of attaining speeds of 19.4 knots. At 208 feet tall they are among the tallest of the Tall Ships.

Today's clippers retain the romance of sailing under canvas coupled with the excitement of participating in the sailing of an authentic square rigger. They are further enhanced by the out-of-the-way Caribbean destinations that the cruises visit. Passangers quickly get to know the youthful crew who double in their duties as deck hands, sports instructors, and in other capacities.

Responding to a changing preference among some vacationers for a deemphasis on ostentatious food and the crowds of big ships, the cruises focus on an active, casual, and even educational, experience, so it's more like being on a private yacht. The food is good but not gourmet. Dress is very casual with shorts and deck shoes the uniform of the day, and only slightly more casual in the evening. Fellow passangers will be kindred souls—you hope—and 50 percent or more might be Europeans, depending on the time of the year. The cruises are also a great environment for families with children ages 7 to 17.

All cabins are carpeted, air-conditioned, and have private bathrooms with showers. Most cabins are outside facing and fitted with twin beds that can be converted to a bed slightly larger than the standard queen size. Eight inside cabins are furnished with upper and lower beds and eight cabins can accommodate three passengers. The top staterooms on the main deck have marble bathrooms with bathtubs and hairdryers. Cabins are equipped with multi-channel radio and video players. Video tapes are available from the ships library. There is storage for luggage, golf clubs, scuba gear, and other such items.

Facilities include a small piano bar, located midship on the main deck. It has brass-framed panoramic windows, carved paneling, and cushioned banquettes. The unusual lighting comes from the skylight overhead, it's actually the transparent bottom of the sun deck pool, one of the ship's two small pools. The piano bar is on the landing of a double staircase leading into the Clipper Dining Room on the deck below. All passangers dine at one seating, although when the ship is full the room can be very crowded. In addition to regular meal service, the dining room converts into a meeting room with screen projectors and video monitors.

Adjoining the aft end of the Piano Bar is the Tropical Bar, protected from the elements by a broad canvas awning, under which is found the bar, a dance floor, and the stage where the

Captain holds his daily talks, and where much of the entertainment takes place during the cruise. Breakfast and lunch buffets are occasionally served here too. Also on the main deck is a library that resembles an English club with large brass-framed windows, carved paneling, and a marble fireplace. It doubles as a reception desk and is used for small meetings.

The *Star Flyer* is based in Antigua in winter, sailing on alternating 7-day cruises in the Eastern Caribbean. An unduplicated 14-day itinerary is possible with back-to-back cruises. The *Star Clipper* spends the winter in Southeast Asia and summer in the Mediterranean. The clippers can anchor in bays that large cruise ships cannot reach. Launches take passengers to isolated beaches, scuba and snorkeling spots, or to enjoy other water sports. Snorkeling gear, water skis, sailboards, and volleyballs are carried on board.

TALL SHIP ADVENTURES, INC.
1010 South Joliet Street, Suite 200, Aurora, CO 80012; 800–662–0090; fax 303–755–9007

Ship (Passengers): *Sir Francis Drake* (36)
Departure port: Tortola
Type of cruises: 3, 4, or 7 days of Virgin Islands
Life-style tips: Sailing under canvas in comfort

Begun in 1988, this cruise line offers short cruises on a classic, three-masted tall ship with comfortable accommodations for 36 passengers. The cruises, evoking the romance of the sea of bygone days, depart twice weekly year-round from Tortola on 3- and 4-day cruises of the British Virgin Islands and can be combined into a week's cruise. The ship's ports of call depend on the winds and weather but most are the hideaways where large ships cannot go.

The 162-foot-long ship is completely air-conditioned and has a wood-paneled lounge with bar, stereo, video, and television. In the evening the salon is transformed into a lovely dining room. Snacks are also served on the topside open deck. The cabins are air-conditioned and have twin or double beds and upper bunks and private toilet with shower.

The ship carries Sunfish sailboats, windsurfing and snorkeling equipment, and a power boat and diving equipment for use by certified divers.

WINDJAMMER BAREFOOT CRUISES,
**Box 120, Miami Beach, FL 33119-0120;
305–672–6453; 800–327–2601**

Ships (Passengers): *Amazing Grace* (96);
supply ship); *Fantome* (126); *Flying Cloud*
(76); *Mandalay* (72); *Polynesia* (126); *Yankee
Clipper* (66)

Departure ports: Cozumel for Western
Caribbean; various ports for Eastern Caribbean

Type of cruises: 6 days for Western Caribbean;
6 and 13 days for various Bahamas and
Caribbean itineraries

Life-style tip: Barefoot adventure for sailors
from 7 to 70 with good sea legs and happy spirits

Windjammer Barefoot Cruises, which celebrated
its fiftieth anniversary in 1992, boasts the largest
fleet of tall ships in the world. The history of each
ship is part of the lore and pleasure of the cruise.
The *Mandalay*, the queen of the fleet, was once
the luxury yacht of financier E. F. Hutton and an
oceanographic research vessel of Columbia
University. The *Fantome*, extensively renovated in
1992, was originally built for the Duke of
Westminster and was later owned by the Guinness
family of brewery fame. They sold it to Onassis to
be given to Princess Grace and the Prince of
Monaco as a wedding present. But, as the story
goes, Onassis was not invited to the wedding, so
the present was never delivered.

Most cabins on all ships are fitted with bunk
beds. They are cozy, not luxurious, and have
private bath facilities and steward service. The
food is good, not gourmet. The atmosphere is
casual—shorts and beachwear on a full-time
basis—and congenial. Most of your time will be
spent enjoying the sun, swimming, snorkeling,
steel band music, barbecues, and picnics on the
beach.

The ships have super itineraries, including sailing from Grenada through the Grenadines, a
route that is often called by yachtsmen the most
beautiful sailing waters in the world. Other members of the fleet visit off-the-beaten-path destinations such as Saba and St. Eustatius, in the Eastern
and Southern Caribbean. Most are 6 days long;
some have different southbound and northbound
legs that can be combined into a two-week cruise.

Windjammer offers several all-singles cruises as
well as fitness cruises for high-energy folks during the year. The cruises appeal most to people
with a sense of adventure who want something
completely different from their routine structured
lives in a relaxed and friendly atmosphere. Fellow
passengers (who return about 40 percent of the
time) come from all walks of life and many countries, although most are Americans. The company
does not take children under 7 years of age.

It's not for everyone, but then, Windjammer
doesn't try to be. If there's a Captain Mitty in you,
though, then here's your chance to stand watch at
the wheel or climb the masts, and to have the kind
of tropical holiday of which dreams and travel
posters are made.

WINDSTAR CRUISES,
**300 Elliot Avenue West,
Seattle, Washington 98119;
206–281–3535; 800–967–8103**

Ships (Passengers): *Wind Star* (148), *Wind
Song* (148), *Wind Spirit* (148); *Wind Surf* (312)

Departure ports: Antigua, Barbados, Puerto
Caldera

Type of cruises: 7 days to the Eastern and
Southern Caribbean; Costa Rica, and Panama
Canal

Life-style tip: Combination of sailing yacht and
deluxe cruise ship, for active people

Imagine a deck one-and-one-half-times the
length of a football field and half its width. Now,
look up to the sky and imagine four masts in a
row, each as high as a 20-story building and each
with two enormous triangular sails. If you can
picture these dimensions, you will have a mental
image of the Windcruiser, which is the newest,
most revolutionary vessel since the introduction
of the steamship in the last century. The six great
sails are manned by computers instead of deck
hands. The computer is designed to monitor the
direction and velocity of the wind to keep the ship
from heeling no more than 6 degrees. The sails
can be furled in less than two minutes.

The windcruiser marries the romance and tradition of sailing with the comfort and amenities of
a Cruise Ship. The ship has 75 identical, outside
182-square-foot staterooms (so they are comparable in size to those on regular cruise ships).

The well-designed cabins make optimum use of space, and are fitted with twin- or queen-size beds, mini-bar, color television, VCR, satelite phone communications, and individual safes.

Cabins, gym, and sauna are on the bottom two of four passenger decks. The third deck has a main lounge and dining salon; both are handsome rooms that have the ambience of a private yacht. The dining room, which has open seating, serves gourmet sophisticated cuisine. The ship has a tiny casino, boutique, and beauty salon. The top deck has a swimming pool, bar, and veranda lounge used for lunch during the day and a disco at night. Through the overhead skylight of the lounge, passengers can have a dramatic view of the majestic sails overhead.

The *Wind Star* has a crew of 81; the officer staff is Norwegian and dining staff are Italian, French, and other nationalities. Cabins are attended by stewardesses. The ship can cruise at a maximum speed of 12 knots. Electrical power and backup propulsion are provided on the 440-foot vessel by three diesel-electric engines.

The vessel has a shallow 13.5-foot draft that enables her to stop at less-visited ports and secluded beaches and coves. She is fitted with a water sports platform that gives passengers direct access to the sea. Sailboats and windsurfing boards are carried on board, as are Zodiaks (inflatable boats) to take passengers snorkeling, scuba diving, waterskiing, and fishing. The gear for these activities is available for use without additional charge. Any passanger lucky enough to hook a fish can have it cooked to order by the ship's chefs.

Cruises are planned to be partly cruise, partly yacht charter, and partly Club Med-type vacation. They are geared to working professionals who can afford to take a cruise and like the luxury of a cruise ship or resort, but who want a more active and unusual vacation than that associated with traditional cruises; thus they attract experienced cruise passengers and boat owners as well as people who may have shunned cruise ships in the past.

The *Wind Star* departs from Antigua and cruises the Caribbean from October or November to April (she sails in the Mediterranean in summer); *Wind Spirit* departs from St. Thomas and Barbados from mid-fall through winter, (she spends the summer in Alaska); and *Wind Song* recently moved to the Western Caribbean from Singapore where she will sail on a new Costa Rica itinerary.

Windstar Cruises was acquired by Holland America Line in 1987, and the following year both companies were purchased by Carnival Cruise Lines. Windstar, however, continues to operate as a separate entity with its own special type of cruises.

In April 1997, Windstar Cruises bought *Club Med I*, one of two identical ships in the Club Med fleet that are large versions of Windstar's ships, and at press time was negotiating for the second ship, *Club Med II*. After some remodeling, *Club Med I* to be renamed *Wind Surf,* will enter service for Windstar Cruises in May 1998 in the Mediterrean for the summer and will return to the Caribbean for the winter season beginning in November 1998.

PART IV
PORTS OF CALL

(PRESENTED COUNTERCLOCKWISE FROM THE BAHAMAS)

The Bahamas

Nassau, New Providence Island, Freeport, Grand Bahama Island, The Out Islands

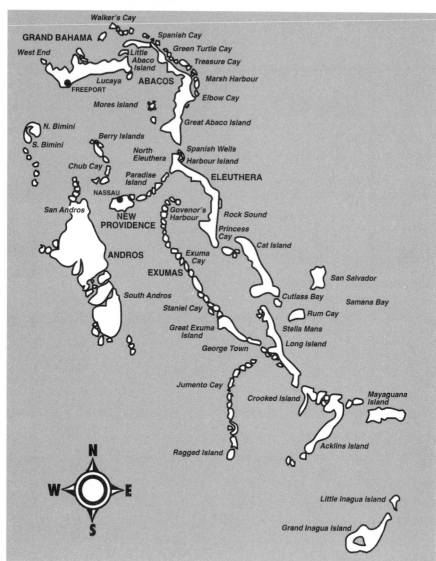

AT A GLANCE

Antiquities ★
Architecture ★★★
Art and Artists ★★
Beaches ★★★★★
Colonial Buildings ★★★★
Crafts ★★
Cuisine ★★
Dining/Restaurants ★★★
Entertainment ★★★★
Forts ★★
Gambling Casinos ★★★★★
History ★★
Monuments ★★
Museums ★
Nightlife ★★★★
Scenery ★★★
Shopping ★★
Sight-seeing ★★
Sports ★★★★★
Transportation ★★

CHAPTER CONTENTS

DISTANT NEIGHBORS

W hether your destination is Nassau, Freeport, or one of the Out Islands, your first impression of the Bahamas and the image you are likely to carry away with you is of water. Intensely beautiful with shades of aqua, turquoise, cobalt, and peacock blue, these waters have long attracted boating and fishing enthusiasts, and now they are being discovered by snorkelers, scuba divers, and cruise passengers.

The Bahamas is an archipelago of more than 700 low-lying tropical islands and islets dotting 100,000 square miles of sea. They start only 50 miles from the eastern coast of Florida and stretch for 750 miles to the northern coasts of Haiti and Cuba. They are strategically situated between the Atlantic on the north, south, and east and the Gulf of Mexico on the west; about half of the archipelago lies north of the Tropic of Cancer.

The Bahamas derives its name from the Spanish, *baja mar,* or shallows, which the early explorers used in mapping the group. Out of the hundreds of islands, islets, and cays that make up the island nation, only about three dozen are populated. Of these, three—Nassau, Paradise Island, and Freeport—get the lion's share of visitors and almost all of the cruise passengers.

The Bahamas is so close to the U.S. mainland that many people hop over for the weekend in their own boats or private planes, and ships board thousands of passengers every week for one-, two-, three-, and four-day cruises between Florida and Bahamian ports.

Yet, the Bahamas is foreign. A British colony for more than two centuries and independent since 1973, the Bahamas in many ways is still more British than the Queen. This, despite the fact that throughout the history of the islands from the time Columbus made his first landfall on the Bahamian island of San Salvador and Ponce de León came in search of the Fountain of Youth, the Bahamas has been as closely linked to events in the United States as with any in Britain.

Today the British flavor combined with American familiarity, the magnificent waters and endless days of clear skies, the outstanding facilities, the variety of sports and entertainment all have made the Bahamas the most frequently visited destination in the tropics, with more than three million visitors a year.

On any given day in port, you can play tennis and golf or bike and jog in the countryside. The shallow, warm waters provide a carnival of life for snorkelers and scuba divers. Protected bays and shallow waters near shore are ideal for windsurfing, waterskiing, jetskiing, and parasailing. There are an abundance of fish in the deep waters only a short distance from port and excellent opportunities for deep-sea fishing year-round.

If the sporting life is not your first requirement, a walking tour of Nassau is a stroll through history and a chance to check out the bargains in the shops and straw markets along the way. You can do it on your own or in the company of a Bahamian host that you arrange through the Tourist Office's People-to-People Program. Evening entertainment in port can range from music of a scratch band in a rustic tavern by the sea to an extravaganza with Las Vegas sizzle at a cavernous casino.

COLUMBUS AND THE AFTERMATH

The diversity of the Bahamas is the result of its variegated past. The islands' recorded history begins on the most significant date in the annals of the New World—October 12, 1492—with Christopher Columbus making his first landfall on an island the native Lucayans called Guanahani and that Columbus christened San Salvador, the Savior.

When the Spaniards who followed Columbus found no gold they abandoned all interest in the Bahamas, but not before enslaving the entire Lucayan Indian population of 20,000 and shipping them to work the mines in Cuba and Hispaniola. Ponce de León was apparently an exception. He came to the Bahamas in search of the Fountain of Youth before moving on to Florida to continue his quest. Today, four places on the island of Bimini claim to have been stops in his epic journey.

A century after the Spaniards departed from the islands, in 1648, English settlers fleeing religious conflict in Bermuda arrived on Sigatoo Island, which they named Eleuthera after the Greek word meaning "freedom." Following a dispute within the group, which was known as the Company of Eleuthran Adventurers, many of the settlers left and founded another settlement at or near Spanish Wells.

In time, the Bahamas was granted to the lords of the Carolinas, absentee landlords whose lack of interest allowed the infestation of pirates, like the infamous Edward Teach, known as Blackbeard, and Henry Morgan. The hundreds of harbors were ideal havens for smuggling and piracy; their reefs and shallows ensured—by accident or design—frequent wrecks.

Finally in 1718 the ironfisted British captain Woodes Rogers took command of the Bahamas and established order. Rogers gave the scavengers a clear choice: Give up piracy and be pardoned or be hanged. Eight who tested Rogers's will were hung in public, thus helping to bring a chapter of the Bahamas' history to a close. Ten years later, the islands were officially made a British colony with Rogers the first royal governor.

In an effort to destroy British supply lines during the American Revolution, the American Navy captured Nassau and held it for two weeks. Later the Spanish held it for a year and did not leave until they were forced out by Col. Andrew Deveaux, a Loyalist from the Carolinas and one of 8,000 who had fled to the Bahamas after the Revolution. Deveaux and the other Loyalists brought with them all their possessions including slaves, and in the Bahamas they replicated the plantation society they had left behind. The old order lasted until slavery was abolished in 1834.

Twice again events in the United States led to direct Bahamian involvement and a boom: gun-running during the Civil War and rum-running during Prohibition. After that, the American–Bahamian connection became more respectable, but no less flamboyant. During World War II, the royal governor of the Bahamas was none other than the duke of Windsor, who along with his glamorous American-born duchess set the style for what was to become the Bahamas' most important postwar enterprise, tourism.

THE NEW BAHAMAS

After the war, a weak and weary Britain welcomed foreign investments that would enable her colonies to become self-supporting. At the same time, several wealthy Americans saw the opportunity to create playgrounds in the Bahamas, which could benefit from the islands' proximity to the U.S. mainland. The most significant venture turned a spit of land facing Nassau harbor into the most complete resort in the tropics.

In the 1950s, A&P heir Huntington Hartford bought most of Hog Island, as it was known, from another millionaire and renamed it Paradise. His estate, set in landscaped gardens adorned with classic marble statues and enclosed with stones from a 12th-century French monastery, became the centerpiece of the fashionable Ocean Club.

During the following decade, Paradise Island was acquired by Resorts International, which added hotels, casino, and extensive sporting facilities. They also made Paradise more accessible by building a multimillion-dollar bridge between the island and Nassau, and later, by adding an airline. Then, in 1989, famed television star Merv Griffin bought Resorts International and put his stamp on the island. But the greatest transformation of all came in 1994 after Sun International bought out Griffin and transformed Resort International's holdings into a new resort named Atlantis, creating an entirely new landscape of lakes, parks, and attractions, and renovated all the hotels for a total investment of $250 million.

About the same time that Hartford was creating Paradise, American financier Wallace Groves was transforming Grand Bahama Island, a little-known stretch of limestone and pine forest situated only 60 miles from the coast of Florida. Freeport, as it is better known, became the showplace of its day with hotels, casinos, a flashy international shopping bazaar, and six championship golf courses.

In the 1970s with the recession, inflation, oil crisis, and competition from newer resorts in Florida and the Caribbean, Freeport lost a great deal of its luster. But by the mid-1980s a renaissance was underway with millions of dollars being invested by the government and private developers.

Another transformation took place in the 1980s at Cable Beach, a 5-mile stretch west of downtown Nassau. The multimillion-dollar Cable Beach Hotel and Casino opened in 1983, (now a Radisson hotel), followed by the thousand-room Crystal Palace Resort and Casino, the largest hotel in the tropics (now a Marriott and extensively renovated).

The Royal Bahamian Hotel, the colonial grande dame of Cable Beach, which served as the fashionable resort of royalty and heads of state in its heyday as the Balmoral Beach Club when the duke of Windsor was governor, was also renovated. In 1994, it was purchased by Sandals, the Jamaican-based, all-inclusive group, and after extensive renovation and expansion reopened in 1996 as the chain's most luxurious resort. Down the road Breezes Bahamas, formerly the Ambassador Beach, is the first Bahamas member of Superclubs, also a Jamaican all-inclusive chain.

As your ship steams into Nassau Harbor, look south and you can spot Cable Beach, on the ship's starboard side. The stretch of green north of the harbor on the port side of the ship is Paradise Island. Long before it became a famous playground, the island served as a natural breakwater for Nassau harbor, protecting the only safe entrance to New Providence. In the distance the arched bridge connecting Paradise Island to Nassau is the most visible evidence of the long-standing American–Bahamian connection.

FAST FACTS

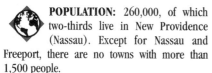
POPULATION: 260,000, of which two-thirds live in New Providence (Nassau). Except for Nassau and Freeport, there are no towns with more than 1,500 people.

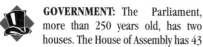
GOVERNMENT: The Parliament, more than 250 years old, has two houses. The House of Assembly has 43 members elected every five years; the Senate is an advisory group of sixteen appointed members. The Bahamas is a member of the Commonwealth and the British queen is its monarch, too.

CLIMATE: Strictly speaking, the Bahamas is not part of the Caribbean, but it enjoys a similar idyllic tropical climate. The Gulf Stream bathes the western coast with clear warm waters, and easterly tradewinds caress the shores. As a result, temperatures in the northernmost islands seldom drop below 60°F and rise above 90°F.

CLOTHING: Casual but proper. Bahamians tend to be conservative and are offended by the overly revealing dress of some tourists on the streets. Informal spring/summer sportswear for day and evening will suit most occasions, although elegant attire is not out of place in the evening, depending on your choice of dining place and activities. Generally, men neatly dressed in slacks, sports shirt, and jacket will be comfortable at any nightspot in the islands. For women, a cocktail dress or stylish pants suit is appropriate.

CURRENCY: The Bahamian dollar (B$) is freely exchanged with the U.S. dollar at par.

DEPARTURE TAX: When you leave the Bahamas by air, you pay $15 per adult and per child, age six and older. Children ages five and under are not charged.

ELECTRICITY: 120 volt, 60 cycle A.C. Standard U.S. shavers, hairdryers, and other appliances can be used.

ENTRY FORMALITIES: U.S. citizens with proof of citizenship or birth certificate do not need passports for visits of up to three weeks.

LANGUAGE: English—more British than American—and with a lilt and influences from the early settlers, African slaves, and Caribbean islanders who came here to work.

POSTAL SERVICE: A letter to the United States costs 55 cents per half ounce; a postcard, 40 cents. The post office nearest the pier in Nassau is at Parliament and East Hill streets, three blocks south of Rawson Square. In Freeport, the post office nearest the pier is at Explorer's Way. Hours: 9 A.M. to 5:30 P.M.

PUBLIC HOLIDAYS: January 1, New Year's Day; Good Friday, Easter Sunday and Monday; Whit Monday (six weeks after Easter); Labor Day (first Friday in June); July 10, Independence Day; Emancipation Day (first Monday in August); October 12, Discovery Day; December 25, Christmas; December 26, Boxing Day.

 TELEPHONE AREA CODE: 242. (Dial exactly as you do for a long distance call within the United States.)

 TIME: Eastern Standard Time. Daylight Saving Time is adopted in the summer months as in the United States.

 VACCINATION REQUIREMENT: None.

 AIRLINES: Direct flights from major U.S. gateways by American Airlines/ American Eagle, Bahamasair, Carnival Air, Comair, Continental, Delta, Gulfstream, Paradise Island Airlines, Taesa, Trinity Air, USAir, USAir Express, and United; and from Canada by Air Canada.

 INFORMATION:

In the United States,
  Bahamas Tourist Offices: 800–422–4262.
  Sports information: Bahamas Sports Line, 800–32–SPORT.
  Atlanta: 2957 Clairmont Rd., No. 150; GA 30329; Tel. 404–633–1793; fax 404–633–1575.
  Chicago: 8600 W. Bryn Mawr Ave., No. 820; IL 60631; Tel. 312–693–1500; fax 312–693–1114.
  Dallas: 2050 Stemmons Freeway, World Trade Center, No. 116; TX 75258–1408; Tel. 214–742–1186; fax 214–741–4118.
  Los Angeles: 3450 Wilshire Blvd., No. 208; CA 90010; Tel. 213–385–0033; fax 213–383–3966.
  Miami: One Turnberry Place, 19495 Biscayne Blvd. No. 809; Adventura, FL 33180;

  Tel. 305–932–0051; fax 305–682–8758; Grand Bahamas Tourist Bureau, Tel. 800–448–3386.
  New York: 150 East 52nd St., 28th Floor; NY 10022; Tel. 212–758–2777; fax 212–753–6531.
In Canada:
  Toronto: 121 Bloor St. E., No. 1101; Ontario M4W 3M5; Tel. 800–667–3777 (Canada only); fax 416–968–6711.
In Nassau:
  The Ministry of Tourism has information booths at Prince George Dock; Tel. 325–9155; Ministry of Tourism Hdqs., Bay St.; Tel. 322–7500.
In Freeport:
  The Tourist Information Centre is located in the Sir Charles Hayward Library, Tel. 352–8044, and there are booths at Freeport Harbor, Tel. 352–9651, and in the International Bazaar. Hours: 8:30 A.M. to 5 P.M., Monday to Saturday.

AN INTRODUCTION TO NASSAU

Old World charm and New World glamour come together in Nassau and its elaborate resorts of Cable Beach and Paradise Island. Nassau is one of the most sophisticated and popular destinations in the tropics.

For most people Nassau *is* the Bahamas. However, Nassau is not an island but a town—to be sure, the main town—on the island of New Providence, located at the center of the Bahamas archipelago. As the seat of government, the hub of commercial activity, and the crossroads of the nation's air and sea lanes, Nassau has acquired the bustle and worldliness of an international capital. Yet it is the only place throughout the 700 islands of the Bahamas archipelago, including Freeport, that comes even close to having this character.

For cruise passengers Nassau's combination of the old and the new in an international city surrounded by lovely beaches is perfect. Stretched along the north coast of the island, the town is compact and easy to explore on foot in a leisurely morning or afternoon. It is situated on a low-lying island only 21 miles long and 7 miles wide that is easy to see by car, bus, or moped in a few hours. It is also possible to combine some sight-seeing with a sport or a shopping expedition and have time at the beach.

Perhaps more than any other place in the Bahamas, Nassau reflects the country's British past visually in the colonial buildings of Old Nassau and in the trappings of tradition that have lasted through three centuries. Cruise passengers encounter the British legacy almost from the moment they step off their ship. Street traffic is directed by "bobbies" whose uniforms—white jacket, blue trousers with a red stripe, and pith helmet—are a tropical version of their London counterparts. Driving is on the left as in Britain.

The graceful colonial buildings of Parliament Square are the backdrop for a statue of Queen Victoria, and visitors on hand for the annual opening of Parliament will see the members of the legislature dressed in striped pants and morning coats. Were you to step into the Supreme Court while it is in session, you would find the judges and lawyers dressed in robes and wearing the traditional white wigs.

NASSAU'S ORIGINS

Nassau, originally known as Sayle's Island, was settled for the first time around 1666 by a group of Bermudians and English, and within five years it had more than 900 settlers. By the time the Bahamas was granted to the Six Lords Proprietors of Carolina by the British Crown in 1670 the population had reached almost 1,000, including slaves. But the settlement developed into a pirate stronghold, which led to Spanish raids in 1684— raids so effective, apparently, that the town was abandoned. Some settlers returned two years later but growth was slow until 1695, when one of the governors, Nicholas Trott, laid out a town plan for Charlestown, as it was called. To protect the western entrance to the harbor he built Fort Nassau, which he named in honor of the Prince of Orange–Nassau who later became William III of England.

Except for Trott, however, the Carolina landlords were not interested in the Bahamas and allowed it to become a haven for pirates and privateers. Finally, from 1718 to 1721 and again from 1729 to 1732, under the first royal governor, Woodes Rogers, Nassau was cleaned up, Fort Nassau restored, an assembly established, and a town plan created, which has remained, more or less, the same to the present day. To protect the eastern entrance to the harbor, Fort Montagu was added in 1741.

Nassau had a burst of prosperity later in the century when Loyalist refugees fleeing the American Revolutionary War came here to settle. Both administratively and architecturally, the new arrivals made a major impact on the island and transformed the scrappy little port into a pretty and prosperous town with new streets and wharfs and city ordinances for fire and health.

In 1787, the last royal governor of Virginia, John Murray, better known to history as Lord Dunmore, became the governor of the Bahamas. Arrogant, incompetent, and thoroughly disliked, Dunmore left an indelible mark on the Bahamas with his passion for building. He cost both the Crown and the Bahamians a great deal of money and grief. To fortify the island he built Fort Charlotte on the west, Fort Fincastle and Fort Winton on the east, and added gun emplacements on Hog (Paradise) Island. His home, Dunmore House, served as the governor's residence until Government House was completed. On the eastern end of New Providence he built the Hermitage as his summer home. The present mansion, reconstructed in the early 1900s, is the residence of the Roman Catholic bishop of Nassau.

 ## PORT PROFILE: NASSAU

EMBARKATION: In Nassau the piers are located on the north side of New Providence Island less than a ten-minute walk from the heart of town. Ships pull dockside to the modern piers, known as Prince George Wharf, one block from Bay Street, the main shopping street of Nassau. An attractive pedestrian walk from the piers to the square was added as part of the port expansion in 1991. Taxis and motorcoaches are waiting for passengers at the dock when ships arrive.

Passengers are allowed to come and go freely between their ship and town. No special identification or security measures are necessary other than those required by your ship for reboarding—usually a boarding card, cabin key, or some other form of identification distributed by your ship. After leaving the pier, en route to Rawson Square, you will pass the Welcome Center of the Bahamas Ministry of Tourism where you can pick up maps, brochures, and other information.

LOCAL TRANSPORTATION: Taxis are readily available and are metered. Rates are supposed to be fixed at $2 flag-fall and 20 cents each one-fifth mile for one or two passengers; $2 for each additional passenger. Unfortunately, some Nassau taxi drivers pretend their meters do not work in order to overcharge tourists.

If you plan to engage a taxi for sight-seeing, negotiate the price in advance. Be aware that there are free-lancers who are not legal taxis and who will charge whatever they think they can get. Look for a taxi with a "Bahama Host" sticker on his windshield. They are reliable and the best informed.

In Nassau, city buses or jitneys (75-cent fare) run frequently throughout the day and early evening from two downtown departure points only three blocks from the pier. At Bay and Frederick streets next to the Straw Market is the station for buses to the north and eastern parts of the island; those to Cable Beach and residential areas on the western side of the island leave from Bay Street and Navy Lion Road, next to the British Colonial Hotel. For Paradise Island, you'll need to take a taxi or ferry. The Paradise Island Bridge toll is $2 per motorized vehicle. Taxis from Prince George Wharf to Paradise Island are likely to charge $6 plus toll, for a one-way trip.

Surreys, the horse-drawn carriages, which can be hired at Rawson Square, are strictly for tourists and cost $5 per person. If you are more than two or if you want to keep the surrey for a longer period than the usual half-hour tour, be sure to negotiate the price in advance.

FERRY SERVICES: Ferries for Paradise Island depart from Prince George Wharf every 20 minutes from early morning until 5:30 P.M. and cost $2.

CAR RENTALS: Car rentals from major U.S. companies are available at major hotels and various locations throughout Nassau. Those with offices nearest the pier are Avis (Tel. 326–6380) and Dollar Rent-a-Car (Tel. 325–3716) at the British Colonial Hotel. Expect to pay $50 and up for a subcompact with unlimited mileage. If you rent a car with a credit card, you must be 21 years or older; without the card, 25 years or older. Americans may use U.S. driver's licenses for up to three months. REMEMBER, Bahamians drive on the **LEFT.** The speed limit is generally 30 m.p.h. but not many drivers observe it, least of all the bus drivers.

MOPEDS/BICYCLES: Rental agencies for motor scooters and bicycles are located by the pier and on Marlboro Road near the British Colonial Hotel. A valid driver's license and a helmet supplied by the rental agency are compulsory for using a motorbike. From Motorscooter Rentals (Tel. 326–8329) at the pier, the price is $26 for half a day, plus $4 insurance, and includes helmet and full tank of gas. You must leave a $10 deposit as well. To repeat, *DRIVING IS ON THE LEFT.*

EMERGENCY NUMBERS: Police: Nassau, Tel. 911 and Tel. 322–4444. Medical Services: Nassau, Princess Margaret Hospital, Tel. 322–2861. Ambulance: Nassau, Tel. 322–2221.

BUDGET PLANNING

Nassau is not a cheap port. Taxis, car rentals, admission fees to privately operated sight-seeing and other attractions, deluxe restaurants, and drinks are usually 20 percent higher than comparable facilities in the United States and other Caribbean ports of call. These costs, however, can be avoided or offset. Here are some ways, particularly for visitors on limited budgets.

- *Walk—Nassau is a compact town that's easy and pleasurable to cover on foot.*
- *Use public transportation, which is good and low cost.*
- *Enjoy the abundant, beautiful, free, easy-to-reach beaches.*
- *Dine in restaurants serving local specialties. They are reasonably priced and clean.*

 DRUGS, CRIME, AND TODAY'S REALITIES

The Bahamas, like other places, is not immune to today's social ills. Although you might be approached to buy drugs, the possession, sale, or purchase of drugs is prohibited. Penalties for breaking the law apply to tourists as much as to Bahamians; they are severe and the jails unpleasant.

Theft and crime, particularly in Nassau and Freeport, are on the rise. As a tourist, you are an easy target. Rented cars and motorscooters, for example, have special plates that make them easy to identify. However, you can reduce your vulnerability with prudence.

Do not park in secluded or isolated areas, particularly on the south coast of Nassau. Never leave valuables in your car or on the beach, including hotel beaches. Do not walk alone in remote or lightly trafficked areas, and most of all, do not engage someone as a guide who approaches you on the street or beach. All guides and taxi drivers in the Bahamas are licensed; if you have any doubt about a person's credentials, you need only step into the nearest tourist office or police station.

 **AUTHOR'S FAVORITE ATTRACTIONS**

WALKING TOUR OF OLD NASSAU
SNORKELING/SCUBA
A DAY AT ATLANTIS RESORT
GOLF
PEOPLE-TO-PEOPLE PROGRAM
FRENCH CLOISTERS AND VERSAILLES
  GARDENS/OCEAN CLUB

 NASSAU SHORE EXCURSIONS

Since Nassau is easy to manage on your own and has a wide selection of activities to enjoy, shore excursions offered by cruise lines tend to be limited. The attractions and sports on these tours are described elsewhere in this chapter.

Combination Tour: 3–4 hours, $25–$36. A drive through Old Nassau and around the island is combined with a visit to the Ardastra Gardens. Some visit Paradise Island, including Versailles Gardens, or Coral World. Suggested for those on their first visit who cannot make the walking tour and whose interest in sports is marginal. A shorter two-hour city tour is hardly worthwhile since most of it can be covered in a walking tour on your own. Coral World's tour with transportation by ferry to and from the port costs US $22.

Atlantis Submarine: $74 adults; $37 child. See description later in chapter.

Seaworld Explorer: $29 adult; $19 child. Semi-submarine drops about five feet below surface of the water for you to view the gardens. Tour begins and returns from the port and goes on a 15-minute ride to the underwater marine park, known as the Sea Gardens, at Athol Island.

Half-day Sail & Snorkel Excursion: 3 hours, $30–$34 adult; $15–$17 child. Several large catamarans and "pirate" sailing ships offer full party cruises to nearby beaches for swimming, snorkeling, rum punch, and/or lunch, $50. Half-day Scuba Dive, $35–$55.

Golf. Most cruise lines offer packages, or you can make your own arrangements. Majestic Tours (tel. 242– 322–2606), one of the major local companies, has golf packages for $90–$110, depending on the course. See the Sports section later in this chapter.

Night Club Tour: $20; $35 with dinner. The tour includes admission to a nightclub with Bahamian and West Indian music and show, drink, tips, and transfers. It is suggested for those who are more interested in local entertainment than casinos but are reluctant to go out on their own.

Casino/Show: $35, cocktail show; $55, dinner show, including transportation to/from hotel at *Crystal Palace* or *Atlantis.* Las Vegas-style musical revue with long-legged showgirls baring lots of "t & a" and visit to the casino. Either can be done on your own, but you will not be saving money, as the round-trip fare by taxi costs $12 or more.

PEOPLE-TO-PEOPLE

The Bahamas Ministry of Tourism gives you the opportunity to meet Bahamians as you would a friend through its People-to-People program, which brings tourists together with Bahamians who have volunteered to host visitors.

People-to-People volunteers, 500 in Nassau and 200 in Freeport, come from a cross section of the community. They might belong to the same service club, such as Rotary or Kiwanis, as you do or practice your profession or trade or share your hobby. Many have traveled themselves and know what it is like to be on one's own in a strange place. They know, too, how much more meaningful a visit can be when it is enriched with a personal experience.

These nice folks are *volunteers.* Although the program is operated by The Bahamas Ministry of Tourism, the volunteers are neither employed nor subsidized by the government. They offer their time and friendship without compensation and neither ask nor expect anything in return. They are involved because they enjoy meeting people from other countries and they want visitors to know their country in a natural, noncommercial atmosphere.

The form that the welcome takes depends on your Bahamian host. Because they, too, work for a living, they generally entertain in the evenings or on weekends. They might take you sight-seeing or to their favorite beach for a picnic or to a Sunday service at their church. Or, your host might invite you to share an afternoon or evening of conversation with light refreshments, join a family gathering or take a meal at their home. If so, you will most likely have a chance

to sample food and drink you will not normally find on restaurant menus. You will be enjoying facets of Bahamian life that most visitors never see.

To participate in the People-to-People program, contact an office of the Bahamas Ministry of Tourism for a request form to be submitted about two to three weeks in advance of your visit, or write to the Ministry of Tourism, P.O. Box N-3701, Nassau, Bahamas; or P.O. Box F-251, Freeport, Bahamas. You will be contacted by a Ministry of Tourism People-to-People coordinator about the arrangements that have been made especially for you.

Cruise directors often have the forms. However, it's better to make your request in advance to give the People-to-People coordinator time to match you with your Bahamian host, especially if you have a particular interest in a social, fraternal, or religious organization, or a hobby, vocation, or profession that you would like to share.

Garden parties, sponsored jointly with the Bahamas Ministry of Tourism, are another part of the People-to-People program. In Nassau, the parties are held on the fourth Friday of the month at historic Government House and hosted by the wife of the governor general. In Freeport, the Garden of the Groves is the venue.

NASSAU ON YOUR OWN

Unless you have already been to Nassau several times, you will probably find a walking tour of Old Nassau or a boat excursion as interesting a way to enjoy your day in port as any alternative. Neither require transportation from the pier, but visiting the attractions east and west of town and on Paradise Island does. Public buses are available but they do not take you directly to the sites; from the main road, you will have a short walk. If you engage a taxi to a specific location, be sure to arrange your return transportation and set the price in advance.

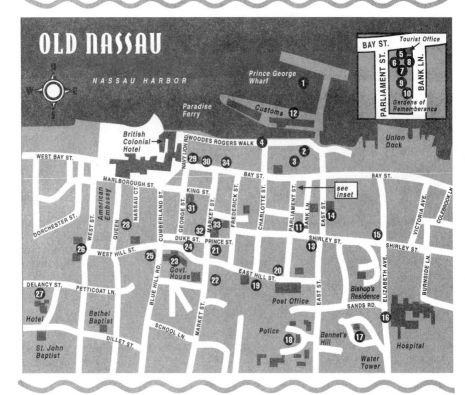

OLD NASSAU

NASSAU HARBOR

Prince George Wharf ❶

Paradise Ferry

Customs ⓬

British Colonial Hotel

WOODES ROGERS WALK ❹

❷
❸

Union Dock

WEST BAY ST.

MARLBOROUGH ST.

BAY ST.

BAY ST.

see inset

DORCHESTER ST.

American Embassy

NASSAU CT.

QUEEN

KING ST.

GEORGE ST.

CUMBERLAND ST.

MARKET ST.

FREDERICK ST.

CHARLOTTE ST.

PARLIAMENT ST.

BANK LN.

EAST ST.

COLEBROOK LN.

VICTORIA AVE.

❸❶

❸❸

❸❷

DUKE ST.   PRINCE ST.

SHIRLEY ST.

❶❹

❶❺

❷❻

WEST HILL ST.

❷❽

❷❺

❷❸

Govt. House

❷❷

❷❶

EAST HILL ST.

❷❹

SHIRLEY ST.

❶❸

BURNSIDE LN.

ELIZABETH AVE.

DELANCY ST.

PETTICOAT LN.

❷❼

BLUE HILL RD.

❷❻

❷❺

❷❹

❶❾

❷❶

Bishop's Residence

SANDS RD.

Hotel

Bethel Baptist

DILLET ST.

SCHOOL LN.

MARKET ST.

Post Office

EAST ST.

❶❻

St. John Baptist

Police

❶❽

Bennet's Hill ❶❼

Water Tower

Hospital

Tourist Office

BAY ST.

PARLIAMENT ST.

BANK LN.

❺
❻ ❽
❼
❾
❿

Gardens of Remembrance

MAP LEGEND FOR WALKING TOUR OF OLD NASSAU

Note: Numbers in the walking tour correspond to the numbers on the accompanying map. An "x" after the number means the house or building is not open to the public; "s" means it can be visited by special arrangement.

1. Prince George Wharf
2. Tourist Information Office
3. Rawson Square
4. Woodes Rogers Walk
5. Parliament Square
6. House of Assembly
7. Senate Building
8. Colonial Secretary's Office and Treasury
9. Supreme Court
10. Central Police Station
11. Public Library
12. Junkanoo Expo
13. Curry House and Zion Church
14x. Cascadilla
15. Bahamas Historical Society
16. Queen's Staircase
17. Fort Fincastle and Water Tower
18. Police Headquarters

19. Ministry of Foreign Affairs
20x. Jacaranda House
21. St. Andrew's Presbyterian Church
22. Gregory's Arch
23s. Government House
24. Christopher Columbus Statue
25. Graycliff House
26. St. Francis Xavier Cathedral/The Priory (Dunmore House)
27. Buena Vista
28. The Deanery
29. Cable Beach/West End Bus Stand
30. Vendue House/Pompey Museum
31. Christ Church Cathedral
32. Balcony House
33. Central Bank/Trinity Place
34. Straw Market/Tourism Ministry; North and East End Bus Stand

A WALKING TOUR OF OLD NASSAU

The entire walk, following the sequence as numbered (see map) takes 3 to 4 hours depending on your pace. At several points along the way, you can stop for a refreshment or break off entirely and return to your ship or to Bay Street for shopping.

A walking tour of Old Nassau in the heart of town is a stroll through Bahamian history, particularly its British past. The town plan, laid out in grid fashion in 1788, is virtually intact and comprises four long, parallel east-west streets crossed by ten small north-south streets running from the harbor and Bay Street on the north to a hillside (East Hill and West Hill streets) on the south. Although modern encroachments are everywhere, many streets have retained enough of their eighteenth- and nineteenth-century buildings, gardens, and broad steps to give visitors a real sense of Nassau in bygone days.

PRINCE GEORGE WHARF (1) From Prince George Wharf where the cruise ships dock it is only a few steps to Rawson Square, the Tourist Information Office (2), and Parliament Square, the heart of downtown. En route you will pass a statue dedicated to the Women of the Bahamas, by Randolph Johnston of Abaco.

The docks have been upgraded with a "Welcome Plaza," a taxi dispatch station, and shelter for the horse-drawn surreys. One building contains a "Welcome Centre," as well as information, communication, and banking services, a Bahamian product gift shop and the Junkanoo Expo (12) (described later in the chapter). Either now or at the end of your walk, a detour to the museum is very worthwhile.

The waterfront between Woodes Rogers Walk and the western end of Prince George Wharf is being transformed into "Festival Place," an urban water park—a themed entertainment attraction with a 315-foot observation tower, an interactive theater, and food and beverage and exhibition spaces—to be completed in 1997.

RAWSON SQUARE (3) In 1985, as part of the beautification project for the visit of Queen Elizabeth II and the meeting of the Commonwealth nations, Old Nassau's stately buildings and monuments in the heart of downtown were spruced up, and a garden and mosaic walkways were laid to connect Rawson Square and Parliament Square on the south side of Bay Street. The square is named for Sir William Rawson, governor of the Bahamas from 1864 to 1869; and it has a small statue of Sir Milo Butler, the first governor-general of the Bahamas after independence in 1973. The Churchill Building on the east side of the square was formerly the prime minister's office. On the west side, you can engage a horse-drawn surrey for a tour or stop to have your hair braided for $2 per braid at the open-air pavilion.

WOODES ROGERS WALK (4) The waterfront walkway west of Rawson Square, known as Woodes Rogers Walk, was named for the first British governor of the Bahamas. The tiny lanes with shops leads to the town's famous Straw Market (34), a lively bazaar of Bahamian crafts. You can also reach the Straw Market by walking along Bay Street, the town's oldest street and main thoroughfare. It is lined with department stores and boutiques selling anything from $2 T-shirts to French perfumes and English china at about 20 percent less than stateside prices.

If you were to continue west on Bay Street beyond the British Colonial Hotel, you would be on West Bay Street, the road leading to Ardastra Gardens and Cable Beach. East on Bay Street about two miles is the bridge to Paradise Island. Potters Cay has a native market where Bahamians buy fresh fish and provisions.

PARLIAMENT SQUARE (5) The traditional center of Bahamian government activity, Parliament Square is graced by a marble statue of a youthful Queen Victoria seated upon a throne and holding a sword and scepter. Framing the statue is the lovely Georgian architecture of the House of Assembly (6) on the west, the Senate Building (7) on the south, and the old Colonial Secretary's Office and Treasury (8) on the east. The buildings were constructed from 1805 to 1813 and are based on Tryon's Palace of New Bern, the old capital of North Carolina, praised as the most beautiful building of its time. South of these buildings facing the Garden of Remembrance, with a cenotaph commemorating the dead of the two world wars, is the Supreme Court (9). The garden with stately royal palms and tropical flowers is one of the prettiest spots in the downtown area. On the east side of the square on Bank Lane is the Central Police Station and International Trust Building (10).

PUBLIC LIBRARY (11) The octagonal structure, built in about 1798 as a prison, was made into a library and museum in 1879. The structure, contemporary with buildings in Williamsburg, is thought to have been modeled after the Old Powder Magazine there. The first and second floors had prison cells on each of its eight sides; a central open area provided fresh air. These alcoves now hold library stacks. A domed gallery on the third floor was originally unroofed; it once held a bell that was rung to summon members of the House of Assembly to meetings. The upper floor has a collection of books and artifacts on the Bahamas, including old maps dating from 1750 and prints from 1891. Hours: Monday to Friday, 10 A.M. to 9 P.M.; Saturday, 9 A.M. to 5 P.M.

Magistrate's Court No. 3 on Parliament Street was originally built in 1894 as a chapel for the Salem Union Baptist congregation on a site known as the "Livery Stable Grounds." It is still owned by the church. South of the library, the old Royal Victorian Gardens was the site of the once grand Victorian Hotel, the center of social activity when it opened in 1861 during the American Civil War. Among its first guests were those fleeing the war; others were blockade-runners, officers of the Confederacy, spies of the Northern States, and "ladies of high quality" who were invited to the nightly parties.

In 1876 the hotel was leased to the brother of Grover Cleveland, U.S. president from 1885 to 1889; and according to a plaque in the gardens, the hotel was purchased in 1898 by Henry M. Flagler. The American railroad czar connected Florida with the rest of the nation and drew up plans for a rail/ferry service to connect the Bahamas to the U.S. mainland. In its heyday, the hotel had a long list of distinguished guests that included Winston Churchill, Prince Albert, and an array of European royalty and celebrities. The

hotel changed hands many times before it closed in 1971 and was later destroyed by fire.

Curry House (13), located on Shirley Street immediately west of Zion Church, is a three-story building which opened in 1890 as a private hotel. Later it became an annex of the Royal Victoria Hotel, and in 1972 it was acquired by the government and is used by the Ministry of Finance.

[From here, you have a choice of walking east to Bennet's Hill and the Water Tower or west to Government House. If you plan to cover this entire walking tour on foot, you might do well to take the uphill climb to the Water Tower first. To reach the Water Tower, walk east on Shirley Street and turn south on Elizabeth Avenue. It leads directly to the Queen's Staircase and hence, the Water Tower.]

CASCADILLA (14x) is one of the Nassau houses thought to have been built by ship carpenters—the island's only craftsmen for many decades. (Certain Bahamian architectural features later transplanted in Key West by Bahamians derive from this origin.) The oldest part of the house dates from 1840, when it marked the eastern boundary of town. The ruins of kitchens and other buildings indicate that it was once part of a plantation house. The property has had many owners over the years and now belongs to a real estate broker.

BAHAMAS HISTORICAL SOCIETY MUSEUM (15) Founded in 1959, the Society is a nonprofit cultural and educational organization dedicated to stimulating interest in Bahamian history and collecting and preserving material related to it. Hours: Tuesday and Wednesday, 10 A.M. to 4 P.M.; Friday, 10 A.M. to 1 P.M.; and Saturday, 10 A.M. to noon. Admission is free, but contributions are welcome. For information: Bahamas Historical Society, Box SS–6833, Nassau (tel. 322–4231).

QUEEN'S STAIRCASE (16) At the head of Elizabeth Avenue is a passageway of 66 steps carved out of limestone, draped with thick tropical foliage, and cooled by a waterfall. Local lore says the steps represent each year of Queen Victoria's reign. Actually, the steps were carved by slaves a century earlier and form a passageway to Fort Fincastle, thus enabling troops to reach the fort from town without being exposed to fire from enemy ships.

FORT FINCASTLE (**17**) Situated on Bennet's Hill overlooking the town, Paradise Island, and the eastern approaches to New Providence, Fort Fincastle was built in 1793 and takes its name from Lord Dunmore's title as the Viscount Fincastle. The fort was constructed in the shape of a ship's bow and has served as a lighthouse and signal station. Hours: Monday to Friday, 9:30 A.M. to 4 P.M.; Saturday, 2 to 5 P.M.

WATER TOWER Next to the fort, the 126-foot Water Tower built in 1928 is the highest point on the island, 216 feet above sea level. An elevator (or a circular stairway of 202 steps) goes to an observation deck at the top for a lovely panoramic view of the city, harbor, and Fort Fincastle below. The tower is open from 9 A.M. to 5 P.M. daily; the elevator ride costs 50 cents. (You may be hustled for tips by the elevator operator and self-appointed guides on the tower's observation deck; you should simply ignore them.)

From the tower, you can continue your walking tour by returning to East Street via Sands Alley or Prison Lane and walking north to East Hill Street. The Police Headquarters (**18**) was built in 1900. The green and white building on the north side of the complex is a typical example of Bahamian wooden architecture and is reminiscent of houses built in Key West by Bahamian transplants.

When the Loyalists came to Nassau after the American Revolution they brought with them ideas about colonial architecture, particularly of the South. Although it evolved into a decidedly Bahamian version with different types of building materials, the influence is evident. Typical building materials included limestone with pink-washed walls and peaked roofs; wood was used in colonnades, fretwork balconies, and jalousies or louvered shutters that shielded the verandas from the hot sun and allowed the air to circulate. In the late nineteenth and early twentieth centuries economic hardship forced many Bahamians to leave the islands. Some became the early settlers of Key West, bringing their building habits with them.

From East Street turn west on East Hill Street. You will pass the modern Post Office building and

the former East Hill Club, which houses the Ministry of Foreign Affairs (**19**). The club was built around 1850 by the socially prominent Matthews family, who were lawyers and government officials. The Georgian colonial-style house was first renovated when it was owned by Lord Beaverbrook.

Jacaranda House (**20x**) on the corner of East Hill and Parliament streets was built about 1840 by Chief Justice Sir George Anderson, of Georgia stone previously used as ship's ballast. During World War II, the house was owned by Capt. Vyvian Drury, aide-de-camp to the duke of Windsor. It was bought in 1949 by the widow of Sir Harry Oakes and later passed to her daughter. The house is furnished with lovely antiques and has exterior features typical of classical Bahamian architecture, such as interlocking corners of large projecting stones used for strength (known as chamfered quoins).

ST. ANDREW'S PRESBYTERIAN CHURCH (21) The pretty, white church at the corner of Duke and Market streets was begun in 1810 and expanded many times over the next five decades. It was completely renovated early in this century.

GREGORY'S ARCH (**22**) Spanning Market Street is a picturesque entrance to Grant's Town, one of the early settlements of former slaves referred to locally as "Over the Hill," as it is literally over the ridge that divides north Nassau from the south side. The arch, named for Governor John Gregory, was built in 1852 by J. J. Burnside, the surveyor general who laid out Grant's Town. The English iron railings were added two years later. Broad stone stairways at the foot of Charlotte and Frederick streets lead from East Hill Street directly to Bay Street.

GOVERNMENT HOUSE (23s) The imposing Government House (at Blue Hill Road and Prince Street) stands on Mount Fitzwilliam, a hillside overlooking Nassau. It is the home of the governor-general, the queen's personal representative to the Commonwealth of the Bahamas. A previous structure is thought to have housed governors from Richard Fitzwilliam in 1733 to Lord Dunmore in 1787. Dunmore moved to the house he built on West Street (now a priory) and sold the former government house and its land to another Loyalist. The present house was built between 1803 and 1806 and expanded several times; the east wing dates from 1909.

The hurricane of 1929 caused a great deal of damage to the structure and, subsequently, the interior and front facade were entirely redesigned, the main entrance changed, and the car porch and main hall added. In 1940 the house was extensively redecorated, and living quarters in the west wing, known as the Windsor Wing, were added for the personal staff of the duke of Windsor who lived here for four years as the royal governor of the Bahamas.

More changes were made in 1964 and again in 1977 for the visit of Queen Elizabeth II. In addition to the queen, many members of the royal family, heads of state including President Kennedy, and other celebrities have been guests here. Monthly, the Bahamas Ministry of Tourism and the People-to-People program hold a garden party for tourists, hosted by the governor-general's wife.

CHRISTOPHER COLUMBUS STATUE (24) The entrance to Government House is marked by a bigger-than-life, 12-foot-tall statue of Christopher Columbus, made in London by an aide to American novelist and historian Washington Irving and placed here in 1830 by Governor Sir James Carmichael Smyth. It commemorates Columbus's arrival in the New World on the Bahamian island of San Salvador. The ceremonial Changing of the Guard with the famous Royal Bahamas Police Force Band takes place on alternate Saturdays at 10 A.M. sharp. (For information, phone 322–3622.)

[From the statue, you can walk down George Street in front of the Columbus statue to Vendue House (30) and the Straw Market on Bay Street, or continue your walking tour to see some of Nassau's oldest and loveliest houses.]

GRAYCLIFF HOUSE (25) This Georgian mansion set in a lovely tropical garden dates from about 1726. Now a hotel and restaurant, it was originally built by a notorious pirate, Capt. John H. Graysmith, as his home. The building may have been used as a garrison for the British West Indies Regiment, judging from the thick walls and other structural elements in the cellars, which are now used by the hotel for its wine collection. The house is known to have been a hotel as early as 1844, but

it became a private residence again in 1937 when it belonged to a Canadian couple who added a swimming pool and made alterations. In 1966, the estate was bought by Lord Dudley, earl of Staffordshire, as his winter home. The present owners acquired it in 1974. Despite the publicity you may have read, Graycliff's restaurant is highly overrated, pretentious, and grossly overpriced.

Farther west on West Hill Street are several beautifully restored private homes and The Priory (**26**), formerly known as Dunmore House. After serving as the governor's residence, the house became the officers' quarters and mess hall for the 22nd West Indies Regiment. It later became a military hospital and in 1893 was purchased by the Roman Catholic church and made into the Priory; the Cathedral of St. Francis Xavier is adjacent.

South of the cathedral on Delancey Street is Buena Vista (**27**), a hotel with one of the town's leading restaurants, housed in a building dating from the mid-nineteenth century.

THE DEANERY (28) From West Street continue north and turn into Queen Street to the Deanery at No. 28 Queen Street. Built in 1710, it is thought to be the oldest house in the Bahamas. The building was acquired by the Anglican church in 1800 and is the Rectory of Christ Church Cathedral. The three-story house is built of stone with chamfered quoins; originally it had three tiers of verandas on three sides. A one-story building on the west side was the stone kitchen with an 8-foot fireplace and a domed oven; it has a small room thought to have been used as sleeping quarters for domestic slaves. Across the street is the U.S. Embassy.

In the next small lane is Nassau Court, built in 1830 as the West Chapel of the Wesleyan Methodist Church. In 1864 it was sold to the government and used as a school for almost a century, although the nature of the school changed several times. In 1960 it was turned over to the Ministry of Public Works and is now occupied by the Ministry of Economic Affairs.

On the north side of Marlborough Street is the British Colonial Hotel, a Best Western Hotel, the pink colonial building which dominates the waterfront. It is on the site of the town's first fortification, Fort Nassau, built in 1670. On its east side is the stand for buses to Cable Beach (**29**).

VENDUE HOUSE/POMPEY MUSEUM (30) At the head of George Street facing Bay Street is the site of the former slave market, originally a colonnade structure without walls dating from about 1769. It was rebuilt in the early 1900s and occupied by the Bahamas Electricity Corporation. In 1992, as part of the Columbus Quincentennial, it was renovated to house a museum—Pompey Museum of Slavery and Emancipation—and art gallery, funded by a grant from Bacardi Corporation.

The exhibit on the African experience in the Bahamas is named after Pompey, a slave on one of five estates in Exuma owned by Lord Rolle and a hero in Bahamian history. Meanwhile, there are changing exhibits on various aspects of the Bahamas and, on the second floor, a collection of paintings by Amos Ferguson, the Bahamas' internationally acclaimed intuitive artist. Hours: Monday to Friday, 10 A.M. to 4:30 P.M.; Saturday, 10 A.M. to 1 P.M.

CHRIST CHURCH CATHEDRAL (31) Turn east on Marlborough Street and walk to the corner of King and George streets to Christ Church Cathedral. In the original layout of the town this area was a park known as George's Square, the site of the colony's first church.

BALCONY HOUSE (32) Facing the Central Bank on Market Street is the two-story Balcony House, whose construction indicates it may have been built by ships' carpenters around 1790. The house was constructed of American soft cedar and has a second-floor balcony that hangs over the street. An unusual inside staircase is said to have come from a ship. The property, which includes three other houses and slave kitchens, was acquired by Lord Beaverbrook, who sold it in 1947. More recently, it was acquired by the Central Bank and renovated as a museum by the Department of Archives to show life of a prosperous family in the nineteenth century. Hours: 9 A.M. to 5 P.M. daily except holidays.

The Central Bank **(33)** has a collection of the Bahamas' leading artists on display in its lobby. The bank is on the corner of Trinity Place, a small street between Market and Frederick streets. One of the oldest streets in Nassau, Trinity Place is home to the Trinity Church.

STRAW MARKET (34) Both Market and Frederick streets lead to Bay Street, directly in front of the Ministry of Tourism Building, the Straw Market, and the local bus stand for buses to the North and East End. You can return to your ship by walking east on Bay Street. Or you can walk through the Straw Market to the north exit and return to the dock via Woodes Rogers Walk and the Junkanoo Expo **(12)**.

NASSAU AND ITS ENVIRONS

New Providence has many good roads, making any section of the island accessible in a few minutes' drive. At least four highways cut the island north-south, making it easy to reach the south coast from Nassau by a direct route.

ATTRACTIONS WEST OF NASSAU

In contrast to the Old World ambience of Old Nassau are the modern resorts of Cable Beach that stretch west from town along five miles of lovely, white sand beaches on the north shore. Dubbed the Bahamian Riviera, they include the eye-popping Nassau Marriott Resort & Crystal Palace Casino, which recently completed a $30 million renovation; Radisson Cable Beach; Breezes Bahamas (formerly the Ambassador Beach Hotel), next to Nassau's oldest golf course; Nassau Beach; and Sandal's Royal Bahamian. Between Old Nassau and modern Cable Beach, in the shadow of Fort Charlotte, there are several attractions that usually can be visited in one tour. *If you visit any of the following places on your own by taxi, be sure to arrange for your return transportation. In most cases, public buses pass within walking distance.*

Ardastra Gardens and Zoo: One mile west of town in the shadow of Fort Charlotte is a nature park with the world's only trained flamingo corps. The pink birds are put through their paces in a 25-minute show thrice daily. The pretty birds, which are the national bird of the Bahamas, have a mating display of strutting that lends itself to being trained to parade. The 5-acre gardens also offer the chance to see in one place a wide variety of tropical plants as well as endemic birds, four species of iguana (which look like miniature dinosaurs), and other wildlife remaining in the Bahamas.

Visitors are allowed to take photographs, including ones of themselves amidst the flapping flamingos. The flamingos come from the southern island of Inagua where 50,000 birds—the world's largest breeding colony—are protected in a nature preserve administered by the Bahamas National Trust. Ardastra also has several beautiful Bahama parrots in a captive breeding program with the trust. This endangered species, one of sixteen Amazon parrot species in the Caribbean, is found only in Inagua and the Abacos in a sanctuary within a large forest reserve. Hours: 9 A.M. to 5 P.M. Admission: $10 for adults; $5 for children. Shows are Monday to Saturday, 11 A.M., 2 P.M., and 4 P.M. (Tel. 323–5806.)

Nassau Botanical Gardens: Adjacent to Fort Charlotte is an 18-acre spread of tropical plants and flowers, a delightful oasis with a large variety of flora typical of the tropics. The gardens are popular for weddings. It also has a re-created Lucayan village. Hours: Daily from 9 A.M. to 4:30 P.M. Admission: $1 for adults; 50 cents for children. (Tel. 323–5975.)

Fort Charlotte: One mile west of town. Named in honor of the wife of George III, the fort was begun by Lord Dunmore in 1787 and built in three stages. The eastern part is the oldest; the middle portion was named Fort Stanley; and the western section, Fort D'Arcy. Much of it was cut out of solid rock; the walls were buttressed with cedar to "last to eternity," according to Dunmore. It still has its moat, open battlements, and dungeons, plus a good view of the harbor. The fort was restored extensively in 1992. Hours: Daily from 9 A.M. to 4:30 P.M.

Coral World: Entrance north of Chippendale Road. Located on Silver Cay and connected to the mainland by a bridge, Coral World is a marine park with an underwater observatory that enables you to walk down into the sea to observe coral reefs and fish through 24 large windows. There is also a reef tank, said to be the largest manmade reef in the world, a shark tank where you can watch sharks being fed by divers, a stingray pool with several kinds of ray, and a turtle pool with breeding populations of rare sea turtles. Visitors may "adopt" a turtle for $50, which helps defray the expenses of a turtle conservation program. Adjacent to the park are shops and walkways among tropical flora that is labeled. Coral World's free shuttle bus stops hourly from 9 A.M. to 4 P.M. at hotels on Cable Beach; its free ferry service departs from the British Colonial Hotel's dock at 10:15 A.M. and 2:45 P.M. and several times daily from Paradise Island. Hours: Daily from 9 A.M. to 6 P.M., and to 7 P.M., April through October. Admission: $15 for adults; $10 for children ages 3 to 12. (Tel. 328–1036.)

From Cable Beach, a road hugging the coast continues west around the island to Love Beach, one of the island's loveliest beaches and the home of the new Compass Point. Created by the Island Outpost Group, the oceanfront resort is made up of 18 huts, cottages, and cabanas painted in the vibrant colors of Junkanoo, the Bahamian carnival, and decorated with whimsical Junkanoo motifs such as owls, roosters, sunbursts, and fish. The resort takes its name from the renowned recording studios across the road, where artists such as the Rolling Stones have recorded. Compass Point's seaside restaurant is very popular for its Caribbean cuisine.

Farther west is Lyford Cay, a private, 4,000-acre residential resort that one can visit only as a guest of a member. Lyford Cay, as much as any development, caused the Bahamas to be called the jet-set capital because of the many famous international personalities who own homes here.

The western end of the island has many elegant Bahamian mansions, frequently painted in the deep-pink color associated with the Bahamas or other pastels with white trim, and surrounded by tropical gardens. Among the loveliest are the home of the former prime minister, on Skyline Drive; the residence of the U.S. ambassador to the Bahamas, on Saffron Hill; and on Sandford Drive, the mansion of Canadian millionaire Sir Harry Oakes, one of the island's most famous residents and benefactors, whose murder in 1943 sent shock waves through the island and continues to be a mystery.

Large areas of the south side of the island are uninhabited and covered by miles of pine forests.

From Adelaide and Carmichael roads you can circle back via Gladstone Road over Prospect Ridge to see one of the island's biggest surprises—Lake Killarney and Lake Cunningham—large bodies of water whose wooded shores are richly populated with birds.

ATTRACTIONS EAST OF NASSAU

Fort Montagu: The first fortification at the northeastern end of the island was built in 1728 to protect the eastern approach to Nassau harbor. In 1741 it was replaced by the present structure, designed by Peter Henry Bruce, an engineer previously employed by Peter the Great of Russia. The fort was seized by the Americans briefly during the Revolutionary War.

The Retreat, Bahamas National Trust: The Trust's headquarters, east of Nassau near Queen's College, is on an 11-acre site where Arthur and Margaret Langlois, beginning in 1925, created one of the world's largest private collections of palm trees—about 175 species from around the world. The property was donated to the Trust and officially opened in 1985. The palm trees grow in a thick coppice forest with other native trees and shrubs. The gardens are maintained by volunteers from local garden clubs. Hours: Monday to Friday, 9 A.M. to 5 P.M. Guided tours

are given on Tuesday, Wednesday, and Thursday at 11:45 A.M., or by appointment. (Tel. 393–1317.)

St. Augustine's Monastery: Near Fox Hill village. Father Jerome, the architect of several Anglican and Catholic churches in the Bahamas, designed the school and cloister of the monastery.

Wealthy colonialists originally settled in the area east of Nassau; there, dozens of fine mansions stand witness to the enormous wealth the early settlers amassed. Some sections also have small settlements of colorful West Indian–style houses built, after slavery was abolished, by former slaves granted plots of land. Four of the original settlements are Adelaide, Carmichael, Fox Hill, and Gambier.

EXCURSION BOAT TRIPS

Glass-bottom boats, catamarans, and other excursion boats depart from the pier area frequently throughout the day for guided tours of nearby reefs, Coral World, and the 40-acre Sea Gardens. Some boats stop for a swim and snorkeling in the vicinity of the north shore; other boats take bathers and sight-seers to Paradise Beach or other nearby islets. Some offer sunset and moonlight dinner cruises as well. Prices range from $40 and up.

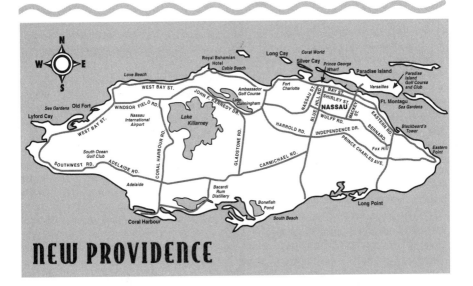

NEW PROVIDENCE

The *Atlantis I* recreational submarine departs from West Bay near Lyford Cay to visit nearby coral reefs. These excursions are sold on almost all cruise ships for $74, adults; $37, children. You will not save money doing it on your own as the departure point is a 20-minute ride from the pier.

ATTRACTIONS ON PARADISE ISLAND

Facing Nassau's north shore is Paradise Island, connected to Nassau by a half-mile bridge and a ferry from Prince George Wharf. Initially, the island resort was put on the map by A&P heir Huntington Hartford, whose home became the centerpiece of the fashionable Ocean Club. In 1994, Sun International acquired Paradise Island, changing the name of the resort to Atlantis and making major changes.

Atlantis Resort and Casino complex includes eight hotels, 12 restaurants, a cavernous casino, an enormous dinner theater, an 18-hole championship golf course, a 12-court tennis complex, horseback riding, a marina, a full range of water sports, and an international airport with flights to several Florida cities. Atlantis' centerpiece is a 14-acre Waterscape, with the largest outdoor, open-water aquarium in the world with six exhibit lagoons, more than forty waterfalls, five swimming pools, three underground grottos, and an underwater walkway with windows for viewing sharks and artificial coral reefs.

The resort has a new day-rate option based on availability, which is especially useful for cruise passengers . For $30 per person, day guests may use any of the water facilities, which include five swimming pools, and have access to the "hospitality cavern," which has changing rooms, showers, and towels. Since the option is extended when the resort is not fully booked and space is available, you may want to call in advance: 809–363–3000. Ask for the Lagun Pool Towel Hut. The hotel also has tours of the resort and aquarium.

Versailles Gardens and French Cloister: Landscaped gardens, adjacent to the Ocean Club on the island's northeast side, are enclosed by the stones and arches of a 12th-century Augustinian monastery, which Huntington Hartford had shipped from France stone by stone and reconstructed here. From the hotel's swimming pool, the gardens rise in seven terraces to the cloisters, which overlook a small garden and the sea; each terrace is embellished with ancient as well as modern statues of historic figures such as Empress Josephine of France, Franklin D. Roosevelt, and Dr. Stanley Livingstone. A visit to the gardens can be combined with lunch at the Ocean Club's Terrace Cafe, one of the Bahamas' prettiest settings.

 ## SHOPPING IN NASSAU

With the increase in the number of cruise passengers in recent years, shopping in Nassau has greatly improved in quality and selection and closely rivals St. Thomas with goods from the four corners of the globe. Now, too, the Bahamas' advertising tagline "It just keeps getting better in the Bahamas" has new meaning. After dropping the duty on most luxury goods—such as jewelry and perfumes—in January 1992, making prices on these items 25 percent or more below those in the United States, the Bahamian government recently passed an ordinance to allow stores to open on Sunday, particularly to accommodate cruise ships that are in port on that day. The Tourist Information Center in Rawson Square can provide information about duty-free shopping.

At Rawson Square, you can turn east or west on Bay Street and you will find every type of shop—dress, sportswear, shoes, men's clothing, liquor, perfume, and more. The newest shops and small shopping plazas are east of the square, while the stores on the west are generally the more established ones. The free promotional booklet *Best Buys in the Bahamas* is useful for maps and store descriptions. It usually has coupons for free gifts and discounts too.

Before the day has ended, you will certainly want to visit the Straw Market on Bay Street; it is open daily. It is one of the best of its kind in the tropics and crammed full of handcrafted baskets, hats, handbags, dolls, and other inexpensive gifts to take home to relatives and friends. You can watch the items emerge from the skilled fingers of a Bahamian craftswoman and even have them handmade-to-order with your own design and initials. Don't hesitate to bargain in the market; the ladies expect it and enjoy the exchange. And it's fun!

In addition to Bay Street, there are shopping arcades in hotels, particularly on Paradise Island and Cable Beach. Stores are open Monday through Saturday from 9 A.M. to 5 P.M. Many also open on Sundays; some close on Thursday afternoons. All stores mentioned below are on Bay Street unless indicated otherwise.

ART AND ANTIQUES: *Caripelago* (East Bay St.) is the new location of the most attractive art store in Nassau. You will find paintings, masks, and carvings along with stylishly designed T-shirts and jewelry by leading Bahamanian artists such as Maxwell Taylor, as well as promising unknowns. At the back of the store is a coffee bar with the latest flavors; it also sells spices and jams from the islands. *Marlborough Antiques* (Marlborough Street) has English antiques, old maps, gifts, and works by local artists, particularly R. Brent Malone, who is best known for his brilliant canvases of Junkanoo. Other names to look for are Manon Selby, who sketches expressive, pensive faces; Reynolds, who uses humorous local settings for subjects; Eddie Minnis, who is also a singer and songwriter; and Chan Pratt.

BAHAMIAN BATIKS: Native Bahamian designs on cotton and other fabrics are printed by *Androsia* on the Bahamian island of Andros and made into sportswear sold in high-quality stores. The widest selections are available at *Mademoiselle.*

BOOKS: *The Island Shop* is something of a department store and sells everything from cameras to cashmeres, swimsuits, and sportswear; the book department on the second floor is the best in town.

CHILDREN: If you want a fun, unusual, and interesting gift for a small child, bookstores, newsstands, and pharmacies stock a series of coloring books on Bahamian flowers, birds and fish, shells, ships, and Junkanoo. For expensive items, *Linen & Lace* has lovely hand-smocked and embroidered children's clothes.

CHINA AND CRYSTAL: For the best selections of English bone china, Waterford, and other fine crystal, *Bernard's China and Gift Shop, John Bull,* and *Little Switzerland* have large selections with savings of up to 35 percent on china and crystal, representing among the best buys in duty-free goods in the Bahamas. You will be better prepared to recognize a bargain when you come with prices from home. Have the name of the pattern as well as the manufacturer for accurate comparisons.

DIVE SUPPLIES: *Bahamas Divers* outfits divers and snorkelers; *Pyfrom's* carries T-shirts, Sea Island cotton shirts, and souvenirs, as well as masks and flippers for children and adults.

JEWELRY: *Coin of the Realm* (14 Charlotte Street) has not only coins but also a large selection of precious and semiprecious stones, gold and silver jewelry, and stamps.

LEATHER: *Leather Masters* (17 Bank Lane) and the *Brass and Leather Shops* (14 Charlotte Street) carry fine Italian bags, briefcases, shoes, and other leather goods. *Fendi* and *Gucci* have their own shops in prime locations. Savings are about 20 percent, if that much, over U.S. prices.

PERFUMES: *The Perfume Shop* has several outlets on Bay Street and in the Paradise Island Shopping Centre. Their prices are as competitive as any we have found. Actually, French perfume prices are set by French perfume makers; any dealer who undercuts the price is cut off from the supply. For local products, *Bahamas Fragrance and Cosmetic Factory* (Charlotte Street) has skin creams, sunscreens, and perfumes.

SPORTSWEAR: Many shops along East Bay Street have inexpensive selections. *Cotton Ginny* has attractive, all-cotton sportswear at reasonable prices. *Everyone's Talking* (Prince George Plaza) has very original playclothes and sportswear for women. *Seventeen Shop* has a large selection of large sizes, along with a full range of standard sizes, in dresses as well as shorts, shirts, and slacks.

SWEATERS AND WOOLENS: *The Scottish Shop* has many of the best-known Scottish cashmeres and a full line of Shetlands.

WATCHES: *John Bull* (Bay Street and Paradise

Island) is one of the oldest and largest stores in the Bahamas. It carries all the famous makes from novelty watches to Corum and Cartier, as well as a full line of cameras and photo equipment.

WOMEN'S FASHIONS: *Cole's of Nassau* (Parliament Street) has the largest selection of sophisticated women's fashions, but many are familiar labels that sell for less in New York. For less expensive clothes, check the shops on Bay Street east of Rawson Square.

DINING AND RESTAURANTS IN NASSAU

Restaurants and hotel dining rooms range from elegant and sophisticated as befits a world capital to simple and unpretentious as suits an unhurried tropical resort. You can enjoy a barbecue on the beach, a fish fry by the harbor, or a gourmet treat in the romantic ambience of a colonial home.

The variety of international cuisine includes French, English, Italian, American, Chinese, Indian, and Greek, but you really should try some Bahamian specialties before the day is out. The best known are johnnycakes, a corn bread; conch chowder, spicy and delicious; conch fritters or deep-fried grouper; or pigeon peas and rice, to mention a few. Prices range from $4 for lunch at a typical local restaurant to $100 for dinner at the top gourmet havens.

Always check your bill before you leave a tip. Many restaurants in the Bahamas and the Caribbean have taken up the European custom of adding a 15-percent service charge to the bill. If so, you do not need to leave a tip, unless the service has been exceptional and you want to leave something more.

Bahamian Kitchen (Trinity Place; Tel. 325–0702), one block from the Straw Market, has Bahamian specialties. Moderate.

Buena Vista (Delancy Street; Tel. 322–2811). Continental cuisine by candlelight in the elegant setting of a historic eighteenth-century house surrounded by beautiful gardens. Dinner only. Expensive.

Coco's Cafe (Marlborough Street, across from British Colonial Hotel) has good salads, sandwiches, and snacks in a cheerful setting resembling a large ice-cream parlor. Inexpensive.

Gaylords (Dowdeswell Street, off Bay Street; Tel. 356–3004). Situated in a 125-year-old Bahamian house, Gaylords is the first member of the international Indian restaurant chain to open in the Bahamas and Caribbean. The menu includes Tandoori, Punjabi, Nepalese, and Mughali dishes. It has carry-out service, too. Moderate. Next door is *Gaylords Spice Shop*, which sells the ingredients for preparing Indian receipes.

Green Shutters (Parliament Street; Tel. 325–5702) is an English pub serving five kinds of draft beer and Bahamian and English specialties. Moderate.

Palm Tree Restaurant (Market and Cockburn streets; not to be confused with one of a similar name on Bay Street) is a local takeout restaurant "over the hill." It's famous among Bahamians for having the best conch fritters in town. Next door, *Mama Liddy's* offers table service. Inexpensive.

Pick-a-Dilly (18 Parliament Street; Tel. 322–2836) has an eclectic menu of Bahamian cuisine and American selections in an outdoor garden, only two blocks from the port. Most of the selections are good original recipes. There is usually music by a guitarist or small combo. Moderate.

Pisces Restaurant & Lounge (West Bay Street; Tel. 327–8827), part of Sun Fun Resorts, is one of Nassau's best restaurants for local dishes, particularly seafood. And Sun Fun's *Seaside Sports Bar* has live satellite sports on a 54-inch TV. Moderate.

The Poop Deck (East Bay Street; Tel. 393–8175). For Bahamian and seafood specialties in a rustic atmosphere at lunch or dinner. The restaurant has great conch chowder, fritters, and key lime pie in a fabulous setting by the water overlooking Paradise Island Bridge. Moderate.

Sugar Reef Harbourside Bar and Grille (Bay & Deveaux Streets; Tel. 356-3065) is one of Nassau's newest restaurants overlooking the harbor. It has a casual atmosphere for enjoying salads, sandwiches, and burgers at lunch; pastas, seafood, and Bahamian and Caribbean specialties for dinner. There's a daily happy hour, 5 to 7:30 P.M.

Sun and . . . (Lakeview Drive; Tel. 393–1205), one of the most popular restaurants in Nassau, serves continental cuisine on the patio of a Bahamian house created by a Belgian chef and his wife. Dinner only; closed Mondays in August and September. Jacket required for men. Expensive.

Tamarind Hill Restaurant and Music Bar (Village Road; Tel. 393–1306), in an old Bahamian house painted up like a tapestry, is breezy and fun. It's a popular stop for happy hour and live guitar music on Wednesday, Friday, and Saturday. The eclectic menu has mango glaze pork, grouper in nut crust, and oven-roasted vegetarian pizza. It's at least a 15-minute drive east of the port.

Traveller's Rest (West Bay Street; Tel. 327–7633) is something of a drive from town, but it's worth it for the food and delightful country setting under huge shade trees overlooking the aqua sea. Here you can try fried grouper with peas and rice, and plantains, which are similar to fried bananas. Moderate.

And lots of places can satisfy your pizza craze—*Domino's, Paradise Island,* and *Swank's,* to name a few.

SPORTS IN NASSAU AND ENVIRONS

The Bahamas has some of the best sports facilities in the tropics, available in or near enough to Nassau or Freeport for cruise passengers to use them with relative ease. When facilities for sports such as tennis or golf are available at a hotel, contact the hotel or the sports operator in advance, particularly during the peak season when demand is likely to be high. When you want specific information on any sport, phone the Bahamas Sports Line, 1–800–32–SPORT.

BEACHES: So fine are the beaches that picking the best is difficult. For hotel beaches, the nearest to the port is the British Colonial, but if you go a little farther west, you have all of Cable Beach, dubbed the Bahamian Riviera. Most of Paradise Island is fringed by white sand.

BIKING: The island is rather flat, and roads away from the main arteries with heavy traffic are easy for biking. Bikes can be rented within walking distance of the pier, at a stand next to the British Colonial Hotel, for about $10–$15 per day.

BOATING: It may seem strange for a cruise passenger to get off one vessel only to climb aboard another, but many people find it a wonderful way to spend their day in port. What better way to enjoy the magnificent waters than by chartering a boat? Almost any size or type, sail or power, with or without crew, is available. You can explore, swim, and picnic at your own pace. *Nassau Yacht Haven* (P.O. Box SS 5693, Nassau; Tel. 393–8173) can provide information on yachts and fishing boats.

DEEP-SEA FISHING: The Bahamas is a magnet for sports fishermen. World records for marlin and other big game are made and broken year after year. Deep-sea fishing can be enjoyed almost anywhere in the Bahamas in ideal weather conditions throughout the year, and the variety of fish is endless. January to late April is the best season for white marlin and amberjack; June through August for blue marlin and kingfish. Ocean bonito, blackfin tuna, and Allison tuna are caught from May to September. Grouper can be found in reefy areas year-round; kingfish are plentiful in winter; dolphin is found in deep waters in winter and spring. And there is bluefin tuna, sailfish, wahoo, and more. Andros calls itself the bonefishing capital of the world.

Boats depart from Nassau Yacht Harbor on regular half-day fishing trips at 8:30 A.M. and 12:30 P.M. for $50 per person, with six persons per boat. The price includes bait and tackle. Contact *Chubasco Charters,* Capt. Mike Russell, 242–322–8148; fax, 242–326–4140. Charter rates, which include tackle, bait, ice, and fuel, range from about $200–$300 for a half day; $400–$500 for a full day for boats accommodating up to six people.

The Bahamas Sports Information Center (800–32–SPORT) has copies of *The Bahamas Fishing Guide* with pictures and descriptions of the main sportfishing targets and their seasons, plus a wealth of other information. The center can provide you with an up-to-date schedule of the fishing tournaments held during the year.

GOLF: A baker's dozen of Bahamian courses, designed by the most famous architects in the world of golf, are as beautiful to see as they are challenging to play. The Bahamas' tropical island landscape provides lovely emerald fairways bordered by flowering trees and palms. Most courses are part of resort complexes and have resident pros, pro shops, and clubhouses.

Nassau/Paradise Island has five courses. The closest to the port is the *Cable Beach Golf Course;* 800–327–6000 (7,040 yards, par 72). This championship course was the Bahamas' first when it was built in 1926. Renovated in 1990 and again in 1996, it has a clubhouse, pro shop, and restaurant. Greens fees for 18 holes are $60 per person; cart for two people, $45.

Paradise Island Golf Course; 800–321–3000 (6,776 yards, par 72). Designed by Dick Wilson and part of the Atlantis Resort and Casino complex. The championship course has what may be the world's largest sand trap—the entire left side of the fifth hole is a white sand beach. The course hosts the PGA-sanctioned Bahamas Classic in January, which attracts many top pros and is carried on ESPN. Greens fees for 18 holes: $100 including cart.

(For Freeport golf clubs, see section on Freeport. For those in the Out Islands, see Eleuthera later in this chapter.)

HORSEBACK RIDING/RACING: *Happy Trails Stables* (Coral Harbour; Tel. 362–1820), open daily except Sunday. A riding tour costs about $40 including round-trip transportation to the stables from town.

PARASAILING: *Paradise Para-sail, Ltd.* (Britannia Towers, Tel. 363–3000) will give you a bird's-eye view of Paradise, and offers waterskiing and windsurfing too. The cost is $20 for five minutes; $35 for 10 minutes.

SNORKELING AND SCUBA DIVING: The spectacular underwater world of the Bahamas has something for everyone, no matter what your level of expertise. Snorkelers and novice divers can simply swim off a beach to discover fantastic coral gardens only 10 or 20 feet below the surface of the water.

More experienced divers can explore drop-offs that start at 40 feet and plunge thousands. They can swim into underwater caverns and tunnels teeming with fish and roam through waters with visibility as great as 200 feet. Masks and flippers are readily available, as are diving equipment and instruction. And those who cannot swim need not miss the fun. At *Coral World* (Tel. 328–1036), one can walk down into the sea in an underwater observatory.

Most ships that sail on three- and four-day cruises from Florida visit their "own" island, usually one of the Out Islands. The highlight of the day is snorkeling or diving directly from shore in water so incredibly clear you don't need a mask to see the colorful fish and fantastic coral. (It is, of course, more practical to wear a mask.)

Bahamas Divers (East Bay Street; Tel. 393–5644); *Divers Haven* (Tel. 393–0869); and *Nassau Scuba Centre* (Tel. 362–1964) have daily snorkeling excursions for $20–$25. They also offer dive trips (all gear provided) with one-tank dives for $35 and two-tank dives for $55 or $60. *Nassau Scuba Centre* has a learn-to-dive course for $50. The selection of dive sites often depends on level of skill of participants. Dive operators offer instruction as well.

The hottest fad is shark diving—yes, shark! *Dive Dive Dive Ltd.* (Tel. 362–1143) takes experienced divers to see bull, reef, and silky sharks, several days a week, for $75.

TENNIS/SQUASH/RACQUETBALL: In the Bahamas, where the weather is ideal for play year-round, tennis is as popular as any water sport. There are no less than 100 courts and excellent facilities with pros and pro shops, instruction and daily clinics available at hotels and resorts in Nassau, Cable Beach, and Paradise Island. Many courts are lighted for evening play. Since most hotels do not charge guests for the use of courts, you will need to make special arrangements in advance by writing or calling the hotel to request court time.

Hotels nearest the port with the best facilities and night lights are on Cable Beach. *Nassau Beach Hotel* (Box N 7756, Nassau; Tel. 327–7711; 800–223–5672) has six Plexipave courts. The resort also offers windsurfing, sailing, snorkeling, and other water sports. The

Palace Spa at the *Nassau Marriott Resort* (Box N 8306, Nassau; Tel. 327–6200; 800–453–5301) has eighteen Har-Tru courts, three squash courts, and three racquetball courts. The sports center has a well-equipped health club, jogging area, spa treatments, and other programs.

On Paradise Island, *Ocean Club* (Box N 4777, Nassau; Tel. 363–2518; 800–321–3000) has nine Har-Tru courts. The lovely setting is the site of the annual Marlboro Open in December, which attracts top-ranked international players. *Atlantis Resort* complex (Tel. 363–3000; 800–321–3000) has twelve Laykold courts. The Bahamas International Open is held here annually in late summer. The resort has water sports on a 3-mile beach, golf, and health club.

WATERSKIING: It is easy to do in the calm Bahamian waters and available at hotels at about $20 for 3 miles or three "falls" in Nassau for up to $40, for 30 minutes.

WINDSURFING: The protection the shallows and reefs give to most parts of the Bahamian coast also makes its many bays excellent places to learn to windsurf. Try it once and you'll be hooked! Instruction is available to get you started. The cost is about $20. The annual Windsurfing Regatta is held in January.

ENTERTAINMENT: CULTURAL EVENTS AND NIGHTLIFE

Bahamians—and visitors—make something of a ritual of watching the pretty sunsets. So when the air begins to cool and the sun starts its fall, you can grab a *Bahama Mama* (that's the local rum punch) and head for the beach. You'll probably be joined by kindred spirits, a scratch band, or other local musicians for some impromptu jamming.

After the sun disappears and the stars are out, you can stay on the beach with the calypso beat or change into something a bit dressier for a round of the Bahamas' razzle-dazzle nightlife. The 1,000-seat theater of *Crystal Palace Casino* and *Atlantis Show Room* (Paradise Island) have Las

Vegas–style shows nightly. Their theaters are adjacent to the casino, where you can choose blackjack, roulette, craps, baccarat, or slot machines to play, and if your luck runs out, you can laugh it off at Atlantis' *Jokers Wild Comedy Club.* The resorts also have discos, several bars, and restaurants. *The Zoo* (West Bay Street; Tel. 322-7195) is Nassau nightlife bigtime—a three-story night club with a tri-level dance floor and one of the biggest sound and light systems in the Caribbean. You can dance to soca, calypso, or reggae or hang out at one of the six theme bars or outdoor section with live entertainment. Happy hour starts at 8 P.M. and the dancing goes to 4 A.M. There is a cover charge of $20 weekdays, $40 weekends.

Rock 'n' Roll Cafe (Cable Beach; Tel. 327–7639) in the Frilsham House, a beautiful Bahamian beachfront mansion next to the Nassau Beach Hotel, is open seven days a week from noon to 2 A.M., with music at a volume that separates generations.

For those who want something on the cultural side, the *Dundas Centre for the Performing Arts* (Mackey Street; Tel. 322–2728) offers plays, musicals, ballets, and folkloric shows.

FESTIVALS AND CELEBRATIONS

Bahamians love to celebrate. From January to December the calendar is full of sporting events, music festivals, historic commemorations, religious feasts, and national holidays. All are windows on island life not open to visitors at other times of the year. You can watch the fun from the sidelines or join the parade, sing along with the music, and try the dances. And if you bring your camera, you'll run out of film before you run out of subjects to photograph.

JUNKANOO, A NATIONAL FESTIVAL

Of all the festivals, none compares to Junkanoo, an exuberant Bahamian celebration full of color and creativity, humor, rhythm and music, dance, fun, and festivity. The national extravaganza traces its origins to the West African dance and mask traditions kept alive throughout the West Indies by slaves brought to the New World in the 17th and 18th centuries. After emancipation in the early 19th century Junkanoo was suppressed by religious zealots, both black and white. It had nearly died out when it was revived in the 1970s as part of the effort to preserve the Bahamas' multifaceted heritage.

Now, once again, Junkanoo is part of the Bahamian tradition reflected in the art, dance, and music. It has been taken into the schools, where the construction of costumes is part of the curriculum, and sent abroad by the musicians and entertainers, where it is receiving international recognition.

Junkanoo is the Bahamian version of Carnival, with parades, costumes, and music, but unlike traditional Carnival, it is held at the end of the year and the start of the new one. The first Junkanoo parade starts at daybreak on December 26, Boxing Day, a public holiday stemming from British tradition. Bahamians and visitors who feel the spirit don brilliant costumes and parade through downtown Nassau to the clatter of cowbells, horns, whistles, and the driving beat of African drums. Prizes are awarded to those with the most unusual and elaborate costumes—all made from cardboard and strips of paper laid down in tight layers. Every display must be able to be carried by one person; nothing on wheels is allowed.

Participants and viewers need to be on the street before daylight—it's all over by 8 A.M. (Photographers need fast film as the light is still low at parade time.) Bleachers are set up in the judging area on Bay Street west of Rawson Square, and the judging takes places from 6 to 7 A.M. Costumes that do not win are often dumped in the street and make fine souvenirs.

The celebration is repeated on New Year's Eve after the private parties at homes and hotels wind down and the streets begin to fill with late-night revelers. It lasts through New Year's Day. But visitors do not have to wait to the year's end to see Junkanoo. They can sample it at some nightclub and folkloric shows and other celebrations throughout the year and visit the Junkanoo Expo by the port, where many of the winning costumes are displayed.

GOOMBAY, A SUMMER FESTIVAL

Goombay Summer Festival is a series of special events for visitors featuring the music of Junkanoo and Goombay. Different events give visitors an opportunity to experience the Bahamians' Bahamas with their music and dance, culture, crafts, and cuisine.

Goombay has several derivations and has come to have several meanings. Historically, it referred to the drumbeats and rhythms of Africa brought to the Bahamas by slaves and free blacks. The term was used during the ring-play and jump-in dances when the drummer would shout *Gimbey* at the beginning of each dance.

Today, Goombay is used to refer to all Bahamian secular music, especially that using the traditional goat-skin drum, a barrel-shaped drum made from wooden kegs with goat or sheep skin covering one end, positioned between the legs and played with bare hands. The word *Goombay* is still used in West Africa, especially by Ibo tribes, who have a similar drum they call Gamby.

OTHER FESTIVALS AND EVENTS

Independence Week in early July is another holiday filled with festivities, parades, and fireworks to celebrate the independence of the Commonwealth of the Bahamas. It culminates on Independence Day, July 10, with fireworks at Clifford Park.

Emancipation Day, the first Monday in August, is a public holiday that commemorates the abolition of slavery in 1834. It is followed on Tuesday by Fox Hill Day. In the old days, Fox Hill was isolated from Nassau; hence, the residents did not learn about the Emancipation until later. And so, symbolically, they celebrate on the second day.

October 12, Discovery Day, is a public holiday with special meaning in the Bahamas. It was on a Bahamian island, which the native Lucayan Indians called Guanahani, that Christopher Columbus landed in 1492. Columbus renamed the island San Salvador.

Another October highlight is the formal opening

of the Supreme Court when the chief justice, dressed in the traditional robe and wig, is escorted by the commissioner of police to inspect the Police Honor Guard while the famous Police Band strikes up the band. An equally colorful event with pomp and pageantry is the formal opening of Parliament, usually in February.

The Christmas festivities begin in mid-December with an annual candlelight procession staged by the Renaissance Singers. The group performs at Government House ballroom and the Dundas Centre for the Performing Arts with a repertoire ranging from Renaissance classics to modern spirituals. For information on tickets, contact the Ministry of Education, Division of Cultural Affairs (Tel. 322–8119). Although the performances are usually sold out early, the ministry makes an effort to accommodate visitors.

FREEPORT

GRAND BAHAMA ISLAND

When American financier Wallace Groves began to turn his dream into reality in the 1950s, Grand Bahama Island, 60 miles from Florida, was little more than limestone, pine trees, and brush. From the money he earned lumbering the pine, he began developing the island. Today Freeport, as it is better known, is the second largest town and largest industrial area in the Bahamas and a major international resort.

Freeport spent the 1960s in the limelight, particularly after Cuba went by the board as an American playground, but by the 1970s it had lost much of its luster. The recession, worldwide economic problems, and competition from new resorts in Florida and elsewhere resulted in a setback for Freeport.

A renaissance began in 1984 with the multimillion-dollar renovation of the Princess Hotels and Casino. This was followed the next year by the $40-million facelift and expansion of the 500-acre Lucayan Beach Hotel and Casino, which had

been closed since 1976. Port Lucaya, a shopping and entertainment complex, was added along with the "Dolphin Experience" attraction.

Freeport also got another boost when it became a popular cruise stop, especially for short cruises from Florida. These cruises bring more visitors to the island in a month than many islands see in a year. And, on a smaller scale, there is as much for them to enjoy here as in Nassau. The island has an active People-to-People program similar to that in Nassau, as well as a large variety of restaurants, two glittering casinos, a famous international shopping bazaar, and six golf courses.

 ## IN BRIEF

LOCATION: Grand Bahama Island is about 80 miles from end to end. The cruise ship port, situated on the south coast at the mouth of Hawksbill Creek, is about 5 miles from the town of Freeport where the Bahamas Princess Hotel and Casino, its golf courses, and the International Bazaar are located. Another five miles east along Sunrise Highway takes you to the Lucayan residential and resort area where major hotels front expansive white sand beaches on the south shore and offer an array of water sports.

TRANSPORTATION: Metered taxis are available at the port, downtown Freeport, and at hotels. Rates are supposed to be fixed at $2 flag-fall and 20 cents each one-fifth mile for one or two passengers; $2 for each additional passenger.

If you plan to engage a taxi for sight-seeing, you should negotiate the price in advance. Rates are $12 per hour for a five-passenger car; $15 for larger ones. Also, you should be aware there are free-lancers who are not legal taxis and who will charge whatever they think they can get. Look for taxis with a "Bahama Host" sticker on the windshield. They are reliable and the best informed.

Town buses or jitneys (65 cents) run during the day from town to Lucayan and West End. However, as a cruise passenger with limited time, you are better off hiring a taxi or renting a car if you want to visit either end of the island.

CAR RENTALS: To rent a car with a credit card,

you must be 21 years or older; without the card, 25 years or older. Americans may use U.S. driver's licenses for up to three months. Car rentals are available from several locations in town and at major hotels. When you have reserved a car in advance with Avis, Hertz, or National, they will deliver your car free of charge to the port. Expect to pay $50 and up for a subcompact with unlimited mileage. Jeeps are available too.

Avis, Tel. 352–7666;

Courtesy Car, Tel. 352–5212;

Hertz, Tel. 352–9250;

National, Tel. 352–9300;

Star Rent a Car, Tel. 352–5953

And remember, Bahamians drive on the **LEFT.** You will need a map and a good sense of direction because even new maps are not up-to-date. Do not hesitate to ask anyone for directions.

MOPEDS/BICYCLES: You can rent a bike at the International Bazaar in Freeport. A valid driver's license and a helmet supplied by the rental agency are compulsory. Prices are about $30 per day. To repeat, *DRIVING IS ON THE LEFT.*

SHOPPING: Freeport has as much shopping appeal as Nassau. The *International Bazaar,* housing dozens of boutiques with merchandise from all over the world, set the standard for other tourist destinations when it first opened in the 1960s. It has since been expanded to hold about 75 shops where you can buy anything from $2 T-shirts to $2,000 emeralds. Among the familiar names are Columbian Emeralds, Fendi, and Little Switzerland. Other shopping centers in the Freeport area are Town Centre and Churchill Square.

Next to the International Bazaar, *The Perfume Factory,* which houses *Fragrance of the Bahamas,* is set in a replica of an old Bahamian mansion, where various scents for ladies and gents are made. Guides dressed in period costumes give visitors a tour and explain how the essences, made only from natural plants, are blended into perfumes and other products. There are six standard fragrances, and you can also create your own scent, which will be officially registered in your name. Perfumes, lotions, and T-

shirts are available for purchase. The fragrance Guanahani—the original name of San Salvador, where Columbus made his first landfall—was created in 1992 to mark the Quincentennial.

Port Lucaya, a waterside shopping, entertainment, and water sports complex in the heart of the Lucayan resort area, has more than 40 stores, snack bars, and restaurants in attractive, colonial-style buildings. "Celebration Circle," the entertainment center, features steel bands, reggae groups, and other entertainment.

Many of the best-known Nassau stores have outlets in Freeport and Lucaya. Generally, shops are open Monday through Thursday, 9:30 A.M. to 3 P.M., and Friday to 5 P.M. However, some shops stay open to 6 P.M., and others, such as Oasis, which sells perfumes, toiletries, and jewelry, are open until 10:30 P.M. Some stores open on Saturday morning; the straw market and pharmacies open on Sundays.

BEACHES AND WATER SPORTS: Grand Bahama has some of the finest beaches in the Bahamas. Among the best with hotels and facilities is Xanadu Beach, south of the Princess Hotel complex, five miles from the port; and Lucayan Beach, 11 miles east of the port. If you prefer an undeveloped beach with miles of sand all to yourself, head toward West End. Several minor roads between Harry's American Bar and Buccaneer lead to lovely beaches. The Lucayan National Park on the south coast is a drive of about 30 minutes from town. Freeport also has terrific fishing, sailing, and sailboarding at prices generally less than in Nassau. All beachfront hotels have sailboarding equipment.

Freeport's facilities for scuba and snorkeling are not only the best in the Bahamas, they are among the best in the world. It is home base for *UNEXSO, Underwater Explorers Society* (Box F–2433; Tel. 373–1244; 800–922–3483). Their facility, adjacent to Port Lucaya, offers eight levels of instruction and includes an 18-foot-deep diver training pool and pro shop. The facility also has a recompression chamber.

An introductory lesson with equipment, three hours of professional instruction, and a dive with your instructor on a shallow reef trip costs $79. There is a daily snorkeling trip for $15. For experienced divers, the society has three dive trips daily, including night dives. A three-dive package with all gear is $75.

THE DOLPHIN EXPERIENCE: UNEXSO has six Atlantic bottlenose dolphins as part of a program to observe how the animals interact with humans under highly controlled circumstances. The dolphins are also released to the open sea daily to swim with scuba divers on the coral reef. Offered in its short form several times daily, the Experience starts with a briefing for participants and is followed by a 20-minute session at the nature reserve created for the Dolphin Experience. Here, a small number of people at a time are allowed to wade into a shallow holding pen to stroke the dolphins while the animals swim in and out on whistle signals from the guide. Cost is $30 adult; no charge for children 5 years or under.

Although the management does not encourage this activity, it advertises that you can arrange—in advance—to swim or snorkel with the dolphins in the reef-protected waters near the reserve. Cost is $85.

TENNIS: Tennis, too, is popular and readily available at the *Bahamas Princess Resort and Casino,* with twelve courts and the most convenient location to the port. Rates are very reasonable.

GOLF: Freeport has almost half the golf courses in the Bahamas. Those nearest the port are the pair of championship courses at the *Bahamas Princess Hotel and Golf Club* (Tel. 352–6721). The Emerald Course (6,679 yards, par 72) designed by Dick Wilson has 84 bunkers and is considered the toughest on the island; the Ruby Course (6.750 yards, par 72) was designed by Joe Lee. Greens fees are $58 for hotel guests, $63 for non-guests with shared cart in winter, $46 and $51 in summer, for 18 holes; $20 club rental.

Lucayan Golf Course (Tel. 373–1066; 6,488 yards, par 72) is a 15-minute drive from the port. Also designed by Dick Wilson, the layout, noted for its fast greens, has several par fives more than 500 yards long. Greens fees and shared cart are $44 in winter, $23 in summer for 18 holes; $22 and $21 for 9 holes. $20 club rental per set.

Some cruise lines have golf packages or will

make arrangements for play for passengers. If not, you should call ahead for reservations. For cruise passengers who are planning to overnight here, some hotels have golf packages.

HORSEBACK RIDING: *Pinetree Stables* (Beachway Drive; Tel. 373–3600) offers trail rides three times daily, except Mondays.

INFORMATION: The Tourist Information Centre is located in the Sir Charles Hayward Library (Tel. 352–8044), and there are booths at Freeport Harbor (Tel. 352–9651), at the airport (Tel. 352–2052), and in the International Bazaar. The offices are open 8:30 A.M. to 5 P.M., Monday through Saturday.

EMERGENCY NUMBERS:

Medical Services: Rand Memorial Hospital, Tel. 352–6735

Police: Freeport, Tel. 911

Ambulance: Freeport, Tel. 352–2689

SIGHT-SEEING

In contrast to its high-living, high-stakes image, Freeport has several attractions that tell its history and highlight its tropical variety.

GARDEN OF THE GROVES This ten-acre park and botanical garden, named for Freeport's developer, is one of the loveliest spots in Freeport. It has footpaths through exotic tropical gardens with ponds and pretty waterfalls and places to sit to enjoy the peace and tranquility of the setting. At the entrance is the Grand Bahama Museum (Tel. 373–5668), a small museum with exhibits of Lucayan artifacts, a reconstructed Indian burial site found in one of the mysterious water-filled caverns that honeycomb the island and probably gave rise to the Fountain of Youth myth that led Ponce de León here in 1513.

The museum has a model of the Pine Ridge lumber railway, the early harbor, and a settlement house that was reconstructed out of Freeport's first airport terminal; a bush medicine garden; a thatch exhibit; and colorful costumes of Junkanoo. The Freeport Story, from the dream of Wallace Groves in 1955 to the three decades of development, is also displayed. Admission is $5 for adults; none for children up to ten years of age.

LUCAYAN NATIONAL PARK Located 25 miles west of Freeport near the former U.S. Army Missile Tracking Base, the Lucayan National Park (Tel. 352–5438) is about a 30-minute drive from downtown. The 40-acre park, opened in 1985, is situated on land donated to the National Trust by the Grand Bahama Development Company and is composed of four different ecological zones. The park, designed by Freeport planner Peter Barratt, has a 1,000-foot-wide beach with some of the highest dunes on the island. Gold Rock Creek, which is bounded by extensive mangroves, flows through the park to the sea. Among the flora are coca plums, seagrapes, sea oats, and casuarinas. Another area has Ming trees, wild tamarind, mahogany, and cedar trees.

The park is also the entrance to one of the world's longest charted cave systems, but access to the caves is restricted to scientists and archaeologists who must have permission from the National Trust. Lucayan Indian relics have been found inside the caverns.

There are footpaths and raised wooden walkways over the mangroves to the beach and a map on display at the car park. Further information is available from the Rand Nature Center. The area is popular with birdwatchers, but the main reason to visit this area of the island is the lovely, untouched beaches.

RAND MEMORIAL NATURE CENTER (P.O. Box F–2954, Tel. 352–5438) Located 3 miles from the International Bazaar, the center, which is also the headquarters of the Bahamas National Trust, comprises 100 acres of tropical plants, trees, birds, and butterflies and is home to hundreds of species of plants and approximately ninety-six species of birds. A preserve for the native pine forests that once covered the island, it contains many species endangered by the island's continuing development.

An hour-long walking tour along winding trails provides an opportunity to see and photograph tropical flora, including many species of wild orchids and a great variety of birds. At the end of the trail, surrounded by numerous flowering

exotic plants, is a pond that is home to a small group of flamingos. Hours: Monday to Friday, 9 A.M. to 4 P.M.; Saturday to 1 P.M. Admission: $5 adults; $3 children ages 3 to 12. Guided tours are available.

BOAT EXCURSIONS Snorkeling trips, picnic trips, and sunset party cruises are available from *Pat & Diane* (Tel. 373–8681) and *Reef Tours* (Tel. 373–5880), all departing from Port Lucaya. The latter also claims to have the largest glass-bottom boat on the seas. It departs daily from the Port Lucaya marina at 10:30 A.M. and 12:30 and 2:30 P.M. on reef cruises. Prices range from $17 to $35, depending on the time of day, length of cruise, and amenities offered.

The Deepstar Submarine (Tel. 373–7934), based in Lucaya, is a new adventure in the first submarine with a completely transparent acrylic hull, which provides passengers with a panoramic view of the magnificent underwater environment. The vessel goes to depths of between 70 and 100 feet, and carries 45 passengers on a two-hour voyage. Operated by Comex Submarines Ltd., the Deepstar departs three times daily from the UNEXSO dock in Port Lucaya onto a ferry that takes them to the *Deepstar.* Cost: $49 adults, $41 children.

DINING AND RESTAURANTS IN FREEPORT

Like Nassau, Freeport has a great variety of restaurants, including inexpensive ones specializing in Bahamian dishes. The International Bazaar, Port Lucaya, and large resorts also provide many choices.

Fatman's Nephew offers patio dining on Bahamian specialties such as cracked conch. Popular in the Lucayan area on Taino Beach are the *Surfside Restaurant,* a rustic seaside tavern known for minced lobster, and *The Stone Crab,* which specializes in lobster and steaks.

On the more expensive side, *Pier One,* just west of the port, has a rustic setting where every table has a pretty view of the sea. The specialty is fresh seafood, particularly fresh oysters and the catch of the day, and there's calypso entertainment most of the time.

Every Wednesday evening a native fish fry dinner is held at *Smith's Point*, a small beachside settlement. Visitors dine on fresh seafood and can meet local residents. It's not an advertized event, but local taxi drivers know about it. Cost is about $6 per person.

Nightlife centers around the large hotels. Princess Casino Show has two shows, nightly except Monday, at 8:30 and 10:45 P.M.

A DRIVE AROUND GRAND BAHAMA ISLAND

To explore the less commercial side of Grand Bahama, a drive of 21 miles to West End will take you to the oldest settlements and some of the quieter corners of this surprising island.

If you are driving from the port or town head west on Queens Highway to Hawksbill Creek, where there are large piles of conch shells and where Abaco fishermen unload their catch. Continue along Fishing Hole Road to Eight Mile Rock, the largest native settlement on the island, aptly named for the 8 miles or so of rocky shore on its south coast. The colorful village of brightly painted wooden houses was settled around 1830. The picturesque *St. Stephens Anglican Church,* built directly on the sea, dates from 1851.

Queens Highway continues to Seagrape, another tiny hamlet with a reputation for making the best bread in the Bahamas. The next town is Holmes Rock where the *Hydroflora Gardens* are growing hydroponic tomatoes, cucumbers, and other vegetables. As you near West End, you pass the saltwater Pelican Lake and Bootle Bay.

West End, hugging the water's edge at the westernmost tip of Grand Bahama Island, is less than 60 speedboat miles away from the Florida coast. It is the oldest settlement on the island and has had at least two fast but fleeting booms—during the American Civil War as a base for southerners running ammunition and supplies through the Yankee blockade to Confederate forces, and during Prohibition when the likes of Al Capone found it a convenient shipping point for liquor from Europe.

After 1933, West End went back to being a sleepy fishing village, attracting such occasional

deep-sea fishermen as Ernest Hemingway. Nothing else much happened until Billy Butlin of British resort fame built one of his holiday retreats, but it never had quite the success of its English seaside counterparts. It was followed by a Jack Tar Village, which also enjoyed a period of success but is now closed.

The road into town takes you by tiny wooden stalls beside mounds of conch shells where you can stop to watch one of the local fishermen prepare his day's catch for tomorrow's market. There's an old church built in 1893 and the *Star Hotel* (Tel. 346–6207), the island's first, built in 1946. The rickety wooden building, no longer a hotel, has a new lease on life. It is being renovated by the grandchildren of the original builder and, at present, houses a bar and a restaurant serving local food.

On your return trip, if you haven't lingered too long, you might stop at *Harry's American Bar* at Deadman's Reef. It's famous for sunsets and Harry's Hurricane—and if you take in too much of either, you are likely to miss your boat.

East End Adventures (242–373–6662): One of Grand Bahamas' newest additions are ecological excursions to the east end of the island, operated by two local residents, Tiffany Barrett and Clarence Bellof. You are picked up in early morning by Jeep for a drive to the east end to McLean's Town where you take a short boat ride to Sweeting's Cay—near yet remote—where you have a glimpse of local life and enjoy a drink, a Bahamian picnic lunch, and swimming and snorkeling at a sublimely beautiful deserted beach. Cost is $100 per adult, $50 per child under 12.

THE OUT ISLANDS

The Other Bahamas—the hundreds of islands, islets, and cays that make up the Bahamas archipelago—are known as the Out Islands (meaning out beyond the main center of Nassau). They are the serene hideaways of our dreams, where endless miles of white and pink sand beaches are surrounded by gin-clear waters and where life is so laid back, ten people make a crowd. Only about three dozen islands have permanent settlements.

No cruise lines offer year-round cruises, but several ships occasionally call at one or two locations, and most ships on three- and four-night Bahama cruises from Florida stop for the day at one of the typical uninhabited islands. These are leased from the Bahamas government for an extended period of time and outfitted with the facilities and amenities to give their passengers a comfortable and fun-filled day at the beach.

THE ABACOS At the northern end of the Bahamas archipelago, a group of islands and cays is strung in boomerang fashion for 130 miles, coupling the Sea of Abaco, whose sheltered waters offer some of the Bahamas' best sailing. Two main islands, *Little Abaco* and *Great Abaco,* are joined by a causeway.

Walker's Cay, a well-known fishing resort, lies off the north tip of Little Abaco; Hole in the Wall at the south end of Great Abaco was a strategic location throughout the eighteenth century for guarding the shipping lanes to Nassau.

Marsh Harbour, the capital and main hub of the Abacos, is the third largest town of the Bahamas and one of the main boat-chartering centers of the Caribbean. It has a resident population of about 1,000 and an airport. Its small resorts are operated by native islanders or American and Canadian transplants. Guests dine on fresh fish and homemade island specialties, and enjoy lazy, sunny days sailing, snorkeling, windsurfing, or doing lots of nothing.

Wallys (on the main road at the edge of town; Tel. 367–2074) is a restaurant/bar in a pretty, pink, attractively furnished villa with a veranda overlooking a flower-filled lawn and the sea. The popular bar is known for its special tropical drinks; the restaurant serves lunch. There is also a boutique.

On nearby Elbow Cay, colonial Hope Town is one of many old settlements in the Bahamas that look like New England villages with palm trees. It is situated on a picture-postcard harbor complete with a candy-striped lighthouse and can be reached by ferry from Marsh Harbour. *Wyannie*

Malone Museum (Tel. 366–0311), set in one of the island's oldest houses—it seems almost like a dollhouse, it is so small—is devoted to the island's history. In 1991, it won the American Express Heritage Award as an outstanding example of a small community's effort at preservation.

Of the Loyalists from New York who came in 1783 to join the English settlers living in the Abacos, some stayed at New Plymouth, another Cape Cod village in the tropics, on Green Turtle Cay. For many years it was the largest settlement and capital of the Abacos. In recent times, the old fishing village has become something of an artist colony whose members were attracted by its beauty and serenity and by two native sons— Alton Roland Lowe, a historian and one of the Bahamas' leading landscape artists, and James Mastin, an outstanding sculptor—who led the way.

The *Albert Lowe Museum,* created by Alton Lowe in honor of his father, who was a noted carver of ship models, is devoted to the history of the Abacos and to shipbuilding. It occupies a pretty Victorian house on the main street, a short walk from the town dock. Lowe's paintings, most of which depict local island subjects and settings, and Mastin's works are on view, and prints are available for sale.

A few steps from the museum on the same street is the *Memorial Sculpture Garden,* Mastin's contribution to the island. Opened in 1983 for the bicentennial of the island's Loyalist settlements, the bronze statues represent the people who shaped the history of the Bahamas down through the centuries from the first settlers to the present. The busts are placed around a central monument of two women—one white, one black—representing the Loyalists, plantation owners who fled the American Revolution with their slaves and were the earliest settlers.

Almost as famous as the artists is *Blue Bee Bar,* whose walls and ceiling are covered with thousands of business cards from around the world. Miss Emily, as Emily Cooper, the former proprietress was affectionately known, is credited with creating the Goombay Smash, a famous tropical drink served in bars throughout the Bahamas— although this churchgoing lady was a teetotaler and never tasted her famous drink. Now, the bar and its traditions are carried on by her daughter. The town also has several tiny hotels situated in houses dating from the eighteenth century. These nestle between the neat white clapboard cottages trimmed with pink, blue, yellow, or green and set in flowering gardens. The neighboring island of Green Turtle Cay, another popular boating center, can be reached by small ferry.

Less than an hour's drive west of Marsh Harbour through forested land is Treasure Cay, where *The Day of the Dolphin* with George C. Scott was filmed. Legend has it that 17 Spanish treasure galleons sank here in 1595. Some have been found; exploration for the others continues. In 1962, two entrepreneurs—one British, one American—developed a self-contained resort, Treasure Cay Beach Hotel and Villas, on 1,500 acres along a three-and-a-half-mile, half-moon beach of powdery sand washed by aqua seas.

Another island south of Marsh Harbour is Man-o-War Cay, famous for its boat builders who craft their vessels by hand. The cay has no cars, but in recent years progress has brought golf carts, which many of the American retirees who populate the island use to get around. One of Man-o-War Cay's enterprising natives has turned the family's sail-making tradition into a prosperous cottage industry producing sturdy tote bags, hats, and a variety of other products that are particularly prized by yachtsmen.

ANDROS A 30-minute flight west of Nassau will bring you to Andros, the largest island of the Bahamas and one of the least developed. The interior of the island is covered with pine forests interspersed with mangroves; other parts are mud flats or barren. Off the east coast of Andros lies the Barrier Reef, more than 100 miles long, the third largest in the world. Just beyond is the Tongue of the Ocean, a depression which plunges as deep as 6,000 feet at the north end. These natural phenomena attract divers and sportfishermen from around the world. Andros also calls itself the bonefishing capital of the world. Among the resorts, *Small Hope Bay Lodge* at Fresh Creek was the first organized diving resort in the Bahamas.

BERRY ISLANDS The group of about 30 islands with a total land area of only 14 square miles is located between New Providence (Nassau) and Grand Bahama Island (Freeport). Most are uninhabited, and several are popular stops for cruise ships whose passengers spend the day on "their" island, enjoying the beaches and swimming and snorkeling in clear water. Their lovely little harbors, coves, and protected waters make them popular with yachtsmen.

THE BIMINIS South of Freeport where the Bahamas Banks meet the Gulf Stream are the Biminis, the Bahamian islands only 50 miles from Florida. Ernest Hemingway was a frequent caller, and his old haunt, *The Compleat Angler*, a wooden frame hotel and bar, displays his paintings and writings from 1931 to 1937. Adam Clayton Powell, the flamboyant Harlem minister and congressman, made Bimini his second home. Long before either of them, however, Ponce de León stopped here in his search for the Fountain of Youth. No less than four places commemorate his landing.

The group is divided into the North Biminis and South Biminis and, along with Cat Cay, are among the prime game fishing centers in the Western Hemisphere. Because of their proximity to the Gulf Stream, Bimini waters teem with sea life. Vestiges of old ships in Bahamian waters number in the hundreds. Among the most famous is the *Sapona*, which lies between South Bimini and Cat Cay. Built by Henry Ford around 1915, the ship served as a private club and is said to have been a rum-runner's storehouse in the 1920s when it was blown ashore by a hurricane in 1929.

The main settlement is Alicetown on North Bimini. You can walk or bike around most of the island in an hour or so. Although the island takes on something of a rowdy party atmosphere in the evening (the fishing crowd at one of their favorite bars), during the day it is a sleepy little place, pleasant for picnicking and lazing on the beach. The best beach is the mile stretch of sand opposite a Cape Cod–type cottage called the Anchorage, which Hemingway used as his setting for *Islands in the Sun*. Another pretty beach shaded with graceful pine trees lies north of town and is reached by a path at the end of the paved road to Bimini Bay. Its calm waters are delightful for swimming and snorkeling.

CAT ISLAND West of the Exumas lies Cat Island

(not to be confused with Cat Cay). It is covered with forested, rolling hills that soar to the great height of 204 feet—the highest natural point in the Bahamas. Once prosperous with sugar plantations of the Loyalists who had fled the American Revolution, Cat Island is largely untouched today and is best known as the childhood home of actor Sidney Poitier. Its four tiny hotels and wide white beaches are made for ardent escapists.

ELEUTHERA First-time visitors to the Other Bahamas often select Eleuthera because of its combination of faraway tranquility, the pretty setting of pastel-painted houses surrounded by gentle green hills, and its 300 years of history. It also has comfortable, unpretentious hotels, good dining and sports facilities, and more roads and transportation than the other islands. The island is famous for its pink sand beaches.

Situated 60 miles east of Nassau, Eleuthera is a 110-mile skinny spine never more than 2 miles wide, except for splays at both ends. It has six official ports of call and three airports with direct flights from Nassau, Freeport, Fort Lauderdale, and Miami.

Eleuthera has three of the Bahamas' oldest and prettiest settlements: Governor's Harbour, the main town near the center of the island and the hub of commercial activity, more than 300 years old; Dunmore Town on Harbour Island; and Spanish Wells.

Harbour Island, almost touching the northeastern tip of Eleuthera, is one of the most beautiful spots in the Bahamas and the site of Dunmore Town, its original capital and now a tranquil village of neat old houses and flower-filled lanes. A high green ridge dotted with pink and white colonial homes separates the seventeenth-century village from a three-mile beach of pink, powdery sand, whose color comes from the coral. The island has eight small hotels.

Spanish Wells, located off the northern end of Eleuthera, is a popular fishing and yachting center. It gets its name from the Spaniards who came ashore here to replenish the freshwater supplies of their ships after making the long voyages between the Old and New Worlds.

The southern part of Eleuthera is slated for major development to create a new resort center that is low-key, tasteful, and ecosensitive, in line with the Bahamas' policy of encouraging development that is compatible with the environment.

PRINCESS CAY The "private island" used by Princess Cruises for most of its Caribbean itineraries is a recreational facility spread along a lovely beach at the southern tip of Eleuthera. Here, Princess has developed excellent facilities for a-day-at-the-beach for its passengers, offering a wide range of water sports, beach games, guided nature walks, several bars, a boutique, small markets for local Bahamian crafts, and local entertainment. Lunch is served at a large pavilion to all passengers who chose to spend the day at beach. Continuous tender service is provided by the line between the ship and the beach.

THE EXUMAS From 35 miles south of Nassau, the Exumas spread southeast over an area of 130 square miles. The group is particularly popular with yachtsmen who say the variety of color and subtle shades of the waters around the Exumas have no equal. Snorkelers and divers sing their praises, too. The *Exuma Land and Sea Park* is a preserve accessible only by boat.

George Town, the capital, is a quiet village of 800 people and several small hotels. Across the bay is Stocking Island whose lovely stretches of white sand beach are rich with seashells. About a dozen resorts are dotted through the Exuma chain, as are hundreds of beaches and coves. This sea-lover's mecca becomes busiest in April, when the islands host the annual Out Islands Regatta, the Bahamas' most prestigious sailing race.

INAGUA The Bahamas' third largest island is one of the least visited. Flamingos outnumber people 40,000 to 1,000. The 287-square-mile *Inagua Park* is the largest flamingo preserve in the Western Hemisphere. *Union Park* is a reserve for giant green turtles.

SAN SALVADOR Situated east-southeast of Nassau and directly east of Cat Island, San Salvador is the island "where it all began," so to speak. Although the island had been neglected, it received a great deal of attention in 1992 when the Bahamas celebrated the Quincentennial as the site of Columbus's first landfall in the New World. The island has four monuments commemorating

Columbus's first landfall. (The landing site has been disputed as much as the landing!)

The San Salvador Museum has a new home in a renovated building that was originally constructed in the early nineteenth century and served until 1966 as a courthouse, a jail, and the Commissioner's Office. The building was restored by the Kiwanis Club of San Salvador with help from other service clubs and private groups. The exhibits are arranged in four groups: Columbus, 1492; The Lucayans, A.D. 600–1492; San Salvador, 1492–1838; and San Salvador in the late-nineteenth and twentieth centuries. The Lucayan exhibit has a map that shows the 48 known Indian archaelogical sites on San Salvador.

San Salvador has a Club Med, which the Bahamian government hoped would bring new life and tourism development to the island, but it hasn't happened yet. There is a small hotel, *Riding Rock Inn,* near Cockburn Town, the main village. The island is prized by scuba enthusiasts because it is almost virgin territory. Both Club Med and the Riding Rock cater to divers.

AIRLINES SERVING THE OUT ISLANDS

Bahamasair (800–222–4262) serves all the airport centers of the Out Islands from Nassau. Same-day connections from U.S. and Canadian gateways are available to Abaco, Andros, Bimini, Eleuthera, and Exuma. Several small airlines offer service to the main Out Islands from Florida.

Haiti

CAP HAITIEN, LABADEE

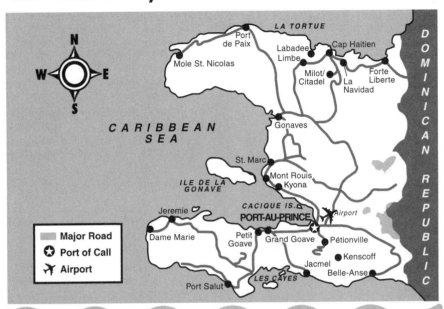

AT A GLANCE

Antiquities	★★★
Arts and Artists	★★★★★
Beaches	★★★
Colonial/Victorian Buildings	★★★★★
Crafts	★★★★★
Cuisine	★★★★
Culture	★★★★★
Dining/Restaurants	★★★
Entertainment	★★
Forts	★★★★★
History	★★★★
Monuments	★★★
Museums	★★★★★
Nature	★★★★
Nightlife	★★
Scenery	★★★★
Shopping	★★★★★
Sight-seeing	★★★★★
Sports	★★
Transportation	★

CHAPTER CONTENTS

A MAGICAL TAPESTRY

The body is French and seductive; the soul is African and mysterious; and the heart is Caribbean, warm and smiling. It's vivid, spicy, heady. It's Haiti and it's like no other place in the world.

Vive la Difference has long been Haiti's national slogan. But this land is not simply different from other places; it is unique in its history, its art, its people, and its attractions. History had a great deal to do with making it that way.

To understand Haiti, do not think of a resort island in the Caribbean but of a country whose people—for better or for worse—have been their own masters longer than any country in the Caribbean and almost as many years as we in the United States. Although the Haitians paid dearly for their independence and freedom, both have often eluded them.

Haiti, less than 1.5-hour flight from Miami, covers 10,714 square miles and occupies the western third of Hispaniola, the island it shares with the Dominican Republic. The native Indians called their country *Haiti,* meaning land of high mountains. It is a fitting description. Haiti's border with the Dominican Republic runs through the Cordillera Central with Haiti's highest peak, *Pic la Selle,* in the south at 8,793 feet.

From the Gulf of Gonave on the west coast where the capital, Port-au-Prince, is situated, Haiti stretches like the open pincers of a crab in two mountainous peninsulas. The northwestern peninsula at its closest point is only 50 miles across the Windward Passage from Cuba; the southwestern extremity of the lower peninsula is slightly more than 100 miles from Jamaica.

Christopher Columbus discovered *La Isla Española,* as he called it, on December 4, 1492, and came ashore for the first time in the vicinity of Mole St. Nicolas, a little town at the extreme northwestern tip of the island. He then sailed along the coast, and at a site near Cap Haitien, the main port of call for cruise ships today, the *Santa Maria,* his flagship, ran aground and had to be abandoned.

AFTER COLUMBUS

After the Spaniards discovered gold in the eastern part of Hispaniola, they largely ignored the western portion, thus enabling French pirates holed up on Tortuga, a small island off Haiti's northwest coast, to prey on Spanish ships, and eventually to settle in pockets on the coast. France, eager to gain her share of the New World, took advantage of the French freebooters to establish her claim and ultimately her control of Hispaniola's western part. In the Treaty of Ryswick (or Rijswijk) in 1697 Spain officially ceded the territory to France.

By then the original Indian population of Saint Domingue, as the French named their colony, had been decimated and replaced with African slaves to work the plantations of sugar, coffee, indigo, cacao, and cotton. Over the next century Saint Domingue became France's richest colony in the New World, earning the title of "the Pearl of the Caribbean."

In contrast with other colonies the number of Frenchmen who came to settle was small, but the number of African slaves imported was exceedingly high. It is said the death rate from toil and inhuman living conditions was so high and required the slave population to be replenished at such a rapid rate that the entire population was replaced in 20 years.

In time the wealthy plantation society that developed became as mulatto as it was white—and just French enough to take on the pretensions of an upper class, calling itself the "Elite." Ultimately, Haiti became a class society which even to this day remains separated by language—French and Creole; education—more than 85 percent of the people are illiterate; and religion—Catholicism and voodoo.

By 1795 when Spain relinquished control of the entire island to France, the ideas stimulated by the French and American revolutions were beginning to erupt in the Caribbean. The planters, now mostly mulatto, asked for the right to vote, but were rebuffed. A series of uprisings by mulattos and free blacks followed, but none was as serious as the revolt by the slaves.

THE HAITIAN REVOLUTION

The Spaniards, ever eager to undermine the French, helped to keep the pot boiling by aiding the slaves who had escaped into the mountains. The British meddled too. In a move to gain the loyalty of their black troops, the French in charge of Saint Domingue declared all slaves free and with the help of Toussaint L'Ouverture, a former slave who had risen through the ranks of the French army to become a general and governor of Saint Domingue, were able to quell the rebellion.

Then, in May 1801, Toussaint L'Ouverture called together an assembly of ten leaders to adopt a constitution. But Napoléon, who wanted to use Saint Domingue as his staging ground for conquering North America, saw L'Ouverture's move as an act of secession. Fearing the loss of his prized New World possession, he sent an armada of 70 warships and 25,000 men to crush the rebels.

Overwhelmed by the French forces, L'Ouverture agreed to a truce, but when he went to discuss peace with General Leclerc, the French commander, he was thrown in chains and carted off to France where he died in prison.

The revolution, however, did not die. After a year of struggle the Haitians, led by two of their generals, Jean-Jacques Dessalines and Alexandre Pétion, defeated the French army, and following an armistice signed on November 18, 1803, all French troops departed.

THE FIRST BLACK REPUBLIC

On January 1, 1804, Dessalines proclaimed the country's independence and took back the island's original Arawak name, Haiti. Following Napoléon's example, Dessalines took the title of emperor under which he ruled until he was killed in a campaign against fresh rebellions in 1806. Then a republic—the first black republic in the Western Hemisphere—was declared. Henri Christophe, a former slave and young soldier who had fought in the American Revolution and had

distinguished himself in the Haitian struggle against the French, was made the first president. But when Pétion, the general who had fought with Dessalines, was elected to succeed him, Christophe didn't like the outcome and proclaimed himself king. Haiti was divided with Christophe ruling the north and west, Pétion the south and east.

Unfortunately, neither peace nor harmony followed. The flamboyant Christophe turned out to be as brutal as he was bold, and it seems he had a mania for building.

Christophe's greatest fear was that the French would return and take his kingdom from him. At least, that's the reason history has given for his building the *Citadel*, the most awesome fortification in the Western Hemisphere and one that rivaled the medieval castle-fortresses of Europe.

Crowning a 3,000-foot mountain peak on the north coast near Cap Haitien, the remarkable structure deserves to be called the Eighth Wonder of the World. Under a ten-year restoration program the Citadel was restored with the help of UNESCO, which named it to the World Heritage List. It is Haiti's major tourist attraction.

Christophe also took on the ways of the French court, surrounding himself with a nobility he created and building himself seven palaces. *Sans Souci*, now a ruin at the foot of the Citadel, was meant to rival Versailles.

After Christophe's suicide and Pétion's death, Jean-Pierre Boyer was elected president and reunited the country, governing it for the next twenty-five years. But Haiti, like its Dominican neighbor, was to experience a century of instability, warring several times with its neighbor. Worried over the country's strategic location in the gathering storms of World War I, the United States occupied the country in 1915. The occupation lasted almost two decades.

After the United States' departure a succession of governments followed—none strong enough to last. Then in 1957, François Duvalier, a country doctor known to his peasant constituents as "Papa Doc," was elected president. At the start of his regime, no one imagined that Haiti had brought to power a man who would become as cruel and ruthless as any in the country's long history of tyrants, establishing a dynasty that would exploit, steal, terrorize, and grind down this once prosperous land into the poorest nation in the Western Hemisphere. The Duvalier chapter closed in 1986, but political turmoil continued to plague the country.

Then in 1992, seven months after Jean Bertand Aristide, the first popularly elected president in Haiti's modern history, took office, he was unseated by a coup of corrupt military and police officials and politicians backed by the equally corrupt and arrogant privileged elite. The group held power for three years through murder, torture, and intimidation while the international community tried, without success, to negotiate Aristide's return. Finally with the waves of Haitian refugees growing to a torrent, the repression and murder worsening daily, and the country's economy at a standstill, President Bill Clinton sent former U.S. president Jimmy Carter and retired General Colin Powell to convince the junta to leave peacefully or face a U.S. armed intervention to remove them. After several intense—and tense—hours of negotiations and only when the Haitian junta got word that U.S. war planes had left their base in North Carolina enroute to Haiti did the chief honcho, General Raoul Cedras, agree to go.

FAST FACTS

POPULATION: 7 million; the most densely populated country in the Western Hemisphere.

MAIN TOWN: Port-au-Prince, Pétionville, Cap Haitien, Jacmel, Gonaives, Les Cayes.

CLIMATE: Haiti has an even temperature between 78°F and 82°F year round on the coast, though it can reach 95°F in summer, and eternal spring in the high elevation of the mountains.

CLOTHING: Dress is informal. Lightweight cottons are recommended and for the trip to the Citadel, comfortable walking shoes are essential.

CURRENCY: The unit is the gourde. The U.S. dollar is freely accepted everywhere. 15 gourdes = US $1. Major credit cards and travelers checks are accepted at hotels, restaurants, and shops on the tourist track, but not in rural, out-of-the-way places.

DEPARTURE TAX: US $25.

ELECTRICITY: 110 volt, 60 cycles, A.C.

ENTRY FORMALITIES: U.S. citizens need proof of citizenship (passport or birth certificate) and a return or continuing ticket.

LANGUAGE: French is the official language, but the language of the people is Creole, a patois evolved from African dialects, Norman French of the buccaneers, classic French, plus some English and Spanish. English is spoken by educated Haitians and on the tourist track.

PUBLIC HOLIDAYS: January 1, Independence Day; January 2, Forefathers Day; Mardi Gras, three days before Ash Wednesday; Good Friday; April 14, Pan American Day; May 1, Labor Day; May 18, Flag and University Day; August 15, Assumption Day; October 17, Dessalines's Death Anniversary; October 24, United Nations Day; November 1, All Saints Day; November 18, Armed Forces Day; December 5, Discovery Day; December 25, Christmas.

TELEPHONE AREA CODE: 509

TIME: Same as Eastern Standard Time

VACCINATION REQUIREMENTS: None

AIRLINES: From the United States to *Port-au-Prince*, American Airlines.

INFORMATION:

New York: Consulate of Haiti, 271 Madison Ave., 17th Floor, New York, NY 10016; Tel. 212–697–9767.

Miami: 444 Brichell Ave., Miami, FL 33162.

Canada: 50 Place Cremazie, Montreal, Quebec H2P 2RA; Tel. 389–3517.

In Port-au-Prince, Rue Legitime 8A, Champ de Mars, PIP.H; Tel. 23–07–23; fax 23–21–43.

HAITI'S UNIQUE CULTURE

There is nothing about Haiti's brutalizing history that should have produced its remarkable people. Yet, if it is ever possible to characterize a whole nation, the Haitians are the most joyous people you are ever likely to meet. They have an extraordinary capacity for love, gaiety, and grace in the face of the worst adversity. This indomitable spirit, which manifests itself in every aspect of Haitian life, has been called the soul of Haiti.

Visitors having only a passing acquaintance with the country have probably seen Haitian art and heard about voodoo. Haiti has the best truly indigenous art, the most creative, imaginative artists, and the best craftsmen in the Caribbean. Their work is everywhere.

Haitian paintings—colorful and primitive to the casual observer—are a tapestry of Haitian life reflecting the vibrant colors one sees in the flowers and fruits of the trees, in women's dresses, on brightly painted buses, in churches, at Carnival, and in the houses of towns such as Cap Haitien and Jacmel from which many artists come.

Rhythm, song, and dance are as much a part of Haitian life as color. Children don't walk or run, they dance. Women on their way to market bearing mountains of baskets on their heads float along the country roads with balletic grace. It's no accident that dancers like Katherine Dunham found their greatest inspiration through their work in Haiti.

The arts all have meanings lost on outsiders who have not been exposed to Haiti or are unfamiliar with its history, particularly the role voodoo has played in the evolution of its culture. To most foreigners, voodoo is some sort of black magic, hocus-pocus to be feared, or at best, a nightclub act which makes an unusual but unconvincing show.

But for Haitians, particularly the uneducated, peasant majority, voodoo is an all-consuming part of their lives. Even Haiti's educated elite which shuns voodoo outwardly does not reject it totally. Indeed, there is a popular saying that Haiti is 99 percent Catholic and 100 percent voodoo.

VOODOO IN HAITI

Volumes have been written about voodoo, as much fantasy as fact. Serious scholars have studied and written about it from religious, sociological, and psychological points of view—advancing different theories and explanations, depending on their perspectives. Yet, it is doubtful if anyone but a practicing Haitian could explain voodoo, and even they have difficulty because of its complexity.

In the simplest of terms, voodoo is a blueprint for life that has its roots in African tribal practices. On its spiritual level voodoo deals with *loas,* deities or spirits, and a set of complex rituals that keep the individual in harmony with them. The word voodoo derives from *vaudoun,* meaning spirits.

Voodoo has three rites: Rada, Congo, and Petro. There is a supreme deity, the Great Master, and secondary *loas* with varying qualities and symbols. The major *loas* are African in origin; the *marassas,* meaning twins in Haitian creole, are said to correspond somewhat to Christian angels. A manifestation can be seen in the reverence which Haitian twins are given. A special rite is held when twins are born.

To enter the priesthood, a novice must undergo three rituals: washing the head—a baptism or trial by water; the *bounsicanzo,* a symbolic form of trial by fire; and the holding of the *asson* or gourd. When these rituals are completed a man is given the rank of *houngan* or priest and a woman that of *mambo* or priestess.

According to experts, a voodoo ceremony can be as brief as two hours or as long as two weeks. It takes place in a ceremonial courtyard or temple with an altar where sacred objects, vases, bells, and ceremonial dresses are placed. The spirits are summoned by *vêvê,* elaborate symbols with hundreds of variations drawn on the ground with cornmeal or flour. There is an offering of food, drink, perfume, or animals to the divinity being summoned, depending on the likes of the *loa.* The beckoning is completed by carefully placing candles around the *vêvê.*

Each god has his own songs and dances. The ceremony begins with a prayer or tuneful invocation. The beat of the drum, considered sacred, by the *hountogui,* an initiated drummer, sets the pace for the dance and songs which are intended to prepare the body for the "possession" which is the essence of voodoo—enabling the initiate to become united with the *loa* who takes control of the individual. The possession causes a transformation of body and facial expressions and culminates in an emotional display of symbolic dance and gesture.

NEW ROOTS IN THE NEW WORLD

There have been periods in Haiti's history when voodoo flourished in the open, and other times when it was suppressed. Even after independence Haitian rulers often prohibited the practice of voodoo, fearing the power of the voodoo priests and their potential to plot the overthrow of the regime. The great slave revolt that led to Haitian independence was hatched at a voodoo ceremony.

Voodoo began in Haiti with the importation of African slaves in the late 17th century. Since the slaves had been brought from different tribes and different parts of Africa, they had no common language and used their rituals for communication and expression of their misfortune.

At the same time, slaves were baptized and forbidden to practice their African cults. With some adjustments and camouflage, however, they often were able under the guise of Catholic ritual to keep their religious concepts alive.

After independence French culture continued to permeate Haitian life but never displaced the African one. Rather, the culture that the Africans brought with them to the New World, torn to shreds in so many other places, had the chance in Haiti to take root in the rich new soil of the Caribbean and to flower.

The class system that separated the mulatto elite and the illiterate peasants, oddly enough, permitted the retention of African roots. And there was also a trick of history: In a fit of pique, Napoléon, embittered by France's defeat and the loss of his richest colony, withdrew the Catholic clergy from Haiti. Their absence, which lasted seventy years, created a vacuum that was filled by various African cults. By the time Christianity returned, the religious synthesis could not be reversed. Christianity and the various African beliefs had become intertwined with many voodoo spirits.

Out of that synthesis has come Haiti's unique blend of French, African, and Caribbean culture that manifests itself in Haitian art, music, and dance; the underlying fabric remains the rhythm, songs, dance, and spirit of voodoo. It is not accidental that the first great Haitian painter to be recognized by the outside world was a voodoo priest, a fact that brings us to the story of Haitian art.

THE BIRTH OF HAITIAN ART

The sudden explosion of Haitian art on the international stage can almost be described as an accident. In 1944 an American artist, DeWitt Peters, on a grant to teach English in Haiti, had seen the lack of a commitment to art in the Port-au-Prince community and opened the Centre d'Art to teach drawing and composition with no more expectation than developing a few talented students.

What happened was totally unexpected. Peters discovered that the subculture of the Haitian peasantry, with its blend of African and Christian cultures, had been nourishing a wealth of artistic talent for more than 200 years. Educated Haitians had dismissed the primitive art as peasant trash; an outsider was needed to recognize its worth and to gain it international attention.

Within a short time word of the school spread, and artists from villages throughout Haiti came to Peters with their works, while others came to paint at the school. In the first phase of the discovery, four remarkable talents, each with his own style, emerged. Two had been working as artists prior to their acquaintance with Peters; two had studied at the centre.

For years Hector Hyppolite, a voodoo priest, had painted, with a brush of chicken feathers, his symbols, flowers, and visions on the doors and altars of his *houmphor* (temple) and elsewhere in his village. Now considered the father of Haitian art, Hyppolite died only two years after he gained international recognition. His paintings have the most direct voodoo application of the early masters.

In Cap Haitien, Philome Obin had set as his goal the documenting of Haitian history. His geometric architectural style began a school of painting known as the Cap Haitien school that flourishes today. Obin, almost blind, worked up until his death in his nineties.

Rigaud Benoit, Peters's driver, had decorated shaving mugs and other objects with his voodoo fantasies. At the centre he applied his talent to the hood and fenders of the Centre d'Art jeep. Today, it would be rare to see a *tap tap*, the truck/bus used as transportation by 90 percent of Haiti's population, without every centimeter painted in an elaborate work of art.

Castera Bazile, Peters's houseboy from Jacmel, was a devout Catholic and painted saints and angels. He, too, is now dead but painted long enough to leave a strong legacy for the new generation of artists.

A second milestone was laid in the 1950s when the Episcopal bishop of Port-au-Prince allowed eight painters working under Selden Rodman, codirector of the Centre d'Art, to create a series of monumental murals in the Cathedral Ste. Trinité. The work was shown in color in *Time* and other magazines and brought immediate international acclaim, particularly for Wilson Bigaud, another of the early Haitian greats. Today, these murals alone would be worth a trip to Port-au-Prince.

Rodman, who has written extensively on Haiti and Haitian painters, explains that he became concerned when he saw all the great art of these newly discovered talents leaving Haiti as fast as collectors, dealers, and museums could scoop them up. His idea for the murals was to create immovable works of art by these masters. He went first to the Catholic archbishop but was turned down flat. "What, voodoo monstrosities on the walls of a Catholic church? *Jamais!*"

The Centre d'Art continues, and in the intervening years dozens of artists and sculptors have emerged. Museums and collectors around the world have selected the most outstanding artists for their permanent collections, and galleries in Haiti, Paris, New York, and elsewhere provided commercial outlets and incentive for others.

Today, the production is so enormous one can easily get the impression that everyone in Haiti is an artist. Some of the art is superb; much is terrible. The majority of paintings sold by street vendors and gift shops are originals in that someone has taken the pains to put paint to canvas, but they are imitations of artists who have established definitive styles, particularly those that sell well. Occasionally, you can happen upon a new artist who is original and distinctive in his own right. If you are wondering how to select, buy what appeals to you. You may discover a budding Bigaud or you may simply go home with a colorful painting.

 FESTIVALS: In the country where Catholicism and voodoo are intertwined, it's no surprise that feasts and pageants are often celebrated in unique ways, particularly on a village saint's day—and every village has a saint and feast day. Best of all, particularly for visitors, is Carnival, which is held during the three days before Ash Wednesday.

CAP HAITIEN

Brightly colored colonial buildings and Victorian gingerbread houses stretching from Mont Joli on the north to the Old City Gates on the south greet cruise passengers as their ship steams into the harbor of Cap Haitien. Behind the town rise green foothills covered with bougainvillea and mango groves, and beyond, the great rugged mountains of the Cordillera Central where the coffee grows. East along the coast extending to Fort Liberté, on the Dominican border, plains of sisal and sugar fields were once the plantations that made the old colony of Saint Domingue such a prize.

Cap Haitien, a town of about 109,638 people, is laid out in grid fashion facing the harbor. From the pier on the east side of town, the east-west streets run 16 blocks deep and are alphabetically named from A Street at the harbor to Q Street at the hills. The intersecting north-south streets are numbered starting with zero on the south and going to 29 on the north.

Cap Haitien is second in size and population to the capital of Port-au-Prince, but certainly it is no second in history and charm. Here, the Spaniards made their first settlement and Christopher Columbus held the first Christmas Mass. The French had their richest colony and suffered their worst defeat. The Haitians declared their independence and created the first black republic in the New World here, too.

Little was heard of the western region after the Spaniards discovered gold in eastern Hispaniola. Pirates from Tortuga under the command of Bertrand d'Ogeron arrived in 1670, and at some later date twelve Frenchmen guided by a Pierre Lelong settled a town they called *Le Cap* in the lowlands. There they built their houses and began to cultivate tobacco, sugar, cacao, and indigo.

Cap Français, as it was known under the French, reached its peak in the 18th century as the political, commercial, and cultural center of the colony—Port-au-Prince was then not even a village. During the revolts against the French that led to independence, the town saw a great deal of fighting. It was burned in 1791, sacked in 1793, and burned again in 1802.

Cap Français had a respite and returned to splendor after the arrival of Pauline Bonaparte, the sister of Napoléon and the wife of General Leclerc, the French commander sent to put down the rebellion. But the interlude ended with the French defeat and withdrawal in 1803.

Under Henri Christophe, the town was renamed Cap Henry and became the capital of his new kingdom. After his demise, Haiti was reunited, and under the new leadership, Port-au-Prince began to eclipse Cap Haitien as the political and economic center of the country. And in 1842 Cap Haitien suffered a violent earthquake which destroyed many of its grand colonial buildings.

Among those destroyed was the cathedral in the center of town. It was rebuilt in 1942 in its original 18th-century style, facing the town square at 18th and F streets. Two blocks west is the town's museum at 18th and I streets.

On the north side of the town beyond Mont Joli are three 18-century French forts at Rival Beach and the ruins of the residence of Pauline Bonaparte.

 INFORMATION: Bureau du Tourisme, Rue 24 Boulevard, Cap Haitien; Tel. 62–0870.

 **IN BRIEF**

PORT/ARRIVAL: Cap Haitien's cruise port was inaugurated in 1984 with the hope of attracting more cruise ships. It is conveniently located only a short distance east of the heart of town. The terminal has separate entrances for buses and taxis and an additional walkway for pedestrians.

TRANSPORTATION: Taxis and tour buses are on hand for the arrival of ships. Car rental is available in Cap Haitien from Hertz, (Tel. 62–0369). If you want to tour on your own, you would be best served by hiring a taxi at the port or in town. Be sure to settle the price before you get into a taxi.

SHOPPING: Cruise ships are greeted by an instant open-air market. Every Haitian with anything to sell is on hand with his or her wares—paintings, straw hats and bags, wooden carvings and bowls, jewelry, leather bags and belts, and more. People have even found antiques in this, Haiti's oldest city. If you must rush off to take your tour, don't worry, the vendors will be there when you return.

Passengers often complain about the persistence of some vendors. Try not to let it bother you. If you will ignore them, keep walking, and call out, *"Non, merci,"* they will usually move on to someone else more promising.

Cap Haitien is one of Haiti's main art centers and the home of the late Philome Obin, whose works are in museums around the world. Obin was the founder of the Cap Haitien school of art, and some of his disciples are artists in their own right. (A great deal of what you will see sold by street vendors and souvenir shops are only copies of the master by those who know that the Obin name sells.)

DINING: Haitian cuisine, like most other things in Haiti, is an unusual French-Creole combination. You can sample it at *Hotel Mont Joli* (Tel. 62–0326), Cap Haitien's main hotel, located on a hillside north of the town. There's a nice pool and a fabulous view of the city, its harbor, and surrounding countryside. Moderate.

In town, *Roi Christophe Hotel* (61 Rue 14-15 H; Tel. 62–0414) is situated in a renovated 18th-century house that was once the residence of the French governor. Moderate.

BEACHES: About 4 miles northwest of Cap Haitien facing the Atlantic coast is pretty Cormier Beach, a drive of about 30 minutes over a bad road. The 32-room *Cormier Beach Hotel* (Tel. 62–1000) is Haiti's answer to Gilligan's Island and caters mostly to a loyal European clientele. Another, Norman Zarchin's Hotel (Village Labadie; Tel. 62–0400), is a small hotel of three antiques-furnished rooms operated by Norman Zarchin, an American who has been in Haiti for many years. It has a bar and restaurant serving Creole cuisine. There are reefs for snorkeling all along the coast.

LABADEE

At Pointe St. Honore at the north end of the Bay of Labadie, about 6 miles west of Cap Haitien, Royal Caribbean International created a port and seaside resort, Labadee, which it opened in 1986 for the exclusive use of its passengers. Some researchers believe *La Badie*, as it was once writ-

ten, was the place where Columbus's ship ran aground. It can be reached only by boat or by an extraordinarily bad road.

The resort, situated on a 260-acre mountainous peninsula covered with tropical forests and unusual rock formations, fronts white sand beaches and small coves along aquamarine waters.

In addition to Dragon's Tail Beach, a long crest of sandy beach on the north side of the point, there are four smaller beaches and secluded coves on its south side. A dive shop supplies the equipment for snorkeling, diving, and other water sports. At *The Marketplace*, a structure of West Indian–style architecture, Haitian craftsmen work and sell their wares, at *Cafe Labadee*, the resort's restaurant, passengers can enjoy Haitian dishes, drinks made from Haitian rum, and other selections. A folkloric group in colorful costumes from Cap Haitien perform traditional dances.

Paths for nature walks pass through the tropical forest that covers the hillsides, and there are ruins of several old landmarks. Due to the difficulty of access between Labadee and Cap Haitien by road, RCCL cruise passengers do not visit the Citadel from Labadee.

THE SEARCH FOR LA NAVIDAD

Near Cap Haitien on the night of December 23, 1492, as Columbus's three ships were leaving the protection of the bay where they had anchored, a shift in the tide caused the flagship, the *Santa Maria*, to slip onto a coral reef that split her hull and filled her with water. Guancanagari, the cacique or Indian chief of the nearby village, quickly sent his people in their large canoes to help rescue the crew and salvage as much of the provisions as they could.

With the wood of the wrecked ship, Columbus built a fort. It was Christmas Day. Columbus, a fervent Catholic who was convinced his ship's demise had been God's will, named the little fort *La Villa de Navidad*, the Village of the Nativity, and celebrated the Christmas Mass, the first in the New World.

Certain he had found the islands fronting the China coast, Columbus left forty of his men at the newly built fort and rushed back to Spain to tell the world of his discovery.

The following year Columbus returned, naively expecting the settlement to be thriving. Instead, he found nothing. All the men had been killed and the fort burned. No one knows for sure what happened but historians theorize that the men's lust for gold and mistreatment of the Arawaks who had been so kind and generous to Columbus had led to conflict, or that the Spaniards struck out in search of gold, encountered less friendly Indians, and were killed.

In the intervening centuries several serious efforts were launched to find the *Santa Maria* and the site of La Navidad but without success. Only the ship's anchor was found at a place about 3 miles inland from the coast. It is one of the main exhibits of the National Museum in Port-au-Prince.

For over a decade a team from Florida State University, headed by Dr. Kathleen Deagan, has been working at a site first uncovered by medical missionary and amateur archaeologist Dr. William Hodges. For more than three decades Dr. Hodges, who comes originally from Chicago, has been caring for Haiti's poor at his clinic, the Hospital of the Good Samaritan, in Limbe, a village about 15 miles south of Cap Haitien. During those years, his passion for history and archaeology led him to devote most of his spare time to excavating sites in the region and searching for the site of La Navidad.

Through methodical work Dr. Hodges identified and documented a site which he and other scholars believe was the village of Guancanagari, the cacique who helped rescue Columbus and his men from the sinking *Santa Maria*. The site is located about 8 miles southeast of Cap Haitien in a marshy area near the shore. Authorities believe the fort of La Navidad was built in or adjacent to the chief's village.

The first evidence that Dr. Hodges uncovered was the cross section of a well built in the manner of Spanish construction of the period. Among the artifacts uncovered were Venetian glass beads, which have been carbon dated to 14 years plus or minus the date of the building of La Navidad.

The antiquities and other artifacts which Dr. Hodges has unearthed over the years are in *Le Musee de Guahaba,* a house he built for them in Limbe. One of the exhibits is a stone gargoyle from Puerto Real, an important Spanish port of the early era of conquest.

EXCURSION TO SANS SOUCI AND THE CITADEL

Cap Haitien's main attraction, *Citadelle la Ferrière,* is a four- to five-hour trip from town. It is the major excursion offered to passengers of cruise ships calling at Cap Haitien. The ascent to the Citadel is made from the village of Milot, about a 12-mile or a 30-minute drive south of Cap Haitien, where the ruins of Christophe's palace of Sans Souci stand. A stop at the palace is better made on the return from the Citadel.

Beyond Sans Souci, taxis or jeeps can drive another 5 miles, or 15 to 20 minutes, over a dirt road to the "parking lot." Cars can go no farther. From here you can walk the last steep mile to the mighty stone fortress crowning the 3,000-foot promontory of Pic la Ferrière. The climb takes about 45 minutes. Alternatively, you can let one of the tired, scruffy old horses or donkeys waiting at the parking lot transport you to the top. No equestrian skill is needed for the bone-crunching ride provided you can hang on to a saddle; the horse's owner or his son walks the horse the entire route.

Much to the consternation of my horse owner (I gave him a tip and asked him to carry my camera bag), I preferred to hike (sneakers will do), as there is more opportunity to enjoy the views, to get a better sense of the incredible effort required to build this colossus, and to photograph it. The assembled equestrians seem to get as many lasting memories out of the comic spectacle of camera-laden tourists lumbering up the precipitous path as they do from seeing the fortress.

You should start as early as possible since tropical rain clouds frequently appear in the early afternoon obstructing the view and making the path slippery. The monuments close at 5 P.M. Be sure to wear slacks, comfortable, sturdy shoes, and a hat for protection against the sun. Bring all your film as there are no shops at the site.

SANS SOUCI PALACE Built in 1807, the Palace of Sans Souci was destroyed by the great earthquake of 1842 and never restored, although the small Catholic church beside it was rebuilt. Yet, even as a ruin, one can easily imagine how grand and glittering a spectacle it must have been.

The palace is said to have been modeled after the Potsdam Palace of Frederick the Great and meant to rival Versailles in size and grandeur. It was three stories high; according to contemporary accounts, the lofty spacious rooms were illuminated by crystal chandeliers and had floors and side panels of polished mahogany and inlaid mosaics. Gilded mirrors, paintings, and silk tapestries decorated the walls, rich brocades covered the furniture, and silk curtains framed the twenty-three windows on each floor. From the palace, sweeping staircases with marble fountains led to the gardens. Mountain streams not only watered the gardens but also were diverted under the marble floors to cool the palace from the heat of the tropical sun.

Guides will show you the room in which Henry I, as Christophe was called, shot himself—with a silver bullet—after word came that a revolt which had been brewing for months had been joined by his palace guards.

With the distance of history Christophe's story might seem heroic had he not been so cruel, if not slightly mad. But the tragedy looks more like a comedy worthy of Molière or Gilbert and Sullivan when the details are revealed. For example, to complement the kingdom he had established, King Henry created a nobility and gave

them land, as any self-respecting sovereign might do. And to the new aristocrats of the New World kingdom who came in their gilded carriages to be feted at the palace, Henry I also gave such incredible titles as the Duke of Marmelade and the Count of Limonade. Little wonder Christophe was the inspiration for Eugene O'Neill's play *Emperor Jones*.

THE CITADEL Throughout the trip up the mountainside and from the summit you will have magnificent views. You will also be haunted by the knowledge of the monumental effort that was required to build the Citadel: thirteen years of toil, 200,000 workers, perhaps as many as 20,000 perishing in the effort. There are 15-foot-thick walls; 365 cannons, some weighing as much as ten tons; 45,000 cannonballs in one room; royal apartments with forty rooms; and space to house and provision an army of 5,000 for a year. And you will ask, how did they do it? Why did they do it?

Christophe had the monstrous fort built to protect his empire against the French. But no cannon was ever fired. The French never came.

In the center of the fortress stands the grave of Christophe. The inscription reads: *Here lies Henri Christophe, King of Haiti. I am reborn from my ashes.*

Today the Citadel is a monument to human endurance, and Sans Souci, a melancholy shell of Haiti's faded glories. The Haitians—ever the optimists—prefer to think of the Citadel as a monument to freedom and independence, to the first revolt in the New World by black slaves that gave birth to a nation.

The Dominican Republic

SANTO DOMINGO, PUERTO PLATA, CASA DE CAMPO/ALTOS DE CHAVON

Major Road
Port of Call
Airport

Monte Cristo
Isabella
Puerto Plata
Sosua
International Airport
ESCOSESA BAY
ATLANTIC OCEAN
Dajaboa
Santiago
La Vega
Samana
HAITI
Punta Cana
Elias Pine
San Juan
SANTO DOMINGO
Airport
La Romana
Higuey
San Cristobal
San Pedro de Macoris
Casa de Campo
Lake Epriquillo
CARIBBEAN SEA

AT A GLANCE

CHAPTER CONTENTS

LAND OF SUPERLATIVES

The Dominican Republic is the oldest European settlement in the New World; it has the tallest mountains in the region. It also has some of the longest beaches, best golf and tennis facilities, best museums, best restaurants, and hottest nightclubs in the region, and about the lowest prices as well. Within its boundaries is a diverse landscape of great green mountains that climb to 10,400 feet, rain forests, rolling hills, plains, lowlands, and a lake, 144 feet below sea level—the only saltwater body in the world with crocodiles. And despite its tourist development of the past decade, which has given it more hotel rooms than any other destination in the Caribbean, it is still the region's best-kept secret for cruise passengers.

The second largest country after Cuba among the Caribbean's island-nations, the Dominican Republic covers 19,000 square miles or about two-thirds of Hispaniola, the island it shares with Haiti. The island lies between Cuba on the west and Puerto Rico on the east and faces the Atlantic on the north, the Caribbean on the south.

Santo Domingo, the capital of this Spanish-speaking country, is located on the Caribbean coast. It is a cosmopolitan and sophisticated city with more than a million and a half people, combining modern comforts and conveniences with the charm of the Old World.

Puerto Plata, an occasional port of call on the island's north coast, is near the site of *La Isabela* where the Spaniards began their first permanent settlement in the New World, and where modern-day Dominicans have developed one of the most extensive playgrounds in the hemisphere along 80 miles of white sand beaches.

A good road connecting the north and south passes over the *Cordillera Central,* the central mountain range which bisects the country from northwest to southeast. Santiago, the principal city of this mountainous region, is the second largest town in the country. It is 36 miles south of Puerto Plata and 93 miles from Santo Domingo.

On the southeast coast near the sugar mill town of La Romana, an 1.5-hour drive from Santo Domingo, Casa de Campo is a 7,000-acre resort developed by Gulf & Western in the 1970s. It helped to launch the Dominican Republic's modern tourism and is a stop for several cruise ships.

The east coast of the Dominican Republic on the Mona Passage facing Puerto Rico is another idyllic setting of palm-fringed beaches. Here, more new resorts have been developed, particularly in the area of Punta Cana, where Club Med has a village, and Samana, on the Bay of Samana, noted for superb fishing. The latter is occasionally visited by cruise ships because of the lovely beaches and some outstanding natural attractions in the immediate area. For one, it has recently become a major whale-watching location from December to March.

Columbus discovered the island which he called *La Isla Española* on his first voyage in 1492. He returned the following year to establish a settlement, *La Isabela,* on the north coast. But within a few years the Spaniards moved south where they founded Santo Domingo. It became their capital and for the next century was their base of operation to explore and conquer the New World.

By 1697, however, the Spaniards were no longer able to hold the entire island and ceded the western part (now Haiti) to France. Spain, due to greater interests in Latin America, gave up the entire island to France a century later in 1795. But France's ownership was not to last either.

Demands by French colonists who sniffed the winds of the French and American revolutions and revolts by slaves in the western portion gave Napoleon all he could handle and enabled the Dominicans to call in the English for help in recapturing Santo Domingo. Over the next fifty years, the island was under the control of the Dominicans, French, Spanish, and Haitians.

Finally, on February 27, 1844, the Dominicans, led by Juan Pablo Duarte and two colleagues in a movement known as *La Trinitaria,* declared their independence. They had great difficulty making it stick, however. Disorder, dictatorships, and intermittent peace characterized the country's history until World War I, when the United States sent in the Marines. The United States administered the country from 1916 to 1924.

In 1930 after a coup d'etat and a rigged election, Rafael Trujillo began what was to become a thirty-year dictatorship during which time he was the president or controlled the person holding the office and was so corrupt and exploitive that even now his name is used almost generically to describe the most ruthless of rulers. His reign ended with his assassination in 1961, by which time he and his family had amassed a legendary fortune.

Two attempts at civilian government were followed by coups and a civil war. In 1965 the United States, worried that another Cuba was in the making, sent in the Marines again. Fortunately, a democratic government was established and has prevailed to the present.

After the Spanish conquistadors had depleted the country of its gold and its native Indian population, they imported African slaves and established a plantation society to exploit the country's rich agricultural potential. To this day, although the country has made great efforts to diversify, its economy is still basically agricultural with sugar the major crop.

The country passed through an extremely difficult period during the early 1990s, when the economy was in terrible shape and inflation was running over 100 percent. Fortunately, the tide turned in 1992, and by 1993 inflation had been reduced to 4 percent and the economy was once again growing at a healthy rate, although unemployment remains high and salaries low.

FAST FACTS

POPULATION: 8,000,000

MAIN TOWNS: Santo Domingo, Santiago, Puerto Plata, La Romana, Sosua, Higuey, San Francisco de Macoris, San Pedro de Macoris.

GOVERNMENT: Democratic form of government with executive, legislative, and judicial branches. Elections held every four years.

CLIMATE: Pleasant, warm weather year-round along the coast and lowlands averaging 77°F in winter, 82°F in summer, and up to 30 degrees cooler in the high mountain regions. January is the coolest month; August is the hottest.

CLOTHING: Casual, informal dress is accepted throughout the country, but in any of the more elegant restaurants one sees patrons always fashionably dressed with women in cocktail or dinner attire and men wearing tie and jacket or the *guayabera*, locally known as *chacabana*, an open-neck shirt with embroidery, popular in Mexico and the Philippines.

CURRENCY: The Dominican peso, which fluctuates around RD $14 to the US $1. Banking hours are from 8 A.M. to 1 P.M. Dollars are readily accepted.

CUSTOMS REGULATIONS: Cruise passengers who disembark in the Dominican Republic to return to the United States by plane must have a tourist card (US $10).

ELECTRICITY: Same as the United States: 120 volts; 60 cycles.

ENTRY FORMALITIES: A tourist card ($10), required for U.S. citizens, is a formality handled by a cruise line for its passengers. However, it is always advisable to carry a driver's license for identification and a passport or birth certificate as proof of citizenship.

LANGUAGE: Spanish. On the tourist track, you will find English widely used, but if you do not speak any Spanish, a Spanish language phrase book or small dictionary is handy.

POSTAL SERVICE: In Santo Domingo, the main post office is located in the Old City at Tejera and Las Damas streets (Tel. 689–4303). Postal service is also available at major hotels. In Puerto Plata, the post office is located on E. Hunhardt Street (Tel. 586–2368).

PUBLIC HOLIDAYS: January 1, New Year; January 6, Kings Day (Epiphany); January 21, Altagracia; January 26, Duarte's Birthday; February 27, Independence Day (which is also the start of Carnival); Good Friday; Easter Sunday; May 1, Labor Day; Corpus Christi (60 days after Good Friday); August 16, Restoration Day; September 24, Our Lady of Las Mercedes; December 25, Christmas.

 TELEPHONE AREA CODE: 809. Direct dial to/from the United States is available.

 TIME: One hour ahead of Eastern Standard Time, November through April; same as Eastern Standard Time, May through October.

 VACCINATION REQUIREMENTS: None

 **AIRLINES:**

From the United States to Santo Domingo, American, American Eagle, Continental, Pan Am–Carnival, and TWA.
From the United States to Puerto Plata, American. The airport in Santo Domingo is 16 miles east of the city, and a cab ride costs about US $18 (RD$250); the Puerto Plata airport is 5 miles east of town, and a cab ride costs about US $7 (RD$100). Air Santo Domingo, a private domestic airline, which begins service in July 1999, connects Santo Domingo with major towns and resorts centers: Puerto Plata, Punta Cana, La Romana, Portillo (Samana), Santiago, and Barahona. It also flies between some towns such Puerto Plata and Punta Cana. Air Santo Domingo has five, seventeen-passenger seat turbo props which fly fifty-four flights daily.

CAR RENTAL: Expect to pay from $50 to $90 per day, depending on the model, for automatic shift and unlimited mileage, including insurance. And remember, gas stations close at 8 or 9 P.M. Gasoline costs U.S. $1.60 per gallon for regular and U.S. $2 for premium. You can drive here with a valid U.S. or Canadian driver's license. The minimum age to rent a car is 25, and you'll need a valid credit card for the transaction. Driving is on the right side of the road.

In Santo Domingo: Avis (Lincoln Square; Tel. 535–7191; fax 535–1747; 800–331–1084 Budget (J. F. Kennedy Ave., Tel. 567–0175; fax 567–0177) Nelly Rent a Car (134 Independence Ave., Tel. 688–3366; 535–8800; fax 535–1233; 800–526–6684, pick up and delivery service). Thrifty (Jose Maria Heredia; Tel. 686–0133; fax 685–4933)
In Puerto Plata: Abbey, (Tel. 586–4436); Budget, (Tel. 586–3141); Nelly, (Tel. 586–0505).

LOCAL TRANSPORTATION: Buses and *collectivos* (seat-in-taxi), known here as *publicos,* are inexpensive, and those which run along major arteries are easy to use with a little Spanish and a sense of adventure. Taxis do not have meters, and they are expensive. An average cab ride with Apolo Taxi (531–3800) costs RD $40 ($3.20) from the port and Old City to the main hotels and restaurants along George Washington Avenue; taxis from the main hotels charge double this amount. A list of taxi fares in Santo Domingo and environs is posted at the port.

 INFORMATION:

In the United States: Travel Hotline: 1–800–752–1151
New York: Dominican Republic Tourist Office, 1501 Broadway, No. 410, New York, NY 10036; Tel. 888–374–6361; 212–575–4966; fax 575–5488. Hours: 9 A.M. to 3:30 P.M.
Chicago: 561 West Diversey Bldg., No. 214, Chicago, IL 60614; Tel. 888–303–1336; 773–529–1336; fax 773– 252–7065.
Miami: 2355 Salzedo St., Coral Gables, FL 33134; Tel. 888–358–9594; 305–444–4592; fax 305–444–4845.
In Canada:
Montreal: 2080 Crescent, Montreal, Quebec, H3G 2B8; Tel. 800–563–1611; 514–499–1918; fax 514–499–1393.
Toronto: 74 Front St. East; Unit 53, Market Sq.,

Toronto, Ontario, M5E 1B8; Tel.
416–361–2126; fax 416–361–2130.

In Santo Domingo:
Consejo de Promocion Turistica and the
Dominican Republic Hotel & Restaurant
Association, 66 Mexico Ave.; Tel. 685–9054;
fax 685–6752; e-mail: cpt@codetel.net.do
Dominican Republic Ministry of Tourism,
Mexico Ave.; P.O. Box 497; Tel. 221–4660;
fax 682–3806
American Chamber of Commerce, Hotel Santo
Domingo.
U.S. Consulate, Maximo Gomez Ave. and Cesar
Nicolas Penson St.; Tel. 541–2171.

In Puerto Plata:
Tourism Information Office, Calle Mirabal,
Parque Costero de Long Beach.

BUDGET PLANNING

As noted earlier, the Dominican Republic is one
of the least expensive countries for visitors in the
Caribbean. Food and restaurant prices are low
compared to most other islands, and Dominican-
made jewelry and crafts are real bargains.

The few cruise ships that stop here do not spend
enough time for passengers to take advantage of
all the attractions and facilities the country has to
offer. But, as is often the case with cruise passengers, if you are looking for places to return for a
longer holiday, the Dominican Republic should
be high on your list for value.

AUTHOR'S FAVORITE ATTRACTIONS

In Santo Domingo
THE OLD CITY: ALCAZAR; MUSEO DE LAS
ATARAZANAS REALES; PLAZA COLON AND
CATHEDRAL OF SANTA MARIA LA MENOR;
TOWER OF HOMAGE; MERCADO MODELO
PLAZA DE LA CULTURA: MUSEUM OF
DOMINICAN MAN
SALA DE ARTE PREHISPANICO
COLUMBUS LIGHTHOUSE

NATIONAL AQUARIUM
LOS TRES OJOS

In Puerto Plata
CABLE CAR TO ISABEL DE TORRES PEAK
AMBER MUSEUM
WALKING/SHOPPING TOUR OF THE TOWN
EXCURSION TO SOSUA
GOLF OR HORSEBACK RIDING AT PLAYA
DORADA

In Casa de Campo
ALTOS DE CHAVON/GALLERIES, SHOPPING,
RESTAURANTS
CASA DE CAMPO/GOLF, TENNIS, POLO,
HORSEBACK RIDING, OR DEEP-SEA
FISHING

SANTO DOMINGO ON YOUR OWN

Santo Domingo is the oldest continuously inhabited city established by the Spaniards in the
Americas. Its precise origins are blurred between
fairy tale and fact, but in 1496, after Columbus
returned to Spain from his second voyage, he sent
word to his brother Bartholomew, whom
Columbus had left to govern in La Isabela, his first
settlement, to go south to find a suitable place for
a new settlement. History is unclear about
Columbus's motives, but he probably wanted to be
closer to the mother lode of the island's gold,
which he had learned was in the south.

Bartholomew selected a site near the mouth of
the Ozama River on the east bank to establish an
outpost and named it *La Isabela Nueva.* Today the
site is marked by the Chapel of the Rosario, near
the enormous Columbus Lighthouse, which was
completed in 1992 to commemorate the 500th
anniversary of Columbus's arrival in the New
World.

In 1498, the settlement was moved across the
river to the west bank, where the Old City now
stands, and was renamed Santo Domingo. In an
area of 1 square mile the Spaniards built their
first fortress, first hospital, first cathedral, and
first university in the New World. Within a decade,

the new town had become Spain's colonial capital, where such men as Hernan Cortés, Diego de Velázquez, Ponce de León, and Alonso de Ojeda planned the conquest of Mexico and the New World. Today such history is a lively part of a modern city that extends 15 miles or more in all directions from its 16th-century origin. With a day in port it is possible, if you move quickly, to see both old and new Santo Domingo.

Santo Domingo is much more than history and sight-seeing. It's lots of fun and has an atmosphere of warmth and friendliness. The city bounces with every sort of entertainment, from romantic piano bars to pulsating discotheques, smart supper clubs to brassy cabarets and casinos. It has a great variety of restaurants to suit most anyone's taste, from hamburgers and pizza to seafood and Dominican specialties. They also have a wide range in price and ambience. The city offers a variety of sports—tennis, golf, bowling, boating, horseback riding, fishing, diving. And then there's baseball.

Baseball is the national sport of the Dominican Republic, with fans as ardent as those in the United States. There are two seasons: the professional winter season, late October through January, when local teams are joined by some greats from the United States; and the summer season, April through September. Many games are played at Quisqueya Stadium; check local newspapers.

SHORE EXCURSIONS

If this is your first visit to Santo Domingo, you will probably want to take a city tour either by motorcoach or private car, since the city is too spread out to cover on foot. However, if you are a history buff and like walking, you can easily cover the Old City on foot. For more adventurous passengers, several tour companies in Santo Domingo offer nature-oriented excursions that must be arranged in advance. Contact the following Santo Domingo-based companies: *Prieto Tours* (Avenida Francia No. 125; Tel. 688–5715); *Ecoturisa SA* (Calle Santiago No. 203–B, Gazcue, Tel. 221–4010); *Metro Tours*

(Avenida Winston Churchill, P.O. Box 303; Tel. 544–4580), or *Turinter Tours* (Leopoldo Navarro No. 4; Tel. 686–4020). *Turenlaces del Caribe* (Avenida Mexico No. 57, Tel. 682–0115) specializes in golf programs.

The newest addition is "Ciudad Colonial Trolley Tours" operated by Edecanes (Calle Isabel La Catolica #5, Colonial Zone, Tel. 687–5245; fax 685–1332). The motorized trolley, which holds up to eight passengers, departs from Edecanes' office daily at 9:30 A.M. and 2 P.M., accompanied by a bilingual guide, and makes a 45-minute drive through the Old City. Cost is $10 per person. When planning your visit, keep in mind that all museums and historic buildings are closed on Mondays.

IN SANTO DOMINGO

City Tour—Old and New: 3 hours, US $32 per person, minimum of two. Visit the colonial section of the oldest city in America, with stops at the Cathedral, Ozama Fortress, and Alcazar, followed by a visit to the modern city, passing by the National Palace and the Cultural Plaza.

City Tour: 3 hours, US $28. Tour by motorcoach with stops at the Aquarium, the Cathedral, Ozama Fortress, National Pantheon, Museum of the Dominican Man, and the shopping street El Conde. Lunch optional. Note: No shorts allowed.

Walking Tour of the Colonial Zone, 3 hours, US $30. Some cruise ships have recently added this tour as a shore excursion. For a self-guided tour, see the next section.

Beach Tour: full day with lunch, US $68 per person, minimum of four. En route to Boca Chica Beach, a 30-minute drive east of Santo Domingo, visit the lush Los Tres Ojos Caverns. At the beach, you have a hotel room for changing and access to the pool, chaise lounges, and other facilities.

Night Tour: 3 hours, US $70 per person, minimum of two. Available Thursday through Sunday, departing at 9 P.M. Most tours include Guacara Taino (a nightclub in a cave), a disco, and the Jaragua Hotel Casino and show or a similar casino and show. Some cruise ships offer this as an afternoon shore excursion when Guacara Taino opens and stages a folkloric show especially for the group.

Jarabacoa, the Dominican Alps: full day, $50. You travel by bus to the countryside with the highest mountains in the Caribbean, ride horses and hike to a waterfall where you can swim in clear—but cold—water. Includes lunch at a restaurant in Jarabacoa village.

A WALK IN THE OLD CITY

If walls could speak, those in the Old City of Santo Domingo would have 500 years of stories to tell. Particularly interesting would be the tales of the city's early years, which would weave a tapestry of the courage and glory, greed and intrigue, triumphs and tragedies that fell on Christopher Columbus and his brothers Diego and Bartholomew, who founded the city, and on all the conquistadors who followed them.

The 16th-century town defined by remnants of the original walls, and now referred to as the "Colonial Zone," covers less than a square mile and contains seventy-six churches, chapels, old houses, palaces, warehouses, monuments, forts, gates, parks, plazas, and other points of interest. In preparation for the Quincentennial in 1992, the entire Old City, or Colonial City as it is also known, was beautifully restored, and its historic buildings and monuments renovated with aid from Spain. The cathedral, the oldest in the Americas, was given particular attention. The waterfront was beautified and made accessible with a new boulevard and several series of steps leading directly from the waterfront into the heart of the Old City. Here, too, a new port for cruise ships was created. The improvements have brought renewed life to the ancient district, where new restaurants, art galleries, shops, and museums are housed in the lovely historic buildings that line the pretty little streets and overlook the graceful parks.

When the new pier is completed in late 1997, passengers will disembark directly at the foot of the Colonial Zone. Meanwhile, cruise ships dock across the river from the Old City, near the Columbus Lighthouse. After visiting the Lighthouse, you will need to take a taxi (or organized tour) to the Alcazar (1) or Plaza Colon (14) to start your walk of the Colonial City. You can cover the main parts on a walking tour of 3 hours or so, but a visit to all the sites with time to linger in the museums and shops and relax over lunch at one of the restaurants needs a full day or more. The big central market, the Mercado Modelo (25), is within walking distance of the Colonial Zone. Admission to museums, churches, and historic buildings is free unless noted otherwise and museums, historic buildings, and sites are closed on Mondays.

CALLE LAS DAMAS The town Columbus knew was a typical walled Spanish town laid out in a grid with the central plaza anchored by a church. You could start at almost any spot, but if you enjoy historic symmetry, Calle Las Damas, which runs north-south paralleling the eastern walls and the Ozama River, is the oldest street of the Americas. It was named for the women brought to the New World to form the court for Columbus's son, Diego—the first viceroy—and his wife, Maria de Toledo, the niece of King Ferdinand of Spain, who financed Columbus's expeditions. Several of the most important landmarks are located along Calle Las Damas; the northern end has been made into a huge esplanade that ends in front of the Alcazar.

ALCAZAR (1) Situated on the edge of the fort overlooking the river, the palace was built in 1514 for Diego Columbus. It is now a museum with reception rooms, galleries, and state apartments furnished with antiques or reproductions of the early Spanish period. Viewers can get a good idea about life at the court in the early history of the New World by wandering through its rooms. Hours: 9 A.M. to 5 P.M. daily except Tuesday. Admission: RD $10 (US $.75) Tel. 689–5946.

Plaza de la Hispanidad, the large courtyard in front of the palace, is frequently used for outdoor concerts. From here, you can look across the Ozama River to the Columbus Lighthouse in the distance and to the *Chapel of the Rosary* (26), the site of Bartholomew's Nueva Isabela, in the foreground. Between the Alcazar and the Ozama River, modern obstructions and centuries of debris were removed in the recent renovations to reveal the old city walls. Steps on both sides of the Alcazar lead through ancient gates in the walls to the new waterfront boulevard and the new cruise ship dock. Cruise passengers on ships using this dock can walk directly from their ship through the gates into the Old City, just as travelers might have done in olden days.

MUSEO DE LAS ATARAZANAS REALES (2) Directly in front of the *Gate of the Royal Arsenals* is the Old City's newest museum, devoted to the history of navigation in the waters of the Dominican Republic. Among the museum's most fascinating displays are the treasures of gold, silver, jewelry, Ming china, and other articles recovered from three sunken galleons, the 17th-century *Concepcion* and the 18th-century *Guadalupe* and *Tolosa,* found only in the late 1970s off the Dominican Republic's north coast and Samana Bay. The museum has miniature models of other galleons and the three ships of Columbus. The oldest artifacts are the cannons from the ship of Nicolas de Ovando, the first governor, dating from 1502 and just discovered on Saona Island off the southeast coast in 1982. Hours: 9 A.M. to 5 P.M. daily except Wednesday, 9 A.M. to 1 P.M. on Sunday. Admission: RD $10.

LAS ATARAZANAS (3) The north and west sides of the plaza in front of the Alcazar are renovated old buildings, Las Atarazanas, which once served as the port's warehouses and the arsenal of the fort. Today they house attractive restaurants, boutiques, art galleries, and shops selling native Dominican crafts. *Fonda de la Atarazana* is a moderately priced courtyard restaurant on the north; *Museo de Jambon* on the west is a tapa bar and sidewalk cafe with amusing decor and musical entertainment several nights. It is one of several sidewalk cafes that line the west side of the plaza and are especially popular in the late afternoon and evening. They also have the best vantage point in town for viewing the cross in the sky formed by the floodlights atop the Columbus Lighthouse Monument, which is lighted on Friday, Saturday, and Sunday nights. *(The view across the river is nicer in the evening, when the*

industrial complexes that blot the daytime landscape are obscured.)

HOUSE OF THE CORD (4) Detouring west from Las Damas to Emiliano Tejera Street, the House of the Cord (*Casa de Cordon*), so named because of the cord decoration on the facade representing the Franciscan order, is thought to be the oldest stone building in Santo Domingo, and thus, the oldest European structure in the Western Hemisphere. Diego Columbus and his wife lived here while the Alcazar was being built. It is now the office of Banco Popular and is open during regular business hours. Free guided tours are available. At the end of Tejera Street are the ruins of the *Monastery of San Francisco* (5) .

DUARTE MUSEUM (6) (138 Isabel La Catolica Street; Tel. 689–0326) Another detour west from the Alcazar is the house where Juan Pablo Duarte, the Father of Dominican Independence, was born on January 26, 1813. After his return from study in Europe, Duarte formed a secret society, *La Trinitaria,* together with Ramon Mella and Juan Sanchez Ramirez, and his house became a center of revolutionary activity against the much-hated twenty-two years of Haitian occupation. In 1844 he led the move to proclaim the nation's independence.

MUSEO DE LAS CASAS REALES (7) At the corner of Mercedes and Las Damas, you will find the Museo de las Casas Reales or the Museum of the Royal Houses, the first Palace of Justice. At a later date, it was used as the headquarters of the colonial government. Today, the stately buildings house a museum covering Dominican history from the Spanish conquest to independence. In the courtyard is a bronze sculpture of the Dominican judge and scholar, Alonso de Zuazo, by Joaquin Vaquero Turcios. Hours: Tuesday through Sunday, 9 A.M. to 6 P.M. There is a small admission fee (Tel. 682–4202).

NATIONAL PANTHEON (8) On the next corner, at Luperon Street, a Jesuit seminary of the 18th century was made into the National Pantheon, a monument to the heroes of the nation where many prominent Dominicans are entombed. The building, which has also been used as a tobacco warehouse and a theatre, was restored in 1955 by

MAP LEGEND FOR WALKING TOUR OF OLD SANTO DOMINGO

1. Alcazar and Plaza de la Hispanidad

2. Museo de las Atarazanas Reales

3. Las Atarazanas

4. House of the Cord

5. Monastery of San Francisco

6. Duarte Museum

7. Museo de las Casas Reales

8. National Pantheon

9. Plaza de Maria de Toledo

10. Hospital of San Nicolas de Bari

11. Casa de Francia (Hernán Cortes House)

12. Hostal de Nicolás de Ovando

13. Casa Quinto Centenario (Borgella Palace)

14. Plaza Colon

15. Cathedral of Santa María la Menor

16. Casa del Sacramento (house of the Archbishop of Santo Domingo)

17. House of Bastidas

18. Tower of Homage

19. Casa Tostado (Museum of the Dominican Family)

20. Las Casas Park

21. Convent of the Dominicans

22. Duarte Park

23. El Conde Gate

24. Independence Park

25. Mercado Modelo

26. Chapel of the Rosary

Trujillo for his monumental tomb. The irony is that one chapel preserves the ashes of the martyrs of the 1959 uprising which tried, unsuccessfully, to overthrow him. Hours: Daily 10 A.M. to 5 P.M. On the south side of the Pantheon, a block of Luperon Street was recently made into a pedestrian walk named *Plaza de María de Toledo* (**9**).

Two blocks west of the Pantheon at Calle Hostos and Calle General Luperon are the ruins of the *Hospital of San Nicolás de Bari* (**10**), the first hospital in the New World.

Farther along on Las Damas, on the corner of Calle de Conde, stands *Casa de Francia* (**11**), the house where Hernán Cortes lived while he prepared for the expedition that led to the conquest of Mexico. Today it houses the French Embassy. Across the street, *Hostal de Nicolás de Ovando* (**12**) was once the home of the city's founder. It has been made into a hotel furnished in colonial style; its inner courtyard and swimming pool overlook the Osama River.

Calle de Conde is the main east-west street of the Old City, running for 10 blocks from Calle Las Damas and the river to *El Conde Gate* (**23**) and *Independence Park* (**24**). In the recent renovations it was converted to a pedestrian mall and is the district's main shopping street. The easternmost end has a pocket park with steps leading down to the waterfront boulevard; the next block passes several popular new restaurants with sidewalk cafes and the *Casa Quinto Centenario* (**13**) on Calle Isabel La Catolica. Formerly the Borgella Palace, it houses the offices of the group that was responsible for the historic restorations in the Colonial City.

PLAZA COLON (**14**) The front of Casa Quinto Centenario faces Plaza Colon, or Columbus Square, the main square of the old city, bordered by Calle Conde on the north and the cathedral on the south. The plaza is dominated by a noble statue of the admiral in bronze made by the French sculptor Gilbert in 1897 to commemorate the 400th anniversary of Santo Domingo.

CATHEDRAL OF SANTA MARÍA LA MENOR (**15**) This church, the oldest cathedral in the Western Hemisphere, is still in use. Built in 1523, it became the Metropolitan and Primate Cathedral of the Indies in 1542. In 1586 the English captain

Sir Francis Drake camped in the church for about three weeks. Drake, who has something of a noble swashbuckler image in English history, was nothing but a scoundrel here, forcing women to give up their jewelry, churches to denude their altars, and the government to empty its treasures to meet his ransom demands. He pressed his point further by burning and destroying most of the town—a siege from which it never quite recovered.

The facade of the cathedral, built of native coral limestone that has mellowed with age, is an outstanding example of Spanish Renaissance architecture. Now cleansed and restored for the first time in this century, it is more beautiful than ever, since the exquisite details of the carved apricot-colored stone can be more easily seen. The interior is Gothic with lovely high pointed arches. It has a high altar of carved mahogany covered with silver and a silver carillon said to have been made by the 16th-century Italian sculptor Benvenuto Cellini.

In addition to the main altar there are fifteen small chapels where María de Toledo, several Dominican presidents, an ancestor of Simón Bolivar, the liberator of South America, and other leaders are buried. The marble sarcophagus of Columbus rested in the nave of the cathedral for more than a century until 1992, when it was moved to the Columbus Lighthouse Monument across the river. Like everything else about the Admiral, his tomb has long been a matter of dispute; Cuba and Spain also claim to hold his final resting place.

In the course of the recent restoration, the tombs of 300 priests, high-ranking military and other government officials, and some of Columbus's descendants were found beneath the presbytery. The catacombs have been renovated extensively and faced with marble and were rededicated during the Pope's visit for the Quincentennial commemorations in October 1992. Cathedral visiting hours: Monday through Saturday, 9 A.M. to 4 P.M.; mass is said at 5 P.M. daily except Tuesday and at noon and 5 P.M. on Sunday.

The south side of the church has another small plaza, and a pedestrian lane next to *Casa del Sacramento* (**16**), the house of the Archbishop of Santo Domingo. Both will return you to Calle Isabel La Catolica.

HOUSE OF BASTIDAS (17) At the end of Calle Las Damas, Fort Ozama and a group of buildings known as *Casa de Bastidas* served as houses, warehouses, and military barracks at different times. Now they are used to stage exhibitions of local artists and to house the *Centro Artesanal*, a shop run by a government-sponsored craft cooperative, which sells pottery, leather, dolls, masks, and other items made by local craftsmen. Hours: Tuesday through Sunday, 9 A.M. to 6 P.M.

TOWER OF HOMAGE (18) At the south end of the complex, overlooking the river, is a military structure known as the Tower of Homage (*Torre de Homenaje*) from which ships entering port were saluted. The tower was significant from its earliest days and was used as a symbol of nobility. As late as the 19th century the queen of Spain conferred upon the governor of Cuba the title of duke of the Tower of Homage of Santo Domingo. From here you can look over the city walls to the Ozama River below and probably see your ship. Hours: Tuesday through Sunday, 9 A.M. to 6 P.M.

MUSEUM OF THE DOMINICAN FAMILY (19) Around the corner from the fort, Calle Billini leads past the Church of Santa Clara to the corner of Padre Billini and Merino streets, where a building dating from 1516 known as *Casa Tostado* stands. It houses the Museum of the Dominican Family and is furnished as it might have been by a prosperous family of the late 19th century. The building is noted for its Gothic double window, an architectural feature said to be unique in the New World. At one time, it was the palace of the archbishop. Hours: Daily from 9 A.M. to 2:30 P.M. (Tel. 689–5057). Admission: RD $10.

LAS CASAS PARK (20) The next block has a small, tree-shaded park dedicated to Bartolomé de Las Casas, the Franciscan friar whose writings are a major source of our knowledge of the Conquest period and particularly of the indigenous people. The sculpture of Las Casas is by Joaquin Vaquero Turcios.

CONVENT OF THE DOMINICANS (21) Next to the park is the *Convento de los Dominicos*, dating from 1510. It once housed the University of St. Thomas Aquinas, the first university in the New World. It is now part of the Autonomous University of Santo Domingo, located west of the Old City. Across the street from the convent is *Duarte Park* (22), which is dominated by a monument and commanding statue of Juan Pablo Duarte, the father of the country.

INDEPENDENCE PARK (24) At the western end of Calle Conde, eleven streets of the city converge at the large square known as Independence Park. It is as much a point of departure from the Old City historically as it is architecturally. Here Independence Day is marked annually by the reenactment of the 1844 events in which the nation's independence was proclaimed by La Trinitaria, a secret society formed by Juan Pablo Duarte, the Father of Dominican Independence, to rid the country of the much-hated twenty-two years of Haitian occupation. The *Monument to the Founders of the Republic* or *Altar de la Patria*, where the three founders of the modern Dominican Republic are buried, was placed here in 1944 to commemorate the 100th anniversary of independence.

 A **T**OUR OF THE **N**EW **C**ITY

Modern Santo Domingo, laid out between wide tree-lined boulevards on both sides of the Ozama River, is a sprawling city that stretches from the sea on the south across more than 15 miles east, west, and north. It cannot be covered except by tour, city bus, or car. But it is worth the effort, as a tour can be a window onto this multifaceted city and a complete contrast to the Old City.

Public buses and collectivos or publicos, shared taxis running on specific routes, are plentiful and reasonable, but given the limited time cruise ships are in port, the use of public transportation is not practical. If you choose not to take an organized tour or to rent a car, you can arrange a city tour with a taxi driver or through a taxi company, but be sure your driver speaks English unless, of course, you are lucky enough to be fluent in Spanish. Information (in Spanish) is available from the Association of Tourist Guides (El Conde Street 53, Second Floor; Tel. 682–0209) from 9 A.M. to

4 P.M. Their guides charge RD $170 (US $12) for 3 hours for up to ten persons, RD $600 to $700 (US $43 to $50) for a full day; transportation is an additional charge.

From the port and Old City, George Washington Avenue, complete with a miniature copy of the Washington Monument, runs along the sea past some of the city's leading hotels and University City, paralleling Independence Avenue to Abraham Lincoln Avenue, a north-south artery that leads to John F. Kennedy Avenue. The names are reminders that Americans will seldom visit a country where they will find a more genuine welcome. And they will probably never meet a Dominican who does not have at least one cousin in the States.

PLAZA DE LA CULTURA Another north-south artery, Maximo Gomez Avenue, leads to the modern Plaza de la Cultura, the heart of the capital's cultural life. Built on a former estate of Rafael Trujillo, the country's infamous dictator for three decades, the plaza is a park with a complex of five buildings of contemporary design.

The *National Theatre* (Tel. 888–637–5347; 687–9131) is used for plays, classical ballet by the National Ballet Company, folkloric performances by the National Folkloric Group, weekly concerts by the National Symphony Orchestra, and chamber and jazz ensembles and visiting artists.

The *Gallery of Modern Art (Galeria de Arte Moderno)* (Tel. 685–2153) is the repository of the nation's leading contemporary artists along with an international collection. Hours: Tuesdays to Sundays from 10 A.M. to 5 P.M.

The *Museum of Dominican Man (Museo de Hombre Dominicano)* (Tel. 687–3622) holds the country's main collection of Taino Indian artifacts and other archaeological exhibits, which constitute the most important collection in the Caribbean on the inhabitants of the Western Hemisphere before Columbus. The museum also houses displays on Dominican history and folklore from earliest times to the present. Hours: Tuesdays to Sundays from 10 A.M. to 5 P.M. Admission: RD $10.

Other buildings hold the *National Library*, a center for West Indies research; *Museum of*

National History and Geography; and *Museum of Natural History* (Tel. 689–0106).

SALA DE ARTE PREHISPANICO This private museum (279 San Martin Avenue at Lope de Vega Street; Tel. 540–7777) is often overlooked because of its unlikely location on the second floor of the Seven-Up Bottling Company. Nonetheless, the collection is outstanding, exquisitely displayed, and should not be missed. (Unfortunately for non-Spanish speakers, the labels here, as in most museums in the Dominican Republic, are in Spanish, but don't let that deter you. The exhibits are worth viewing if you have even a passing interest in and knowledge of pre-Columbian art.) You need to call in advance to visit. Hours: 8 A.M. to noon, Monday through Saturday. Admission is free.

COLUMBUS LIGHTHOUSE MONUMENT In a large park near the site of the founding of Santo Domingo on the east bank of the Ozama River stands the colossal monument commemorating the 500th anniversary of Christopher Columbus's discovery of the Americas. It was inaugurated in October 1992 with the transfer of Columbus's mortal remains from the Cathedral in the Old City to the $70 million memorial. The Lighthouse, first conceived in 1852 and designed in 1926, was a long-time dream of Dominican president Joaquin Balaguer, who predicted the monument would become "the greatest tourist attraction in the Caribbean."

The gargantuan structure is 693 feet long and 132 feet wide at the widest point; it rises to 99 feet in 7 stories. Designed in the shape of a cross, it reclines at a 45-degree angle on a base with steps resembling those of an Aztec or Mayan pyramid, as if to suggest the overlaying of Christianity on the pagan culture of the New World.

Columbus's marble sarcophagus is at the center. On the roof directly above the sarcophagus is a crown made up of linked arms, one for each country of the Americas, and a center light with a rotating beam like the beacon of a lighthouse. The roof has 149 floodlights that are beamed to the heavens on Friday, Saturday, and Sunday; they project the shape of the cross into the sky (which depending on the clouds, can be seen from miles away).

Columbus died in 1506 in Valladolid, Spain, and was buried there; but in 1544 his remains were taken to Santo Domingo, as he had requested, by his daughter-in-law, Maria de Toledo, on her fifth and last voyage to the New World, and buried in the cathedral. Then, in 1795, Columbus's remains—or what were thought to be his remains—were removed from the cathedral and taken to Havana and later to Seville. However, in 1877 the Dominicans discovered in the cathedral a coffer with an inscription which they believe proves conclusively that its contents are the bones of the great explorer. Dominican scholars have concluded that the remains in Seville are those of Columbus's grandson.

Intended solely as a tomb by its original designer, the Lighthouse has exhibits in the tomblike interior that are meant to enhance its role as a tourist attraction; but most are disappointing, and the U.S. exhibit is so puny it's embarrassing. The most interesting display deals with the Lighthouse's history, including drawings and models of earlier commemorative projects. The most valuable artifact is an anchor said to be from the *Santa Maria*, Columbus' flagship, which went aground off the coast of Hispaniola on his first voyage. The anchor was taken to Chicago for The World's Exhibition in 1892 and remained with the Chicago Historical Society, which returned it to the Dominican Republic in 1992.

Hours: Tuesday through Saturday, 10 A.M. to 5 P.M. Admission: RD $10 adults, RD $2 children. Tel. 592–2517. No shorts, tank tops, or bare feet allowed.

THE AQUARIUM By the sea, about a mile east of the Columbus Lighthouse, is one of the Caribbean's best aquariums, with large windows onto a great variety of Caribbean sealife, including stingray and moray eels. At the center of the building, a glass tunnel passes directly through an area of the sea. An orientation film (in Spanish) is shown frequently each day in the center's auditorium; English-speaking guides are available for visitors. Hours: Tuesday to Sunday from 9:30 A.M. to 6 P.M. Admission: RD $10 adults, RD $2 children.

LOS TRES OJOS Before you leave Santo Domingo be sure to visit Los Tres Ojos, "the

Three Eyes," a grotto at the edge of town on the airport road. At the entrance, steps lead down 50 feet through tropical foliage to an underground world of stalactites and stalagmites and three pools of water: one sweet, one salt, one sulphur. Hours: 9 A.M. to 5 P.M. Admission: RD $5.

PASEO DE LOS INDIOS Located on the west side of town, Paseo de los Indios is a linear park that runs for 8 miles through residential sections to the western edge where the industrial district begins. The park, which is especially popular with Dominicans on weekends, has playgrounds, a miniature lake that represents Lake Enriquillo in the western part of the country, and samples of trees and flowers which grow in the Dominican Republic.

At the entrance to the park stands a statue of an Indian in chains, meant to represent the native Tainos whom Columbus took back with him from Hispaniola to prove to his Spanish backers that he had found the Orient; a belief he carried with him to his grave.

NATIONAL BOTANIC GARDENS Located on the northwest side of town at Colombia Avenue, the tree-shaded lawns and gardens of the National Botanic Gardens *(Jardin Botanico Nacional)* are popular with residents as places for relaxing and picnicking, but are little-known to tourists. Named for a prominent Dominican botanist—Dr. Rafael Moscoso, author and founder of the Botanical Institute of the Autonomous University of Santo Domingo—the 445-acre gardens have a pretty entrance with colorful bougainvillea and stately palms leading to fountains and pools and a large floral clock. There are ten dioramas representing the exotic vegetation of the country.

Here, and on many streets of the capital, you can see Dominican mahogany, which blooms from February to April. Its tiny blossoms are the national flower and are used in the design on Dominican money. The gardens have a stream with rowboats available for rent, a Japanese garden with an arched bridge over a pond, and a small train that provides transportation through the gardens. There are many exhibits of Dominican plants, flowers, and herbs. An annual flower show is usually held in April. Hours: Tuesday to Sunday from 9 A.M. to 5 P.M. Admission:

RD $10 adults, RD $5 children. Train costs RD $10 adults, RD $7 children. Tel. 567–6211.

NATIONAL ZOO Situated on 400 acres on the north side of town at Arroya Salado Avenue, the zoo has many native animals as well as elephants and hippos in simulated natural settings without cages. There are ponds with swans, geese, ducks, and the West Indian flamingo, and a serpent and reptile house with the native American crocodile; the Hispaniolan hutia, a rodent; an anteater from the Los Haitises region in the northeast; and two native iguana. There is a large walk-through aviary with exotic and native birds, including the Hispaniolan parrot and the palmchat, the national bird. Known as *cigua palmera* in Spanish, it builds its unusual nest, sometimes 6 feet long and 3 feet wide with many compartments, in the palm trees. A small train provides transportation around the grounds. Hours: Daily from 8:30 A.M. to 5:30 P.M. Admission: RD $10; train service costs RD $10 adults, RD $3 children. Tel. 562–2080.

SHOPPING

Shopping for Dominican products can be a highlight of a visit to Santo Domingo if you make your way to the big central market, *Mercado Modelo* (**25**) on Mella Avenue, which is within walking distance of the Old City. You'll know you are in the right place when you smell freshly roasted Dominican coffee. It's on sale at the entrance and can be bought by the pound in bags or vacuum-packed tins for about half the price of coffee in the United States. Dominican coffee is excellent and is a wonderful gift to take home to friends who like espresso.

The Mercado covers a city block and is crowded with stalls stacked with pyramids of fruits and vegetables in the central aisles, and grains, groceries, and handicrafts along the sides. Look around and bargain hard. There are so many great buys you could stock up on a year's worth of presents and pay for your trip with the savings! A cruise ship shore excursion is unlikely to bring you here; buses have no place to park or discharge passengers because the streets around the market are often very busy with traffic and the small stalls in the market are not the type that would pay the cruise lines commissions or that cruise lines would recommend.

ART AND ARTISTS: The Dominican Republic has a very active art community and exhibits are held year-round at galleries, museums, and sometimes hotels. The Old City has many galleries that feature Dominican artists. Among the best are *Galeria Toledo and Bettye's Cafe* (Isabel La Catolica 163/Plaza Maria de Toledo; Tel. 688–7649), which fills two floors of a restored townhouse and spills onto a tree-shaded pedestrian lane where gallery owner Bettye Marshall, a native of Tennessee, has a sidewalk cafe serving light meals. The gallery features works by established Dominican and Haitian artists, in a wide range of styles and prices, and crafts of artistic merit. Among the award-winning artists represented are Alberto Ullao, Miguel Valenzuela, Mary Nuñez, and Jose Perdomo. Prices range from US $5 to $5000. *Nader Gallery* (9 La Atarazana Street; Tel. 688–0969) is one of the oldest galleries; and next door, *Sala de Arte Rosemaria* features outstanding art and gaily painted, life-sized wood sculpture from a school of art and sculpture which has come to be known as *Prats Ventos,* after one of the Dominican Republic's best-known sculptors, Antonio Prats-Ventos, who created a series of figures meant to represent the women of the court in colonial times. The faces of the women are white on one side, black on the other, and have been interpreted to mean the embodiment of the country's European and African heritage—a duality that has permeated all of Dominican life. In the next block, members of the School of Dominican Plastic Arts (58 Calle El Conde) exhibit their work in shows that are changed monthly. *Miniaturas* (Calle Padre Billini No. 54; Tel. 686–3498) is the gallery of Martha de Bido, the daughter-in-law of Candido Bido, whose work, along with works by other Dominican artists, is available in oils, prints, and miniatures. The artist has his own shop, *Candido Bido Gallery* (5 Calle Dr. Baez; Tel. 688–3098) near the Sheraton Hotel. Other shops near hotels are *Deniels* (1201 Independence Avenue; Tel.

533–6688); *Nouveau Centro de Arte* (354 Independence Avenue; Tel. 689–6869), which specializes in young artists; and *Arawak* (104 Pasteur Avenue; Tel. 685–1661). For readers who are visiting La Romana/Casa de Campo, see information about Altos de Chavon, an art center, later in this chapter.

CIGARS: The cultivation of tobacco, which Columbus learned about for the first time from the natives he encountered in Hispaniola, and the making of cigars are time-honored traditions here. Dominican cigars are sold in most souvenir shops, but for a selection of the finest Dominican and Cuban cigars, *The Cigar Shop* in the Jaragua Renaissance Hotel is the best, and they are not cheap. Prices for Dominican cigars range from about US $4 for one cigar and US $107 for a box of Leon Jimenez, No. 5 to US $20 for one cigar and US $500 for a box of Arturo Fuente–Heminway. Cuban cigars are about double the cost. Top-of-the-line Cohio Esplendidos cost US $42 for one cigar; US $1,000 for one box of 25 cigars. Remember, it is illegal to bring Cuban (but not Dominican) cigars into the United States. Miami customs officials are particularly apt at sniffing them out and confiscating them.

CLOTHING: Dominicans shop in the market for fruits and vegetables and other groceries, but for clothing they either go to a dressmaker or tailor or to the modern shopping centers, such as Plaza Centro, which are popping up in residential areas at an astonishing rate. There, you will find such brand names as Liz Claiborne and Benetton, which has three stores in the city; some locally made apparel; and a few fashionable stores of young Dominican designers. Except for T-shirt shops, jewelry stores, and a few recently opened high-fashion boutiques, such as *Gianni Versace* (Padre Bellini and Calle Merino) housed in a restored 16th-century building, the stores in the Colonial Zone are stocked with cheap quality merchandise of little interest to most visitors. As more cruise ships bring visitors into the Old City, though, this is likely to change.

CRAFTS: Local crafts, such as ceramics, straw bags, baskets and planters, macrame, and hand-carved mahogany salad bowls are well made and sell for one-third of their U.S. prices. Ladder-back chairs and rockers are sold disassembled and neatly boxed for easy carrying; they cost about $50. A craft shop next door to the Museo de Las Atarazanas Reales has a very good selection of ceramics from artisans around the country; *Casa Verde* (Calle Isabel La Catolica 152), a craft and souvenir shop, features a large selection of Carnival masks—a specialty of Santiago and La Vegas—and other folk art. A variety of local crafts is available at the Mercado Modelo and at the *Centro Artesanal* (Calle Las Damas), and there are many craft and souvenir stores along Calle El Conde, the main shopping street of the Old City. At Altos de Chavon, *La Tienda* is the official outlet for crafts made at Altos based on designs created by the Dominican artists at the *Central Design Center*, which include weaving, pottery, and silk-screening.

JEWELRY: Two Dominican gemstones—larimar and a special type of amber—are unique to the Caribbean. Amber, a fossilized resin, ranges in color from pale yellow to dark brown and is embedded with particles of plants and insects millions of years old. Recently two small, private amber museums, *Amber World Museum* (452 Calle Merino; Tel. 682–3309; fax 688–1142) and *Amber Art Gallery and Museum* (107 El Conde; Tel. 221–1337; fax 682–5101) have opened in the Colonial Zone; both have jewelry shops on the ground floor and museums on the upper level. (For details on amber see the information on the Amber Museum in the section on Puerto Plata.)

Larimar, a milky blue stone similar to turquoise found in the Bahoruco Mountains near the Haitian border, was discovered to be suitable as a gemstone in 1974 by Miguel Mendez, a well-known jeweler, and Norman Rilling, a Peace Corps volunteer. The name larimar came from a contraction of Mendez's daughter's name, Larissa, and *mar*, the sea, suggested by the color of the stone.

Amber and larimar are fashioned into bracelets, necklaces, and earrings by local craftsmen and range from as little as $1 to $100 and more. Most sold in tourist gift shops are in the $10 to $50 range. The Mercado is full of cheap jewelry, cheaply made. If you like the unusual amber or larimar stones and want to buy a good piece of jewelry with Dominican gold or silver, go to a real jeweler such as *Amber Colonial Gift Shop* (Old City), *Mendez Artesania* (Tel. 567–9652), or *Joyas Criollas* (Plaza Criolla); and top stores at *Plaza Naco* (Tiradentes Avenue) in the city's most elegant residential area of Naco.

Shops with the most artistic, high-fashion design are found at Altos de Chavon at Casa de Campo. *Everett's* is the boutique of Bill and Rosie Everett, world-class custom jewelry designers who use locally mined semiprecious stones and coins set in gold. Their sophisticated designs are a match for Bulgari but at affordable prices.

A word of caution: Jewelry, combs, and other gifts made from tortoise shells are Dominican crafts. It is illegal to bring these items into the United States as tortoises are on the endangered species list. Items made from tortoise shells will be confiscated by U.S. customs officials. Similar items made from animal horns are not illegal to import into the U.S.

DINING AND EVENING ENTERTAINMENT

Santo Domingo has a large number and variety of restaurants, patronized by Dominicans as much as, if not more than, by tourists. Dominicans tend to follow their Spanish ancestors when it comes to lunch and dinner hours, seldom having lunch before 1 or 2 P.M. and dinner at 9 or 10 P.M. Music, which is so much a part of Dominican life, is often provided in restaurants by strolling troubadours, guitarists, or dance bands. Dominican cuisine is Spanish-influenced, too, but the nation has a cuisine of its own. Annual events celebrating the food are the Dominican Gastronomic Festival in late May and the Native Cuisine Contest in mid-October.

OLD CITY

Bachata Rosa Café Concierto (9 Calle La Atarazana; Tel. 688–0969), an eclectic bar and restaurant named after an album by the wildly popular Dominican musical group Juan Luis Guerra y 4–40, and where the tables are designed by Dominican artists inspired by Guerra's songs. You can catch his videos on three different screens while you dine on Caribbean cuisine and sip a "Bachata Rosa" cocktail. Moderate.

La Cocina (Calle El Conde 56; Tel. 689–7231), set in a renovated colonial house, is a new restaurant specializing in very good Dominican cuisine with selections not usually found outside the home. Open for lunch and dinner. Moderately expensive. The owners also operate *Salon de Te*, a popular Chinese restaurant in the Old City.

La Bricciola (103 Padre Billini; Tel. 688–5055), is one of the city's best eateries for Italian specialties; it is set in a beautifully restored townhouse.

Museo de Jamón (Atarazana 17; Tel. 688–9644) is a tapa bar with a sidewalk cafe on the large plaza in front of the Alcazar. The inside bar is decorated with dozens of hanging smoked hamhocks, and the restaurant serves a variety of meat and cheese sandwiches. Several evenings during the week, and on Sundays, a folkloric group performs Spanish dances at 10 P.M. The owner also operates two popular restaurants, *Reina de Espana* and *Cantabrico*, near the hotel district.

Cafe Coco (53 Calle Padre Billini; Tel. 687–9624) is an inviting bar and restaurant in a restored colonial house, which boasts a courtyard garden and attractive decor that reflects the tastes of its British owners, chef Christopher Gwillym and Colin Hercock. The menu, which changes daily, is an international mix that stresses fish and poultry dishes. Reservations are required. Moderately expensive.

Retazos (Calle Padre Billini at Duarte; Tel. 688–6140) serves Dominican cuisine in a pleasant setting with two small dining rooms cooled by ceiling fans and flower framed windows. Moderate.

CENTRAL AREA—WASHINGTON/ INDEPENDENCE AVENUES

The area commonly referred to as the Malecon, which is the seaside boulevard where some of the city's leading hotels—Jaragua, Santo Domingo, and Sheraton—are located, also has some of the city's most popular restaurants. Others are within easy reach of this core.

El Castillo del Mar (2 George Washington

Avenue; Tel. 688–4047) serves great seafood al fresco by the sea. Open from 11 A.M. to 3 A.M. Moderate.

El Conuco (Casimiro de Moya 152; Tel. 686–0129). Superior, authentic Dominican cuisine in a residential neighborhood, in a house made to look like a farmhouse but with lots of whimsy. It has only one drawback: The music is oppressively loud. Open for lunch to 2:30 P.M. and dinner to 3 A.M. Moderate.

Fellini (Robert Pastoriza and Winston Churchill Ave.; Tel. 540–5330), an excellent new restaurant, is currently the *in* place for Santo Domingo's movers and shakers. It offers a large menu of fish, pasta and other Italian specialties. Open for lunch and dinner. Moderately expensive.

Lina (Lina Hotel, 27 Maximo Gomez Avenue; Tel. 689–5185) has the longest-standing reputation for good Dominican cuisine in the city. It also has a piano bar. Moderately expensive.

Lumi's Park (809 Avenida Abraham Lincoln; Tel. 540–4584) serves grilled-meat specialties, as well as some Dominican favorites, al fresco in a garden setting that it calls a "steak park." Open daily to the wee hours. Inexpensive.

Meson de Castilla (8 Dr. Baez Street; Tel. 688–4319) specializes in Spanish food and is popular with Dominicans. Moderately expensive. Open from noon to midnight.

Cafe Jaragua (Jaragua Renaissance Hotel). For a quick meal, the cafe is like a coffee shop with salad, sandwiches, and a variety of hot selections.

Scherezade (226 Calle Roberto Pastoriza; 227 2323) is an Arabian palace out of *A Thousand and One Nights* where Chef Santos Aquinos serves up Middle Eastern and Continental fare.

Vesuvio (Malecon/George Washington Ave. 521; Tel. 689–2141). Long-established favorite of Dominicans for hearty Italian food. Moderately expensive.

In addition to entertainment at popular restaurants, the city has any number of discos, nightclubs, and casinos. The leading big cabaret show is at the *Jaragua Renaissance Hotel*. Its casino is the largest in the Dominican Republic and one of the largest in the Caribbean. Note: No sneakers, shorts, or tank tops are permitted at discos and nightclubs.

Meson de la Cava (Mirador Sur Avenue; Tel. 533–2818) is a popular restaurant/nightclub in a cave. That's right, a cave! You enter via a circular stairway. The menu is steaks and lobster. Live dance music/disco after 9 P.M. Reservations necessary. Moderately expensive.

Guacara Taina (Mirador Sur Avenue; Tel. 530–2666) is an equally popular restaurant/ nightclub in a gigantic cave that's worth seeing even if you don't like discos. Under the stalactites and stalagmites, the multilevel air-conditioned showplace pulsates with Latin rhythms and Dominican fun. It has three levels—each with a different ambience—containing three bars and two huge dance floors and can seat more than 1,500 people. One of the cave's big attractions is an hour-long folklore show staged by the Ballet de la Cueva that runs through the country's dance history, from the Taino Indians' ceremonial ritual and Spanish court influences of colonial days to modern times. Check locally for times.

The sidewalk cafes and tapa bars on the Plaza de la Hispanidad are a popular sundown rendezvous for Santo Domingo's diverse expatriate community of artists and writers. Among the top nightclubs are the *Merengue Lounge*, the lobby bar of the Jaragua Renaissance Hotel, which has a hot musical group and dancing nightly, and *L'Azotea*, the seventh-floor nightclub of the Dominican Fiesta Hotel (Anacaona Avenue; Tel. 562–8222), where authentic Dominican music is featured Thursday to Saturday from 9 P.M.; no cover.

Berimbau's (Avenida Abraham Lincoln; Tel. 567–2565) is a Brazil bar with happy hour nightly, 6 to 9 P.M. where drinks are named after national soccer idols and the music brings on the spirit of Rio Carnival. Other popular spots include *Las Palmas*, the bar of the Hotel Santo Domingo (Tel. 532–1511), and the discos *Jubilee* (Jaragua Renaissance), *String Fellow* (23 Avenue Pasteur; Tel. 685–9728), open daily from 9 P.M., and *La Bella Blue* (George Washington Avenue; Tel. 689–2911), open daily from 10 P.M. *Vesuvio*, a long-established Italian restaurant and traditional favorite of top Dominican families, also has entertainment.

The main casinos are in hotels: Embajador, V Centenario Fiesta, Dominican Hispaniola, Jaragua, Lina, Naco, Napolitano, Santo Domingo Sheraton, and San Geronimo.

SPORTS IN SANTO DOMINGO AND ENVIRONS

BEACHES: The most accessible beaches are about 30 to 45 minutes east of Santo Domingo beyond the airport at Boca Chica where the water is calm and shallow. Several hotels have packages that enable day visitors to use their facilities, including a room for changing. Next to the airport is La Caleta Marine Park *(Parque Nacional Submarino La Caleta)*, an underwater park created in 1987 to protect three miles of the coastline. A wrecked ship was sunk here to create an artificial reef. Although the Dominican Republic is bordered by reefs along much of its coasts, diving is a fairly new sport.

GOLF: The Dominican Republic has twenty golf courses, including some of the best courses in the Caribbean. Those convenient for cruise passengers—at Casa de Campo, Puerto Plata, and Santo Domingo—are among the best. There is a Dominican Golf Association: Tel. 563–7228; fax 567–3447.

Cayacoa Golf Club (Tel. 561–7288) is the capital's newest beauty. Designed by Pete Dye to offer a variety of hazards, the course (par 71, 5,869 yards) is challenging and blends in with its tropical setting and a breathtaking view. This is a private club but visitors who have made prior arrangements are admitted. Green fees for 18 holes, RD $600; cart rental, RD $250; club rental, RD $250. A golf pro is available.

Casa de Campo (Tel. 523–3333; 800–877–3643) has two of the most beautiful courses in the Caribbean: The Links, and its companion course, The Teeth of the Dog. Famous for its natural beauty and challenge, the latter is considered one of the best in the world. The Links (par 71, 6,461 yards) is an 18-hole manicured layout. Green fees, 18 holes RD $800 (US $57), cart, RD $365 (US $26) for 2 persons; club rental, 18 holes RD, $280 (US $20). Resident pro available. The Teeth of the Dog (par 72, 6,888 yards) has seven holes next to the Caribbean, making it a memorable experi-

ence. Green fees, 18 holes $RD 1,200 (US $90), cart, $RD 365 (US $26) for 2 persons. A third course operates as a private club for members only. The resort hosts many international tournaments annually, featuring the top pros of the game.

DEEP-SEA FISHING: The clear waters off the Dominican shores teem with fish. Excursions can be arranged through *Mundo Submarino* (Tel. 566–0340). Two boating clubs at Boca Chica are *Andres Boca Chica Club* (Tel. 685–4940) and *Santo Domingo Nautical Club* (Tel. 566–4522; 566–1684). You can also arrange in advance a day of deep-sea fishing through the Jaragua Renaissance Hotel; the cost is US $150 per person.

OTHER SPORTS: Tennis is available at the Jaragua Renaissance Hotel, which has four courts and is conveniently located near the city center.

There is horse racing at the *Perla Antillana Race Track* (Avenue San Martin) on Tuesdays, Thursdays, and Saturdays at 2 P.M. Cockfighting can be seen at the *Coliseo Gallistico* (Avenue Luperon) in Herrera, a suburb on the northwest side of the city.

As noted earlier, baseball is a national passion and can be enjoyed year-round. During the professional winter season from late October through January, well-known players from the United States join local teams. Check local newspapers.

For biking, jogging, rollerblading, walking, and the best view of Santo Domingo, you can join the Dominicans in the *Mirador del Sur Park*, a 3-mile-long linear park, which is closed to traffic from 5 to 8 A.M. and 5 to 8 P.M. daily. At about the 1 km post, near the entrance to Guaina Taino, bikes are available for rent, provided you can show a valid credit card, for about US $2.50 per hour for adults; US $2, children. There are tandem bikes, too. Hours: Monday to Friday, 3 to 8 P.M.; Saturdays, Sundays, and holidays, 9 A.M. to 8 P.M. The park, which is known locally by the district of its location, Mirador, and the panoramic view for which it was named, starts at Churchill and Anacoana avenues at the entrance to *Meson de la Cava* and is usually shown on maps as *Parque Paseo de los Indios*.

CULTURAL EVENTS AND FESTIVALS

The performing arts are very important in the Dominican Republic. The country has its own national symphony orchestra, chamber orchestra, opera company, ballet company, folkloric company, and national theater, plus a number of smaller groups. The Plaza of Culture is the center of activity, but there are concerts, ballet, folklore, and other performances in other parts of the city. Check the local English-language newspaper, *Santo Domingo News,* for events during your visit.

Casa de Teatro (Arzobispo Merino No. 110; Tel. 689-3430) is the gathering place of avant-garde artists, actors, and musicians. It stages art and literature exhibitions and offers painting, drama, and dancing courses and monthly contests for poetry, short stories, and other writings. On weekends there are plays and concerts. Performers that you might see here and around town, known as *Perico Ripiado,* are genuine campesino (country) scratch bands that play traditional merengue on homemade instruments of African origin. Casa de Teatro is open from 8 A.M. to 6 P.M. on weekdays; check locally for the weekend schedule.

For other Dominican popular artists, Wilfrido Vargas y Los Beduinos is one of the most exciting, syncopated groups around. Grammy-winner Micheal Camilo, a composer and pianist of sophisticated jazz, is a recognized force in the jazz world. His composition "Caribe" is samba, merengue, and jazz that melts in your ears. He now lives in New York but performs often in Santo Domingo. Juan Luis Guerra y 4-40 (Cuatro-Cuarenta), a group with an international following that blends original music with jazz and Latin rhythms, is easy to like.

Villages throughout this country of rich traditions mark their patron saints' days with feasts and festivals. Independence Day, February 27, one of the largest festivals, marks the start of Carnival and is celebrated with several days of festive parades. The religious procession of

Epiphany (January 5) and Holy Week just before Easter are also colorful occasions in Santo Domingo.

The annual Merengue Festival in late July in Santo Domingo and the first two weeks of October in Puerto Plata offers concerts, ballet, craft and food fairs, folk dancing, parades, and other events. The fiesta takes its name from the *merengue,* the dance that originated in the Dominican Republic two centuries ago.

CASA DE CAMPO (LA ROMANA)

Casa de Campo, a 1.5-hour drive east of Santo Domingo near the sugar mill town of La Romana, is the most elaborate resort in the Dominican Republic, set on 7,000 acres of a former ranch near miles of sugar plantations. Developed by the U.S. conglomerate Gulf & Western in the 1970s, the resort was sold in 1984 to the Florida-based Premier Hotel Corporation. The group also has Hotel Santo Domingo and Hotel Hispaniola in the capital.

In addition to its magnificent championship golf courses, Casa de Campo has a tennis village with thirteen courts, some lighted for night play, and a full-time pro and professional staff; horseback riding and polo; sailing and deep-sea fishing; more than a dozen swimming pools; a fitness center; a secluded beach; and its own airstrip. The hotel interiors were created by the fashion designer Oscar de la Renta, who is Dominican. No structure is more than two stories high.

On the north side of the resort is Altos de Chavon, an artisans' village, unique in concept and design. It is a 16th-century Mediterranean village built entirely in the 20th century from the imagination of its architect. Here, noted artists, writers, and performers are in residence for several months during which time they both teach and do their own work. Three times annually the artists-in-residence show their works; year-round the art galleries exhibit the works of well-known and emerging Dominican talent.

Altos has a craft center and silk-screen workshop to train young Dominicans in their craft heritage. Altos's affiliation with the Parsons School of Design in New York and a university in Santo Domingo enables it to offer an associate's degree for its two-year university program.

The *Regional Museum of Archaeology*, a teaching museum, grew from a private collection of a La Romana resident who had gathered the unusual and valuable Indian artifacts from the immediate area. They are beautifully displayed, and the labels, fortunately, are in English.

Altos has a small inn, four restaurants, art galleries, craft and gift shops, an Oscar de la Renta boutique, and a 5,000-seat amphitheatre which was inaugurated in 1982 by Frank Sinatra. Performances by international artists such as Sergio Mendes, Julio Iglesias, and the Dance Theatre of Harlem are part of a year-round calendar of events.

Altogether, Casa de Campo has nine restaurants and cocktail lounges. *Casa del Rio*, at Altos overlooking the Chavon River, is the gourmet restaurant—one of the most expensive in the Dominican Republic—where you dine on international cuisine in a candlelight setting with troubadour music in the background. It is open for dinner only.

A number of cruise ships that call at Catalina Island offer shore excursions and golf packages for Casa de Campo. They arrive about mid-morning to spend the day, which is about enough time for passengers to play a round of golf or some tennis, or to enjoy the hotel's other facilities and explore Altos de Chavon.

In the case of Costa's ships and perhaps some others, passengers are not allowed to disembark for Casa de Campo unless they have bought one of the cruise ship's shore excursions. We have not been able to find out if this is Costa's policy to ensure that the activities are purchased from Costa or Case de Campo's policy to control the number of cruise ship passengers at the resort at any given time.

CATALINA ISLAND/ SERENA CAY

Off the coast at La Romana is the small, deserted island of Catalina, which has become a stop for the ships of Costa Cruises and several other cruise lines, and has been renamed Serena Cay by them. It is scalloped with pearly white beaches and surrounded by crystal clear waters. Here passengers spend a day at the beach, with water sports, a buffet, an open bar, and entertainment by a merengue dance group on the beach. (You will need your sunscreen and insect repellent.) Or they take excursions to Casa de Campo and enjoy the resort's facilities.

SHORE EXCURSIONS FROM SERENA CAY

The following tours are sold on board the Costa Cruises' ships that stop at Serena Cay.

Casa de Campo/Altos de Chavon Village Tour: 4 hours, US $25. Passengers are tendered to the pier, where a motorcoach takes them on a tour of the resort and village.

Golf: 18 holes 5 hours, US $113. You play one of Casa de Campo's famous courses, depending on availability. (See the section on golf in Santo Domingo for a description of these courses and their fees.)

Horseback Riding: 4 hours, (1.5 hours riding time), US $44. Casa de Campo's Equestrian Center offers facilities for riders of all levels. Tours through the fields and along the Chavon River are accompanied by experienced guides; both English and Western saddles are available.

Tennis: 4 hours, (2 hours playing time), US $31. In addition to courts and ball-boy service, the tennis club has a swimming pool and bar.

Fishing: 3 hours, US $119. Passengers depart from Serena Cay on a fully equipped sportfishing vessel that provides captain and mate, tackle, bait, beer and soft drinks, and box lunch.

SAONA ISLAND

The southeast corner of the Dominican Republic, beyond La Romana and Casa de Campo, is a large dry forest protected by the Eastern National Park. Offshore is Saona, the Dominican Republic's largest island, which is part of the park. The island, covered with dry vegetation and encircled by beautiful beaches, hosts several endemic species of birds. The island was once a refuge for the native Arawak Indians and is now inhabited by about 600 people. Local travel companies offer full-day excursions from La Romana/Casa de Campo for about US $70. From the fisherman's village of Bayahibe, you board a motorboat or catamaran for a 2-hour trip to the island.

PUERTO PLATA

A popular cruise ship port of call for years, Puerto Plata, on the north coast, is now on hold until its facilities, which were allowed to deteriorate from neglect by the previous regime, are renovated; a move that the director of the Dominican Republic Port Authority has promised. When the port returns to Caribbean cruise itineraries, passengers will find it a charmer.

Puerto Plata, seemingly plucked from another century, delights cruise passengers with its surprises.

The first surprise is its dramatic location. Hugging the shores of the north coast, the white-washed village is surrounded by towering green mountains on whose highest peak stands a monumental cross, reminiscent of the famous Christ the Redeemer statue overlooking the harbor of Rio de Janeiro.

MT. ISABEL PEAK AND CABLE CAR The second surprise is the cable car which runs from the foot of the mountains to the foot of the cross where

there is a spectacular view of the Atlantic coast and the golden sand beaches of Puerto Plata. They stretch east to the holiday villages of Playa Dorada and Sosua and west to Cap Isabel, the site where the Spaniards made their first settlement. Behind the coast rise the mountains and foothills of the Cordillera Septentrional that slope on their south side into green valleys watered by dozens of small rivers running down from the mountain peaks.

A third surprise comes as you ride the cable car from the warm tropical sun of the coast. Twenty minutes later when the car has reached the mountain peak at 2,565 feet, you will be reaching for a sweater to face the bracing air that's at least 30 degrees cooler than at sea level. At the top you can stroll around the four acres of botanical gardens that seem more Alpine than Caribbean. (The cable car runs daily, except Monday and Wednesday, from 9 A.M. to 2 P.M. There is a small fee.)

Back in town, you will be greeted by more surprises. Puerto Plata is one of the most attractive little ports in the Caribbean, oriented not to the sea but to its plaza, as is so often the case with Spanish colonial towns. And the plaza is pure Victorian, complete with a gingerbread-trimmed gazebo and gaslight lamp posts decorating the walkway. Around the square a mélange of colonial and Victorian structures have been renovated, as have many of the buildings throughout the town.

AMBER MUSEUM Your first stop should be the Amber Museum (61 Duarte Street; Tel. 586–2848). It is situated on the second floor of *The Tourist Bazaar* in a grand Victorian house only 2 blocks from the square. Dominican amber is the petrified resin of an ancient tree, *algarrobo,* and created by the earth's violent eruptions and drastic changes 50 million years ago. Scientists explain that the resin dripping from the trees entrapped insects, flies, spiders, and leaves, giving the amber its unusual character.

Some of the best examples of these pieces— with insects perfectly intact—are displayed in the museum. The most valuable piece is a tear drop of clear amber with a tiny lizard entrapped; others of remarkable quality have a mosquito, a tiny scorpion, and a grasshopper. The amber ranges in color from bright lemon yellow to dark brown and, more rarely, white, green, red, black, blue, and opaque. The different colors result from the nature of the soil where it was buried.

The discovery and commercial development of amber in the Dominican Republic is less than fifty years old. The mineral is mined in three places: in the Cordillera Septentrional at Palo Alto; near Santo Domingo; and in Samana. Similar amber is found only in two other places in the world, Germany and Russia.

The museum was conceived by Aldo and Didi Costa, owners of The Tourist Bazaar and well-known personalities in the Dominican tourism industry who operated the town's main hotel for many years. The museum, which opened in 1982, was organized by Chief Curator Brandt Gephardt of the Museum of Natural History in Cleveland. His objective was conservation as well as appreciation. The admission fee of RD $15 includes a tour in English by a knowledgeable guide. Hours: Monday to Friday from 9 A.M. to 6 P.M. and Saturday from 9 A.M. to 5 P.M.

On the ground floor, The Tourist Bazaar has a workshop for jewelry design and sells amber, larimar, and many other Dominican products. From my experience, this is the best craft store in the country; it is full of wonderful products not available elsewhere, and at reasonable prices.

CENTRO ARTESANAL Your next visit will take you walking through the city to Centro Artesinal (3 Calle Kennedy, near the corner of 30th of March Street, and a 5-minute walk from the port). Here in a restored tobacco warehouse is a craft school of the government-sponsored cooperative, Planarte, where young Dominicans are trained in jewelry-making, woodcarving, stone cutting, and other crafts from which they will be able to make a livelihood.

The school was partially financed by the World Bank and run by German artisan Heinz Meder with the aid of a Peace Corps volunteer. It stresses the adaptation of native Taino Indian designs to practical application in gifts, household items, and jewelry. Those on display are exquisite.

SAN FELIPE FORT Before you leave town to discover the other surprises of Puerto Plata (the name applies to the north coast district as well as the town), you may want to visit a landmark at the extreme west end of the Malecon, the boulevard of the town which runs along the sea.

The Fort of San Felipe, completed in 1577 to protect the harbor of Puerto Plata, is the only fortification the Spaniards built on the north coast that survived and, as the story goes, it was conquered only once when the city was overrun and looted by pirates a thousand strong.

It has an unusual feature. Instead of using a water-filled moat which usually surrounded a fortress such as this, the engineers created a moat by taking advantage of nature, using the bed of jagged coral rock which was there. A guided tour of the fort includes displays of old weaponry; the cell in which Juan Pablo Duarte was imprisoned in 1844 has been made into a memorial. Hours: Daily except Wednesday from 9 A.M. to 4:30 P.M. Admission: RD $10.

RESTAURANTS Other pages from the past can be found in some of the town's leading restaurants. *De Armando* (23 Avenue Mota; Tel. 586–3418) offers steak, lobster, and Dominican specialties with serenading by a guitar trio in the attractive setting of a Victorian house; and *Valter's* (Hermanas Mirabal Boulevard; Tel. 586–2329) has al fresco dining on a wide, wraparound Victorian veranda and garden and serves French and Italian specialties created by its owner-chef. Prices are moderate.

CASINOS In the resort area east of Puerto Plata, there are casinos at Jack Tar Village and Playa Dorada Hotel.

TOURIST OFFICE The Tourist Office is located on Calle Mirabal at the eastern end of the Malecon, next to the Costero Park and across the street from the Montemar Hotel.

SHORE EXCURSIONS FROM PUERTO PLATA

In anticipation of the return of some cruise ships to Puerto Plata soon, we have retained the Shore Excursions section, with estimated prices solely as a convenience for readers.

The prices are likely to be higher by the time cruises return to the area.

City and Cable Car Tour: 3 hours, US $25. Because of the brevity of cruise stops in Puerto Plata, you may find it easier to take the tour to the cable car and town rather than go on your own, unless you speak Spanish or know how to arrange such excursions quickly. The port is convenient—only a few blocks from the town center—but you will need transportation to the cable car station.

City Tour and Beach: 4 hours, US $30. There are beaches to the east and west of the city, but those to the east are far superior. The excursion takes a brief tour of town and the fort, followed by a beach party with a show of native merengue music and dancers and drinks.

Tour by Horseback: 3.5 hours, US $40. Experience the Dominican countryside by horse- back. The group is led by experienced guides.

OTHER TOURS

Apolo Tours (15 Kennedy Street; Tel. 586–2751) has a variety of tours; you need to book them in advance of your arrival. Other travel agencies in town can arrange similar tours as follows.

Sosua Beach: full day, US $40. A day at the beach resort of Sosua includes water sports, snorkeling, a glass-bottom boat ride over coral reefs, and a visit to a craft market.

Playa Grande: full day, US $50. Near Rio San Juan, an optional boat ride takes you through the Gri-Gri Lagoon, a mangrove swamp, to the Atlantic. After lunch at a countryside restaurant, you visit a farm to see how the tropical fruits are cultivated, then spend time at the beach.

Santiago: full day, US $60. From the north coast you travel through the fertile valley of Cibao, the main agricultural area of the island, to Santiago, the Dominican Republic's second largest city, where two of the country's main exports, rum and tobac- co, are produced. At the Bermudez Rum Distillery, founded in 1852, you learn how rum is made, and at the Cigar Factory you see how Dominican cigars, as popular as Havana cigars, are made by hand in the traditional way. Lunch at a Chinese restaurant

and time for shopping are included.

ON YOUR OWN IN PUERTO PLATA

An alternative would be to engage a taxi for 2 hours or half a day for sight-seeing on your own and return to the town for shopping. The cost is about RD $400 to $600 for 2 hours. Another option is to take one of the privately owned minibuses that travel east to Sosua, Cabarete, and beyond. They leave frequently from the town's central plaza and make frequent stops to pick up and let off passengers along the way. The fare from Puerto Plata to Sosua is RD $10; to Cabarete, RD $20.

Local buses from Puerto Plata to the resorts at Playa Dorado run from 6 A.M. to 6 P.M. and cost RD $5. There are also motorscooters and trail bikes for rent for about US $40 to $50. However, no insurance is available, and theft is a problem, particularly in Sosua.

For a few hours at the beach, the hotels at Playa Dorada offer a fabulous beach, tennis, sailing, windsurfing, swimming, riding, and golf at the 18- hole course used by all the hotels of the resort area. You should make arrangements for a day visit in advance because most of the resorts in the area are all-inclusives and are not set up to accommodate individual visitors without prior arrangements.

GOLF: Designed by Robert Trent Jones, the Playa Dorada Golf Course (par 72; 6,990 yards) has four holes located directly by the sea, where strong Atlantic tradewinds blow frequently, and ten holes with water hazards. Inquire through *Alegro Resorts/Jack Tar Village* (Tel. 800–999–9182) in advance for green fees and to make arrangements to play.

SAILBOARDING: The north coast is world famous as a windsurfing location, particularly at Cabarete, 2 miles east of Sosua, or about a 1.5- hour drive from Puerto Plata. All the seaside resorts of the north coast have boards for rent. The *Cabarete Surf Sail Center* gives lessons to beginners. The annual Puerto Plata Windsurf Tournament is held in June.

PLAYA DORADA

E ast of Puerto Plata at Playa Dorada a series of attractive resorts were developed in the 1980s by the Dominican Republic government with the help of the World Bank. All of the resorts are situated along a lovely 2-mile-long beach, but one is hardly aware of the others because of their layout, architecture, landscaping, and the restrictions on building heights. All the resorts have an informal atmosphere with pool- or beach-side restaurants and offer swimming, tennis, sailing, windsurfing, and share an 18-hole Robert Trent Jones golf course.

SOSUA

A pproximately 15 miles east beyond Playa Dorada is one of Puerto Plata's biggest surprises—the seaside resort town of Sosua. Its story is unique.

When U.S. president Franklin Roosevelt asked Allied leaders gathered in Evian, France, to address the plight of the Jews under Hitler, the only one to offer concrete help was Trujillo. He offered the Jews citizenship and parcels of land on the north coast.

In the 1940s approximately 1,000 Jews emigrated to the town of Sosua, and under difficult conditions of a hot climate to which none was accustomed, they transformed the 27,000 acres of tropical wilderness into a farming community which became the country's meat and dairy capital. In the early 1980s, Sosua, with its slightly St. Tropez–like character, became something of a haven for artists and writers, but more recent resort development has changed the town's character considerably.

Sosua is set on a ½-mile-long crescent beach of fine white sand tucked under a hillside of lush gardens with brilliantly colored bougainvillea and other tropical flowers. At the lower level of town, *Los Charamicos,* whose name is taken from the beachside vendors who cook local specialties on their charcoal fires, is a colorful medley of lilliputian houses and cafes in a maze of narrow streets filled with children and chickens, a cockfighting arena, and a brightly painted yellow church.

"Uptown," the upper part of the hillside known as *El Batey,* is not only at the other side of the beach but the other side of the world. Here, wide shaded streets are bordered by flowering trees and graced by pretty homes and gardens. Many are "country" houses owned by wealthy Dominicans who come to the north coast to escape the bustle of the capital. Very few of the original Jewish settlers are still here, but their forty-year-old synagogue remains.

Sosua has swimming, sailing, snorkeling, waterskiing, and windsurfing. The beach at Sosua, one of the best on the coast, has a small reef suitable for snorkelers. There are unpretentious restaurants which specialize in fish, Dominican dishes, or American selections.

Another hour's drive east, at the town of Rio San Juan (72 miles from Puerto Plata), there is a mangrove swamp known as *Gri Gri Lagoon* through which you can ride in a small boat to a secluded beach that you will probably have all to yourself. Allow four to five hours for the round trip from Puerto Plata, bring beach towels and a picnic lunch, and be sure to arrange your return transportation or you will most surely miss the boat!

CABARETE

A short distance east of Rio San Juan and Playa Grande is a beautiful stretch of sand known as Cabarete with a tiny seaside village that is growing daily as the word gets out about its great attraction: windsurfing. Already discovered by the avant garde enthusiasts who put Cabarete on the windsurfing map, the area has the ideal combination of wind and wave to claim itself the windsurf capital of the Caribbean. Several international competitions are held here annually.

As might be expected, an increasing number of outfitters—there are already eight windsurfing schools—are finding their way here too, along with resorts, an assortment of small inns, shops, car rentals, restaurants, bars, and cafes. At some time or other, everyone seems to make his or her way to the *New Wave Café*, located right on the beach in the center of town. It has a long thatch-roofed bar overlooking the sea that's a welcome refuge from the sun and, at night, becomes the setting for an instant beach party. It attracts some of the best reggae, rock, and Latin-rock bands in the country, several nights a week.

If you are in Sosua or Cabarete long enough for hiking and biking, *Iguana Mama* (Tel. 571–0908), on the main highway through Cabarete, rents mountain bikes and offers adventure tours.

Puerto Rico

SAN JUAN • PONCE

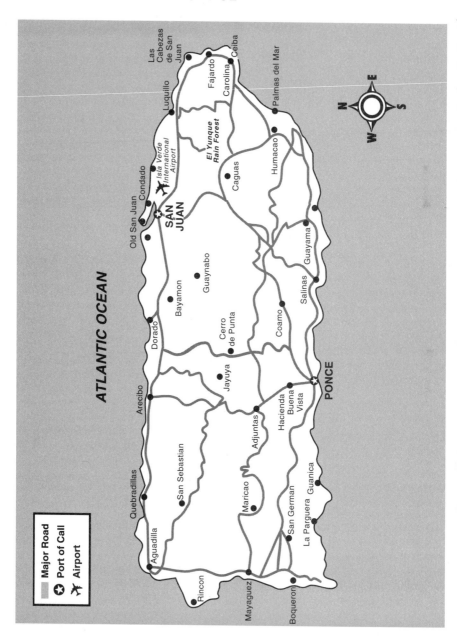

ATLANTIC OCEAN

Las Cabezas de San Juan
Fajardo
Ceiba
Carolina
Luquillo
Palmas del Mar
Condado
El Yunque Rain Forest
Isla Verde International Airport
Humacao
Old San Juan
Caguas
SAN JUAN
Guaynabo
Guayama
Bayamon
Salinas
Dorado
Cerro de Punta
Coamo
Arecibo
Jayuya
PONCE
Hacienda Buena Vista
Adjuntas
Quebradillas
Guanica
San Sebastian
Maricao
San German
La Parguera
Aguadilla
Mayaguez
Boqueron
Rincon

Legend
- Major Road
- ✪ Port of Call
- ✈ Airport

AT A GLANCE

Antiquities	★★★★★
Art and Artists	★★★★
Beaches	★★
Colonial Buildings	★★★★★
Crafts	★★★★
Cuisine	★★★
Dining/Restaurants	★★★★
Entertainment	★★★★★
Forts	★★★★★
Gambling Casinos	★★★★
History	★★★★
Monuments	★★★★★
Museums	★★★★
Nature	★★★★
Nightlife	★★★★★
Scenery	★★★★
Shopping	★★★
Sight-seeing	★★★
Sports	★★★★★
Transportation	★★★★

CHAPTER CONTENTS

THE COMPLETE ISLAND

"We proceeded along the coast the great part of that day, and on the evening of the next we discovered another island called Borinquen . . . All the islands are very beautiful and possess a most luxuriant soil, but this last island appeared to exceed all others in beauty."
(From a letter by Dr. Diego Alvarez Chanca, who accompanied Columbus on his second voyage to the New World in 1493)

Like Columbus, cruise passengers sailing into San Juan Bay have a breathtaking view of Puerto Rico. From afar the green peaks of the thickly wooded Cordillera Central, rising 4,398 feet at their highest point, are outlined against the blue Caribbean sky; palms etch miles of white sand beaches washed by the sea.

As the ship approaches the harbor it passes the colossal fortress of El Morro, strategically located on the northwest side overlooking the Atlantic Ocean, to dock in Old San Juan, the oldest city now under the American flag. Beyond the ramparts of the fortress, the skyline of new San Juan with its glittering resorts of Condado Beach and its modern high-rises of Hato Rey is juxtaposed against the Old World grace of the colonial city.

Puerto Rico, the easternmost island of the Greater Antilles, is a commonwealth of the United States. Although it has been under the American flag since 1898, it was under Spanish rule for almost four centuries. From the intermingling of the two cultures comes modern Puerto Rico. For visitors, it offers the best of both worlds—the familiarity of home in a setting that is distinctly foreign. And it offers a great deal more.

Puerto Rico has greater variety of activity and attractions than any place in the Caribbean. For sports enthusiasts, there are miles of beaches for swimming, windsurfing and sailing, and even surfing. The World Surfing Championships were held in 1988 for a second time in two decades on the west coast.

The Puerto Rico chapter has been prepared with the assistance of San Juan resident Kathryn Robinson, the author of The Other Puerto Rico.

Anglers can try to beat one of the three dozen sportfishing world records previously set in Puerto Rican waters. Golfers have fourteen courses to test, including the famous Robert Trent Jones quartet at Dorado. Tennis buffs can choose from dozens of courts at hotels in San Juan or within easy reach of the capital. Several resorts have complete tennis complexes with clinics, instructors, pro shops, and courts lighted for night play.

The diving around Puerto Rico and her satellite islands is good, too, with a dozen places suited for snorkelers and novice divers, and an even greater choice for those with experience. And there are mountains for hiking, caves to explore, horseback riding, and horse racing. Puerto Rico even has its own special breed of horses, Paso Fino, which are shown at horse shows frequently throughout the year.

In a country whose culture stretches over 500 years there's plenty for history buffs to explore. Shoppers can be diverted at street markets and boutiques in the Old City, arcades in hotels, or the Texas-size shopping centers of the suburbs. But what will interest them most are the crafts made in Puerto Rico. Santos, hammocks, and cuatros are a few in which local artisans excel.

Entertainment and nightlife offer so much variety, you could stay in Puerto Rico for a month, try a different restaurant and nightclub every night, and still have plenty left for your next visit. There are discos, cabarets, and casinos, but the Puerto Rican specialty is a lobby bar with live salsa and other Latin beats where you can start moving your feet in the afternoon and dance the night away.

The variety of arts and cultural attractions is equally impressive. No week goes by without an exhibit in a gallery, museum, or hotel. The performing arts calendar is filled year-round with concerts, opera, ballet, and theater, and highlighted by the annual Casals Festival in June.

The scenery is immensely varied. The rectangular-shaped island is only 100 miles long and 35 miles wide, yet it has the range of geographic features of a country fifty times its size. From the quiet, palmed beaches on the east the land rises to two rugged mountain ranges that fall off in an ocean of rolling surf on the west where the Mona Passage separates Puerto Rico from the Dominican Republic. A spine of mountains separates the north coast on the Atlantic Ocean from the south which faces the Caribbean Sea.

The mountain slopes are thick with breadfruit and mango trees and coffee bushes, while large stretches of flat land and rolling hills are planted with sugar, pineapple, and vegetables. There are deserts, salt flats, and two phosphorescent bays that glow in the night. The west end of the island has the Maricao State Forest, a tropical forest at 2,625 feet; and near the east end is the 28,000-acre Caribbean National Forest, known locally as *El Yunque,* the only tropical rain forest in the U.S. Forest Service system.

For those planning a stay before or after their cruises, Puerto Rico offers a large variety of hotels in San Juan and around the island—large, small, beachside, mountainside, modern, or historic—to suit any lifestyle or pocketbook. Remember, too, that it's part of the U.S., so you can use your U.S. dollars, credit cards, and driver's license.

THE ARRIVAL OF THE SPANIARDS

At the time of its discovery by Columbus on November 19, 1493, Puerto Rico was inhabited by the Tainos, a branch of the Arawak Indians who had pushed north from South and Central America to flee the pursuing Carib Indians, the fierce warrior tribe from which the Caribbean Sea takes its name.

Columbus renamed the island San Juan Bautista in honor of St. John the Baptist, but in time, it became known as Puerto Rico, meaning "rich port." The Spaniards found gold in the mountains on the north coast, but more importantly San Juan became an important storage and transit harbor for the gold and silver shipped from the mines of Mexico and South America to fill the king's coffers in Spain.

In 1508, one of Columbus's companions, Juan Ponce de León, returned to Puerto Rico with fifty Spaniards to establish a settlement at Caparra on the southwestern side of San Juan Bay. The following year Ponce de León was appointed the country's first governor by the Spanish Crown. Twelve years later the settlement moved to the north side of the harbor at the present site of Old San Juan.

Because of its strategic location as a gateway to Spain's New World empire, Puerto Rico played a central role in the European rivalry for control of the Caribbean. Many European commanders, including England's Sir Francis Drake in 1595, attempted to wrestle the island away from the Spaniards, but none succeeded.

Under the iron fist of Spain, Puerto Rico developed a plantation society based on sugar and imported black slaves, but it never really flourished as did other parts of her empire. Spain's highly restrictive economic policies limited the ability of her colonies to trade with other countries and required all their goods to be carried in Spanish ships.

By the mid-19th century with the abolition of slavery throughout the Americas and England's supremacy on the seas, Spain's empire days were numbered. The 1868 uprising proclaiming Puerto Rico a republic was unsuccessful, but it foreshadowed coming events.

Slavery was abolished in 1873, and in 1897 Spain granted Puerto Rico autonomy and established a new government. For the Puerto Ricans, it was too little too late. In the same year the Spanish-American War ended Spain's empire in the New World and in 1898, Puerto Rico was formally turned over to the United States.

In 1917, Puerto Ricans were made U.S. citizens and given the right to vote in local elections, and a senate and house of delegates were created; but the people had to wait until 1948 before they were allowed to elect their own governor. He is empowered to appoint his cabinet and members of the Puerto Rico supreme court. In 1952, Puerto Rico was made a Commonwealth; it is represented in the U.S. Congress by a resident commissioner with a voice but no vote, except in committees on which he may serve.

Currency, immigration, customs, postal services, international relations, and the armed forces are shared with the United States, but the island enjoys one big difference: residents pay no federal income tax on income earned in Puerto Rico. They do, however, pay a local tax.

OPERATION BOOTSTRAP

Five decades ago, Puerto Rico was an extremely poor country with a meager economy based on agriculture. The major crop was sugar, raised on the coastal plains and harvested by the backbreaking, handcut method. Other crops were coffee and tobacco. Per capita income was about $121 per year; life expectancy was around 45 years. Doctors were few, hospital care limited, and illiteracy widespread.

Operation Bootstrap, started in 1947, transformed Puerto Rico into a modern society. Through a program of industrial development, it was able in three decades to attract seven billion dollars of investment which resulted in the creation of 2,600 new plants, equipment, machinery, and other facilities and thousands of jobs.

Life expectancy has risen to 72 years, and illiteracy has been reduced to under 2 percent of the population. Puerto Rico has pushed its per capita personal income to about $7,800—a figure considerably lower than that of the U.S. mainland, but one of the highest in Latin America.

Operation Bootstrap was followed by Operation Serenity, which sought to do for Puerto Rico's culture what the industrial program had done for its economy. As a result, the Institute of Puerto Rican Culture was created to help bring about a renaissance of the island's folklore, crafts, music, dance, sculpture, painting, theater, and architectural preservation. Today visitors, along with the warm and outgoing people of Puerto Rico, can enjoy the fruits of the renaissance in museums, galleries, concerts, and a year-round calendar of festivals and cultural events.

After a well-spent day in this port of call with its array of sports, activities, and attractions, and the wealth of its history and culture, you too may agree, Puerto Rico *is* the "Complete Island."

FAST FACTS

POPULATION: 3.6 million

SIZE: 3,421 square miles

MAIN CITIES: San Juan, Ponce, Mayaguez, Caguas, Arecibo

CLIMATE: Average yearly temperature, 78–83°F. December to April are coolest months; July to September are hottest

with average temperatures over 80°F. Mountain regions are cooler and in winter require sweaters and blankets at night. Annual rainfall, about 59 inches; rainy season is mainly May through October but short rains are characteristic at other times as well. The dry season is January to March.

CLOTHING: Informal dress is accepted throughout the country, but in more elegant restaurants and nightclubs, patrons are fashionably dressed with women wearing cocktail or dinner attire and men in tie and jacket or a *guayabera*, an open-neck embroidered shirt popular in Mexico.

CURRENCY: U.S. dollar

CUSTOMS REGULATIONS: Cruise passengers who disembark in San Juan to return to the United States by plane after visiting other islands and countries must go through U.S. customs.

ELECTRICITY: 60 A.C.; 110 volts

ENTRY FORMALITIES: None for U.S. citizens. Driver's license or voter's registration suggested.

LANGUAGE: Spanish. English widely spoken.

POSTAL SERVICE: Same as U.S. mainland

PUBLIC HOLIDAYS: January 1, New Year's Day; January 6, Three Kings Day; January 11, Patriot de Hostos; February, Presidents' Birthday; March 23, Emancipation Day; Good Friday; April 16, Patriot de Diego Day; May, Memorial Day; July 4, U.S. Independence Day; July 17, Muñoz Rivera Day; July 25, Constitution Day; July 27, Barbosa Day; September 1, Labor Day; October 14, Columbus Day; November 11, Veteran's Day; November 19, Discovery of Puerto Rico (by Columbus); November, Thanksgiving; December 25, Christmas.

POSTAL SERVICE: Same as U.S. mainland.

TELEPHONE AREA CODE: 787

TIME: One hour ahead of Eastern Standard Time.

AIRLINES: *From the United States mainland:* American, Continental, Delta, Northwest, Pan Am Carnival, Tower, TWA, United, and US Airways. *Regional and Domestic:* American Eagle, Carib Air, Flamenco, LIAT, Vieques Air Link.

INFORMATION:

In the United States,
Puerto Rico Tourism Company:
New York: 575 Fifth Avenue, 23rd Floor, New York, NY 10017;
Tel. (800) 223–6530; fax: (212) 818–1868.
Los Angeles: 3575 W. Cahuenga Boulevard, No. 560, Los Angeles, CA 90068;
Tel. (213) 874–5991; fax: (213) 874–7257.
Miami: Peninsula Bldg., 901 Ponce de Leon Boulevard, No. 604, Coral Gables, FL 33134;
Tel. (305) 445–9112; fax: (305) 445–9450.

In Canada: 2 Bloor Street West, No. 700, Toronto, Ont. M4W 3R1;
Tel. (416) 368–2680; fax: (416) 368–5350.

In San Juan: La Casita, Puerto Rico Tourism Information Center, Comercio Street, Old San Juan; (Tel.722–1709; fax: 722–5208.) Hours: Tuesday to Saturday 9:00 A.M. to noon and 1:00 to 5:00 P.M.

Que Pasa, the free quarterly official tourist guide, maps, and brochures are available. On Saturday and Sunday, from 3 to 5 P.M., the *Festival La Casita* takes place here, combining street theater with an arts fair.

BUDGET PLANNING

Costs in Puerto Rico are similar to those on the mainland. There are no particular items of unusually high cost that need to be noted. You can compare costs in San Juan to a large metropolitan area such as New York or Chicago, and those in the Puerto Rico countryside to small-town America.

The best way to save money is to walk, which is delightful in Old San Juan, and to use public transportation, which is inexpensive and plentiful. Restaurants, with the exception of the most deluxe, are reasonably priced and those that cater mainly to a local clientele are inexpensive. Outside of San Juan, they are cheap by any standard. Most museums and other tourist attractions are free or have a nominal charge. The cost of sports is comparable to other places in the Caribbean. However, tennis and golf at posh resorts are expensive.

INTRODUCTION TO SAN JUAN

San Juan, with a population exceeding one million, is one of the largest and most sophisticated Caribbean cities. Its deluxe resorts, nightclubs, cabarets, casinos, and discos live side by side with its history, culture, and Old World charm. More than any place in the Caribbean, San Juan combines the bustle of a large American city (plus good communications facilities) and the grace of its Spanish heritage with the beat of the Caribbean.

The city has an incredible range of activity and attractions with every kind of sport for active people or spectators; elegant shops and trendy boutiques or colorful Caribbean markets; restaurants with as many different cuisines and types of ambience as in New York or Miami; and a nightlife that outshines both. Yet it is no more than a stone's throw from quiet fishing villages and little towns hidden in forest-clad mountains.

San Juan, 1,040 miles southeast of Miami and

40 miles west of the U.S. Virgin Islands, is the transportation hub of the Caribbean. It is 2 hours by air from Miami, 1 hour from Caracas, 20 minutes from St. Thomas—with a dozen airlines connecting it with the mainland, other islands of the Caribbean, and Latin America.

San Juan now vies with Miami for the highest number of cruise ships using it as home port. The numbers vary by season, but more than a dozen cruise ships are based here for part or all of the year and depart weekly to the Eastern Caribbean; another two dozen or more ships call weekly from Florida ports; and even more call intermittently throughout the year.

One of the biggest attractions of San Juan for cruise passengers is the location of the port. Quite literally, you step off your ship into the oldest, most interesting part of the city, Old San Juan. Indeed, until this century, it *was* the city. As new areas sprang up after World War I, the old district decayed and might easily have been lost to the bulldozers had it not been for some farsighted Puerto Ricans who banded together to save it. Today, Old San Juan is a living city once again with its old buildings beautifully restored and bursting with activity from morning to night.

Yet, if you are not interested in Old World charm and instead want beaches, sports, or nightlife, you need go no farther than one of San Juan's two main hotel areas. These, too, are within easy reach of the port. Many of San Juan's hotels are self-contained resorts offering tennis, deep-sea fishing, and every kind of water sport; most have casinos, cabaret-style nightclubs featuring big-name entertainment, and nonstop music and dancing in lively lobby bars and discos.

A short taxi or bus ride east from Plaza Colon in Old San Juan will take you to Miramar and the resort area of Condado, where several of the city's best hotels, beaches, restaurants, and shops are located. The Condado area became fashionable in the 1920s and held its own until after World War II, but suffered when the center of social activity shifted. In the 1980s, the district received a facelift that started with the Condado Beach Hotel, the island's Art Deco gem. Its restoration sparked similar action on the part of its neighbors.

East of Condado, the main highway takes you through Santurce, a business center, and along

the San José Lagoon. Almost parallel to San Juan International Airport is Isla Verde, another resort area which peaked in the 1960s and then slipped badly after the recession and the oil crisis of the 1970s. Like other parts of San Juan, Isla Verde has made a comeback with a renovation and beautification program that received its biggest boost in 1986 with the reopening of the totally renovated El San Juan Hotel, the darling of celebrities and other vacationers in the 1960s.

For a totally different kind of day, ferries leave every half hour from the pier next to your cruise ship for Cataño across San Juan Bay. Here you can have a free tour of the Bacardi Rum Distillery, sample the rum, and lunch at a waterfront seafood restaurant in the fishing village of Palo Seco, with a view of San Juan and the Fortress of El Morro in the distance. The ferry also goes to Hato Rey, another suburb on the southeast, passing through pretty mangroves and bayous en route.

San Juan has a lot to offer whether you prefer to enjoy it as part of a group or on your own.

PORT PROFILE: SAN JUAN

LOCATION/EMBARKATION: All ships pull in dockside at the Port of San Juan. In recent years, the port and its surrounding area have been extensively renovated and beautified, enhancing the pleasure of passengers' arrival.

In preparation for its 500th birthday, in November 1993, Puerto Rico was spruced up with more than $700 million in renovations and new attractions. The bulk of the money was spent in Old San Juan and Ponce, Puerto Rico's second largest city, and now Old San Juan looks more beautiful than ever, with redesigned streets and many new attractions.

The port of San Juan, situated at the foot of Old San Juan, is the most conveniently located one in the Caribbean for passengers, giving them the choice of taking tours or exploring on their own with equal ease. The piers are within walking distance of the city's most interesting sight-seeing and some of its best shopping and dining, and they are convenient to transportation to other parts of the city as well.

For those who arrive in San Juan by air to join their ship, the ride from the airport to the pier takes 25 to 40 minutes depending on traffic. A taxi from the airport to the pier costs about $16. If you are arriving as part of an air/sea package, the transfer from the airport to the pier is handled for you by your cruise line.

In the immediate area of the piers, there are shops, banks, the new *Wyndham San Juan Hotel* with attractive restaurants and a large casino, and *La Casita*, the Puerto Rico Tourism Information Center, open Tuesday through Saturday, 9 A.M. to noon and 1 to 5 P.M. Tourist Police (wearing white hats) are available to help visitors. Passengers are allowed to go and come from their ships freely, provided they show proper identification issued by their cruise ship.

LOCAL TRANSPORTATION: Fleets of taxis are on hand to meet all ships. Taxis operate on meters and are comparable in price to those in stateside cities. You can hire them by the hour or half day, but *settle the price in advance*. A taxi dispatcher is available to help passengers. City buses to Condado and all parts of San Juan leave frequently throughout the day from their station slightly east of Pier One.

To help alleviate traffic in Old San Juan, motorized trolleys for shoppers and people who work in the district are operated by Goya and the Old San Juan Merchants Association. They, too, leave from just north of the piers and make a round-trip on two routes: The center one runs via San Francisco Street, Plaza de Armas, and Fortaleza Street; the other follows a more northern route to Boulevard de Valle and Calle Norzagaray to Calle Cristo and Fortaleza Street.

CAR RENTALS: All major U.S. rental firms are represented in San Juan, but unfortunately, none has offices at the port. The nearest offices are in Condado, a 10-minute taxi ride from the port. There are also local companies with lower rates. A list appears in *Que Pasa*.

Avis, Tel. 791–0426, 721–4499
Budget, Tel. 791–3685
Hertz, Tel. 791–0840
National, Tel. 791–1805

FERRY SERVICE: The Agua Express leaves from Pier Two every half hour, from 6 A.M. to 9 P.M., to Cataño across the harbor. Cost is 50 cents. Tel. 788–1155.

DOMESTIC AND REGIONAL AIR SERVICE: *American Eagle* (Tel. 749–1747) offers daily flights to Mayaguez and Ponce. *Flamenco Air* (Tel. 723–8110) flies to Puerto Rico's satellite island of Culebra; *Vieques Air Link* (Tel. 722–3736) serves Vieques. American Eagle and LIAT have flights to nearby islands. San Juan is American Eagle's main hub for flights throughout the Eastern Caribbean.

EMERGENCY NUMBERS:
   Medical Service, Tel. 754–3535
   Police, Tel. 343–2020;
   Tourist Zone Police, 24 hours, emergencies, Tel. 722–0738
   Ambulance, Tel. 343–2550
   Alcoholics Anonymous, Tel. 723–4187

AUTHOR'S FAVORITE ATTRACTIONS

OLD SAN JUAN:
   EL MORRO FORTRESS;
   PASEO DE LA PRINCESA, LA PRINCESA, AND CITY WALLS;
   CHURCH OF SAN JOSE;
   LA ROGATIVA;
   LA FORTALEZA ART MUSEUMS AND ART GALLERIES;
   SHOPPING IN OLD SAN JUAN
EXCURSION TO PONCE VIA PANORAMIC HIGHWAY
GOLF: HYATT REGENCY DORADO BEACH
DEEP-SEA FISHING
SAN JUAN NIGHTLIFE
HIKING IN EL YUNQUE

SHORE EXCURSIONS

The first several tours listed are available from almost all cruise ships, but the others may not be or they may have slight variations in length and price, depending on the operator. A few have been included here for those planning a pre- or post-cruise visit in San Juan; they can be booked through your hotel or directly with the local travel company. Prices per person may be slightly higher when purchased aboard ship, but the extra cost is usually offset by the cost of a taxi from the port to a hotel or local travel agency.

City Tour—Old and New San Juan: 2 to 2.5 hours, $19–$25. As San Juan is a large, sprawling metropolis, a brief introduction by motorcoach can be useful for those on a first visit. The tour is also recommended for those who do not have a sport, activity, or special interest to pursue, or who are unable to walk comfortably for extended periods.

El Yunque Rain Forest: 4 hours, $24–$30. One of the most popular tours offers an eastward drive through San Juan to the Caribbean National Park, which covers the peaks and slopes of the Luquillo Mountains. Better known as El Yunque, it is the only rain forest in the U.S. Forest Service. Longer tours stop at Luquillo Beach to allow participants to swim. Further description of these attractions is provided later in this chapter.

Horseback Riding in El Yunque: 4 hours, $54–$60. A riding excursion in the foothills of the Luquillo Mountains and along the beach is offered several days per week and leaves from the Caribe Hilton and El San Juan hotels. It is also offered by some cruise lines.

San Juan by Helicopter: 45 minutes, $67. A flight-seeing trip over the city and bay to see Old and New San Juan is an excursion not to be missed.

Old San Juan Walking Tour: 2 hours; $20; Colonial Adventures (201 Recinto Sur St., Old San Juan; Tel. 729–0114) offers a variety of guided walking tours of Old San Juan geared to special interests: art, history, photography, and so on. The basic tour departs twice daily at 9:30 A.M. and 2 P.M.; other tours should be booked in advance.

City Tour and Rum Distillery: 3 hours, $30. The tour combines sightseeing in Old San Juan with a visit to the Bacardi Rum Distillery in Cataño across the bay. It is recommended for those who prefer touring with a group; the excursion can be made on one's own using public transportation, too.

El Commandante Racetrack: half day, $30. If not

available on your cruise ship as a shore excursion, this trip can be booked at the Caribe Hilton (Tel. 791–6195) and other major hotels. It departs from the Hilton at 12:30 P.M. on Wednesday, Friday, Sunday, and holidays and includes round-trip transportation and clubhouse admission.

San Juan Night Life Tour: 3 hours, $35–$40. For those who might prefer to sample San Juan nightlife with others rather than on their own, the tour usually takes in a cabaret with a Las Vegas–type show, time at a casino, and a drink. Or try "Ole Latino," a musical revue featuring Latin American dances, at the Condado Convention Center.

Golf Tour: See Sports section later in this chapter.

Camuy Cave Tour: full day, $50. Rio Camuy Cave Park, with a surface area of 268 acres, is a showcase of Puerto Rico's elaborate network of caves. The Camuy Caves, the largest of the 220 caves which have been documented, have chambers as high as a 25-story building. The Camuy River, the third largest underground river in the world, passes through the system. (See description later in chapter.)

Trans-Island Tour to Ponce: 8 hours, $50. The tour reveals the island's beauty and great diversity and is highly recommended for those on a second visit to Puerto Rico or as a trip for those spending extra days in San Juan before or after their cruise. The drive to Ponce on the south coast crosses the Cordillera Central mountains and offers lovely panoramic views of the countryside. It is followed by a city tour of Ponce, Puerto Rico's second largest city, which has a wealth of attractions.

Snorkeling and Diving Tours: See Sports section later in this chapter.

SAN JUAN ON YOUR OWN

San Juan, the air and cruise hub of the Caribbean, with a population exceeding one million, has the bustle of a large American city, the grace of its Spanish heritage, and the beat of the Caribbean. It also has a wonderful variety of big-city activity and attractions, yet it is only a stone's throw from quiet fishing villages and quaint mountain hamlets.

Beautifully restored Old San Juan is a living city bursting with activity from morning to night and ideal for walking. (For more than 350 years it was a walled and fortified city.) Then, beginning in this century with growth and expansion to new areas along Condado and Isla Verde beaches, the old part of San Juan became seedy. It might easily have been lost to the bulldozers, had it not been for some farsighted Puerto Ricans who banded together to save it, by first getting it made a protected historic zone in 1949. In 1955 the Society for the Development and Conservation of San Juan got a ten-year tax exemption for those restoring Spanish colonial buildings, and the Institute of Puerto Rican Culture designed a twenty-year plan to guide the preservation effort.

The renovations sparked a renaissance that has recaptured the town's old charm and ambience. Along streets paved with the blue cobblestones and in lovely old Spanish houses with flower-filled balconies and colonnaded courtyards, you can browse in shops, museums, and art galleries, enjoy lunch or refreshments at restaurants and cafes, and visit some of the oldest monuments in the Western Hemisphere.

A WALKING TOUR OF OLD SAN JUAN

Travelers who like to walk and sight-see on their own will probably find San Juan the most satisfying port of call in the Caribbean.

San Juan was a walled and fortified city for more than 350 years. Then, beginning in this century with growth and expansion to new areas along Condado and Isla Verde beaches, the old part of San Juan started to deteriorate and parts of it became seedy. Reversing the trend has taken time and hard work. In 1949 the government passed legislation establishing Old San Juan as a protected historic zone. This did not, however, stop misguided owners and builders from destroying some fine old structures to make way for new buildings.

In 1955, a sufficiently aroused citizens' group,

the Society for the Development and Conservation of San Juan, got legislation enacted which provided for a 10-year tax exemption on Spanish colonial buildings whose restoration met the guidelines established by the society. In the same year, the Institute of Puerto Rican Culture took over the responsibility for Old San Juan's preservation, culturally as well as architecturally, and designed a 20-year plan to guide the effort.

Government renovation of major public buildings and private restoration of homes and other structures sparked a renaissance in the city's most beautiful district, which has now recaptured its old charm and ambience, and made it a place that is as much fun as it is interesting to visit.

Here, along streets paved with the blue cobblestones once used as ballast by the trading ships of yore, in lovely old Spanish houses with flower-filled balconies and colonnaded courtyards, you can browse in shops, museums, and art galleries, enjoy lunch or refreshments at restaurants and hotels, and visit some of the oldest monuments in the Western Hemisphere.

There are any number of ways to route one's walking tour and so many interesting shops and detours that one can easily get sidetracked and miss some of the best parts. It is almost impossible to see all the important sites in the Old City on foot in one day, even if you have extraordinary stamina. Two, or preferably three days are needed to cover it all.

Old San Juan was laid out in typical Spanish colonial fashion as a grid and built on a hill which slopes from El Morro fortress on the northwest and San Cristobal fortress on the northeast, south to the port. With the exception of the perimeter roads which follow the contours of the old city walls, streets run north-south and east-west, making it easy to find one's way. However, the walk can be tiring when too much of the route is directed uphill. If you prefer to have a guide contact, *Colonial Adventure* (201 Recinto Sur St.; Tel. 729–0114). The firm offers 2- to 3-hour walking tours for $20.

If you get tired from walking or would like to conserve energy at points along the way, you can ride the motorized Goya trolleys, operated free of charge by the Merchants Association of Old San Juan. They start from just north of the

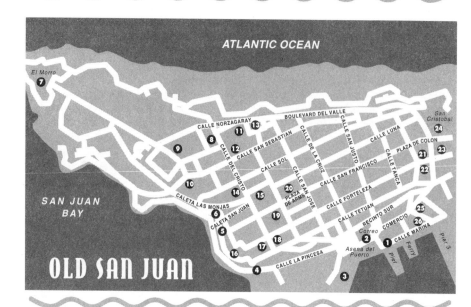

MAP LEGEND FOR WALKING TOUR OF OLD SAN JUAN

1. San Juan Piers and Plazoleta del Puerto
2. La Casita
3. Museum of Puerto Rican Culture (Arsenal)
4. La Princesa Jail and City Walls
5. Parque de Isabel and Gate of San Juan
6. Plaza de La Rogativa
7. El Morro Fortress
8. Quincentennial Plaza
9. Museum of the Americas
10. Casa Blanca
11. Church of San José and Dominican Convent
12. San José Plaza, Casals Museum, Casa de Los Contrsfuertes
13. San Jose Museum of Art and History
14. El Convento (Hotel)
15. San Juan Cathedral
16. La Fortaleza
17. Pigeon Park and Christ Chapel
18. Casa del Libro and National Center for Popular Arts
19. Department of State and Provincial Deputation Building
20. City Hall
21. Plaza Colon
22. Tapia Theatre
23. Old Casino of Puerto Rico
24. Fort San Cristobal
25. Municipal Bus Station
26. Wyndham San Juan Hotel

piers on two routes: one runs via San Francisco Street, Plaza de Armas, and Fortaleza Street; the other follows Boulevard de Valle and Calle Norzagaray to Calle Cristo and Fortaleza Street. The streets on which the trolleys run are usually closed to other motorized traffic during the day. There is no consistency in the Old City regarding the opening/closing hours and

days of important buildings, museums, galleries, and shops. Also, the buildings which are currently closed for renovations have been retained in this listing.

You can start your walk anywhere along the route but the plan I suggest, beginning at the piers (1) and continuing to Fort San Cristobal (26), avoids the uphill direction as much as possible, minimizes backtracking, and emphasizes the scenic and historic highlights with time for browsing and shopping. Stops along the route which should be given top priority are starred (*); the others can be added to your itinerary if time permits.

If you plan to spend a few days in San Juan prior to boarding your ship, you are most likely to arrive in Old San Juan for the first time at the Plaza Colon (23); your walk can start here and be made in reverse order.

From your ship, the 25-minute walk west-north-west along the old city walls to El Morro is a lovely introduction to Old San Juan, and indeed, the way visitors in olden times had to approach it. If you want to conserve time and energy, take a taxi to El Morro ($6) and start your walking tour from there.

LA CASITA (2) Assuming it is a beautiful morning and you are able to start your walking tour by 8:30 A.M. or so, upon leaving the piers turn left to Plaza de Hostos and continue along Calle La Princesa. You will pass La Casita, housing the Puerto Rico Tourist Office. You can stop here to get the latest copy of *Que Pasa*. The terminal for buses to Condado and other parts of San Juan is about a block north of Pier 3 (25).

The most recent renovations of the Old San Juan waterfront, part of the $700 million project celebrating Puerto Rico's 500th anniversary in 1993, cover an area of more than a mile, from La Puntilla, the small peninsula fronting the Old City Walls on the west, to the capitol building on the east.

Barrio La Marina, a 10-acre area fronting the cruise ship port from Piers One to Six, was the most ambitious part of the program. A $100 million urban renewal plan that won the American Institute of Architects' 1991 Citation for Excellence in Urban Design, the Barrio is in the fashion of Baltimore's Harborfest and has transformed an eyesore into an invitation to the city for arriving cruise ship passengers. Realigned streets connect the tree-lined seaside boulevard with Old San Juan and Plaza Colon.

The next phase of the program will extend the renovations for another mile east along the waterfront where more hotels and a new convention center are planned. The area is to be connected to Condado and Isla Verde by water taxi.

THE ARSENAL (3) South of the large parking lot on your left is the 18th-century building known as the Arsenal (yellow building on the waterfront). It was here in 1898 that the last Spanish general, Ricardo Ortego, turned Puerto Rico over to U.S. Commander General John R. Brooke. It was renovated to house the *Museum of Puerto Rican Culture*, which has changing exhibits of the works of Puerto Rican and other artists. Hours: Wednesday through Sunday, 9 A.M. to noon and 1 to 4:30 P.M.

LA PRINCESA AND CITY WALLS (4*) The Paseo de la Princesa is a broad walkway stretching from the cruise port to El Morro along the massive old *City Walls* which once completely surrounded the city. Now restored to its 19th-century elegance, with fountains and stately palms, the Paseo has a charming gazebo serving light food. Also, specially designed food carts with gaily colored awnings dispense "criollo," or local dishes, and the island's rich coffee. There are tree-shaded tables with umbrellas where folks can relax while they watch their children playing in the playground nearby.

On the west end of the Paseo is La Princesa, constructed in 1837 as a prison, just outside the original 16th-century City Walls. The magnificent building, now the home of the Puerto Rico Tourism Company, has huge mahogany doors, beautiful stairways, arcades and patios, and a spacious courtyard with a portion of the 70-foot-high old walls forming its northern enclosure. Several jail cells were preserved for their historic value. In addition to a Tourism Information Center, the ground floor has exhibition halls where works by contemporary Puerto Rican artists are on display. A children's theater with puppets, clowns, and other programs is staged on Sundays at 3:30 P.M.

Next to La Princesa is a monumental bronze fountain by the Spanish artist Luis Sanguino. Titled "Raíces" ("Roots"), the fountain depicts the epic history of the island and its diverse heritage—Indian, Spanish, and African—through human figures with dolphins cavorting at their feet. Viewed from afar the ensemble is meant to suggest a caravel being steered out to sea by the dolphins, setting its course for the 21st century. The Paseo's east side has a group of five allegorical pieces on the island's heritage.

The Paseo rounds the walls beneath *La Fortaleza* (**16**), the governor's residence for almost 500 years, and continues north along the sea. After 5 minutes, you will come to the small *Parque de Isabel la Catolica* and the *Gate of San Juan* (**5***), one of the four original gates to the city. An inscription on the south wall inside the doorway records that the gate was built in 1639 and its wooden doors mounted in 1749. Stop here to admire the view along the walls, which rise to 60 feet above the sea.

Overhead to the south you see La Fortaleza, originally the fort where the early Spaniards stored their gold and silver. Look north and you will see the massive city walls, which extend to the magnificent fortress of El Morro. Later, when you are at El Morro, you will be able to look back at this route and appreciate the enormity of this fortification.

LA ROGATIVA (**6***) After you have passed through the Gate of San Juan, turn left to *Plaza de La Rogativa*. The spectacular sculpture of La Rogativa is one of the most forceful, inspired works in iron ever conceived. It was done by Lindsay Daen and presented by the Development Corporation of Puerto Rico to mark the city's 450th anniversary in 1971.

La Rogativa, meaning The Procession, commemorates the saving of San Juan when the British had laid siege to it from the sea in 1797. After two weeks of being pounded by the guns of British warships lying off the coast, as the saga goes, city leaders thought their defeat was imminent and asked the bishop to lead a night vigil in honor of St. Catherine, the governor's patron saint.

Marchers bearing torches started from San Juan Cathedral at the top of the hill above La Rogativa, proceeded through the streets and returned to the church for Mass. The British commander, seeing the lights of the torches and hearing the continuous ringing of church bells, thought reinforcements had arrived by land from the east. Rather than face an uncertain battle, he hoisted anchor and quietly slipped away under the cover of night. The next morning the townspeople found their prayers had been answered; the British were gone and their city saved. On the small street leading to the cathedral is an alternate stop, the *Felisa Rincon de Gautier Museum*, the home of the

mayor of San Juan from 1946 to 1968. Hours: Monday to Friday, 9 A.M. to 3:45 P.M., Saturday and Sunday, 12:30 to 4 P.M.

North of the Rogativa, the street forks: the fork on the east leads to Casa Blanca, the ancestral home of Ponce de León, who colonized the island; the one on the left passes Casa Rosa and leads directly to El Morro, passing the most recent and most extensive renovations in this area, known as the Ballaja District (see below, nos. 8–12). The gate to Casa Blanca (open from sunup to sundown) leads directly into the mansion's beautiful gardens from where there are magnificent views across San Juan Bay (see no. 10).

EL MORRO (**7***) Begun in 1539, El Morro Fortress was part of the Spanish defense system, which stretched from Puerto Rico on the Atlantic to the coast of South America and was intended to protect the ships carrying gold and silver from Mexico, Colombia, and Peru to Spain. When danger approached from the sea, El Morro's mission was to close the entrance to San Juan harbor with its firepower.

El Morro is built on a promontory, or *morro*, in the shape of a head of a longhorn steer. If you can picture this image, the entrance gate leads directly into the steer's forehead with the snout jutting out to sea; the horns are the ramparts on the north and south of the entrance.

The fortress was built with such strength that it withstood all attempts to take it from the sea for over 350 years. Indeed, the only time the fort was captured was in 1598 when it was attacked by the British from the land side on the east. (In 1625, the Dutch also took the city from the same side but were forced to retreat.)

To protect its eastern flank, the city began to construct walls in 1633. Later, Fort San Cristobal on the northeast corner of the peninsula was added. During the Spanish-American War, the U.S. Navy bombarded El Morro, and after the war, when the Spaniards left Puerto Rico and the Americans took over, the U.S. Army occupied the site for several years.

El Morro was a living citadel. It has seven levels of tunnels, storage rooms, barracks, artillery emplacements, plus kitchens, a chapel, and foundry to see. Be sure to go up to the level of the lighthouse for the splendid view of old and new

San Juan and the cemetery along the north wall. The fort has been beautifully restored and is maintained by the U.S. National Park Service. It, along with the City Walls, Fort San Cristobal, and La Fortelaza, is listed on the National Register of Historic Sites and on UNESCO's World Heritage List. Orientation and slide presentation are available in English and Spanish. There is a museum and bookshop where specialized books, maps, and souvenirs are available. Allow one hour or more to see El Morro, depending on your interest. Hours: 8 A.M. to 6 P.M.

QUINCENTENNIAL PLAZA (8) Among the largest undertakings in Old San Juan in connection with the Columbus Quincentennial were those in the Ballaja Barrio, the district in the northwest corner of Old San Juan whose buildings and grounds once comprised Fort Brooke. They have now been transformed into a park and cultural complex, making use of some of Old San Juan's largest historic buildings, most dating from the 19th century.

Ballaja was the name of the barrio or district as early as the 18th century. The name is thought to be derived from its inhabitants, who were mostly immigrants from a town of the same name in the Dominican Republic. The area is known to have had Arawak settlements, as their artifacts have been uncovered in the archaeological excavations made alongside the renovations.

In 1857, after the construction of the Ballaja Military Barracks (El Cuartel de Ballaja) as the headquarters of the Spanish Army, the barrio became more integrated with its contingent areas, and the Dominican Convent (1523), Conception Hospital (1774), and other nearby buildings were taken over by the military. After the Spanish-American War, the U.S. Army occupied the buildings and added three small structures. All were turned over to the Commonwealth in 1976.

Ballaja covers the 5 blocks from the Church of San José, the second oldest church in the Americas, and the Dominican Convent on the east to Casa Blanca on the west. Calle Norzagaray and El Morro Fortress are on the north and Calle San Sebastin on the south. Some streets of this area were redesigned as pedestrian walkways, and an underground parking lot was created.

The $60 million Ballaja project centers around the Quincentennial Plaza, or the Plaza of Five Centuries, a three-tiered urban park dominated by a 40-foot monumental sculpture by Jaime Suarez, one of Puerto Rico's leading artists. An earthen totem pole, the sculpture is meant to represent the origins of Puerto Rico. Because the massive structure is totally divorced from its Spanish colonial setting, most people have trouble relating to it and find it an eyesore. Even more unforgivable are the arcades lining the plaza's east and west sides, which intrude and partially block the sightlines to the Church of San José, one of the most beautiful buildings in the Western Hemisphere.

On the east side of the plaza is the Dominican Convent, adjacent to the Church of San José and San José Square. West of the plaza are the district's two largest buildings, the former Ballaja Barracks and the Casa de Beneficencia, whose facades define a triangle encompassing another plaza and a street leading to El Morro, which is in full view. Casa de Beneficencia has become the new home of the Institute of Puerto Rican Culture, and the Dominican Convent, which it had occupied, has been made into the National Art Museum for Puerto Rican painting and graphic arts.

MUSEUM OF THE AMERICAS (9) The imposing Barracks has become the new Museum of the Americas, directed by Ricardo Alegria, the founding head of the Institute of Puerto Rican Culture. Under Alegria's stewardship, Old San Juan was restored and Puerto Rico's cultural institutions were nourished for more than two decades.

The museum is in formation and is envisioned as a panorama of New World cultures from prehistoric times to the present, as well as a living institution with year-round cultural activities and facilities that include a theater, library, restaurants, and shops. Its placement here, according to Alegria, was inspired by San Juan's unique geographic and historic position as the second oldest city in the Americas, coupled with Old San Juan's inherent quality as living history—it spans the 16th to the 20th centuries—and the monumental size of the Ballaja structures. The Popular Art Exhibit can be seen on the second floor.

CASA BLANCA (10*) From the Museum of the Americas, a lane on the south leads to Casa Blanca, built in 1521 as Juan Ponce de León's residence and hence considered the oldest continuously occupied residence in the Western Hemisphere. The first structure was a modest wooden house, but Ponce de León never occupied it, as he was felled by a poison-tipped arrow and died in Cuba that year. After the first house was partially destroyed by fire, Ponce de León's son-in-law replaced it with a stone and masonry structure that also served as a fort against Indian attacks. In 1540, when La Fortaleza was completed Casa Blanca became the Ponce de León family home and so remained until 1779, when it was sold to the Spanish government for use as a residence by the army corps of engineers.

From 1898, after the Spanish-American War, Casa Blanca was occupied by the U.S. military until 1967, when all such buildings were handed over to Puerto Rico. The following year, the house was declared a National Historic Monument, and the Institute of Puerto Rican Culture was given responsibility for its restoration. Recently renovated and furnished with 16th- and 17th-century antiques, the mansion juxtaposes two quite different collections—the Juan Ponce de León Museum and the Taino Indian Ethno-Historic Museum. Hours: 9 A.M. to noon and 1:30 to 4:30 P.M.

CHURCH OF SAN JOSÉ (11*) Return to Calle San Sebastián and walk one block to the Church of San José, the second oldest Roman Catholic church in the Americas and one of the purest examples of Gothic architecture in the world. Built in the early 16th century as a chapel of the Dominican monastery on land donated by Ponce de León's family, it was used as a family church until the last century. Ponce de León was buried here after his remains were brought from Cuba in 1559. Later, his body was moved to San Juan Cathedral.

The Church of San José has undergone lengthy renovation to strip away centuries of coatings on the walls and reveal the beautiful apricot stone and the magnificent cross vaulting of the ceiling. The original altar, too badly damaged to be retained, has been replaced by an authentic 15th-century Spanish one. A lovely figure of Christ on the Cross on the north side of the church is said to date from the mid-16th century. Hours: Monday through Saturday from 8:30 A.M. to 4 P.M., and Sunday for Mass at noon.

DOMINICAN CONVENT On the north side of the Church of San José is the convent, which dates from 1523. It was one of the first buildings constructed after Ponce de León moved his settlement from Caparra to establish San Juan. It remained one of the most important Catholic centers in the New World until its closing in 1838. It was then converted into a barracks for the Spanish army and after the Spanish-American War became the headquarters of the U.S. Antilles Command. The large interior patio is often used for concerts and the cloister walls for art exhibits.

(History buffs may be interested to know that the site of *Caparra*, Ponce de León's first settlement, is preserved by the ruins of the first house [1508], cathedral [1512], and the *Museum of the Conquest and Colonization of Puerto Rico*, located on the southwest side of San Juan. Hours: Monday to Friday from 9 A.M. to 5 P.M., and Saturdays, Sundays, and holidays from 10 A.M. to 6 P.M.)

SAN JOSÉ PLAZA (12) On the south side of the church, San José Plaza has a statue of Ponce de León made in 1882 and said to have been cast from the melted-down cannons used by the British during their attack on San Juan in 1797. The square, fronting San Sebastián Street, was renovated by the Institute of Puerto Rican Culture to resemble a typical plaza of colonial times. The plaza and San Sebastián and adjacent streets are the setting for the *Festival of San Sebastián Street,* an annual art and music show held during the last two weeks in January, when artists and artisans from all over Puerto Rico come to show their wares and musicians play every evening.

CASALS MUSEUM A townhouse on the east side of the plaza is the location of the Casals Museum, devoted to the great Spanish cellist who made his home in Puerto Rico for more than 20 years. Pablo Casals was the spearhead for a festival of the performing arts which bears his name; it has become one of the island's most important cultural events and is held annually in June. Hours: Tuesday through Saturday from 9:50 A.M. to 5:30 P.M.; Sunday 1 to 5 P.M.

CASA DE LOS CONTRAFUERTES The corner building of the Square, on Calle San Francisco, dates from the early eighteenth century and is said to be the oldest private residence in the city. The first floor houses the recently renovated Pharmacy Museum, a replica of a colonial-era apothecary. Hours: Wednesday to Sunday from 9 A.M. to 4:30 P.M. The second floor is devoted to the Latin American Graphic Arts Museum, where there are exhibits from time to time.

SAN JUAN MUSEUM OF ART AND HISTORY (13) Next to the convent but facing Calle Norzagaray is a large structure originally built in 1855 as a marketplace. Restored by the city of San Juan in 1979, it is used as a cultural center (closed temporarily). The museum is being housed temporarily at 200 San Francisco Street, second floor. Hours: Monday through Friday from 8 A.M. to 4 P.M.

CALLE DEL HOSPITAL Walking west on Calle San Sebastian, you will reach a set of stone steps, Calle del Hospital, leading to Calle Sol and a second set of stairs, *Stairway of the Nuns,* leading directly to Hotel El Convento.

If you have taken a taxi to El Morro to start your walking tour, you should detour down Calle Sol, a pretty lane leading to La Rogativa and San Juan Gate (described earlier), and return via either of two beautiful small streets, Caleta Las Monjas or Caleta San Juan to Hotel El Convento. If you made these visits earlier, continue to the second stairway leading directly to El Convento.

EL CONVENTO (14) Built in 1646 as a convent for the Carmelite nuns, El Convento was made into a deluxe hotel after extensive restoration guided by the Institute of Puerto Rican Culture. The lovely colonial architecture of the old building was retained and furnishings throughout are antiques or authentic reproductions from the 17th and 18th centuries.

The Carmelite order gave up the building in 1903 after it could no longer afford the maintenance. The building had deteriorated so badly by 1957 that it was going to be demolished to make way for a parking lot until the Institute of Puerto Rican Culture stepped in to save it. Now, after extensive renovations, the hotel has reopened under new ownership. The first and second levels have boutiques, restaurants, and a casino; the third to fifth floors house the new deluxe hotel with a small rooftop fitness room, pool, and sunset terrace overlooking the sea. The project was directed by Jorge Rosello, the architectural and interior design genius behind the renovation of El San Juan and El Conquistador hotels.

SAN JUAN CATHEDRAL (15) Facing El Convento on Calle Cristo, San Juan Cathedral enjoys a commanding position at the top of the hill leading up from San Juan Gate. It was from here the procession commemorated by La Rogativa set out in 1797 and miraculously saved the city. The present structure, dating from the mid-19th century, stands on the site of the first chapel built soon after the city was founded. The cathedral was renovated in 1979; the remains of Ponce de León were moved here from San José Church in 1908.

On the west side of the pocket park in front of the Cathedral and El Convento is the Museo del Nino (Museum of the Child), which features fun and educational hands-on exhibits and a staff of youth counselors to help kids get the most out of their visit. The museum is most appropriate for three- to seven-year-old children.

Continuing south on Calle Cristo, you will pass some of the best shops and art galleries in the city. If you have stuck with the itinerary until now, you might want a break from history to catch up on the San Juan of today. (See Shopping section for suggestions.)

LA FORTALEZA (16*) When you are ready to resume sight-seeing, visit La Fortaleza, the official residence of the governor of Puerto Rico located at the west end of Calle Fortaleza. It is considered to be the oldest executive mansion in continuous use in the Western Hemisphere. Hours: Monday to Friday, 9 A.M. to 4 P.M. (Tel. 721–7000, ext. 2211, 2323, and 2358). Tours in English are available every hour, when guides take visitors through the ceremonial rooms and the lovely grounds. Tours that include a visit to the mansion's second floor are available in English only at 10 and 10:50 A.M. Visitors are required to be properly dressed. La Fortaleza, El Morro, and its companion fort, San Cristobal, San Juan Gate, and the City Walls have been designated by UNESCO as landmarks on the World Heritage List.

PIGEON PARK (Las Palomas Park (17*)) After viewing La Fortaleza, return to Calle Cristo and turn right at the corner on the pretty little street with outdoor cafes leading to Pigeon Park, where you get a lovely view of San Juan harbor. You will probably be able to spot your ship at the pier. *Christ Chapel* has a pretty altar made of silver. The chapel is said to have been placed here after a horseman, racing down the hill from El Morro, missed the turn in the road and was thrown over the wall to the sea below to seemingly certain death. But miraculously, he did not die, according to the legend.

CASA DEL LIBRO (18) (255 Calle Cristo; Tel. 723–0354) Two adjoining homes from the 18th century house a rare-book museum and a section devoted to the art of printing and bookmaking. Hours: Tuesday through Saturday, except on holidays, from 11 A.M. to 4:30 P.M. Next door, the *National Center for Popular Arts* (253 Calle Cristo; Tel. 723–2320) sells the island's traditional crafts. Hours: Monday to Saturday from 9:30 A.M. to 5:30 P.M., and Sunday from 11 A.M. to 5 P.M.

Returning to Calle Fortaleza, walk east. *The Butterfly People* (No. 152, second floor) is an art gallery with an attractive restaurant. *The Bookstore* (255 Calle San José; Tel. 724–1815) has a good selection of books on Puerto Rico in English.

STATE DEPARTMENT (19*) At Calle San José, turn left (north) for a brief stop at the recently restored Department of State, whose interior courtyard is one of the loveliest examples of colonial architecture in San Juan. Note especially the staircase on the right of the entrance. A similar building across the street is the Provincial Deputation Building, so called because it served for eleven days as the headquarters of Puerto Rico's first representative body formed in 1897 when Puerto Rico gained autonomy from Spain. The building is also used by the State Department.

CITY HALL (20) Across Plaza de Armas is City Hall, one of the first important public buildings to be renovated three decades ago, helping to spur other activity in Old San Juan. The building, dating from 1602, has been the site of many important events in Puerto Rico's history, including the abolition of slavery in 1873. Be sure to walk through the building to see the lovely colonnaded rear entrance and stained-glass windows. Guided tours are available for groups but not for individuals. A *Municipal Tourism Information Office* (Tel. 724–7171) is located left of the entrance. Hours: Monday to Friday, 8 A.M. to 4 P.M.

Here on the square you can pick up the trolley to return to the port or walk east 2 blocks to Calle Tanca and head south. The street leads directly to the pier where you started. If you want to continue sight-seeing, continue east on either Calle San Francisco or Calle Fortaleza.

PLAZA COLON (21) The Plaza, dominated by the statue of Christopher Columbus (whose Spanish name is Colon), was erected in 1893 to mark the 400th anniversary of Columbus's discovery of Puerto Rico. Plaza Colon is one of two stations in Old San Juan for taxis and public transportation to all parts of the city; the other terminal (25) is at the port facing the passenger piers.

TAPIA THEATRE (22) On the south side of Plaza Colon is the Tapia Theatre, built early in the last century. It has been renovated many times, but claims to be the oldest theater in continuous use in the Western Hemisphere. The theater has a year-round schedule of concerts and drama. Check *Que Pasa* or the newspaper for performances during your visit (Tel. 722–0407).

OLD CASINO (23*) On the east side of the Plaza is the Old Casino of Puerto Rico, built in 1915 to be the most elegant social hall in the Americas. Unfortunately, the building never had the chance to realize its potential because of the war, and came to be used for many purposes, deteriorating all the while. The building was completely renovated in 1985, and its magnificent drawing rooms restored to their former elegance. It is used mainly by the Department of State of Puerto Rico for special occasions and receptions. Hours: Monday to Friday, 8 A.M. to 4 P.M., when not in use for special events. The building has been renamed the *Manuel Pavia Fernandez Government Reception Center.*

FORT SAN CRISTOBAL (24*) Northeast of Plaza Colon is the entrance to Fort San Cristobal, part of the defense structure begun in 1633 after the city's eastern flank was found vulnerable to capture by land. The impressive fortress is larger than El Morro, with several levels of ramparts, moats, tunnels, and storerooms, and is considered a masterpiece of strategic military design. Like its companion, it is maintained by the U.S. National Park Service. Hours: Daily 8 A.M. to 6 P.M. Orientation is available in English and Spanish.

From Plaza Colon, you can return to your ship by any of the east-west streets, turning south on Calle Tanca or Calle San Justo for the most direct route. Calle Fortaleza ad Calle San Francisco between Plaza Colon and Calle Cristo are the heart of the shopping area. The Goya trolleys run along this route and will take you back to the pier where you started your walk.

 ## SHOPPING

Old San Juan is the best area of the city for shopping. Most of the stores are boutiques and specialty shops; prices cover a very wide range. The Condado hotel area also has a large selection of stores, including branches of Old San Juan shops. San Juan has large, Florida-style shopping centers; the best known, Plaza Las Americas, has 192 shops and is located in Hato Rey, about a 25-minute taxi ride from the pier. For those last minute needs, there's also a *Walgreen's* (Plaza des Armes) in Old San Juan, a short walk from the port.

Art, crafts, clothing, and shoes made on the island, and, of course, rum are the best buys. And remember, on return to the U.S. mainland, there are no customs duties on goods bought in Puerto Rico.

Because passengers on cruises visit ports such as the U.S. Virgin Islands, which are duty-free, it is not surprising that some are confused about Puerto Rico's status as a port. Puerto Rico is NOT a duty-free port. Imported goods such as gold jewelry, Scottish cashmeres, and Italian leather have had the same duties levied on them here as those in New York or Miami. Advertisements for "duty-free" merchandise mean only that you will not have to pay additional tax upon your return home and, of course, you are saved any state and local taxes which you might have to pay at home. Also, sometimes, stores import directly from foreign manufacturers and can realize savings which they pass on to customers. Generally, locally made products are the best buys if you are looking for bargains. There are new duty-free shops at port.

ARTS AND ARTISTS: If you take the Walking Tour of Old San Juan, you will pass several art galleries and will have a chance to discover many fine Puerto Rican and other artists living and working here. All media—oils, watercolors, ceramics, sculpture, photography, and graphic arts—are represented. With the possible exception of a few artists who have achieved international recognition, prices are reasonable. Store hours vary but most are open Monday through Saturday from 9:30 or 10 A.M. to 5:30 or 6 P.M.

Coabey Galleries (101 Calle San José) specializes in international contemporary art. *Fenn Studio/Gallery* (58 Calle San José) is the studio and gallery of artist Patricia Fenn, a painter of the local scene who has lived in Puerto Rico most of her life. The gallery also displays and sells the works of other local artists.

Galeria M. Rivera (107 Calle Cristo) belongs to native son Manuel Rivera, who lived in New York for many years. Rivera makes inexpensive, small Old San Juan houses with the colors and architectural details of the originals you can see on a walk around the Old City. In the past few years, such houses have become commonplace and are available in many souvenir shops.

Galerias Botello (208 Calle Cristo) belonged to the late Angel Botello, one of Puerto Rico's best-known artists who had a very distinctive style; it is now operated by his son. You will enjoy a visit to see the display even if you cannot afford the prices—and no one seems to mind your browsing. The gallery carries other Puerto Rican artists and Haitian paintings of good quality and has another shop in the Plaza Las Americas.

Galeria San Juan (204 Blvd. del Valle; Tel. 722–1808) is as interesting to visit for its ambience as its art collection. It is set in three restored 17th-century buildings that were originally used as a lookout and officer's quarters for the Spanish Artillery.

The gallery is owned by American-born artist Jan D'Esopo, who is known for her Old San Juan street scenes and who has her home, studio, and small inn here as well. In addition to her own paintings, works by young artists are on display. The gallery is open Tuesday through Saturday from 10 A.M. to 5 P.M. The artist organizes and caters private lunches, dinners, and cocktail parties at the gallery too.

The Butterfly People (152 Calle Fortaleza) is a

second-floor art gallery with a pretty restaurant, where all art work on display have butterfly designs.

CIGARS: Cigar stores, along with cigar bars, have proliferated around the city. The closest to the pier is *Cigarros Antillas,* a small shop on the side street facing Pier 3, opposite the new *Wyndham San Juan Hotel.* Here you can watch the Dominican craftsman at work, rolling and pressing tobacco leaves from the Dominican Republic, Honduras, and Equador into shape and purchase the finish product. One cigar costs $2.50; box of 25 cigars costs $55.

CRAFTS: Puerto Rico has dozens of artisans that are encouraged and assisted by the government through Fomento, the Puerto Rico Economic Development Administration, and the Tourism Office. Although on a cruise, time does not permit your seeking out the artisans, those willing to do the spade work in advance and who are planning a pre- or post-cruise visit could conceivably create their own "Craft Tour" of Puerto Rico. Crafts fairs are held frequently in different parts of the city and throughout the island.

Out of the dozens of crafts practiced by local artisans, the carving of *santos,* small wooden figures representing a saint or depicting a religious scene, is considered Puerto Rico's most distinctive craft, and the best *santeros* are held in great esteem. The *santeros'* style and techniques have been passed down from father to son for generations and account for their highly personalized, emotional nature.

The making of musical instruments and masks are two of the oldest crafts. The *cuatro* is a five-double-string instrument that evolved from the Spanish guitar; the *guiro* or gourd comes from a tradition that goes back to the Taino Indians. *Mask-making* stems mainly from Loiza, a town east of San Juan which has maintained its African heritage more than any other place on the island and is famous for its annual feast in July when masks made from coconuts are used. Papier-mâché masks, a tradition from Spain and the Mediterranean, are used during Carnival, particularly in Ponce. *Hammock-making* is another Puerto Rican tradition taught to the early Spaniards

by the Taino Indians. *Mundillo,* handmade bobbin lace, was brought to Puerto Rico by the Spaniards and Portuguese. The fine threads are worked on a frame into bands of lace, collars, handkerchiefs, and tablecloths. Aguadilla in the western part of the island is the center for the craft.

The *National Center for Popular Arts* (253 Cristo Street; Tel. 723–2320) has exhibits of the island's best crafts and a shop. Two stores specializing in Puerto Rican crafts are *Aguadilla en San Juan* (352 Calle San Francisco) and *Puerto Rican Art & Crafts* (204 Calle Fortaleza). The former carries the famous traditional *mundillo* lace and an array of inexpensive but fairly low-quality crafts; the latter store has a more sophisticated selection.

On Calle Fortaleza, a few steps from the corner of Calle Cristo, is a tiny lane, known simply as La Calle, where there are a variety of attractive shops selling jewelry, leather belts and other accessories, masks, and other crafts.

Ole (107 Fortaleza) is crammed full of handcrafts from South America, particularly Ecuador and Peru.

CLOTHING: A *Ralph Lauren* outlet is at the corner of Calle Cristo and San Francisco. *London Fog Factory Outlet* (156 Calle Cristo) has the best bargains of all. Snow and rainwear imperfects (but almost impossible to spot the imperfections) are as much as 50 percent off retail prices; shirts, sweaters, and accessories are also available. *Big Planet* (205 Cristo St.; Tel. 725–1204) carries good quality sports wear, but unlike its sister store on St. John, U.S. Virgin Islands, it does not offer kayaking and other adventure excursions.

T-shirt shops are everywhere. The most attractive shirts have designs adapted from Taino Indian petroglyphs. Hand-painted T-shirt dresses and bathing coverups are also popular.

On Fortaleza between Calle San José and Calle Tanca, there are several shoe stores featuring inexpensive ladies', men's, and children's shoes. Almost always they have racks of sale shoes as well. Dexter Shoes (across the street from The Bookstore) are among those made in Puerto Rico; others are imported from Brazil and Spain.

Guayaberas is a style of embroidered, dressy but informal man's shirt which the Caribbean borrowed from Mexico and the Philippines. They are available in department stores and specialty shops and vary widely in price from $10 to over $100 depending on fabric and quality of the design.

Not to be overlooked are Puerto Rico's designers. Nono Maldonado, a former fashion editor of *Esquire*, is known for the classic, tropical look of the clothes sold from his boutiques on Ashford Avenue in Condado and at the El San Juan Hotel. *Lisa Campelli* (206 Calle O'Donnell, Old San Juan; Tel. 722–5784) is a young designer who creates fun, fresh, funky outfits that are sold in several shops around town.

JEWELRY: Calle Fortaleza has so many jewelry stores, especially for gold, you might think they were giving it away! (A check of stateside prices, however, would convince you they are not.) Some cruise directors and guides direct passengers to certain stores where they have something to gain. The practice is no different here than in countries around the world, so a good dose of skepticism on your part is healthy, particularly if a specific store is recommended to the exclusion of all others. If you have any intention of buying expensive gold jewelry, become familiar with prices at home first, and do not buy in San Juan or any other Caribbean port without first looking around and comparing prices.

Boveda (209 Calle Cristo) features unusual, one-of-a-kind mod jewelry and accessories, dolls, and women's clothing of good design.

LEATHER: Several shops in Old San Juan import leather goods from Colombia. Prices are about the same as those in the United States. *Coach* (158 Calle Cristo; Tel. 722–6830) has a wide selection of fine leather goods from wallets to handbags and briefcases. Most prices are about 20 percent less than those on the mainland, but some are up to 40 percent lower, depending on the item. *Dooney & Bourke* (200 Calle Cristo; Tel. 289–0075), a factory-outlet shop, has similar articles.

SPORTSWEAR: Many shops in Old San Juan and hotel arcades sell moderately priced sportswear, but two standouts for style and quality are *Wet* (150 Calle Cruz) for swim and beachwear; and *Soho* (258 Calle Fortaleza) for handpainted knitwear.

DINING & RESTAURANTS

Puerto Rico has a cuisine of its own which you will be able to enjoy at attractive restaurants set in townhouses of Old San Juan within walking distance of the pier and at specialty restaurants throughout the island. The Puerto Rico Tourism Company publishes a list of over forty *mesones gastronomicos*, which are moderately priced restaurants outside of San Juan that specialize in *cocina criola* (creole cooking), as native cuisine is known, and comply with certain standards.

Traditional Puerto Rican cuisine is a potpourri of the island's Spanish, African, and Taino Indian heritage plus the inventive additions of resourceful people living on a tropical island and other influences that crept in over the centuries through trade and immigration. The Tainos thrived on corn, root vegetables, tropical fruits such as pineapple, and fish, and they taught the early Spaniards how to *barbacoa*, or barbecue, as we know it. One of their dishes which Puerto Ricans still eat is *sancocho*, a thick vegetable and meat stew.

The Spaniards introduced beef, pork, rice, wheat, olive oil, and new spices. Typical Spanish favorites today are *arroz con pollo* (chicken with rice), *asopao* (a hearty gumbo-like soup or stew with chicken or seafood), and flan (custard). With the Africans, who were brought in large numbers as slaves in the early 17th century to replace the decimated Indian population, came such items as okra and taro, known as *yautia* in Puerto Rico. They also added the popular *tostones* (crisp fried flat cakes of green plantains) and *guineos verdes* (boiled green bananas).

Puerto Rican cuisine relies on herbs, savory sauces, and special spice blends. *Sofrito* is a basic seasoning of onions, garlic, peppers, and sometimes ham browned in oil. *Adobo*, a dry marinade made by crushing together peppercorns, oregano, garlic, salt, olive oil, and lime juice or vinegar, is rubbed into meats before they are roasted. *Mojo islena*, a flavorful sauce, is made from slowly cooked onions, tomatoes, olives, chopped garlic, and fresh coriander and is served with fish. *Achiote*, a cooking oil colored with annatto seeds, gives a deep yellow color to rice, stews, and fried dishes.

Lunch or dinner will likely begin with hot appetizers such as *bacalaitos* (crunchy cod fritters), *surullitos de maiz* (cornmeal fingers), and *pastelitos* (half-moon pastry turnovers filled with meat or seafood).

Among the most popular dishes are *mofongo* (plantain pounded with pork rind and served in a mold); *conejo* (rabbit cooked with raisins in port); and *lechon asado* (spit-roasted suckling pig), a traditional Christmas special. Other dishes you might find on the menu are black bean soup; *pionono,* a ripe plantain stuffed with ground beef; *mechada,* stuffed eye of round beef; *pernil,* roast pork; and *arroz con gandures,* rice with pigeon peas.

Not to be overlooked is the bounty from the sea, particularly in restaurants by the seashore where you know the daily catch is fresh. It might include red snapper, squid, conch, and Caribbean lobster, to name a few. A favorite dessert is sliced guava or papaya with white cheese. The island has abundant tropical fruits such as mangos and pineapples.

More recently, a new style of Puerto Rican cuisine has evolved at the hands of young, imaginative Puerto Rican chefs—often foreign trained—as well as foreign chefs working in Puerto Rico, who have taken an interest in native culinary traditions. They have adapted many of the old recipes to new eating trends and created a new Puerto Rican cuisine, *la nueva cocina criolla,* that is lighter and leaner, with less fried food and a lower salt content than was typical in the past. Their efforts have met with enthusiasm from Puerto Ricans and visitors alike. And whatever the style, you will want to finish the meal with a cup of rich and full-bodied Puerto Rican coffee.

OLD SAN JUAN

Amadeus (106 Calle San Sebastian, at San José Plaza) offers its own sophisticated creations based on local products. Moderately expensive.

Cafe Berlin (407 San Francisco/Plaza Colon; Tel. 722–5205), a patisserie and sidewalk cafe with light fare and vegetarian specialties. Great people-watching spot. Moderate.

Il Perugine (105 Calle Cristo; Tel. 722–5481) is a small restaurant of chef/owner Franco

Seccarelli in a lane of smart, trendy shops, serving the best, most stylish Italian haute cuisine in Old San Juan, perhaps in Puerto Rico. Dinner nightly. Reservations suggested. Expensive.

La Mallorquina (207 Calle San Justo; Tel. 722–3261) has been in operation for more than 140 years and claims to be the oldest restaurant in Puerto Rico. Its menu has the most typical of Puerto Rican dishes. It is open Monday through Saturday from 11:30 A.M. to 11 P.M. Moderate.

The Parrot Club (363 Calle Fortaleza; Tel. 725–7370), a new overnight success, offers an eclectic menu inspired by spicy Caribbean cuisine in arty, colorful decor. Moderate for lunch; expensive for dinner.

La Zaragozana (356 Calle San Francisco; Tel. 723–5103) is owned by Spaniards originally from Cuba. Hence, the menu has Cuban, Spanish, and Puerto Rican specialties; black bean soup is a treat. It is open daily from 11:30 A.M. to 1 A.M. Moderately expensive.

For a snack or light meal on your walking or shopping tour, try *El Patio de Sam* (102 Calle San Sebastian); or *The Butterfly People* (152 Calle Fortaleza), where you can dine to the accompaniment of classical music (which was much too loud on my last visit). If you want to try a Puerto Rican breakfast, *La Bombonero* (259 Calle San Francisco; no phone) is the cognoscenti's mecca for rich Puerto Rican coffee and *pan de Mallorca,* a melt-in-your-mouth pastry.

CONDADO AND BEYOND

Aquarella (El San Juan Hotel; Tel. 791–1000). The new venture of Doug Rodriguez of New York's *Patria* and Miami's *Yuca* fame replaced the hotel's *Bar Tiffany,* and no ordinary hotel restaurant this. Stunning, ultra-modern, understated decor provides the right setting for the chef's wide ranging unorthodox creations that emphasize seafood and South American dishes with Pacific Rim touches. Very expensive.

Augusto's Cuisine (Excelsior Hotel, Miramar; Tel. 725–7700) is headed by the former executive chef of the Caribe Hilton, August Schreiner, who creates his own European-inspired specialties. Expensive.

Chayote (603 Avenida Miramar, Olimpio Court Hotel; Tel. 722–9385) features chef Alfredo Ayala's Caribbean cuisine inspirations, which use fresh local fruits, vegetables, and fish. Expensive.

Cobia (Condado Plaza Hotel, 999 Ashford Avenue, Lagoon Annex; Tel. 721–1000). Seafood lovers will do themselves a favor if they try this new San Juan addition. Select from a great variety of fish and have it prepared to order: baked, broiled, blackened, brochette, grilled, steamed, fried, or as you like. If you can't decide on one fish, you can have a medley, each prepared a different way. Expensive.

Compostela (106 Avenue Condado, Santurce; Tel. 724–6088) is often named by San Juan's movers and shakers as the best in the city for classic Spanish cuisine. The attractive, sophisticated decor of its new location matches the superior quality of the food and impeccable service by tuxedoed waiters. Lunch and dinner daily except Sunday. Expensive.

Pescaderia Atlantica (2475 Calle Loiza, Atlantic View/Isla Verda; Tel. 728–5440) is located next to a fish market, ensuring fresh seafood. It has a casual setting, popular with local businessmen. Valet parking. Moderately expensive. Its sister restaurant *Puerta de Tierra* (7 Calle Luap Vina; Tel. 722–0890) is located at the eastern entrance to Old San Juan.

Pikayo (1 Joffre St., Condado; Tel. 724–4160). Situated in the Tanama Princess Hotel, the restaurant with contemporary decor is tops with fans of chef and television personality Wilo Benet. Benet, a graduate of the Culinary Institute of America and director of its Puerto Rico program, is also a former chef to the governor of Puerto Rico. He considers it his mission to develop a contemporary Puerto Rican cuisine and is known for his innovative dishes that fuse French and Californian with Caribbean creole cuisine.

Ramiro's (1106 Magdalena Avenue; Tel. 721–9049) is one of the city's leading gourmet restaurants, on par with top restaurants in New York. Set in a house in the Condado area, the restaurant features classic recipes along with its own creations, which are best described as nouvelle Puerto Rican cuisine—*la nueva cocina criolla*—inspired by fresh local ingredients and their traditional uses with a creative flair. Lunch and dinner daily. Expensive. Reservations required.

Yamato (El San Juan Hotel; Tel. 791–8152). You'll not find fresher, better sushi and sashimi in Tokyo than here in this quiet oasis. There's also a wide selection of other Japanese dishes, all excellent and expensive.

San Juan also has Argentinian, Chinese, French, Italian, Mexican, Middle Eastern, and Swiss restaurants as well as the well-known American fast food chains and a New York deli. For variety, the Condado area is best. Details are available in *Que Pasa*.

 **SPORTS**

Puerto Rico has some of the best sports facilities in the Caribbean, in or near enough to San Juan for cruise passengers to use them with relative ease. You should contact the hotel or sports operator in advance to make arrangements, particularly during the peak season when demand is likely to be high.

BEACHES/SWIMMING: In Puerto Rico, all beaches are public, including hotel beaches. Public beaches operated by the government or municipality have *balneario* facilities (lockers, showers, and parking) at nominal rates; they are open daily, except Monday, from 9 A.M. to 5 P.M. during winter and from 8 A.M. to 6 P.M. in summer.

Hotels on or near *Condado Beach* are the closest to the port: the *Caribe Hilton* and *Condado Plaza* are the most popular. *Isla Verde Beach,* where The Sands and *El San Juan Hotel* are located, is 6 miles west of the port and 1 mile from the airport. The beachfront *El San Juan*, a famous pleasure palace of the 1960s which fell on hard times, reopened in 1986 after a complete renovation by its new owners. It's worth a visit. Next door, the *Sands Beach Hotel and Casino* has a beach and swimming pool garden setting that's right out of a Hollywood movie set.

DEEP-SEA FISHING: Clean, deep water only 20 to 30 minutes from shore is just one reason San Juan is one of the favorite sportfishing spots of the world. Fish are abundant and world records are set and broken in these waters year after year. Half- or full-day and split-boat charters with crew and equipment are readily available from these operators; expect to pay about $400 and up for a half day and $600 and up for a full day for up to six people.

Benitez Fishing Charters (Club Nautico San Juan, Miramar; or P.O. Box 5141, Puerta de Tierra, San Juan 00906; Tel. 723–2292). 53-foot custom-built fishing yacht. Also, daily harbor wine and cheese sunset cruises, 5 to 7 P.M.

Castillo Watersports (ESJ Towers, Isla Verde; Tel. 791–6195). Half- and full-day and split-boat charters; small and big-game fishing. Also offers sailing and dive trips and snorkeling and dive instructions.

GOLF: The classic quartet of Robert Trent Jones 18-hole championship courses at *Hyatt Regency Cerromar Beach* (Tel. 796–1234) and *Hyatt Dorado Beach* (Tel. 796–1234) are not only among the best in the Caribbean but in the world. Located at Dorado 15 miles west of San Juan, these courses are famous for their layouts and spectacularly beautiful natural settings. Pro shop, clubhouse, and restaurants are excellent. You would be wise to book a reservation in advance, particularly in high season. Greens fees are $53 for hotel guests and $115 at Dorado and $85 at Cerromar for visitors, plus a fee for carts, depending on season.

Westin Rio Mar Resort and Country Club (Tel. 888–6000), a resort east of San Juan (a 40-minute drive from the port), has villas designed by Edward Durell Stone and two 18-hole courses: one designed by George Fazio; and a new one by Greg Norman, his first in the Caribbean. Both are dotted with lakes and have the El Yunque mountains as a backdrop and a palm-fringed beach as the foreground.

Wyndham Palmas del Mar in Humacao on the southeast coast has a lovely, 18-hole Gary Player resort course laid out on palm-lined rolling terrain with mountain scenery in the background. The clubhouse has an open-air restaurant overlooking the greens and a pro shop. The drive is about an hour from the city, depending on traffic.

The 18-hole championship course at the fabulous *El Conquistador Hotel Resort and Country Club* is located on the east coast near Fajardo.

HIKING: The best trails are available at the Caribbean National Forest, better known as El Yunque, and range from an easy 15-minute walk to more difficult 2- and 3-hour hikes. El Toro, the

highest peak, is an arduous 8-hour trek. Information and maps are available from *El Portal* (Tel. 888–1810), the new visitors and interpretive center opened in 1996. Hours: Daily 9 A.M. to 5 P.M. Admission: $3 adults; $1.50 senior and children under 12. Some cruise lines have recently added hiking in El Yunque as a shore excursion sold aboard ship. Along with hiking, local specialized tour companies such as *Adventours* (Tel./fax 881–6447), *Copladet Nature and Adventure Tours* (Tel./fax 765–8595), *Explora* (Tel. 751–9647; fax 250–1998), and others, offer biking, birding, spelunking, kayaking and a host of other adventure and nature-oriented excursions. See section, "El Yunque," for more information.

HORSEBACK RIDING: East of San Juan near Luquillo Beach, *Hacienda Carabali* (Tel. 889–5820) offers group riding along the coast and foothills of El Yunque rain forest. You must call in advance when you are going on your own. There is no organized transportation; you will need to engage a taxi for the round-trip, rent a car, or use a *publico* (shared taxi) from Pier One. A practical alternative is an excursion which leaves on several days each week from the Caribe Hilton and El San Juan Hotel. Recently, too, some cruise lines have added horseback riding as a shore excursion sold aboard ship.

KAYAKING: Kayaks are available at the *Condado Plaza Hotel* water-sports center where they can be rented by the hour, and from specialized tour companies (see Hiking above).

SCUBA AND SNORKELING: Puerto Rico's best snorkeling and diving are found on the east coast around the tiny coral-fringed islands like Icacos and Palominitos facing Fajardo. Boats operated by water sports centers at resort hotels depart daily for these locations from Fajardo and San Juan. Equipment is available for rent for certified divers, and the centers offer diving courses to obtain certification. *Barefoot III*, a 46-foot catamaran, runs a full-day picnic sail with snorkeling from Fajardo to Icacos for $55 per person (Tel. 791–6195). *Spread Eagle*, a 40-foot catamaran, has a similar excursion for $55 departing from Fajardo at 10 A.M.; transportation from San Juan can be arranged (Tel. 863–1905). Other excursions are listed in *Que Pasa*.

Caribe Aquatic Adventures (San Juan Bay Marina, Miramar; Tel. 729–2929 ext. 240) is one of the oldest dive operations on the island and a member of the Puerto Rico Water Sport Federation. It has daily excursions for novices as well as experienced divers and can also arrange kayaking, sailing, windsurfing, and other water sports. For information write: C.A.A., Box 1872, San Juan, Puerto Rico, 00903. *Mundo Submarino* (Laguna Gardens, Isla Verde; Tel. 791–5764) offers trips and instruction including underwater photography. *San Juan Water Sports* (Condado Plaza Hotel; Tel. 721–1000) offers snorkeling, diving instruction and trips, sailing, and fishing.

Puerto Rico's newest dive location, dubbed the Puerto Rico Wall (and as exciting for divers as the Cayman Wall), is off the south coast at La Parguera, already famous for its bioluminescent bay. Several miles offshore, the continental shelf drops and extends for approximately 20 miles out to sea. The wall, thickly encrusted with a great variety of corals and teeming with marine life, descends in slopes and sheer drops ranging between 60 to 120 feet before disappearing into the depths of the sea. Other popular diving and snorkeling locations are the islands of Vieques and Culebra.

TENNIS: Courts and full-time pros are available at more than a dozen San Juan hotels. Those nearest the port are *Caribe Hilton*, six courts with night lights; *Condado Beach* and *Condado Plaza*, each with two courts. *El San Juan Hotel* (Isla Verde) has three courts, while nearby, the new *Ritz-Carlton* (scheduled to open in early 1998) has two night-lit courts.

Hyatt Regency Cerromar Beach (15 miles west of San Juan at Dorado; Tel. 796–1234) has fourteen Decoralt courts, some with lights; fee $15 per court per hour in daytime, $18 at night. Next door, the *Hyatt Dorado Beach* (Tel. 796–1234) has seven Laykold courts. The program is operated by Peter Burwash International.

San Juan Central Park (Cerra Street; Tel. 722–1646) has 17 public courts with night lighting. Open daily. For those planning an extended stay, *Wyndham Palmas del Mar* at Humacao on the southeast coast has the largest layout in Puerto Rico with twenty courts.

SURFING AND SAILBOARDING: Every beachfront hotel, particularly on the north coast, offers sailboarding, and the Hyatt hotels in Dorado even have a sailboarding school. Less known to most people is that Puerto Rico is a popular location for surfing, particularly on the northwest coast. Twice, Rincon has been the setting of the Annual World Championships.

SPECTATOR SPORTS

Puerto Rico is a sports island for spectators as well as players. Baseball fans already know the names on the roster of Puerto Rican greats, and fans here are every bit as passionate about the game as their stateside counterparts .

BASEBALL In the winter season all eight of the local professional teams have major league players in their lineups. (Each team is allowed six major league players for the season.) The season begins in October after the World Series and lasts through January, when Puerto Rico holds its own playoffs and competes in the Caribbean Series. Games are played at night at San Juan-Santurce Stadium, which seats 25,000. Check newspapers or call the Professional Baseball League of Puerto Rico (Tel. 765–6285) or write P.O. Box 1852, Hato Rey, San Juan 00919, for a schedule.

COCKFIGHTS One of Puerto Rico's most popular sports, cockfighting, is held on Saturdays from 1 to 7 P.M. at Club Gallistico, Isla Verde (Tel. 791–1557).

RACING Horse races are held on Wednesday, Friday, Sunday, and holidays at El Commandante (Tel. 724–6060), one of the most beautiful race tracks in the Americas. Starting time is 2:30 P.M.; Wednesday is ladies' day. Buses leave from Plaza Colon timed for the starting race and return according to the racing schedule.

PASO FINO Horse shows are popular too and are often held when a village celebrates a saint's day or festival. The local breed, Paso Fino, is a small spirited horse noted for its gait. The annual *Dulce Sueño* is a Paso Fino horse show held in early March in the coastal town of Guayama, 40 miles south of San Juan; the Paso Fino Horse Show in San Juan takes place in November and is one of several competitions held in the area of the capital; check *Que Pasa* and local newspapers.

ENTERTAINMENT

CULTURAL EVENTS

Puerto Rico has a full calendar of seasonal concerts by the Puerto Rico Symphony Orchestra, the San Juan Opera Company, several ballet and theater groups, Broadway productions, and performances by visiting artists. Most are given at the new *Fine Arts Center (El Centro de Bellas Artes)*, which is also known as the Performing Arts Center. The multi-auditorium center is the best-equipped facility in the Caribbean. Another venue for the performing arts is the *Tapia Theatre*, reputed to be the oldest theatre in the Western Hemisphere.

The year starts with the *Arts Festival of San Sebastian* in January, *Carnival* is in February or March, followed by the *Puerto Rican Music Festival* in May and June, and the *Casals Festival of the Performing Arts* in June, which is the year's biggest cultural event. The *Summer Arts Festival*, which provides free entertainment on Sunday afternoons on the grounds of El Morro, runs from August to October; and the Interamerican Arts Festival is held annually at the Fine Arts Center in September and October.

LeLoLai Festival performances highlighting the country's folklore with song, dance, and crafts are staged at participating hotels. The festival, sponsored by the Puerto Rico Tourism Company, is available to cruise passengers as part of their shore excursions. Each show has a different theme reflecting the island's rich heritage, which is a blend of Spanish, African, and Taino Indian cultures.

Tickets and information are available by phone (Tel. 723–3135) from the festival office (Condado Convention Center, Ashford Avenue, Condado) open Monday to Friday, 9 A.M. to 5 P.M.

NIGHTLIFE

If you are eager to check out the nightlife, you have a choice of small bars with Spanish guitars or jazz in the Old City, and there's even a *Hard Rock Cafe* with a cigar bar! Or, you can take in nightclubs, discotheques, big-name cabarets, and casinos, most centered in or near large hotels in the Condado or Isla Verde areas.

Some of the liveliest action is at lobby bars which have combos playing salsa and other Latin and disco beats. *La Fiesta Lounge* in the newly renovated lobby of the Condado Plaza is an experience no salsa lover should miss. The action gets underway at 5 P.M. and goes to the wee hours. The hotel's newest addition is a sophisticated nightclub where the music is quiet enough for conversation.

Small-scale and low-key in Old San Juan is *Le Bistrot de San Juan* (152 Calle Cruz; Tel. 724–1198), the place to hear jazz nightly except Sunday and enjoy an open jam session on Wednesday. Among the other night spots with jazz are *Cafe Matisse* (Ashford Avenue, Condado; Tel. 723–7910) where jazz is featured on Wednesday evenings and blues on Fridays; and *Vivas* (Condado Beach Hotel; Tel. 721–6090) where jazz with a Latin flavor can be enjoyed on Friday and Saturday nights.

The *Caribe Supper Club* (Caribe Hilton) has big-name entertainers, and its *Juliana's* is the leading discotheque in the city—and packed on the weekends. It is followed closely by the disco at the *El San Juan Hotel*, particularly for the under-25 crowd. For everyone else, the hotel has the city's largest selection of nightlife from the rooftop *Tequila Bar and Grill* where sunset views over the city and sea are as fabulous as the margaritas, to the nightclub with headliner entertainment, to the lobby bar that offers the best people-watching spot in town. Never a place to let a new fad pass by, the El San Juan Hotel's *Cigar Bar* wins the blue ribbon for elegance and panache. Situated by the entrance to the casino, the clubby corner has as a backdrop, a wall of private humidors, which can be rented for $1,250 per year.

Closer to the port, the Condado Convention Center (Tel. 722–8433) offers "Ole Latino," a Latin American musical revue, which is often included on "San Juan-by-Night" cruise ships' shore excursions. In the same complex, *Red* (Tel. 722–5430) is an entertainment center with a dance floor, game room, sports and cigar bar, and cafe. Special entertainment, such as Spanish rock on Sunday, is featured most nights.

GAMBLING CASINOS

All San Juan casinos are in hotels and some, such as the *Condado Plaza* and *El San Juan*, are practically in the lobby. These two also happen to be among the most popular. In San Juan and vicinity, casinos are found at the *Ambassador Plaza*, Tel. 721–7300; *Caribe Hilton*, Tel. 721–0303; *Condado Plaza*, Tel. 721–1000; *Dutch Inn and Tower*, Tel. 721–0810; *El San Juan Hotel*, Tel. 791–1000; *Hyatt Dorado Beach*, Tel. 796–1234; *Hyatt Regency Cerromar Beach*, Tel. 796–1234; *Condado San Juan*, Tel. 724–5657; and *Sands Beach Hotel and Casino, San Juan*, Tel. 791–6100.

FESTIVALS AND CELEBRATIONS

The exact dates for most festivals and celebrations change each year. Consult the quarterly tourist publication, *Que Pasa*, for special events during your visit. Also, see "Fast Facts" for public holidays.

JANUARY: 6, Three Kings' Day, when the governor holds a party for children on the grounds of El Morro and La Fortaleza, as do mayors in their municipalities throughout the country. Two weeks in mid-January, San Sebastian Street Arts Festival; Puppet Theatre Festival (Old San Juan); Artisan and Troubadours Festival (Bayamon).

FEBRUARY: Carnival (date according to Lenten observation); Coffee Festival (Yauco and Maricao). Ponce has the biggest celebration.

MARCH: Annual Orchid Show (San Juan and Ponce); annual "Dulce Sueño" Paso Fino Horse Fair (Guayana). Crafts Fair (Ponce and Cayey).

APRIL: Holy Week (sometimes in March) with religious processions through streets of all towns on Good Friday at 3 P.M.; Tropiflora (Roberto Clemente Coliseum).

MAY: Semana de la Danza (Dominican Convent, Old San Juan); Puerto Rico Theatre Festival (Tapia Theatre); Puerto Rico Weaving Festival (Isabela and Cabo Rojo); Annual Music Festival (Dominican Convent, Old San Juan).

JUNE: Aibonito Flower Festival; Casals Festival, held in San Juan, Ponce, Mayaguez, and other locales; San Juan Bautista Day, the capital's patron saint's day, is a ten-day festival culminating on the eve of June 23 at midnight and celebrated throughout the island.

JULY: 13–17, National Crafts Fair (Barranquitas); 19–28, Festival de Loiza Aldea.

AUGUST–OCTOBER: Summer Arts Festival; late August, International Billfish Tournament.

SEPTEMBER: Opening of season for Puerto Rico Symphony; Annual Copa de Palmas Sailing Regatta; Interamerican Arts Festival (Fine Arts Center).

OCTOBER: Bomba y Plena Festival (Ponce); October–November, Annual Ceramic Festival; International Theatre Festival.

NOVEMBER: 15–18, Yuca Festival (Coamo); mid-November, World Paso Fino Horse Show; Jayuya Indian Festival (Jayuya); November 18–December 2, Festival of Puerto Rican Music; late November, International Women's Marathon (Ponce); 28–30, Thanksgiving Day and weekend; Palmas del Mar Deep Sea Fishing Tournament.

DECEMBER: 1–8, Bacardi Arts Festival (Catano); early December, Crafts Fair (Mayaguez); December 15–January 6, Navidades. The festivities continue through to the weekend after January 6. The entire period (i.e., eight days of celebration) is called Octavistas. One of the most colorful festivals is the annual Innocents' Day in Hatillo, December 27–28, highlighted by a parade of masqueraders in fabulous costume.

SAN JUAN'S ENVIRONS AND EAST

CATAÑO AND PALO SECO

Across the bay from San Juan in Cataño is the home of the *Bacardi Rum Distillery*, the largest single producer of rum in the world. On a free 45-minute tour conducted by Bacardi guides you are driven around the distillery's manicured grounds and taken through its modern plant, where the rum-making process is explained. You may also visit its museum and shop.

About a mile or so from the distillery is the tiny fishing village of Palo Seco noted for its waterfront seafood restaurants. Each has a fresh fish specialty and a loyal clientele. An easy way to start an argument is to ask devotees which restaurant is the best. It's difficult to recommend one over the others. That would be like asking someone if he preferred lobster or shrimp. The restaurants are side by side along the road. Take a look and decide on the spot. Prices are reasonable. Southwest of Palo Seco there are beaches which, though not San Juan's best, are unpopulated on weekdays and have a lovely view looking back at El Morro and Old San Juan.

FERRY SERVICE The Agua Express for Cataño departs every half-hour from 6 A.M. to 9 P.M. from a dock by Pier Two. The ride takes only a few minutes. At the landing on the opposite side of the bay, *publicos* (shared minibuses) to the Bacardi Rum Distillery are available. From the factory, you can take a *publico* or taxi to Palo Seco, if you do not want to walk. To return to the ferry landing, take a *publico* or ask the restaurant where you have lunch to call a taxi.

BOTANIC GARDENS

In the San Juan suburb of Rio Piedras, about a 30-minute drive from the port, is the Agricultural Experiment Station Botanical Garden, which belongs to the University of Puerto Rico, and the Institute of Tropical Forestry, which is part of the U.S. Forest Service. Spanning both sides of a stream and a series of ponds, the gardens cover an area of 270 acres, 45 of which are developed in a park setting, providing an oasis in this sprawling city and a delightful introduction to the enormous variety of flowers, trees, and other vegetation of Puerto Rico and the Caribbean.

Along tree-shaded walkways you can see native trees such as the *ausubo,* a strong termite-proof wood used for house beams, and the Puerto Rican royal palm. A palmetum near the main entrance with 125 species, thousands of orchids,

a bamboo grove, and a chapel are highlights. In addition to the many kinds of trees common to the Caribbean, the gardens have tropical fruit trees and herbs from around the world.

Two libraries, among the best in the hemisphere, are housed here: one belongs to the institute which conducts research on tropical flora and wildlife; the other is for tropical agriculture. Both are open to the public on weekdays. The garden is open Tuesday to Sunday from 9 A.M. to 4:30 P.M. and on Monday holidays (followed by Tuesday closings). At Casa Rosada (Tel. 766–0740), the headquarters building, an orientation and a leaflet guide in Spanish is available.

GARDEN OF SAN JUAN

The most imaginative of all the projects inaugurated to mark Puerto Rico's 500th anniversary in 1993 is the scheme to create an 11-mile linear "Central Park" through the heart of the city, stretching from the Luis Muñoz Rivera Park, between Old San Juan and Miramar on the north, to the Botanic Gardens on the south. The ten-year, $10 million Garden of San Juan will link the city's existing parks by ribbons of green space into one long, continuous park that snakes through urban areas, creating a traffic-free pedestrian path and jogging and biking trail.

The existing parks are being renovated and embellished with sculptures, fountains, and recreational facilities, and the connecting green ribbons lighted. Basically, though, the architects are working with what is already in place—integrating open spaces and enlisting local businesses and residents to create focal points.

The first section, Luis Muñoz Rivera Park at the north entrance just west of Old San Juan, has been completed. Its focus is a 55-foot-high stainless steel sculpture designed by Puerto Rican artist Pablo Rubio and dedicated to Puerto Rico's 500th anniversary. The sculpture, set next to a large bronze compass, is composed of three steel sails representing Columbus's ships; each sail turns on its own axis in the wind.

PIÑONES AND ESPIRITU SANTO

A few miles east of Isla Verde, a paved road on a strip of land between the ocean and the Piñones marshes winds through 6 miles of old coconut plantation and skirts uninterrupted beach. Slightly farther east, the Espiritu Santo, the only navigable river in Puerto Rico, tumbles down the El Yunque mountains through rocky ravines to empty into the Atlantic Ocean. Near the town of Rio Grande, the river flows gently into marshland where the water is navigable. Kayaks are available from a mooring at Km. 25.2 off Route 3, the main east-west artery, for trips along a pretty stretch of the river that passes through mangroves down to the mouth of the river on the Atlantic. You can see water birds and even an occasional native Puerto Rican woodpecker.

EL YUNQUE

In the Luquillo Mountains, about 30 minutes east of San Juan, is the Caribbean National Forest more commonly known as El Yunque, the only tropical rain forest in the U.S. Forest Service system. Long a research center on tropical flora and fauna, El Yunque has 240 species of trees, more than 200 types of fern, and sixty species of birds. One of the most important projects undertaken here has been the effort to save the Puerto Rican parrot, decimated from an estimated one million birds at the time of Columbus to only 22 in 1975. Now the bird's numbers are slowly being rebuilt.

El Yunque has a recreation area with well-defined and maintained trails. La Mina/Big Tree Trail, a paved path leading to La Mina Falls, takes about an hour, round-trip. It runs along the Mina River, which has small pools of water created by large rocks that have tumbled down from the surrounding mountains, and passes through a forest of stately *tabonuco* trees, one of the four types of forest found in the reserve. Named for a common native tree and containing the greatest variety of plants and trees, this forest grows on lower elevations and most closely resembles the rain forests found in other parts of tropical America.

El Yunque Trail, a steeper path of three hours, leads through *palo colorado* to cloud-thick dwarf forest, two types of forest found at higher elevations. Typically, trees are shorter and thick with mosses and surrounded by dense undergrowth. Tree ferns which look like lacy parasols add to the trail's exotic beauty. Sierra or cabbage palm, a type of forest that grows on steep slopes and gulleys, provides another distinctive element in the lush appearance of the forest. On clear days there are splendid views down the north slopes to the Atlantic coast from lookouts on the trail.

Longer and more difficult trails are El Toro/Tradewinds Trail, a six-mile trek to 3,532-foot El Toro, the highest peak in El Yunque; and La Coca Trail, which crosses several streams on its way to remote pools and waterfalls.

You can also drive through El Yunque on a tarmac road (No. 191) into the heart of the rain forest and pass waterfalls, lookouts, and picnic areas. After the turnoff from the main highway (Route 3) onto Route 191, you should drive about 5 miles to *El Portal* (Tel. 888–1810) the new interpretive and visitor's center, where exhibits on the rain forest can be seen and maps and information are available. Hours: Daily 9 A.M. to 5 P.M. Admission: $3 adults; $1.50 senior and children under 12. There is also a bookstore and gift shop. Look for *Where Dwarfs Reign: A Tropical Rain Forest in Puerto Rico* by Kathryn Robinson (University of Puerto Rico Press, 1997). Written in readable layman language, it is the most comprehensive book available on El Yunque.

For tour companies that specialize in nature-oriented excursions and offer hiking in El Yunque, see the Sports section in this chapter.

In a day's outing, it is easy to combine a visit to El Yunque with a stop at Luquillo Beach, a beautiful stretch of palm-fringed sand that sweeps around a perfect crest of tranquil waters at the foot of the El Yunque mountains. It is the island's most popular *balneario,* or public beach, and is crowded on weekends.

LAS CABEZAS DE SAN JUAN NATURE PARK

One of Puerto Rico's newest attractions, Las Cabezas de San Juan Nature Park, is a 316-acre nature reserve located on a peninsula on the northeast corner of the island, north of Fajaro. A stop here can also be combined with a visit to El Yunque. Created by the Conservation Trust of Puerto Rico, the reserve covers mangroves, coastal forests, cliffs, a phosphorescent lagoon, scenic beaches, and coral reefs. There are walkways through the mangroves and brochures for self-guided hikes; the beach is very popular with local people on weekends.

The park is marked by a 19th-century lighthouse, El Faro, on a hill above the reserve. Built in 1880 in the neoclassical style by the Spanish colonial government, El Faro has been renovated and serves as the visitor's center. It has a nature exhibit and an observation deck, from which you can enjoy majestic views with El Yunque's rainforested slopes in the background, the Nature Park and the Icacos islets in the foreground. On a clear day, the expansive seaviews can stretch as far as the Virgin Islands.

FAJARDO: South of the reserve on the coast is Fajardo, home to Puerto Rico's largest marina and an occasional port of call for small cruise ships. Nearby is *El Conquistador Resort, Casino and Golf Club,* a large, elaborate resort with a championship golf course and excellent tennis and water-sports facilities.

A DRIVE WEST OF SAN JUAN

RIO CAMUY CAVE PARK

Opened in 1986, the Rio Camuy Cave Park, with a surface area of 268 acres, is a showcase of Puerto Rico's elaborate network of caves and tropical karst terrain that pockmark the island. Of the 220 caves which have been documented, the Camuy Caves are the largest. Seven miles of passageways have been explored, including chambers as high as a 25-story building. The Camuy River, the third largest underground river in the world, passes through the complex system.

Cueva Clara de Empalne, the first of a series of chambers opened to the public, was followed in 1989 by Tres Pueblos Sinkhole, which measures 650 feet in diameter and 400 feet deep—large enough to contain all of El Morro Fortress. It takes its name from the three municipality borders—Camuy, Hatillo, and Lares—that it touches.

At the visitor's center you will find a film that provides an orientation and literature that illustrates and describes the cave system. Here, too,

visitors accompanied by knowledgeable bilingual guides board a tram for the tour. The tram winds through a ravine with rain forest vegetation to the first of several chambers where passengers begin a 45-minute walk. The room is illuminated by natural light that penetrates the entrance and is 200 feet wide and 700 feet long with a 170-foot-high ceiling with stalactites. It leads to another huge chamber, tall enough to hold a 17-foot-high stalagmite—the largest known in the island. The walk continues to another gallery with a pool which reflects the 400-foot walls of a sinkhole rising above it. From here, the trail goes up stairs and down along a winding path from which the Camuy River, 150 feet below, comes into view.

In addition to these chambers, others are to be added in the future. The park is open Wednesday to Sunday; Tel. 898–3100. From Old San Juan, it is about a 2-hour drive west via Arecibo and inland on Route 129. In the town of Camuy, do not be misled by a sign to "La Cueva de Camuy." This is a small, private cave, not the government park.

ARECIBO OBSERVATORY

Nearby, the Arecibo Observatory is the largest radar/radio telescope in the world—a 20-acre dish set in a sinkhole equal in size to thirteen football fields—where scientists listen for signs of intelligent life in the universe and many exciting discoveries have been made. They include the mapping of one of the largest structures in the universe—a cluster of galaxies—and observations from which scientists determined the true rotation of the planet Mercury. Here, too, the first planets outside the solar system were found; and the first evidence of the existence of gravitational waves was uncovered, the latter lead to the Nobel Prize in Physics for scientists Joe Taylor and Russell Hulse.

Operated by Cornell University, the observatory has a wonderful new visitor's center, the *Arecibo Observatory Visitor and Educational Facility,* which opened in 1997. It makes the research being undertaken here more accessible, understandable, and interesting to the non-scientific community. The new building houses interactive exhibits, a theater, meeting rooms, work space, and a science-related book and gift shop. A variety of exhibits and video displays in English and

Spanish introduce visitors to the basics of astronomy, the radio telescope, and more. A second level is devoted to the work being done at Arecibo. Hours: Wednesday to Friday, noon to 4 P.M.; weekends and holidays, 9 A.M. to 4 P.M. Admission: $3.50 for adults; $1.50, seniors, students, children under 12.

Deeper in the mountains, near Utuado, the Caguana Indian Ceremonial Park preserves a recreational and ceremonial site of the Taino Indians, the inhabitants of Puerto Rico at the time of Columbus. Stones with petroglyphs line some of the ten courts outlined on the 13-acre grounds, and there is a small museum.

CORDILLERA CENTRAL AND PANORAMIC ROUTE

Crossing the center of Puerto Rico, dividing the north and south coasts, is a spine of tall green mountains, Cordillera Central, whose peaks are often concealed by clouds. The Panoramic Route, a 165-mile road made up of forty different routes, winds its way through the mountains from Yabucoa on the southeast to Mayaguez on the west coast and provides spectacular panoramas through forest reserves and rural landscapes, light-years away from the bustle and glitter of San Juan. The route divides easily into three sections, each needing a day to cover with stops along the way. There are hiking trails, picnic areas, a natural spring-fed swimming hole, and man-made lakes that are part of the system created in the 1930s to harness the island's water resources.

SAN CRISTOBAL CANYON

The central section, starting at Cayey on the main highway between San Juan and Ponce, is the most picturesque and passes through villages and rolling hills on its way to the island's highest peaks. Between Albonito and Barranquitas lies San Cristobal Canyon, the island's deepest gorge. Roads skirt the canyon and provide views; steep

paths for agile hikers lead to the canyon floor and a 100-foot waterfall, the highest on the island.

TORO NEGRO FOREST RESERVE

Almost in the center of the island is the 7,000-acre Toro Negro Forest Reserve containing the Cordillera Central's tallest peaks. Lake Guineo, the island's highest lake, is near Divisoria where Route 143 crosses Route 149, a scenic cross-island road that winds through the densely forested mountains. Farther west on Route 143 a short, very steep paved spur leads up 4,390-foot Cerro de Punta, Puerto Rico's highest peak. Here, on a clear day, you can have a grand panorama of the island from the Atlantic on the north to the Caribbean Sea on the south. The walk takes about 20 minutes.

 # PONCE

THE DESTINATION OF TOMORROW

Ponce, Puerto Rico's second largest city, earned the title of "Pearl of the South" in the late 19th century during its heyday as the center of the sugar, rum, and shipping industries. An intellectual center as well, Ponce was home to many of Puerto Rico's most famous poets, artists, and politicians. But today, this jewel on Puerto Rico's south coast might be called the best-kept secret in the Caribbean.

A treasurehouse of architecture, Ponce's streets are lined with colonial houses whose balconies and wrought iron railings are reminiscent of Savannah and New Orleans; turn-of-the-century Victorian gems with gingerbread trim similar to houses in Key West; and others built in the art deco style of the 1930s and 1940s.

After half a billion dollars' worth of renovations to restore Ponce's lustre and a celebration of the city's 300th anniversary in December 1992, the city nurtures the hopes of becoming the "Destination of Tomorrow." The addition of the Ponce Hilton International by the sea at La Guancha and of American Airlines service between Miami and Ponce should make it easier for others to discover the secret, too. The improvements—among the most comprehensive ever undertaken in the Caribbean—range from the restoration of historic buildings to the construction of new roads, schools, and hospitals to the creation of parks and improvement of the port. But the main focus was the National Historic Zone, a 66-block area in the heart of the old city where 1,046 buildings—more than half of them private homes—constitute an architectural treasure of unusual diversity. Along with the renovation of the area came beautification of the streets: telephone and power lines were buried, 19th-century gas lamp replicas added as street lights, and pedestrian walkways paved with cobblestones and pink marble.

Ponce was founded in 1692 by a great-grand-son of Ponce de León, for whom it was named. But from the Amerindian artifacts found in the vicinity, we know that the site was inhabited from ancient times. Although Ponce was once a major port, the town is not oriented toward the sea. Rather, its heart is a typical Spanish colonial square dominated by a cathedral and bound by streets laid out in a grid. These streets are lined with townhouses built mostly in the late 19th and early 20th centuries, when Ponce enjoyed great prosperity, by plantation owners and wealthy merchants who, in something of a keeping-up-with-the-Joneses mentality, engaged the most prominent architects of their day. Today, a walk along these tree-lined streets is like a tour through the architectural history of the Americas, where six styles—Spanish colonial, New Spain Revival, Ponce Crillo, neo-classic, art nouveau, and art deco—can be seen within only a few blocks.

A WALKING TOUR OF PONCE

PLAZA LAS DELICIAS (1) Shaded by large Indian laurels, cooled by fountains, and brightened with tropical flowers, the central square has two sections: Muñoz Rivera Plaza on the north, named for Luis Muñoz Rivera, a prominent statesman whose statue is here; and Degetau Plaza, the south section, with a fountain from the New York World's Fair, placed here in 1939. The fountain is decorated with

recumbent lions—the symbol of Ponce. There is also a monument to the composer Juan Morel Campos, the father of the "danza," one of Puerto Rico's main folk dances, which is celebrated in an annual festival. The west side of the plaza has the Cathedral of Our Lady of Guadalupe, built in the last century on the site of a 17th-century chapel and named for Ponce's patron saint.

OLD FIREHOUSE On the east side of the main square—you can't miss it—is the Old Firehouse (also known as Parque de Bombas), another of the town's emblems. Painted bright red and black—Ponce's colors—it is all the more startling standing as it does next to the classic Cathedral. Built in 1883 as an exhibition booth for an agricultural fair, the building served as the town's firehouse until 1990, when it was made into a museum to house memorabilia on Ponce's history and on its volunteer fire brigade.

Plaza Las Delicias is bordered on all sides by buildings that reflect the town's architectural diversity. On the south, *City Hall* (Alcaldia) (**2**), built as a jail and military headquarters in 1843, houses the mayor's office and the municipal assembly. Its interior courtyard, with a two-story arcade, is typical of Spanish colonial government buildings. In contrast, *Banco de Santander* (**3**) on the southeast corner has a spectacular art nouveau window dating from 1922 over its glass and brass entrance.

CASA ARMSTRONG (4) On the west, facing the Cathedral, the renovated neoclassic Casa Armstrong-Poventud mansion, designed by Manuel V. Domenech in 1901, is the headquarters of the Institute of Puerto Rican Culture, which supervised the Ponce renovations, and the Tourist Information Center, which is open Monday to Friday from 8 A.M. to noon and 1 to 4:30 P.M.

The north side of the plaza experienced the most radical change over the years, succumbing mostly to cheap commercial storefronts. Building owners were encouraged and aided through a grant from the Spanish government to renovate their facades in the style—or at least the spirit—of the colonial architecture that once typified the square.

Slightly recessed from the street, *Fox Delicias* (**5**) is a former movie theater from the 1930s with an ornate facade designed by Francisco

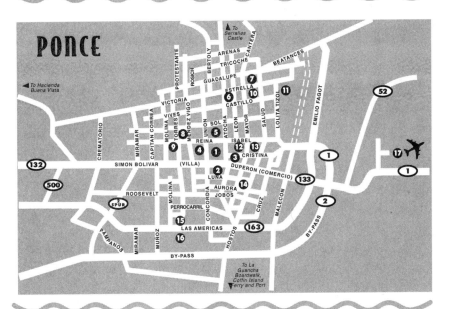

MAP LEGEND FOR WALKING TOUR OF PONCE

1. Plaza Las Delicias
2. City Hall
3. Banco de Santander
4. Casa Armstrong-Poventud
5. Fox Delicias
6. Paseo Atocha/Plaza del Mercado
7. Plaza de los Perros
8. Casa Villaronga
9. Residence Frau
10. Casa Virgilio Monsanto
11. Carcel del Castillo
12. Museum of Puerto Rican Music
13. La Perla Theatre
14. Casa Paoli
15. Ponce Museum of Fine Arts
16. Catholic University
17. Airport

Porrata Doria, the architect of the Banco de Ponce and Melia Hotel, two landmarks on the east side. The theater has been renovated as a small mall.

PASEO ATOCHA/PLAZA DEL MERCADO (6)
An old commercial street, Paseo Atocha, which connects the town square with the town market, Plaza del Mercado, was renovated as a cobblestone pedestrian mall with wrought iron benches and gas lamps. The old market, one of the town's largest buildings, has a handsome art deco facade that was added in the 1930s.

A block to the north, *Plaza de los Perros* (7) (which means Dogs' Square) was the former meat market. A block-long corridor between two streets,

it is entered at each end through beautiful Moorish keyhole doorways, created in 1923 by Rafael Camoega, who also designed the University of Puerto Rico in San Juan. The doors are framed by mosaics made from colored crystals rather than ceramics, as is traditional in New Spain Revival design. The renovated corridor is now a vegetable market.

Calle Reina Isabel, the east-west street along the north side of the Plaza Las Delicias, was the most fashionable thoroughfare of town during its heyday. Today, the western extension is called simply Calle Reina; the eastern one, Calle Isabel. Some houses of special architectural interest represent particular styles, but it will be obvious that the architects had no hesitation about mixing styles.

Casa Villaronga (8) was created in 1910 by Alfredo Wiechers, an architect of German origin and one of the most prolific of his time. The fanciful facade with its wedding cake trim has art nouveau elements such as the rounded front and oval windows, but its most distinctive feature is the colonnade ring on top. *Residence Frau* (9) combines neoclassic design in the porch and stairs with art nouveau features, particularly the Tiffany-style windows over the doors. Designed by Blas Silva in 1910, it was a wedding present to the bride from her parents. Casas Gemelas on Calle Reina are twin 19th-century townhouses with balconies and slim cast-iron railings in a style known as Ponce Crillo (reminiscent of the townhouses in Savannah and New Orleans).

Calle Castillo, north of Calle Isabel, is another street with a great variety of styles: art deco, Ponce Crillo, and New Spain Revival. *Casa Virgilio Monsanto* (10), one of the town's most ornate buildings, dates from 1913, as indicated on the facade. The mansion has two round protruding porches supported by fluted Corinthian columns and an abundance of wedding cake trim. It was the work of Blas Silva, the architect of the Frau house.

At the eastern end of Calle Castillo, the *Carcel del Castillo* (11), a former jail, has been renovated and expanded to house the School of Fine Arts. On the street's north side, a group of low-income houses was restored for the owners by the municipality. The aim was to retain the mixed-housing nature of the district and not allow gentrification to drive lower-income families from their homes.

MUSEUM OF PUERTO RICAN MUSIC (12)

(Cristina 70; Tel. 848–7016) Among several mansions which house new museums, this one is devoted to different Puerto Rican musical traditions: "La danza," the Spanish-influenced ballroom dance of the 19th century; "bomba and plena," the African-influenced popular song and dance; "seis charraos" dances from the mountain villages, which blend Indian, African, and Spanish cultures; and classical music, including the works of Puerto Rican composers. Musical instruments from the 19th and 20th centuries as well as those played by the Taino Indians are displayed. It has a gift shop, a library, small auditorium, and a "phonotheque" where people can listen to music.

Exhibits and concerts are here throughout the year. It is open Tuesday to Sunday from 9 A.M. to noon and 1 to 4:30 P.M.

LA PERLA THEATRE (13)

(Calle Major and Cristina) The city's cultural center, used year-round for concerts, plays, and other cultural events, La Perla Theatre was originally built in 1864. The structure was destroyed by fire and rebuilt with a colonnade front in 1941. It was restored in 1989.

CASA PAOLI (14)

(Calle Mayor 14; Tel. 840–4115) The home of Antonio Paoli, Puerto Rico's most famous opera star, who was born in Ponce in 1871, Casa Paoli underwent extensive restorations before being opened in 1990 as the headquarters of the Puerto Rico Folklore Research Center, a nonprofit organization founded in 1976 and devoted to the study of all aspects of Puerto Rico's folk heritage. The center holds seminars and exhibits and publishes studies on the island's folklore. Restoration of the house was a project of the Puerto Rican Commission for the Quincentennial.

Among Ponce's best-known folk traditions are the horned masks for Carnival in Ponce. The artists who create them are famous and highly regarded. They follow a tradition handed down from generation to generation. Some masterpieces are on view in Casa Paoli, and miniatures are on sale in its small bookstore. Hours: Weekdays, 8:30 A.M. to noon and 1 to 5 P.M.

PONCE MUSEUM OF FINE ARTS (15)

Poncenos, as the natives of Ponce are known, are especially proud of their Fine Arts Museum and believe it reflects the city's sophistication and longtime cultural focus. Founded in the 1950s by former governor Luis A. Ferre, the museum contains the largest collection of Western art in the Caribbean and a Latin American gallery.

The museum, housed in a building designed by Edward Durell Stone, is considered something of a work of art itself. It consists of seven interconnected hexagons, each with a domed skylight that provides natural light as the main source for lighting the collections. A graceful "welcoming arms" staircase gives access to the upper galleries. The museum has three gardens, each with a different focus. The Granada garden, in the style of its namesake, is on the east; another, dedicated to the presidents of the United States, is on the west; and the third and largest, featuring Puerto Rican flora, is at the center. Located on the south side of the city in the modern section near *Catholic University* (16), the museum is open Monday through Friday from 9 A.M. to 4 P.M., Saturday from 10 A.M. to 4 P.M., and Sunday from 10 A.M. to 5 P.M.; closed Tuesday.

SERRALLÉS CASTLE (El Vigia Hill; Tel. 259–1774) Perched on a hillside north of Ponce, Serrallés Castle was the former mansion of the Serrallés family, the owners of Don Q, one of Puerto Rico's oldest and largest rum distilleries. It is now a museum, furnished mostly with the family's collection from the 1930s. The palatial Spanish-style home has an elegant open courtyard with fountains and a magnificent carved wooden ceiling in the dining room. There is a cafe and an arts-and-crafts shop. Hours: Wednesdays to Sundays, 10 A.M. to 4:30 P.M.

PONCE ENVIRONS

INDIAN CEREMONIAL PARK One of the oldest and most important burial grounds ever discovered in the Caribbean is the Tibes Indian Ceremonial Park, located about 2 miles north of town. It was uncovered in 1976 after a heavy rainstorm. Here, seven ceremonial plazas belonging to the Igneri culture dating from A.D. 600 to 1,000 were found. Guides are available to take visitors through the park and explain the site and how it was discovered. In the Indo Museum at the entrance a film on the first Puerto Ricans is shown every 45 minutes as an orientation to the site. The museum's displays pertain to the Taino Indians and other pre-Columbian cultures.

HACIENDA BUENA VISTA In the foothills of the Cordillera Central north of Ponce is an estate, Hacienda Buena Vista, which was once one of the largest working plantations in Puerto Rico, growing coffee and other cash crops. Now a property of the Puerto Rico Conservation Trust, it has been extensively renovated and opened as an interpretive center and museum.

A pretty footpath through the woods to a waterfall goes along an aqueduct that once carried water to the huge waterwheel that supplied the estate with power. Multilingual guides and descriptive brochures for a self-guided tour are available at the entrance. The hacienda is located on Route 10 at Km. 16.8. The drive from Ponce takes about 20 minutes and is signposted—all but the last turnoff (!), which is easy to miss. It is open to groups on Wednesday and Thursday and to the general public on Friday to Sunday. Reservations are required: Tel. 722–5882.

GUANICA RESERVE West of Ponce lie the coastal forests and mangroves of the Guanica Reserve, with half of all Puerto Rico's terrestrial bird species. This birdwatcher's mecca has been designated an International Biosphere Reserve, protecting endangered species found only in Puerto Rico. The 10,000-acre reserve has more than 700 plant species, of which sixteen are endemic. Among the endangered species are the nightjar and the yellow-shouldered blackbird. Several species of sea turtles nest on its beaches, and the endangered West Indian manatee is sometimes found in its waters. The Copamarina Resort, the area's first deluxe beachside resort, is a pleasant place to lunch and swim.

LA PARGUERA West of Guanica near La Parguera is one of Puerto Rico's three bioluminescent bays. The luminescence is caused by microorganisms in the water that light up like shooting stars with any movement. This fragile phenomenon, found in shallow tropical bays surrounded by mangroves, occurs in only a few places in the world.

La Parguera with more than fifty dive sites along the newly explored Puerto Rico Wall, is rapidly becoming a mecca for divers.

TRANSPORTATION Ponce is a 1.5-hour drive from San Juan over the scenic cross-island expressway and can be reached by car, public transportation, or motorcoach tours. A visit to Ponce can be covered on one's own by rental car or taxi with three or four sharing the cost. American Eagle has daily flights between San Juan and Ponce. To visit the sites in the Ponce vicinity requires a car; some stops are available on tours that depart from San Juan and from Ponce.

The Virgin Islands

U.S. VIRGIN ISLANDS

CHARLOTTE AMALIE, ST. THOMAS; CRUZ BAY, ST. JOHN;
FREDERIKSTED, ST. CROIX; CHRISTIANSTED, ST. CROIX

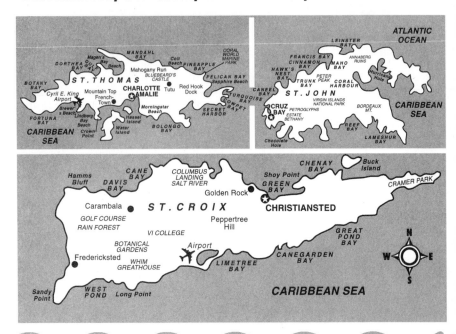

AT A GLANCE

Antiquities	★	Forts	★★★★
Architecture	★	History	★★★★
Art and Artists	★★	Monuments	★
Beaches	★★★★★	Museums	★★
Colonial Buildings	★★★★	Nature	★★★★★
Crafts	★	Nightlife	★★
Cuisine	★★	Scenery	★★★★★
Culture	★★	Shopping/Duty-free	★★★★
Dining/Restaurants	★★★	Sight-seeing	★★★★
Entertainment	★★	Sports	★★★★★
		Transportation	★★★

BRITISH VIRGIN ISLANDS
TORTOLA, NORMAN ISLAND, JOST VAN DYKE, VIRGIN GORDA, ANEGADA

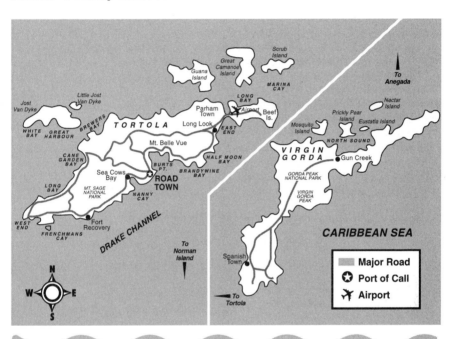

CHAPTER CONTENTS

U.S. VIRGIN ISLANDS

THE AMERICAN PARADISE

Their license plates say *American Paradise.* They are our corner of the Caribbean and, topside or beneath the sea, there isn't a more beautiful place under the American flag. Every turn in the road reveals spectacular scenes of white beaches washed by gentle turquoise water, backed by forest green hills, and colored by a rainbow of flowers with such marvelous names as Catch and Keep, Jump Up and Kiss Me, Clashie Melashi, and Cock-a-Locka. Easy breezes carry the delicate scent of jasmine and frangipani and cool the air.

The Virgin Islands, volcanic in origin, are divided between the United States and Britain into two groups of about fifty islands, islets, and cays each. They are situated in the northeastern part of the Caribbean adjacent to the Anegada Passage, a strategic gateway between the Atlantic Ocean and the Caribbean Sea, 990 miles from Miami, 1,400 miles southeast of New York, and 40 miles east of Puerto Rico where the Lesser Antilles begin.

The U.S. Virgin Islands comprise a "territory" rather than state; out of the group only the three largest islands are populated: St. Croix, the largest of the trio, lies entirely in the Caribbean and can claim to be the easternmost point of the United States; St. Thomas, the most populated and developed, is 35 miles north of St. Croix between the Caribbean and the Atlantic Ocean; and neighboring St. John, the smallest, is 3.5 miles east of St. Thomas.

Two islands at the mouth of Charlotte Amalie harbor are Water Isle, developed as a resort, and Hassel Island, given to the government by a private owner and made into a national park. Buck Island Reef National Monument faces the north coast of St. Croix and is surrounded by the only underwater park in the U.S. National Park system. The other islands are either uninhabited or uninhabitable.

The three largest islands are so close to one another that a day visit to St. John or St. Croix can be arranged easily from St. Thomas. And after a visit, you will see that no three islands in the Caribbean are more different from one another than our American trio.

On the northeast side of St. Thomas is the island of Tortola, capital of the British Virgin Islands, a British crown colony. Farther north, Virgin Gorda, known for its luxury resorts, is the second most populated of the group. Several tiny islands have been developed as private island resorts, but for the most part the British Virgin Islands are almost as virgin as the day Christopher Columbus discovered them.

DAY OF DISCOVERY

Columbus first sighted the Virgin Islands on November 13, 1493, on his second voyage. He arrived at the island known to its native Carib Indians as *Ay Ay,* and named it Santa Cruz or Holy Cross (we call the island by its French name, St. Croix). There, Columbus sailed into the Salt River estuary on the island's north side to replenish his ships' supply of fresh water. (And thus, St. Croix's second claim is that it is the first land now under the American flag to have been visited by the great explorer.)

But the fierce Caribs did not welcome Columbus as the peaceful Arawaks had done elsewhere. Instead, they came on the attack in their small canoes, firing a hail of arrows at Columbus's men who repulsed them, and as the story goes, continuing to shoot their arrows even after their fragile craft had been sunk. The attack, the first of his expedition, was substantial enough for Columbus to name the spot *Cabo de la Flecha,* the Cape of the Arrows.

Columbus made a hasty withdrawal from St. Croix, sailing north and west to St. Thomas, St. John, and the multitude of islands that make up the archipelago. The admiral, like all those who have followed him, was dazzled by the exquisite beauty of the islands; seeing so many clustered together inspired him to name the group the Virgin Islands after the ancient legend of St. Ursula and the 11,000 beautiful virgins.

In the legend, the son of a powerful pagan prince demands the hand in marriage of Ursula, the beautiful daughter of the king of Britain. Ursula, who has pledged herself to a saintly life, consents to the marriage to save her father and his kingdom from the pagans—on one condition. Eleven thousand of the most beautiful virgins in the two kingdoms must be her companions for three years. At the end of that time, she will marry the prince.

For the next three years, so the legend goes, Ursula trains the virgins into an army of amazons and then sails with them up the Rhine to Basel. From there they travel by foot to Rome to pledge their Christian allegiance. The outraged pagan prince waits with his army near Cologne for the virgins' return, and in the battle that follows all the virgins are martyred. To this day the Virgin Islanders like to say, "the beauty of the Virgins is legendary."

Although Columbus claimed the Virgin Islands for Spain as he did all the islands, the Spaniards were more interested in the potential riches of Cuba, Mexico, and other lands and paid the islands little or no attention for a century or more. At the same time the Caribs, who had quickly gained a reputation for their ferocity among European adventurers, discouraged settlement.

Raids by the Caribs from St. Croix on the early Spanish settlement in Puerto Rico were frequent. La Fortaleza, one of the first fortifications built in San Juan, was intended principally as a protection against the Caribs from St. Croix. Indeed, the Caribs were so troublesome that the king of Spain gave Ponce de Leon a special license to hunt them.

Sir Francis Drake, the dashing corsair of English history, was among those who sailed the Virgins' waters, long enough, it seems, to form the basis of England's claim to the islands too.

Finally in 1625 the English and Dutch, having recognized the islands' strategic location and eager to extend their territories in the New World, established settlements in St. Croix at approximately the location of Christiansted and Frederiksted today. They found no Indians, and the assumption is the Spaniards had raided the island and either had killed the inhabitants or had taken them off in bondage to work the gold mines of nearby Hispaniola.

A Checkered History

That the conditions under which the Caribbean was colonized were treacherous can be seen in a series of events in the history of St. Thomas and St. Croix. In 1645 the Dutch governor of St. Croix was accused of killing his English counterpart. This brought reprisals from the English settlers who attacked the Dutch settlement, killing the Dutch governor and others.

The Dutch soon appointed a new governor, and the English as a gesture of friendship invited him to visit. But instead of being received amicably, he was publicly tried and shot. The Dutch, who were outnumbered by the British, got the message and quickly left for safer territory on the nearby Dutch island of St. Maarten.

Meanwhile, a group of Frenchmen who earlier had deserted their ship in St. Thomas also decided to flee. They bartered all their properties in St. Thomas with an English captain in return for safe passage to the French West Indies. But upon his arrival in Guadeloupe, the French threw the English captain in chains and sold his ship and its goods to the highest bidder.

For a while, at least, the British, who were constantly trying to drive the Spanish out of Puerto Rico, had the Virgin Islands to themselves. In 1650, however, the Spaniards returned 1,200 strong from nearby Puerto Rico and drove them away. Thinking the Spaniards had no lasting interest in the Virgin Islands and would withdraw after driving away the English, the group of Dutchmen who had been chased away earlier returned to reclaim their land. But the Spaniards had no intention of relinquishing the islands and wiped out the Dutch instead.

Meanwhile, the French sent two ships to attack the Spaniards. One of the ships strayed off course, but the second was able to land 65 soldiers on St. Thomas without being detected by the Spaniards. During the night they surrounded the Spanish fort and at dawn demanded its surrender.

The Spaniards returned to Puerto Rico, and the Virgin Islands became French. The following year, 1651, the French king sold St. Croix to Count De Poincy, later governor of the French West Indies, as a private kingdom. Two years later the new owner ceded the island to his religious order, the Knights of Malta, who sent a group of emigrants there to establish a colony. The noble knights, unable to scratch out a living in the tropics, sent desperate messages to De Poincy for provisions. A ship was sent to save them but when the ship arrived, the knights locked the French captain in irons, seized his ship, and sailed off to Brazil.

The many islands, with their jagged coastlines, good harbors, and proximity to major shipping lanes, became natural havens for pirates and privateers. For most of the 17th century official authority over piracy was almost nonexistent.

In 1665, the French West Indies Company bought St. Croix from the Knights of Malta. Within a decade, however, the company had fallen into so much debt that the king of France was forced to repossess the island and settle its accounts himself. By 1695, the French king had had enough of St. Croix and ordered all inhabitants to leave. He reclaimed it in 1720 only long enough to do battle with the British.

Meanwhile the Dutch and British had been battling over Tortola (capital of the British Virgin Islands today), but by 1672 the British were able to make their claim stick. In the same year, the Danes took possession of St. Thomas and began colonizing it, dividing the land into 170 plantations of 125 acres each. They added St. John in 1717, and in 1733 the Danish West India and Guinea Company bought St. Croix from the French and started colonizing it as well.

Two decades later, Denmark declared the islands a crown colony and subsequently made St. Thomas a free port. Denmark's liberal trading laws and her neutral stance amidst the rivaling Europeans enabled St. Thomas to flourish as the center of contraband for the entire Caribbean. Twice again, in 1801 and 1807, the British came back to capture the islands but returned them to the Danes in both instances.

While St. Croix and St. John became rich with sugar plantations, St. Thomas became the chief trading station and slave market of the region. Slaves were imported from Africa not only to work the sugar plantations in the West Indies but to be reshipped to other areas of the New World as well. By the late seventeenth century, sugar had become the West Indies' most important commodity and the linchpin in the lucrative triangular trade which brought slaves from Africa to the colonies to work the plantations and returned molasses and rum (and later, cotton, tobacco, and indigo) to Europe, whose products were then bartered for more slaves in Africa.

The importance of sugar and the strategic role of the Caribbean in the high-stakes power game that raged in Europe and on the seas can be gleaned from the negotiations between England and France at the conclusion of the Seven Years' War in 1763. The English actually seriously considered exchanging Canada for the island of Guadeloupe in the French West Indies. After 1848 when slavery was abolished, the plantations were gradually abandoned and the economy withered away. Some plantations on St. Croix, however, continued to operate even until the early part of this century.

Equally devastating to the islands' economy was the invention of the steam engine. When ships could run on steam, they no longer needed the tradewinds or the strategic haven which St. Thomas had provided. Although it took 50 years from the time the first steamship arrived in St. Thomas in 1823 for the full impact to be felt, the handwriting, one might say, was in the sand.

UNITED STATES PURCHASES ISLANDS

After years of negotiations with Denmark to purchase the Virgin Islands, the United States finally bought them in 1917 for $25 million—or about $300 an acre—a high price at the time. The U.S. government, whose priority was the protection of the Panama Canal, worried that Germany might seize the islands for a base in World War I.

The islands, whose residents were made U.S. citizens in 1927, were administered by the U.S. Navy until 1931 when they were placed under the Department of the Interior. The present structure of territorial government with its three branches was established by Congress in 1954. Executive power is vested in the governor who appoints the heads of his twelve departments. Residents were granted the right to vote for their governor in 1970.

The legislature, which has convened since 1852, is a single body of 15 senators from the three islands elected for two-year terms. The district court of the Virgin Islands has certain local jurisdiction. Residents vote in local elections and since 1972 they have sent a representative to Congress. Residents pay federal income tax, but they cannot vote in national elections and their congressman does not have a vote on the floor of the House of Representatives.

In December 1996, the U.S. Department of the Interior transferred ownership of 50 acres of Water Island, a former World War II military installation, to the Virgin Islands government. Located ¼ mile off St. Thomas' Charlotte Amalie harbor, the island's remaining 440 acres will be transferred as agreements with homeowners are finalized.

U.S. citizens visiting the U.S. Virgin Islands, of course, do not need passports or visas; the language is English, and the currency is the American dollar. There is a bonus customs allowance (double that of other places) for returning U.S. residents.

Although they have become Americanized, with fast food, supermarkets, direct dial, and cable television, the U.S. Virgin Islands have retained enough of the atmosphere and attractions of their past to give visitors a sense of being in a foreign yet familiar place.

FAST FACTS

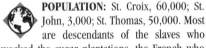

POPULATION: St. Croix, 60,000; St. John, 3,000; St. Thomas, 50,000. Most are descendants of the slaves who worked the sugar plantations, the French who migrated from the French West Indies, the Danes who held the islands the longest, and Spanish, Scottish, Portuguese, and other European traders and settlers. More recent arrivals are the large number of mainlanders who have come to live on one of the islands for part or all of the year, and residents of neighboring Caribbean islands who come to work, particularly in the tourist industry.

MAIN TOWNS: Christiansted and Frederiksted, St. Croix; Cruz Bay, St. John; Charlotte Amalie, St. Thomas.

CLIMATE: The Virgin Islands have some of the nicest weather in the Caribbean with temperatures ranging from 77°F in January and February to 82°F in July and August. The humidity is relatively low; tradewinds blow generally from the northeast and east.

CLOTHING: Dress is comfortable and casual. In the winter season you may need a sweater or light wrap in the evenings because there is often a big drop in temperature after the sun goes down. At fashionable restaurants and resorts gentlemen are asked to wear jackets for dinner.

CURRENCY: U.S. dollar. Most shops and restaurants accept major credit cards and traveler's checks. If you need to do any banking, Bank of America, Chase Manhattan, Citibank, and First Pennsylvania are among the major banks with branches here. Hours are Monday through Thursday, 9 A.M. to 2:30 P.M.; Friday, 9 A.M. to 2 P.M. and 3:30 to 5 P.M. American Express is represented by Tropic Tours, with offices at the airport and port, if an emergency arises.

CUSTOMS REGULATIONS: Cruise passengers who disembark in the U.S. Virgin Islands and plan to return to the United States by plane pass through customs here rather than on the mainland. The U.S. Virgin Islands have a special status, enabling U.S. residents to bring back up to $1,200 worth of goods duty free—twice that of other islands in the Caribbean. The next $1,000 over the amount is taxed at a 5 percent rate (rather than the 10 percent levy applied elsewhere). Persons over 21 years old are allowed five fifths of liquor plus a sixth one of a Virgin Islands spirit such as Cruzan Rum and five cartons of cigarettes or 100 cigars. Major retailers deliver liquor purchases to your cruise ship free of charge. The cartons are designed to withstand reasonable abuse. In addition you can mail home to friends and relatives an unlimited number of gifts (other than perfume, liquor, or tobacco), each valued up to $100.

If you have any questions whether items such as plants and fruit can be taken back to the States, the Agriculture Department and Bureau of Customs are located in the Federal Building at the waterfront (Tel. 774–2510).

ELECTRITY: 120 volt A.C., 60 cycle

ENTRY FORMALITIES: None for U.S. citizens. Driver's licenses, voter's registrations, or passports are suggested for proof of citizenship and identification.

LANGUAGE: English. Don't be surprised, however, if you have trouble understanding some Virgin Islanders. Their patois or local dialect is a corrupted English-Creole which has had a profound influence on the pronunciation and enunciation of local speech. Also, many residents come originally from other islands where English was not their native language. If you have trouble with the dialect, ask the person to speak slowly—and you should do the same.

 POSTAL SERVICE: Same as United States; the British Virgins issue their own stamps.

 PUBLIC HOLIDAYS: January 1, New Year's Day; January 6, Three Kings Day; third Monday in January, Martin Luther King's Birthday; February 17, Presidents' Day; Good Friday, Easter Sunday and Monday; March 31, Transfer Day (from Denmark to United States); May 26, Memorial Day; June 16, Organic Act Day (granting V.I. self-government in 1945); July 3, Emancipation; July 4, Independence; July 28, Hurricane Supplication; September 1, Labor Day; October 13, Columbus Day; October 20, Hurricane Thanksgiving; November 1, Liberty Day; November 11, Veteran's Day; Thanksgiving Day; December 25, 26, Christmas. Banks and stores are closed on the major holidays; on local ones, stores remain open.

 TELEPHONE AREA CODE: 340. Direct dial to/from the U.S. mainland is available. The code for St. Thomas is 77; local numbers are five digits, but more and more frequently they are written with the 77 as well, as in 774–1234. If you do not reach your number when dialing five digits, try it with the 77 prefix.

TIME: The Virgin Islands are in the Atlantic Standard Time Zone, which is one hour earlier than Eastern Standard Time. When Daylight Saving Time is in effect on the mainland, the V.I. time is the same as that on the U.S. East Coast.

VACINNATION REQUIREMENTS: None

  AIRLINES:

From the United States to the U.S. Virgin Islands, American, Delta, and US Airways
To the British Virgin Islands, no direct flights.
Interisland, Air Guadeloupe, American Eagle, LIAT, Air St. Thomas, Air Sunshine, Carib Air, and Seabourne Seaplane.

INFORMATION:

In the United States, nationwide: 1–800–372–USVI
U.S. Virgin Islands Tourist Information Offices:
Atlanta: 225 Peachtree St. N.E., No. 760; GA 30303; Tel. 404–688–0906
Chicago: 500 N. Michigan Ave., No. 2030; IL 60611; Tel. 312–670–8784; fax 312–670–8788.
Los Angeles: 3460 Wilshire Blvd.; CA 90010; Tel. 213–739–0138; fax 213–739–2005.
Miami: 2655 Le Jeune Road, No. 907; Coral Gables, FL 33134; Tel. 305–442–7200; fax 305–445–9044.
New York: 1270 Ave. of Americas; NY 10020; Tel. 212–332–2222; fax 212–332–2223.
Washington: 444 N. Capital St., No. 298; DC 20001; Tel. 202–624–3590; fax 202–624–3594.
In Canada: Toronto, 245 Britannia Rd. East, Missassauga, Toronto, Ont. L4Z 2Y7; Tel. 416–233–1414; fax 416–233–9367.
In St. Croix: Christiansted, P.O. Box 4538, USVI 00822; Tel. 773–0495.
In St. John: Cruz Bay, P.O. Box 200, USVI 00830; Tel. 776–6450.
In St. Thomas: Charlotte Amalie, P.O. Box 6400, USVI 00804; Tel. 774–8784; fax 774–4390.

 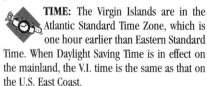

BUDGET PLANNING

Generally, prices for sports and tours in St. Thomas and St. John are typical for the Caribbean. The largest expenses for visitors are taxi fares and fancy restaurants. Some of those with gourmet pretensions can cost as much as $80 per person for dinner and wine.

On the other hand there is an ample selection of moderately priced, attractive restaurants serving local dishes; public transportation is plentiful and inexpensive; and beaches are free or have minimal charges. Generally, prices in St. Croix are slightly lower than in St. Thomas.

We have listed prices of shore excursions and other facilities to enable readers to budget their expenses in the three ports of call. However, the prices are intended as guidelines only and will probably vary depending on the time of the year and other factors. With judicious planning and the use of moderately priced facilities, you and all the family should be able to enjoy your visit to the U.S. Virgin Islands on a modest budget because they offer so many options.

AN INTRODUCTION TO ST. THOMAS

St. Thomas, the capital of the Virgin Islands, is the perfect cruise port. It is steeped in history yet as up-to-date as Fifth Avenue; it has stunning tropical scenery and is small enough to see in a day; it has the diversity to ensure universal appeal and the range of facilities to offer cruise passengers a wide choice.

The green mountainous island, only 13 miles long and up to 4 miles at its widest, rises dramatically from the deep turquoise sea to peaks of 1,550 feet that frame an irregular coastline of fingers and coves, idyllic bays, and white sand beaches. Perhaps because it is the most developed and populated of the trio St. Thomas gives the impression of being much larger than its 34 square miles.

Cruise ships steam into the lovely, yacht-filled harbor of Charlotte Amalie, set in a deep horseshoe bay with mountains rising behind it. The heart of town, which is both its historic district and commercial center, hugs the shore and climbs the mountainsides overlooking the port. Located on the south side of St. Thomas about mid-island, Charlotte Amalie (pronounced Ah-

mahl'-ya) was named in honor of the consort of King Christian V of Denmark under whom the first settlement was made in 1672. It is the busiest cruise port in the Caribbean, a familiar role. For two hundred years it was a major trading port on the sea lanes between the Old and New Worlds.

First settled by the Danish West India Company for the purpose of growing sugar, the island's mountainous terrain was such tough going that soon the colonial governors were looking for other ways to make a living. The easiest and most lucrative was to give their unwritten consent for pirates to use it as a haven.

In time, Charlotte Amalie collected quite an assortment of buccaneers, gunrunners, pirates, and privateers, as well as slave traders and religious zealots. Some of that legacy is still around at Drake's Seat, a strategic peak from which the English buccaneer is said to have watched his fleet pursuing Spanish treasure galleons. On another hill is Blackbeard's Tower, which legend claims the infamous pirate used as a lookout and hiding place for his stolen treasures.

By 1754 mismanagement of the Danish West India Company led the Danish king to reestablish his sovereignty and move the capital to Christiansted on St. Croix. Less than a decade later, St. Thomas was declared a free port— another continuing historic tradition—and a century of prosperity followed.

But two occupations by the English when the Danes broke their traditional neutrality in the wars among the Europeans, a devastating hurricane, an earthquake, and five disastrous fires were to test the islanders' mettle. These were followed by the abolition of slavery and the decline in the sugar economies of the West Indies, resulting in the loss to St. Thomas of its most lucrative sources of trade. The final deathblow was the conversion of ships to steam power. Even after the United States purchased the islands in 1917, St. Thomas languished as a backwater port until after World War II, when the tourist boom put it back at the center of the Caribbean's sea lanes.

Charlotte Amalie's lovely old buildings, now part of the National Historic Trust; the names of districts and streets; and driving on the left side of the road are today's reminders that the Danes, English, Spanish, and French were here long before the Americans. In colorful historic buildings which were once the warehouses of the old port, attractive boutiques selling an array of high-quality goods from around the world have helped to reestablish St. Thomas's prosperity as a free port and its premier position as the shoppers' mecca of the Caribbean.

Additionally, St. Thomas offers every kind of warm-weather sport a visitor could want—swimming at pretty beaches, deep-sea fishing, golf, hiking, horseback riding, sailing, snorkeling, scuba diving, tennis, waterskiing, and windsurfing. Dive experts have called the Virgin Islands one of the three best dive areas in the Caribbean and have identified more than 100 sites in their immediate vicinity; facilities are excellent. For those who do not snorkel or dive there are coral garden tours by glass-bottom boats and Coral World, the first underwater observatory in the Western Hemisphere.

For history buffs there are enough colonial buildings, old homes, forts, and monuments to fill your day easily. There are also many activities for those interested in the arts. Carnival, an exuberant display of island talent, takes place during the last two weeks of April; more than 50 local artists exhibit their works three times a year at the Arts Alive Festival; and the College of the Virgin Islands' Reichhold Center for the Arts, with its magnificent outdoor theater, provides an arena for local and regional talent, as well as a full program of the performing arts by international artists.

St. Thomas is crisscrossed by good roads that make travel to any part of the island a matter of a few minutes (except during morning and afternoon rush hours!) and a leisurely drive around the island a delightful activity of a few hours.

PORT PROFILE:
CHARLOTTE AMALIE

LOCATION/EMBARKATION: Sailing into the pretty harbor of Charlotte Amalie is a delightful experience no cruise passenger should miss. You will see whitewashed, red-roofed houses against the forested mountains set on a sapphire sea. Charlotte Amalie's harbor is horseshoe-shaped and has three docks; the size of your ship usually

dictates which dock is used. Ships enter the opening of the horseshoe from the south; straight north is the town. On the east side of the horseshoe is the West Indian Company Dock where the majority of ships arrive. It is about 1.5 miles east of downtown. Five cruise ships can berth here at one time. If your ship is small (under 200 passengers) it will probably sail directly to King Wharf on the waterfront in town. If your ship is one of the largest vessels, such as the *Norway* or *QE2*, you may have to tender.

Another dock on the west side of the harbor, Crown Bay Dock, about 1.5 miles west of town, was built especially to accommodate large ships. Since more cruise ships call at St. Thomas than any other port in the Caribbean, it is not surprising to find five or six ships in port at one time. The system operates more or less on a first-come, first-served basis, so the number in port will determine whether your ship draws dockside or tenders. There are no embarkation formalities required to leave your ship.

FACILITIES: At the West Indian Company Dock there are telephone facilities for local and long distance calls, a mobile U.S. Post Office, a new, much improved tourist information center, and a large shopping complex, *Havensight Mall.* The transportation system is well organized and convenient. Crown Bay Dock's facilities are much more limited. Private communications facilities are offered by The Calling Station (Cohens Liquor Mall, Havensight, Tel. 777–8205; Bakery Square Mall, Back St., Tel. 776–8355). It has direct-dial phones in private air-conditioned booths, fax service, and video rentals.

ACCESSIBILITY: All three docks are easily accessible, enabling passengers to come and go from their ship with ease. You need only your cruise ship embarkation card or cabin key to reboard your ship.

LOCAL TRANSPORTATION: *Taxis:* Taxis and minibuses, which are mostly either 8-seaters or open jitneys for 20 passengers, are lined up by the dozens for transportation from the port to Emancipation Square in downtown Charlotte Amalie. Cost is $2.50 per passenger one-way. The square is a central location at the head of Main Street, the central shopping street. It is also the ideal place from which to start a walking tour. For the return trip to your ship, jitneys leave frequently from the square to the docks, and you can almost always share a taxi with other returning passengers. Be sure to give yourself ample time to return to your ship particularly from 4 to 6 P.M. when local traffic is extremely heavy and moves at a snail's pace. It can easily take 30 minutes or more to drive the 1.5 miles between town and the West Indian Company Dock.

Taxi rates are based on destination rather than mileage and are set by the government; a copy of the rates should be available from the driver. Rates for most locations beyond town are $7 to $11 oneway. Coki Beach, for example, is $7.50. Taxis are available for tours of the island; drivers are usually informed on the basics and also act as guides. Some are definitely better than others; you'll get potluck. Cost is $30 for two persons for a two-hour tour and $12 for each additional passenger.

Several St. Thomas transportation and sightseeing companies have service in St. John and can combine the two islands into one package. Drivers take and return you to the ferry docks on both islands. After a two-hour tour of St. John the driver will leave you at a beach and fetch you at a mutually agreed time for the return trip.

BUSES: Regular bus service connects Charlotte Amalie with Red Hook at the eastern end of the island where ferries leave for St. John, and with Bordeaux at the west end. The buses run about hourly with the last returning to town about 10 P.M.; cost is $1. Tel. 774–5678 for schedule. The "Open Air Taxi" buses or jitneys from Market Square to Red Hook leave hourly until 5:15 P.M.; the last returns from Red Hook to town at about 9 P.M. A one-way fare is $3.

CAR RENTALS: Driving is on the **LEFT** side of the road. Some say it's a colonial legacy; others maintain it is the terrain, theorizing that left-hand driving better enables one to follow the precipitous mountain roads than right-hand driving. You need only a valid U.S. driver's license. Expect to pay about $45 to $65 per day for a compact with unlimited mileage from a brand name company and about $40 from independent dealers. Some car rental companies have agreements with local merchants which offer discounts on rental and/or

merchandise. Several companies have jeep rentals, too, which cost about $65. Some car rental firms have free pickup and delivery service at the port; however, during the winter season when demand is greatest, the availability of cars is uneven, and pickup service unreliable. Unless you have had experience with driving on the left and with roads as mountainous as those on St. Thomas, it may be wiser for you to hire a taxi.

ABC Auto & Jeep, Tel. 776–1222;
  800–524–2080;
Avis, Tel. 774–1468;
Budget, Tel. 778–4663;
Caribbean AMC Jeep, Tel. 776–7811;
  800–524–2031
Dependable, Tel. 774–2253;
Discount, Tel. 776–4858;
Dollar, Tel. 776–0850;
Hertz, Tel. 774–1879;
National, Tel. 776–2557;
Thrifty, Tel. 776–3500

FERRY SERVICE: Ferry service is available between the downtown waterfront and Frenchman's Reef Hotel for $4 every half hour, 9 A.M. to 4 P.M. daily except Sunday. St. John is connected by hourly service from Red Hook from 6:30 A.M. to 7:30 P.M.; the trip takes 20 minutes. Another ferry, less frequent but more convenient for cruise passengers, leaves from the downtown waterfront (8:30 A.M. to 4:30 P.M.) several times daily.

Katron Hydrofoil has service between St. Thomas and St. Croix, twice daily: from St. Thomas, 7:15 A.M. and 3:15 P.M.; from St. Croix, 9:15 A.M. and 5 P.M. The trip takes 1 hour 15 minutes. Cost is $37 one way; $70 round trip; seniors $33 and $63 respectively.

Ferries to the B.V.I. are the *Bomba Charger* (Smithy's Ferry; Tel. 775–7292) and *Native Son* (Tel. 774–8685). They leave from the Charlotte Amalie waterfront on frequent schedules and take 45 minutes to reach Tortola; some continue to Virgin Gorda. You will need your passport or proof of citizenship. Complete schedules of ferries are printed in the weekly publication, *St. Thomas This Week,* a free booklet widely distributed in stores, hotels, and tourist offices.

INTERISLAND AIR: *Seaplane Service* (Tel. 777–4491) flies between St. Thomas and St.

Croix almost hourly during the day. Air Sunshine (Tel. 776–7900) has daily flights between St. Thomas, St. Croix, and San Juan. Carib Air (Tel. 777–1944) has service between St. Thomas, San Juan, Virgin Gorda, Culebra, and Fajardo daily. American Eagle, LIAT, Sunaire Express, Virgin Air, and Winair fly on regular schedules between the Virgin Islands, Puerto Rico, Antigua, the French West Indies, and other Eastern Caribbean islands.

EMERGENCY NUMBERS:

Medical Service/St. Thomas Hospital,
   Tel. 776–8311
Ambulance, Fire, Police: Dial 911
Recompression Chamber, 776–2686
Alcoholics Anonymous, Tel. 776–5283

INFORMATION: When you step off your ship at the West Indian Company Dock, you are a few steps from the Virgin Islands Tourist Bureau where you can get maps and brochures and ask questions. The bureau's town office is in the Territorial Building at the corner of Post Office Alley and Veterans Drive (Tel. 774–8784). Also in the latter location on the ground floor is a Hospitality Lounge (Tel. 776–9493; 774–5639) with a hostess on duty daily except Sunday from 9 A.M. to 5 P.M. Among its facilities is a place to check luggage and shopping bags for a small charge.

AUTHOR'S FAVORITE ATTRACTIONS

WALKING TOUR OF CHARLOTTE AMALIE
   HISTORIC DISTRICT
DAY SAIL WITH SWIMMING AND
   SNORKELING
VIEWS FROM DRAKE'S SEAT AND PARADISE
   PEAK
HIKING IN THE VIRGIN ISLANDS NATIONAL
   PARK ON ST. JOHN
SEA LIFE: *ATLANTIS II,* A RECREATIONAL
   SUBMARINE; RESORT DIVE COURSE AT
   COKI BEACH FOR NONDIVERS; WRECK OF
   THE RHONE (FOR DIVERS)
WINDSURFING AT COWPET BAY OR
   SAPPHIRE
DEEP-SEA FISHING
GOLF AT MAHOGANY RUN

ST. THOMAS SHORE EXCURSIONS

What to do during your visit to St. Thomas largely depends on your personal interest—the choices are here. Be sure to plan some activity because despite what you have heard about the wonderful shops in Charlotte Amalie, most people find they can complete their shopping in under two hours and are disappointed when they have not planned another activity as well. For those on a first trip to the island, we suggest a drive on your own or a tour to enjoy the beautiful scenery and spectacular views. If you have no sport in mind, a visit to Coral World is suggested. St. Thomas and St. John have lovely beaches.

Shore excursions most frequently offered by cruise ships follow; prices are per person and will vary according to the cruise line. Recently, I found a sharp increase in the prices being charged by some cruise lines—up to 40 percent over prices offered by local companies for the same tours. Sites mentioned here are described in more detail elsewhere in the chapter.

St. Thomas Island Tour: 2.5 hours, $26. The introductory drive starts from the port and goes to Bluebeard's Castle for the view; continues to Mafolie Hill and Drake's Seat with panoramic view of Magens Bay Beach, one of the Caribbean's prettiest; and back to town. Same drive available with local taxis for $30 for two.

St. John Land Safari: 4.5 hours, $40. For those who have visited St. Thomas before or those who are more interested in outdoor activity than shopping. The excursion goes by ferry from St. Thomas to Cruz Bay, tours the island, and visits Trunk Bay for a swim, snorkel, and refreshment. Snorkeling equipment and lessons available. Take a towel and plastic bag for wet swimsuits. The U.S. Park Service does not permit more than twenty snorkelers from one group in the water at one time.

Underwater Life: 4 hours, snorkelers, $36; introductory dive lessons, $65. Some cruise ships send snorkelers and divers in separate groups; others combine them depending on the number of people and their proficiency. In either case, they are accompanied by a professional instructor; children under 18 usually have to be accompanied by an adult.

Atlantis Submarine: 2 hours, $68 adults, $34 teens, children, $25. For those who do not snorkel or dive, the Atlantis II, a recreational submarine, takes passengers over the reefs at 150 feet below sea level, about 20 minutes south of the West Indian Dock. The 50-foot vessel is air-conditioned and has all its systems duplicated to ensure safety.

Sailing: 3.5 hours, $40–$50; full day $55–$75. Your yacht (with crew) sails to a nearby uninhabited island to anchor while you swim and snorkel. Usually limited to 6 or 10 people, it has an open bar; light snacks are served. A 2-hour party version on a boat for 120 people is also available for $28.

Island Bike Adventures: $50–$60. Enroute to your biking adventure, you get an island tour in an open-air safari van. At the starting point you receive a twenty-one-speed mountain bike, helmet and water bottle plus an orientation to the bike and route. The guided tour, followed by a support vehicle, travels on secluded roads and trails and ends at Magens Bay beach for a swim. You can return to your ship or stay at the beach. Participants need to be in good health, thirteen years old or older. Wear tennis shoes and light clothing. Currently the tour is sold only through cruise lines. (Tel./fax 776–1727.)

Sight-seeing by Air: It's a fantastic way to see our American Paradise. *Air Center Helicopters* (Box 6186, St. Thomas 00804; Tel. 775–7335) has charters. For up to four people the cost is $340 for half-hour; $685 for 1 hour. Some cruise ships contract with Air Center Helicopters to provide short air tours, thus enabling passengers to buy a tour on an individual basis.

ST. THOMAS ON YOUR OWN

T he U.S. Virgin Islands began to preserve and restore its historic buildings in the 1960s and was inspired by the Bicentennial to move full steam ahead. Today the historic old towns of Charlotte Amalie on St. Thomas and Christiansted and Frederiksted on St. Croix are listed in the National Register of Historic Places.

These towns are not museums; rather, most of the restorations were done by private owners who preserved the old structures, giving them new life as stores, business and government offices, hotels, restaurants, and residences—uses not far removed from their original purposes. A walk through these streets is a chance to learn something about the island's history and have fun shopping in areas made charming by their past.

The layout of historic Charlotte Amalie is a grid running three blocks deep from the waterfront on the south to the hillsides on the north, intersected by long east-west streets extending from old Hospital Gade on the east to just below General Gade on the west.

A CHARLOTTE AMALIE WALKABOUT

A walking tour takes 2 to 3 hours, depending on your pace. The route begins at Emancipation Garden (1), but it can be picked up at any point. The most difficult part, numbers (8) to (9), which lie between Government House and Hotel 1829, can be eliminated if the walk becomes tiring. Most of the information on the buildings and sites described here is based on a study of the Historic District by the Virgin Islands Planning Office, Division of Archaeology and Historic Preservation (774–7859).

Open-air jitneys and taxis from the West Indian Company Dock or Crown Bay discharge passengers at Emancipation Garden at the head of Main Street or in front of the Post Office (17). If your ship has docked at Kings Wharf, you are already in the heart of downtown one block south of Main Street and can start your walk at the Legislative Building (4).

EMANCIPATION GARDEN (1) A small park which was originally the town square is called Emancipation Garden, named to commemorate the emancipation of the slaves by Governor Peter von Scholten on July 3, 1848, a date celebrated as a holiday today. The park has a bandstand and an open-air market for T-shirts and souvenirs. There is a bust of the Danish King Christian IX and a small replica of the Liberty Bell in Philadelphia. Across from its southwest corner is the Tourist Hospitality Lounge, operated by Project St. Thomas, a citizen's group.

GRAND HOTEL (2) On the north side of the park, the Grand Hotel, built in 1839–40 as the Commercial Hotel, was the town's leading accommodation for over a century. Originally the Greek Revival structure occupied an entire block at the end of Dronningens Gade (Main Street) and overlooked the town's main square. It is now a commercial building with shops and a new interior courtyard with a sushi bar and an outdoor cafe. The structure, combining classical and West Indian architectural elements, was originally three stories high. The top story was lost sometime after 1896, presumably from damage caused by a hurricane. The first floor had arched openings, now filled in by shops, and entrances on the north, south, and west sides, each framed by jutting columns. The corners are accented by thick rounded columns partially attached to the building. The second floor has a ballroom; the south side facing the gardens has an arcaded loggia.

FORT CHRISTIAN AND MUSEUM (3) East of the park is the entrance to Fort Christian, the oldest building in the Virgin Islands. It was declared a National Historic Landmark in 1977. The red brick fortress, built between 1666 and 1680, was named for Denmark's King Christian V and was the focal point of the community for three centuries. Through the years it housed the colony's first governors and officers, served as a church, surgeons' quarters, shipwatch, and garrison. In 1874 the fort was greatly altered when the watchtower was removed and replaced with a crenellated clock tower and the present facade on the north side of the building was added. The fort was then converted and used for almost a century as a prison, police station, and local courthouse.

In 1977, when the fort was designated a historic landmark, the police and prisoners were moved out, and in 1982 extensive renovations began that are still in progress. Now, as funds become available, the entire fort is being made into a museum with each room focusing on a different period of Virgin Island history and culture, from the pre-Columbian period, particularly that of the Arawaks, to the present. Local families whose ancestors came to the island have donated locally made furniture and utensils. The part of the fort that was formerly the police station is now a gift and book shop. Hours: Monday through Friday from 8:30 A.M. to 4:30 P.M. and Saturday from 9:30 A.M. to 4:00 P.M.

LEGISLATIVE BUILDING (4) After leaving the fort, turn left on Fort Pladen Street and continue south along the fort past the fire station and cross the street to the waterfront. The bright lime-green structure by the water is the Legislative Building, home of the 15-member Virgin Islands Legislature. Here in 1917, the Danish flag was lowered for the last time, transferring ownership of the Virgin Islands to the United States. The two-story arcaded Italian Renaissance structure was built in 1874 as barracks for the Danish police. It served as a U.S. Marine Corps barracks from 1917 to 1930 and as a public school until 1957, when it became the home of the legislature. It has a graceful winged staircase and an attractive wrought iron gate at the entrance. Hours: Monday through Friday.

KINGS WHARF Facing the Legislative Building is the headquarters of the Coast Guard on Kings Wharf, a dock for small ships and departure point for some ferries.

You can return up the same street, Fort Pladen, by the fire station and turn right on Norre Gade (the eastward extension of Main Street) to the Bethania Frederick Lutheran Church and Parish Hall.

FREDERICK LUTHERAN CHURCH (5) This church, built in 1820 to replace an earlier one destroyed by fire, is the oldest on the island. It was originally established in 1666, the year Erik Nielson Smith took formal possession of St. Thomas in the name of the Danish West India Company. Two earlier churches dating from 1750 and 1789 are known to have been on the site.

The Lutheran church was closely allied with the development of the colony in the early period. The charter which the royal government granted

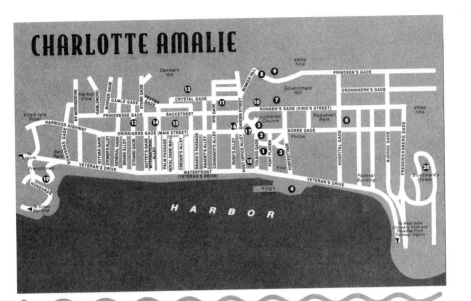

MAP LEGEND FOR WALKING TOUR OF CHARLOTTE AMALIE

1. Emancipation Garden
2. Grand (Commercial) Hotel
3. Fort Christian and Museum
4. Legislative Building
5. Frederick Lutheran Church and Parish Hall (Jacob H.S. Lind House)
6. Moravian Memorial Church
7. Government House
8. The 99 Steps
9. Fort Skytsborg or Blackbeard's Tower
10. Hotel 1829 (formerly Lavalette House)
11. St. Thomas Dutch Reform Church
12. Synagogue Hill
13. Market Square
14. Enid M. Baa Public Library (formerly Large Residence)
15. Pissarro Birthplace (Tropicana Shop)
16. Danish Harbor Office (Gucci Store)
17. Post Office
18. Virgin Islands Tourist Information Office
19. Bluebeard's Tower
20. Paradise Paint

to the stockholders of the Danish West India Company included a provision that the Lutheran church, the state church of Denmark, would be maintained with appropriate ministers to serve it.

At first, services were held in the homes of planters and soldiers; later, a small chapel was built in the courtyard of the fort. Danish, Creole, and English were used in the services. When St. Thomas became a Crown colony in 1754, the church quickly expanded its role in the commu-

nity, increasing the number of schools it operated and adding a hospital.

The present buff-colored brick building is Gothic Revival in design and has a rather grand entrance which was added during remodeling after the church was damaged by the hurricane of 1870. The entrance, approached by a wide set of stairs, has a projecting central pavilion with an arched door and bell tower. A vestry was added to the rear of the building in 1951 and a sacristy in 1954. The wood in the chancel and pulpit is local mahogany. Among the church's heirlooms are a gold-plated, solid silver communion chalice and paten that were presented to the congregation by the Danish Crown in 1713 and used until 1977. Hours: Monday through Saturday, 8 A.M. to 5 P.M.; Sunday services are at 8:00 and 10:30 A.M. (Tel. 774–1741).

The Parish Hall, formerly the Jacob H. S. Lind House, was built between 1806 and 1827 as a residence and has been used as a post office, an old people's home, and a school. The two-story masonry building is U-shaped in plan and has a hip roof, a feature characteristic of West Indian colonial architecture.

The Parsonage, 23 Kongens Gade, is located behind the church across from Government House. The building is more than 250 years old and is one of the oldest structures in continuous use on the island. The original walls, partially exposed in several rooms, consist of bricks and stones brought from Denmark as ballast for sailing ships. They were left for building purposes in exchange for cargoes of sugar, cotton, and rum. During the remodeling of the building in 1960, the original fireplace and brick oven in the kitchen were removed, but the huge beams across the opening and the chimneys are still there. A cell used to lock up rebellious slaves can be seen in the first floor courtyard.

MORAVIAN MEMORIAL CHURCH (6) If your time permits, there is another nineteenth-century church, the Moravian Memorial Church, farther east on Norre Gade. The two-story building is constructed of a hard volcanic local rock known as blue-bitch stone and has rusticated or beveled sandstone quoins or cornerstones. The windows of the upper story are framed with similar stone and triangular pediments. Atop the hip roof is a small bell tower with a delicate wooden cupola dating from 1882. Inside the church there are balconies on three sides supported by columns.

A few steps east of the Lutheran church a small street, Lille Taavne, leads north up the hill to a short flight of stairs to Kongens Gade (King's Street) and Government Hill.

GOVERNMENT HOUSE (7) Built between 1865 and 1867 for the Danish Colonial Council to replace an earlier building used by them,

Government House is the official residence and office of the governor of the U.S. Virgin Islands. The first two floors are open to the public and have paintings and objets d'art relating to the islands' history, and a collection of works by the French Impressionist Camille Pissarro who was born on St. Thomas in 1830.

Architecturally, the freestanding, three-story masonry structure is neoclassical in design and has a hip roof and an unusual two-story verandah of cast iron. The brick walls are covered with stucco and have a decorative belt of exposed brick and traditional cornerstones. Hours: Monday through Friday, 8 A.M. to noon; 1 to 5 P.M. Closed holidays.

Returning to Kongens Gade, walk west and you pass Quarters B, 32 and 33 Kongens Gade, a Greek Revival two-story masonry house with a hip roof, originally constructed as a residence in 1816. It was reconstructed as the German Consulate early in this century. It was built on the slope of the hill, and the upper floor is entered through a recessed gabled archway supported by two Ionic columns. The interior is noted for its large mahogany stairway leading to the traditional "welcoming arms" staircase at the lower landing.

The area around Government House, known as Government Hill, has attracted prosperous merchants, government officials, and professionals throughout the island's history. From here and higher up the hill houses enjoy grand views of Charlotte Amalie and the harbor, and, of course, catch the breezes.

A short detour east of Government House is the *Seven Arches Museum,* (Tel. 774–9295), a private residence open to the public as a lived-in museum. It is a modest example of Danish West Indian architecture; some rooms are furnished with antiques. A thick vine growing on the wall of the garden is full of iguana. Hours: Tuesday through Saturday, 10 A.M. to 3 P.M.

THE 99 STEPS (8) Since the hills are so steep, it was difficult to build roads; access between the higher and lower parts of town was gained by a series of stone stairs. Two of the best preserved ones, built by the Danes in the mid-18th century, are west of Government House—one immediately west of the mansion and a second, known as the

99 Steps, a short walk beyond. (Another set of stairs can be seen next to the Cathedral of St. Peter and St. Paul on Main Street.)

FORT SKYTSBORG (9) Both passageways lead to Fort Skytsborg, a five-story conical watchtower built by the Danes in 1678 and known as Blackbeard's Tower. Legend has it that the infamous pirate used the tower to watch his prey and hide his treasures. Today a gourmet restaurant is adjacent to the tower. The view from here is magnificent and reward enough for climbing the 99 Steps.

On the south side of the street, Crown House is one of the few authentic Danish mansions remaining from the eighteenth century. (Most buildings in Charlotte Amalie were destroyed in a series of devastating fires prior to the early 1800s when more stringent building codes were introduced.) The lovely old mansion, built in 1750, was used as the residence of the Danish governor and other Danish officials and is now a private home.

HOTEL 1829 (10) If you walk back down the 99 Steps (there are actually 103) to Kongens Gade, you come to Hotel 1829. Formerly known as *Lavalette House* after its builder, a French sea captain of the same name, the townhouse was begun in 1819 and took ten years to complete. The two-story stucco structure was designed by an Italian architect in a Spanish motif. The initial "L" of the original owner can still be seen in the wrought iron grillwork at the entrance.

The hotel is particularly noted for its restaurant. The building has had extensive restoration, down to the 200-year-old Moroccan tiles that are used as trim in the bar and patio. The bar is in the original Danish kitchen. The original part of the building was U-shaped in plan; a molded brick cornice defines the height of the second-floor ceiling. Across the central part of the front facade is a two-story balcony, a feature characteristic of houses from this era. It is supported by brick pilasters or columns with molded capitals and bands.

ALL SAINTS CHURCH Continue west about 50 paces and go down the stairs on the north side of the street to Garden Street. If your interest is keen and time permits, you can take a detour north to the 19th century All Saints Church; otherwise turn west onto Crystal Gade and continue to the corner of Nye Gade.

ST. THOMAS DUTCH REFORM CHURCH (11) The St. Thomas Dutch Reform Church, a Greek Revival building constructed in 1846, has such classical features, it looks more like a temple than a church. At the top of its two-story facade is a large triangular pediment supported by four Doric columns. Its doors are framed by pilasters or columns with typical classical cornices and moldings. Parts of the stucco facade are marked with lines and grooves to imitate dressed stone.

SYNAGOGUE HILL (12) Farther along on the north side of Crystal Gade, also known as Synagogue Hill, is the Beracha Veshalom Vegmiluth Hasidim Synagogue. Built in 1833 on the site of two earlier structures dating from 1796 and 1804, it is the oldest synagogue on American soil, the second oldest in the Western Hemisphere, and the oldest in continuous use in the Americas.

The Jewish community on St. Thomas is one of the oldest in the Caribbean. As early as 1684, Gabriel Milan, a member of a prominent European Jewish family, was appointed governor by the Danish Crown; and in 1734, another member of the Jewish community, Emanuel Vass, was sent to Martinique on behalf of the Danish West India and Guinea Company to handle the transfer of St. Croix from France to Denmark. The Synagogue marked its 200th anniversary in 1996.

The synagogue is a freestanding, one-story structure of cut stone and brick believed to have been brought as ballast by trading ships. A wrought iron fence encloses a small patio at the entrance and marble steps lead to its impressive and unusual entrance. The front doorway, a high pointed arch, is covered by a porch supported by four columns from which the plaster has been removed to expose its composition of red bricks. Similar columns are repeated at the entrance; the arched windows on either side are framed with matching brick.

Inside, the exposed walls are composed of native stone with a mortar made of sand and molasses. Mahogany pews face the center of the sanctuary; the *m'chitzot* which once separated the men and women can be seen behind the fourth row. All the furniture and many of the fixtures and ornaments date from 1833, according to the synagogue's literature. On the east wall the Holy Ark contains scrolls of the Torah, three of which are over 200 years old; one set of *rimonim* (handles of the scrolls) were saved from the fire of 1831; the lovely old mahogany doors have ivory insets. Above the Ark are the blue and gilded Tablets of the Decalogue; the lamp of eternal light hanging in front has an unusual design by which it can be raised and lowered with a counterweight.

On either side are benches originally intended to seat the synagogue's leaders. Overhead in the center of the dome is a Magen David encircled with designs; from it hangs an eighteen-armed candle chandelier with Baccarat crystal hurricane shades. The candles are still used for special services.

There are four corner columns with Doric capitals which are said to represent the four mothers of Israel: Sarah, Rebecca, Rachel, and Leah. Several interpretations have been given for the sand floors but according to the synagogue's historian, Isidor Paiewonsky, they are meant as a reminder of the time when the Jews of Spain were forced to pray in unfinished basements. Another interpretation is that the sand symbolizes the exodus of the Jews from Egypt and the forty years of wandering in the wilderness. Hours: Weekdays 9:30 A.M. to 4:30 P.M. A small guidebook by Mr. Paiewonsky with an introduction by Herman Wouk is available from the synagogue.

The *Weibel Museum* (Crystal Gade, adjacent to the synagogue; Tel. 774–4312) covers the 300-year-old history of the Jews of St. Thomas. Hours: Weekdays, 10 A.M. to 4 P.M.; weekends, 12:30 to 4 P.M.

MARKET SQUARE (13) Now, backtrack to the corner and start downhill on Raadets Gade for 1 block and turn west (right) on Backstreet to Market Square, the site of the notorious slave market, one of the biggest in the West Indies. Today, the old auction blocks are covered by an iron market shed built earlier in this century and used as the town's open-air fruit and vegetable market. Saturday is market day. The south side of the market faces Dronningens Gade (Main Street). One block west on Main Street is the Cathedral of St. Peter and St. Paul, built in 1844.

PUBLIC LIBRARY (Lange Residence) **(14)** One block east of Market Square is the large pink corner building facing Main Street, the Enid M. Baa Public Library. Built around 1800 as a residence, it was the town's first recorded fireproof building. The library is named for one of the island's first female university graduates, who served as librarian for many years and was instrumental in creating its von Scholten Memorial Collection.

The collection does not contain the former governor's private papers, as is sometimes thought, but rather is an important group of books, prints, and documents on the Virgin Islands and the West Indies. They are available to researchers and were used extensively in the preparation of the Archaeology and Historic Preservation Division's study on the Historic District.

PISSARRO'S BIRTHPLACE (15) East 1 block is No. 14 Dronningens Gade, the birthplace of the Impressionist painter Camille Pissarro (1830–1903). Pissarro, a Sephardic Jew, lived here until the age of 12, when he went to Paris to study. Although he lived in Paris most of his life, he retained his Danish citizenship and is known to have returned to St. Thomas at least once.

By now you will probably be ready to do some shopping. If you continue east on Main Street to its end you will come to the Emancipation Garden where your walk began. Along the way, on both sides of Main Street you will find small lanes and passageways that have been made into lovely palm-shaded shopping plazas where many shops are in renovated warehouses built in the 18th century as part of the old port. Some, however, are recent structures made to look old.

RIISE ALLEY Riise's Store and Alley, which belongs to the Paiewonsky family, was one of the first old structures to be renovated and helped inspire the renaissance of the historic district. In the old days each warehouse had its own lift to haul cargo from the ships at the waterfront and load it onto a flatbed car that ran on rails through the alleyway to Main Street. Only one sample of these relics remains.

At the entrance to Riise Alley is an art gallery where you can see and buy the works of local artists as well as those from other Caribbean islands. The 18th-century building at the end of Riise Alley, which now houses the Gucci store, was formerly the *Danish Harbor Office* (16).

POST OFFICE (17) The Post Office has murals painted by illustrator Stephen Dohanos in the 1940s as a WPA project before he gained a reputation as an illustrator for the *Saturday Evening Post* and other publications. The *Continental Building* (18), a yellow building on the south side of the Post Office, is the old *Danish Customs House,* and next to it is the Territorial Building, which houses the *Virgin Islands Tourist Information Office.*

OTHER LANDMARKS

FRENCHTOWN At the west end of town is the old fishing village of Frenchtown, settled by French immigrants fleeing the Swedish invasion of St. Barts in the late 18th century. Some of their descendants continue to speak a Norman dialect of French. While many of the old structures have given way to new houses and buildings, Frenchtown still retains a community feeling, and fishermen can be seen any day bringing in their catches to sell on the dock. This small area has a concentration of restaurants popular with islanders and a pretty village church, the Church of St. Anne, built in 1931. Frenchtown is also known as Cha Cha Town for its pointed straw hats called *chas chas* that are woven by the town's women and sold at craft stores in Charlotte Amalie. (The Norman women who live on St. Barts make a particular type of straw hat, too.)

BLUEBEARD'S TOWER (19) High on a hill at the east end of town, Bluebeard's Tower is another watchtower built by Danes in 1678; it, too, may have been used as a pirate's dwelling. It is now the honeymoon suite of Bluebeard's Castle Hotel.

PARADISE POINT (20) On another hilltop directly above the port is a restaurant/bar with the best view of Charlotte Amalie and the port; this spot is particularly popular at sunset. From the station (Tel. 774–9809) directly behind the West Indian Dock, a cable car whisks passengers in four minutes up a steep mountainside to the summit from where there are spectacular views. Cost

is \$10 round trip. Paradise Point can also be reached by a road from the harbor. The road to the top is directly in front of the entrance to the Havensight Mall, which fills the area between the dock and the main road into town.

CARIFEST Also behind the dock to the south is the site of Carifest, a Caribbean heritage village in West Indian design. Entertainment and cultural events will be staged here when the center opens in 1998.

DRIVING TOUR OF ST. THOMAS

KEEP TO THE LEFT *Generally, roads on St. Thomas are well-marked with route signs but you do need to pay close attention because the roads are very winding and branch onto small roads frequently. Also, it is very easy to get distracted by the views. Be sure to have a good route map in hand; they are readily available from tourist offices and shops.*

Two roads (No. 38 and No. 40) traverse the island east-west from Charlotte Amalie to the east end of the island. Route 38 is a four-lane highway part of the way and leads northeast to Coki Point and Coral World, or at the junction of Route 32, bears southeast to Red Hook. Route 40, known as Skyline Drive, travels along the north side of the mountains from where one gets magnificent views, particularly of the island's famous Magens Bay, and lcads to Mountain Top, the highest accessible point on the island.

If you begin at the waterfront on Veterans Drive and drive east along the harbor, turn north (left) 1 block before the Federal Building, go 1 block to the first stoplight and turn east (right). This street leads up the hill to Bluebeard's Castle Hotel. From here, you can have one of the best panoramas on the island—a spectacular view of Charlotte Amalie harbor—and you will be able to spot your ship at the West India Company dock directly below. (A similar view is available from the hilltop known as Paradise Point, directly above the port.) The hotel is surrounded by gardens of tropical plants and 200-year-old banyan trees. Look closely among the hibiscus and you might see an iguana, a small reptile that

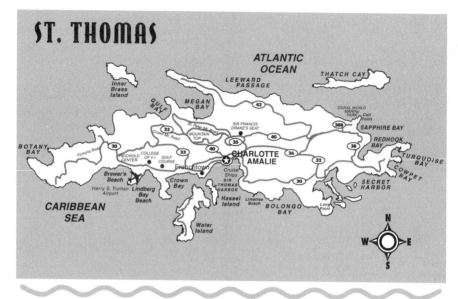

MAP OF ST. THOMAS

looks like a miniature dinosaur. They are green when young, but turn grey with age. Unlike other Caribbean islands where the iguana is elusive and endangered, it is something of a pet on St. Thomas and will often remain still for a photograph. They frequent these hotel grounds as well as those of Coral World and Lime Tree Beach. (As noted previously Bluebeard's Tower, built as a lookout in 1678, is now the hotel's honeymoon suite.)

To go from Bluebeard's to Mafolie Hill, follow Route 35 to its junction with Route 40 at the top of the hill. Turn left and follow Route 40 to *Drake's Seat,* a small lookout named for the British sea captain Sir Francis Drake who is said to have used this vantage point to watch for the Spanish treasure galleons on which he preyed.

You may not see any treasure ships but you will be richly rewarded with a magnificent view of Magens Bay Beach, once cited by *National Geographic* magazine as one of the ten most beautiful beaches in the world. In the panorama, the island directly ahead (north), Hans Lollick, is uninhabited. On the northeast slopes of St. Thomas is the Mahogany Run Golf Course; and offshore in the background is Drake's Passage, a sea channel

first explored by Drake in 1580. You can also see the British Virgin Islands of Tortola, Jost Van Dyke, and Little Jost. St. John lies to the east-southeast.

Drake's Seat is one of the favorite picture-taking spots on St. Thomas; usually there are several boys with their flower-crowned donkeys waiting for you to use them as the foreground for your picture—all, of course, for a tip.

After continuing along the narrow road, Route 40 turns left and then right at the next intersection to St. Peter Mountain Road. You will come to *Fairchild Park,* a lovely little mountaintop oasis named for the philanthropist who donated Magens Bay to the public. From here you can see both the north and south coasts.

On Route 40, the *Estate St. Peter Greathouse and Botanical Garden* (St. Peter Mountain Road; Tel. 774–4999; or 690–4499), which was once part of an 18th-century plantation, is now a 12-acre landscaped spread 1,000 feet above Magens Bay Beach. It has a modern West Indian-style house, furnished with works by fifty local artists and self-guided nature trails. Hours: Daily, 9 A.M. to 5 P.M. Admission: $8 adults; $4 children.

Turn left off Route 40 onto the first narrow road

and continue along this one-way road uphill to the yield sign. From here, follow Route 33 south along winding roads to the intersection of a secondary road on the right leading to *Mountain Top,* where a lookout point at 1,500 feet offers another fabulous view. Mountain Top is also a bar and shopping center.

You can continue west on Route 33 along Crown Mountain Road, which circles Crown Mountain at 1,550 feet—the highest peak on St. Thomas—and return to the south coast at a point near the airport. Or, if your time is limited, turn right at the end of Mountain Top Road and continue to the intersection of Routes 33 and 40 from where you came and follow Route 40 south on Solberg Hill Road. At several points along the road you will have more extensive views of Charlotte Amalie, the harbor, and Hassel Island in the foreground and Water Island beyond. If you continue to the bottom of the hill, you end up back in Charlotte Amalie in the center of town.

Another road, Route 30, runs east along the south coast past the West India Company dock and Frenchman's Reef Hotel to Bolongo Bay and ultimately intersects Route 32 (which goes to Red Hook). Several of the most popular beaches— Secret Harbor, Cowpet, and Sapphire—are on the southeast corner of the island.

The waterfront road west of town (also Route 30) leads past the ferry docks, Frenchtown, and the airport, and continues to the *University of the Virgin Islands* and the *Reichhold Center for the Arts,* an outdoor amphitheatre of modern design in a lovely wooded setting. The college, situated on 175 acres, was founded in 1963 and offers a four-year curriculum. Reichhold Center is the island's main venue for the performing arts for local and visiting artists. Walking tours are available by appointment, Monday through Friday from 9 A.M. to 4 P.M. (Tel. 774–8475).

Route 30 continues west along *Brewer's Beach* and the west end of the island. *Botany Bay* at the westernmost tip has one of the most secluded beaches on the island. There is no road directly to the beach; you must park your car and walk approximately a quarter mile. Local residents advise against going to this area alone.

REMEMBER, driving is on the **LEFT.**

Shopping

Because the U.S. Virgin Islands has a special tax status allowing returning U.S. residents a generous customs duty exemption for goods bought here, St. Thomas has turned shopping into its leading attraction. You can start spending your duty-free allowance the moment you get off the ship at a shopping plaza next to the port, but you should wait until you have been to the downtown shopping district, which is both one of the most attractive and competitively priced in the Caribbean.

On a walk down Main Street (and down side lanes such as newly renovated Palm Passage), in pretty stores and smart boutiques housed in renovated 18th- and 19th-century warehouses from the city's heyday as a trading post, you will find top-quality, brand name watches, jewelry, cameras, electronic equipment, china and crystal, designer clothes and accessories, leading makes of perfumes, cosmetics, and a variety of other gift items at prices ranging from 20 percent and more off those in the mainland. The international character of the selections often makes them as attractive as their prices.

Duty-Free Shopping

The matter of "duty-free" needs some explaining. All stores in the U.S. Virgin Islands are duty-free. Even so, the goods they sell are not entirely without import taxes. Local merchants pay taxes on the merchandise they import but the levies are much lower in the U.S. Virgin Islands than on the mainland. The goods are also free of state and city sales taxes, the principal reason cigarettes and liquor are bargains.

A word of caution: As tempting and attractive as the merchandise in St. Thomas stores may be, it is not always the bargain it is claimed to be. The proliferation of discount houses in the United States, particularly those carrying such items as cameras, electronic equipment, china, and crystal, has cut into the traditional savings on duty-free merchandise. If you are looking for real bargains and not just gifts and souvenirs to take to friends and relatives, come prepared with prices from home and do some comparative shopping before you buy.

Generally in the U.S. Virgin Islands, cigarettes, wine, and liquor are the lowest priced in the Caribbean and represent the greatest savings. Perfume is discounted about 20 percent, depending on the type, size, and make. For example, a $40 bottle of French eau de toilette at home will probably be $34 in St. Thomas, but a one-ounce bottle of perfume that sells for $250 in New York costs $195 in St. Thomas. Riise Gift Shops (Main Street) publishes a brochure listing the prices of most leading perfumes. Use this list to compare prices from home.

Another point: If three or more cruise ships are in the port at one time, the streets and shops can be as crowded as Macy's at Christmas. Since the shopping district is also the historic area for the walking tour, you would be smart to do your sight-seeing first and wait for the crowds to leave.

Finally you will discover the shopping area is quite compact; even the most ardent shoppers can easily cover the district in an hour or 2. Be sure to plan another activity or a sight-seeing tour as you could be disappointed with your visit to St. Thomas if you plan to do nothing more than shop.

Store hours are Monday through Saturday, 9 A.M. to 5 or 5:30 P.M. Some stores stay open until 6. Stores close on Sunday unless a cruise ship is in port. Several booklets published locally, such as *Best Buys in St. Thomas,* have discount coupons.

ART AND ARTISTS: *Mango Tango* is the best place in St. Thomas to buy quality art by local artists. The gallery has frequent shows and helps promote the best artists as well as young unknowns who show the greatest promise. The gallery also carries quality art and crafts from other Caribbean islands, from masks and wall hangings to replicas of West Indian houses. *A. H. Riise Gift Shops and Art Gallery* (Main Street; Tel. 800–524–2037) has a collection of local artists as well as those from around the Caribbean. *The Gallery* (Down Island Traders on the waterfront at Post Office Alley, second floor; Tel. 776–4641) has a large collection of art from around the Caribbean.

The Kilnworks (Route 38 #4H Smith Bay near Stouffers Resort; Tel. 775–3979) is the workshop and gallery of potter Peggy Seibert. Works by other local sculptors, jewelry designers, batik artists, and painters are also on display. Hours: daily except Sunday, 9 A.M. to 5 P.M.

In late March, mid-August, and November, *Tillett's Gardens* (Route 38, Tutu; Tel. 775–1929), where some artists and jewelry designers work and sell their products year-round, holds an arts fair, *Arts Alive,* in which more than fifty local artists exhibit their paintings, sculpture, ceramics, jewelry, needlecraft, novelties, and other crafts. (See the section on cultural events.) The complex includes *El Papagayo,* a tropical restaurant for light snacks, which is open daily from 9 A.M. to 5 P.M. and Monday, Wednesday, and Friday to 7:30 P.M.

BOOKS: *Dockside Bookshop* (Havensight Mall; Tel. 774–4937) and *Island Newstand* (Grand Hotel) have the largest selection of books and carry stateside newspapers—costing $2 or more.

CAMERAS/ELECTRONICS: All leading makes are available, but bring along stateside prices for comparison. The largest selections are at *Boolchand's* (31 Main Street and a branch at the Havensight Mall next to the West India Company dock). Prices generally are comparable to those of discount houses in New York.

CHILDREN'S TOYS/CLOTHES: *Mini Mouse House* (Trompeter Gade) is the place to find clothes and toys for tots.

CRAFTS: Don't overlook locally made products, especially for gifts and souvenirs. What's more, you do not have to count any of these products in your $1,200 customs allowance. Straw hats, mats and other household items, candles with scents of local herbs and spices, candies and preserved fruits and spices, pottery and ceramics, folkloric dolls, particularly the Mocko Jumbi stiltwalkers, macrame and scrimshaw, and perfume and suntan lotions made from native flowers and herbs are some of the products available. Limited selections are available in gift and souvenir shops all over the island, but *Caribbean Safari* (35 Back Street) has a selection of straw crafts from around the Caribbean. *Cowboys and Indians* (Grand

Hotel Court) specializes in Native American art.

Down Island Traders on the waterfront has preserves, herbs, and spices as well as imported teas and coffees and an array of crafts and Caribbean art. Similarly, *Caribbean Marketplace* (Havensight Mall) has an array of products from throughout the Caribbean, particularly Tortola-based Sunny Caribbee, which packages fabulous herbs, spices, and condiments, guaranteed to add zest to almost anything you cook, and a new line of cosmetics, Sunsations, made from tropical fruits and flowers.

CHINA/CRYSTAL: *Little Switzerland* (Main Street) has a wide selection of English bone china, French crystal, and similar high quality goods. You can get a catalog by calling 800–524-2010. *A. H. Riise Gift Shops* (Main Street) is something of a department store with a collection of boutiques for jewelry, gifts, perfume, and liquor as well as china, silver, and crystal.

CLOTHING: Boutiques with designer fashions can be found in the narrow passageways between Main Street and the waterfront. *Fendi, DKNY,* and *Polo Ralph Lauren* (Palm Passage) have their own stores. *Nicole Miller* (Main Street) is a new addition, as is *Bisou-Bisou* (Palm Passage) which had young, trendy fashions. *Local Color* (Hibiscus Alley) has handpainted T-shirts, dresses, and sportswear; look for the label, *Sloop Jones,* based at Hansen Bay, St. John. *Cosmopolitan* (Drakes Passage) has designer sportswear, including Gottex swimwear at about 30 percent less than U.S. prices, as well as shoes.

JEWELRY: Several stores such as *Cardow, Cartier, Colombian Emeralds,* and *H. Stern* (all on Main Street) have international reputations; *A. H. Riise Gift Shops* has a large jewelry department and is the exclusive Mikimoto dealer. *Blue Carib Gems* (Bakery Square Mall) has jewelry designed by Alan O'Hara, who uses gemstones and coral found in the Caribbean. You can watch craftspeople cutting gemstones and design your own jewelry. There are many smaller jewelry stores on Main Street and adjacent malls, too. All stores stock selections of gold, pearl, and semi-precious rings, bracelets, and earrings. Look around before you buy.

LEATHER/LUGGAGE: Several shops in Royal Dane Mall have attractive high quality Italian and Spanish handbags. *The Leather Shop* (Main Street) is the dealer for Fendi and Bottega Veneta. *Gucci, Louis Vuitton,* and *Coach* (Hibiscus Alley) have their own stores. *Cosmopolitan* (Drakes Passage) carries Bally shoes for men and women and Bruno Magli for men. *Stepping Out* (Havensight Mall #5) has moderately priced shoes.

LINENS: Table linens are among the best bargains. Most come from India and China. *Linen House* and *Mr. Tablecloth* (Palm Passage) have large collections and you might check some of the general stores on Main Street, too.

LIQUOR: Prices are very competitive. *Al Cohen's* near the port claims to have the best prices in St. Thomas, but *Sparky's* and *Bolero,* both on Main Street, are usually the same. Check *St. Thomas This Week* or *Best Buys in St. Thomas,* free pamphlets distributed for tourists. The centerfold or back page has a list of the current liquor prices. Liquor stores will deliver your purchases to your ship.

PERFUMES: *Tropicana Shop* (Main Street) has nothing but perfume; *St. Thomas Cosmetic & Fragrance Factory* carries locally made items. The *West Indies Bay Company* (Estates Thomas, formerly at Havensight Mall) makes *St. Johns Bay Rum* for men and *J'Ouvert* for women. The fragrances are packaged in bottles with handwoven palm fronds in a design taken from the traditional one used by Caribbean fishermen for their fish pots.

WATCHES/CLOCKS: *Little Switzerland* and *A. H. Riise Gift Shops* carry famous high-quality names, but there are any number of stores on Main Street and at the International Bazaar which have lesser known brands at considerably lower prices. High quality watches and clocks are among the best buys, but check hometown prices in advance if you plan to buy a watch in St. Thomas, and shop around before you buy.

 **Sports**

St. Thomas has good facilities for almost every warm-weather sport one could imagine—fishing, golf, horseback riding, tennis, parasailing, waterskiing, windsurfing—and those for sailing and diving are outstanding.

BEACHES AND SWIMMING: The irregular coastline with its coves and bays that sheltered pirates in the old days is one of St. Thomas's biggest attractions for tourists today. The most celebrated—and the most crowded—beach is at *Magens Bay* on the north side of the island. For the reader's convenience, the main beaches are listed here according to location starting with those closest to Charlotte Amalie.

In the South/Southeast:

Morningstar: Chairs, umbrellas, and equipment for sailing, windsurfing, snorkeling for rent; restaurant; weekend entertainment; shower/changing facilities.

Tranquil Honeymoon Beach: On Water Island, it is earmarked to get a $3.3 million facelift by the Interior Department. The beach is open to visitors and can be reached by a ferry from town.

In the North/Northeast:

Magens Bay: Chairs and equipment for sailing, windsurfing, snorkeling for rent; restaurant; dressing rooms. Admission: $1 adults; 25 cents per child under age 12; $1 per car. Less crowded in the morning.

Coki: Especially popular with snorkelers and used frequently by dive instructors for their classes; therefore, likely to be busy. Snorkel gear for rent; snack cart.

Renaissance Grand Beach Hotel: Chairs, umbrellas, and equipment for sailing, windsurfing, snorkeling for rent; restaurant.

In the East End/Red Hook:

Sapphire, Secret Harbor, and half a dozen places in between are popular with snorkelers and divers; most have equipment for sailing, windsurfing, and snorkeling for rent. There are about a dozen hotels and as many restaurants in the vicinity. Sapphire Beach on Sunday has a brunch where you can meet local folks and enjoy island music and dancing. Blackbeard's Beach is the windsurfer's favorite.

In the South/Southwest:

Lindberg: South of airport; sports equipment

for rent from Island Beachcomber and Emerald Beach hotels; restaurants.

Brewer's: South of the University of the Virgin Islands, it is popular for shelling.

BIKING: See Shore Excursions elsewhere in this chapter.

BOATING: The Virgin Islands with their calm seas and year-round balmy weather are well known as boating meccas and have a large number of charter operations based here. Every type of craft from small sailboats to large ocean yachts is available and can be chartered any way you want—from bare boat to full crew with all provisions. Many charter operators have stateside offices and toll-free numbers for information and reservations.

Ramada Inn Yacht Haven Marina is homeport for the V.I. Charter Yacht League (Tel. 774–3944). The marina is always full of boats and is the venue for the league's annual boat show in mid-November. The east end of the island has the *American Yacht Harbor* (Red Hook, Tel. 775–6454) and *Charter Boat Center* (Piccola Marina; Tel. 800–866–5714; 775–7990) among others. In April the annual Caribbean Ocean Racing Triangle begins in St. Thomas and moves to Tortola and Antigua for another series of meets.

Day Sailing Excursions: More than two dozen boats operate day sails which take passengers to pretty beaches for swimming and snorkeling and serve lunch and refreshments. Some take only up to six people; others are party boats which take more than a dozen. There are also several large sight-seeing boats which offer dinner cruises.

DEEP-SEA FISHING: Experts say the Virgin Islands are one of the best places in the world for blue marlin and the records set here support the claim. Other fish—dolphin, kingfish, white marlin, sailfish, wahoo, yellowfin tuna, blackfin tuna, and skipjack—are plentiful too.

American Yacht Harbor (Red Hook; Tel. 775–6454), *St. Thomas Sports Fishing Center* (Tel. 775–7990), and a dozen or more boat operators offer half- and full-day deep-sea fishing trips and provide bait, tackle, ice, and beer. For example, *Boobie Hatch* (Red Hook, Box 79, St. Thomas, USVI 00802; Tel. 775–6683) runs half-day fishing trips for $325 to $375; full-day, $550 to $750 for a maximum of six people; and $600 and $750 for marlin. The time of year can make a difference in the prices; the marlin season is mainly July and August.

GOLF: *Mahogany Run Golf Course* (Route 42; call Tel. 777–6006 for tee times) is St. Thomas's only 18-hole championship golf course, and one of the Caribbean's most challenging layouts. It was completely renovated in 1996 and a new watering system installed to ensure optimum conditions year-round. Located about 15 minutes from Charlotte Amalie, the spectacular course (6,100 yards, par 70) designed by George and Tom Fazio extends over verdant mountains, valleys, and rocky cliffs overlooking the ocean. Difficult terrain and tight runways make accuracy the golfer's most essential tool. The famous 13th, 14th, and 15th holes, known as Devil's Triangle, are laid out along sea cliffs with breathtaking views of the ocean and surrounding islands; they are cliff-hangers in every sense of the word. Both 9- and 18-hole greens fees are available. There is a resident pro, clubhouse with bar and grill, fully equipped pro shop, driving range, and practice putting green. Greens fee: Winter, $75 plus $15 for cart (required). After 2:30 P.M. you can play as much as you want for $60. Ship golf packages cost about $130 but will include transportation from the port.

HIKING: A few trails have been opened on Hassel Island, now being developed as a national park in Charlotte Amalie Harbor. More interesting and extensive trails are available in the national park on St. John. (See St. John section later in this chapter.)

JOGGING: Beach areas are best as St. Thomas is very mountainous. A 1-mile jogging track along the National Park Road at East End begins at the park entrance, marked by a sign on Route 32. Local residents use it, particularly in the early morning.

KAYAKING: *Virgin Island Ecotours* (Nadir, Route 32; Tel. 779–2155; fax: 774–4601) offers 2.5-hour guided kayak tours of the Virgin Islands Marine Sanctuary, Mangrove Lagoon, led by marine biologists and naturalists from the University of the Virgin Islands. The company uses single or two-person ocean kayaks that are easy for anyone with little or no experience to paddle and provide a treat for adventurers. No motorized vessels are allowed in the lagoon; so kayakers can enjoy the quiet atmosphere in an area of calm waters. The tours start from the Holmberg Marina and cost $50, with a 15-minute orientation and slide show to introduce kayakers to local flora and fauna. Kayaks may also be rented for individual exploration.

SNORKELING AND SCUBA DIVING: The Virgin Islands are consistently rated by dive experts among the best in the world for both novice and experienced divers. Visibility ranges from 50 feet to 150 feet; water temperatures are warm, averaging 82°F in summer and 78°F in winter; there's great variety; and the facilities are excellent. The St. Thomas Hospital has a recompression chamber.

Three dozen of the Virgin Islands' one hundred dive sites lie within a 20-minute boat ride of St. Thomas. On the southeast shore, *Cow and Calf,* only 25 feet deep, has a variety of corals and schools of fish and is well suited for snorkelers and novice divers. *St. James Island* has rocky shelves, tiny caves, and sea whips in a vast sweep of coral reef. *Stevens Cay,* a beautiful reef crowned with seafans and mountain coral, abounds with angelfish and triggerfish.

For experienced divers, the north side of St. Thomas, where the Atlantic and Caribbean meet, is a prime location. Here, water rushes in and out carrying with it tremendous amounts of fish. *Thatch Cay,* just north of St. Thomas, has a series of tunnels divers can swim through. *Congo Cay,* only 30 feet down, has huge boulders and lava archways.

Most dive operators have their own tanks and boats and offer packages and instructions ranging from a half-day minicourse to a week-long course with certification and advanced instruction. A complete list is available from the U.S. Virgin Islands tourist offices. The half-day minicourse is ideal for cruise passengers as an introduction to scuba diving; they are given instruction in the use of dive equipment and make a supervised shallow-water dive at a location abundant with fish and coral.

Chris Sawyer Diving Center (Stouffer Grand Beach Resort; Tel. 775–7320) has daily dives of 4 hours in the morning for $65; 2 hours in the afternoon for $40; and on Fridays, a special all-day excursion to the Wreck of the Rhone in the British Virgin Islands for $95. Night dives are also offered several times weekly. Similarly, *Aqua Action* (Secret Harbour Beach Hotel; Tel. 775–6285) has daily departures at 8:45 A.M. for a two-tank dive for $70 and at 1:30 P.M. for a single-tank dive for $50.

The *St. Thomas Diving Club* (P.O. Box 7337; Tel. 776–2381) is located at the Bolongo Bay Beach Resort on the south coast. The diving club is a PADI five-star facility and a training school. The club offers a daily introductory scuba resort course, 3.5 hours long, at 9 A.M. for $70. The class begins with a 1.5-hour lesson at the hotel pool followed by a beach dive usually at Coki Point; snorkelers, $25. For certified divers the club offers daily dives at specific locations. A one-tank dive is $55; two-tank dive, $80; and night dive, $65. Also for certified divers, Cartanser Senior Wreck Trip goes to a 190-foot-long wrecked ship lying in shallow, calm waters about 15 minutes by boat from Bolongo.

For snorkelers and divers, the club's custom-built boat makes all-day cruises to the British Virgin Islands to dive the Wreck of the Rhone ($125), while snorkelers and nondivers visit Tortola and the Baths ($130). Lunch is provided on both all-day trips.

Joe Vogel Diving Company (12B Mandal Road, P.O. Box 7322, St. Thomas 00801; Tel. 775–7610) is owned by a professional diver with over thirty years of experience. He does not offer packages but prefers to tailor trips to the individual's needs and level of proficiency. Vogel offers five hours of beginner's instruction for $50.

Virgin Islands Diving Schools (Vitraco Park, one block north of Yacht Haven, across from Pueblo Supermarket; Tel. 774–8687) offers Scuba Adventure, a half-day dive for noncertified divers at Coki Beach, for $45 including all gear. It is available twice daily, 9 A.M. to noon and 1 to 4 P.M. For advanced divers, a one-tank dive departs at 9 A.M. and costs $50; a two-tank dive is $70. Snorkeling trips depart at 9 A.M. and 1 P.M. and cost $25.

While divers are searching for sunken treasures and snorkelers are mesmerized by the fish and coral, those who don't swim need not miss the excitement. They can opt for the comfort of a glass-bottom boat. An alternative is the *Atlantis II,* a recreational submarine which dives to a depth of 150 feet. The 50-foot-long ship holds twenty-eight people and a two-member crew and has 8 large viewports along the sides from which passengers can see nature's magical display. The ship is air-conditioned and all its systems are duplicated to ensure safety. *Atlantis II* makes its dives at Buck Island, about a 20-minute boat ride from its station next to the West India Company Dock. To add interest and excitement, a diver plays the role of the Pied Piper, feeding the fish which swarm to him in great numbers. You will see schools of yellowtails and blue chromis, an occasional barracuda, and other species typical of the Virgin Islands reefs. The dive lasts about an hour and costs $72 for adults; $36 ages 13 to 18; $27 ages 4 to 12.

Coral World, an underwater observatory at Coki Point and once St. Thomas' most popular attraction, was badly damaged in the 1995 hurricane. In spring 1997, it was purchased by a group of local investors with the aim of renovating the facility and reopening it for the 1998 season. Check locally.

TENNIS: About three dozen hotels have tennis courts. Those closest to the West India Company Dock and open to nonguests are at *Marriott's Frenchman's Reef Hotel* (Tel. 776–8500), two courts, $10 per hour. Those nearest to Crown Bay Dock are two public courts, lighted until 8 P.M. On the eastern end, the new *Sugar Bay Plantation Resort* has a large tennis complex with seven courts, $9 per hour; and *Stouffer Grand Beach* has six courts, $10 per hour.

SAILBOARDING: *Morningstar Beach* (Tel. 776–5860) is nearest the West India Company Dock, but the eastern end of the island has the best windsurfing. *Sapphire Beach* (Tel. 775–6100) offers instruction on a simulator in the water. *West Indies Windsurfing* (Tel. 775–6530) on the beach in Red Hook, has the best rentals. For those with experience, Vessup, an area on the southside of Red Hook known locally as Bluebeard's Beach, is a popular venue for windsurfing contests.

DINING AND NIGHTLIFE

The Virgin Islands do not have a big nightlife scene like that of Nassau or San Juan. Rather, the action is small-scale—steel bands, small combos, guitarists, or discos—and mostly revolves around the entertainment offered at hotels and restaurants. As a result, the sections on dining and nightlife have been combined, with notations on entertainment made as appropriate. You should have reservations for dinner, particularly in the winter season.

As for the dining, the U.S. Virgin Islands, alas, did not gain their reputation as Paradise in the kitchen. It's not that innkeepers and restaurateurs don't try. They try very hard, perhaps too hard, to create gourmet havens. But for a myriad of understandable reasons (Herman Wouk's hilarious *Don't Stop the Carnival* was written from his trials and tribulations in trying to operate a hotel in St. Thomas), they are unable to maintain a consistently high level; instead, such places can quickly become pretentious disappointments at very high prices. (Expensive means more than $30 per person. If wine is added, the bill can quickly climb to $50 per person and more.)

Beni Iguana (Grand Hotel Court; 777–8740). A sushi bar in an historic Danish building has umbrella tables outside in a pretty courtyard. There are cooked dishes and daily specials, as well. The bar serves domestic and Japanese beer and sake. Live classical and jazz guitar on Friday evenings. Closed Sunday.

Berry's Farm Garden Bar and Restaurant (Route 33; Tel. 774–3020) offers a grand view over the north coast and the neighboring islands while you enjoy salads featuring the farm's home-grown vegetables, along with local fare. Lunch and dinner daily. Moderate.

Craig and Sally's (Frenchtown; Tel. 777–9949). A family-run restaurant/bar with owners Craig at the door and Sally in the kitchen. The bar, open daily 11:30 A.M. to 1 A.M. except Monday, serves wine by the glass. The restaurant offers an eclectic menu that changes daily. Closed Saturday and Sunday lunch. Moderate.

Cuzzen's (7 Back Street; Tel. 777–4711). In the heart of Charlotte Amalie, this lively restaurant-bar specializes in West Indian dishes and has sandwiches and pasta. Moderate.

Gladys' Cafe (Royal Dane Mall; Tel. 774–6604). A charming cafe in town, it serves lunch plus dinner on Friday with jazz (6 to 9 P.M.). Lunch offers fresh fish, salads, hamburgers, and local specials. Gladys's own hot sauce, attractively packaged for gifts, is on sale for $6 a bottle. Moderate.

Hervé Restaurant and Wine Bar (Government Hill; Tel. 777–9703). St. Thomas' hottest new restaurant is set in a renovated 18th-century building with a panoramic view of Charlotte Amalie. *Hervé* is Hervé Paul Chassin, a St. Thomas restaurateur with twenty-five years experience. You lunch and dine in an informal ambience on contemporary American and classic French selections, all touched by a bit of Caribbean. The bar serves wines by the glass. Closed Sunday. Expensive.

Hotel 1829 (Government Hill; Tel. 774–1829). Set in a historic landmark, classic international selections are served in a pretty setting. Very expensive.

Old Stone Farmhouse (Mahogany Run; Tel. 775–1377). St. Thomas habitués will welcome the recent return of this former island favorite. In its rustic yet elegant setting, you can select from an eclectic array of French, Asian, and Caribbean dishes as well as steak and seafood dishes. Expensive.

Paddy O'Furniture's Irish Brew Pub (East End; Tel. 779–1760). USVI's first "Irish brew pub" makes four different beers. Pitbull Irish Stout, the most popular brew, combines four malts. The waterfront restaurant serves lunch and dinner and has take-out service. Closed Sunday. Moderate.

Victor's New Hideout (Sub Base; Tel. 776–9379). West Indian specialties and fresh fish; the setting has a panoramic view of the bay. Lunch and dinner served daily. Moderate.

Zorba (2B Commandant Gade, Government Hill; Tel. 776–0444). The rustic outdoor patio setting helps give this unpretentious restaurant an authentic flavor of Greece as much as the food, which is good and inexpensive.

Bluebeard's Castle or *Paradise Point* are good perches for cocktails at sunset; and on different nights of the week, you will find steel band entertainment at different hotels. Several nights a week, *Smuggler's* at Renaissance Grand Beach Hotel has one of the best West Indian musical groups on the island, and on Wednesdays the hotel features West Indian night, with steel band music and the Mocko Jumbi stilt dancers, beginning at 7 P.M. Check local publications such as *St. Thomas This Week* for what is happening during your visit.

CULTURAL EVENTS AND FESTIVALS

St. Thomas has a rich year-round calendar of cultural activity, festivals, and sporting events.

Reichhold Center for the Performing Arts

During the season from October through May, the Reichhold Center for the Performing Arts (Tel. 693–1559) features concerts, opera, ballet, Broadway musicals, jazz, gospel, and plays at its wonderful outdoor theater. Performances are by college and visiting artists. Past events have featured such diverse talents as Ray Charles, Golden Dragon Acrobats of Taiwan, Senegal Dancers, and the Boy's Choir of Harlem, among others.

St. Thomas Arts Council (Bakery Square, No. 330, St. Thomas; Tel. 776–0100; contact: John Jowers) is a private, nonprofit organization with over one hundred members that encourages the preservation of Virgin Islands arts and crafts, while promoting the discovery and training of local talent, and that sponsors artistic events throughout the year.

Cultural Dancers

Three Virgin Islands dance groups perform at different venues throughout the year.

Caribbean Dance Company of the Virgin Islands (Tel. 778–8824) based in St. Croix has twelve dancers and ten singers and musicians. They perform in both St. Thomas and St. Croix and on various cruise ships and give two major performances (February and November) each year. The company has a new dance center in St.

Croix in a 200-year-old building renovated for them. Visitors are welcome to participate in any of the forty classes taught weekly.

Mungo Niles Cultural Dancers and Musicians (Tel. 774–3366) are based in St. Thomas and directed by Magnus "Mungo" Niles. The nonprofit group whose purpose is to preserve the dance traditions of the island has members ranging in age from twenty to seventy and dances to Quailbay, or scratch, music.

Mocko Jumbi Dancers (Tel. 774–1968) directed by Hugo Moolenaar are the most colorful stiltwalk dancers in the Americas. Their dances and costumes derive from ancient cult traditions brought to the islands by African slaves. Their name, meaning "mesmerizing spirits," is appropriate as they never fail to fascinate their audiences when they dance around on 17-foot-high stilts.

Arts Alive

More than fifty local artists exhibit their works at the popular Arts Alive Festival at the Tillett Gallery (Tel. 775–1405) on St. Thomas. The festival is a three-day potpourri of the arts with artists, sculptors, and crafts people from the three islands on hand to display their paintings, pottery, sculpture, handcrafted jewelry, needlework, and photography. There are also craft demonstrations. The fair started as an annual event in 1980 but has become so popular that it is now held three times a year in late March, mid-August, and mid-November. Performances by brilliantly costumed Mocko Jumbies, clowns, acrobats, and the Quadrille Dancers folkloric group are part of the entertainment. Admission is free.

Classics in the Garden is a special classical music series held on Wednesday afternoons during the winter season at the Tillett Gallery.

Three Carnivals

The Virgin Islands observe all the U.S. national holidays, plus a few of their own. Leading the list on all three islands is Carnival. On St. Thomas, Carnival is held in the spring during the last two weeks of April and gives everyone on the island the fever.

Carnival begins officially with the opening of Calypso Tent, a weeklong calypso song competition for the coveted title of the Calypso King. It is followed by a week of festivities including the crowning of a Carnival queen, food fair, children's parades, and J'Ouvert morning tramp. The celebration winds up with one of the most elaborate all-day parades in the Caribbean featuring the Mocko Jumbi Dancers.

On St. Croix, the big festival is the Crucian Christmas Fiesta, a two-week affair beginning on Christmas and culminating on Three Kings Day, January 6, with a parade. Children and adults dressed in richly decorated costumes of silk and satin dance through the streets of Christiansted to the rhythm of calypso. July 3, Emancipation Day, is another important day on St. Croix with a moving ceremony in Frederiksted on the site of the freeing of the slaves in the Danish West Indies in 1848.

St. John holds a mini-Carnival as part of its July 4th Independence Day celebrations.

Sporting Events

Among the most prestigious sporting competitions are the Blue Marlin Fishing Tournament in August; International Rolex Cup Regatta in March; Annual Caribbean Windsurfing Championships in June; Mahogany Run Golf Classic on St. Thomas in October; and V.I. Charter Yacht League Boat Show in November.

ST. JOHN A GIFT OF NATURE

Serene St. John, the quietest, least developed, and most secluded of the U.S. Virgin Islands, is truly America the Beautiful. Almost one-half of the heavily forested, mountainous island—9,485 acres—is covered by national park on land donated in 1956 by Laurance Rockefeller.

The island is edged by lovely little coves and pristine, white-sand beaches and some of the most spectacular aquamarine waters in the Caribbean. Beneath these waters is a tropical wonderland of fish and coral, also protected by the national park. Hidden in the park on the north side of the island are two camps—the rustic Cinnamon Bay and the more deluxe Maho Bay, about 6 miles from town. Both sites have watersports facilities.

St. John lies between the Caribbean and the Atlantic Ocean, about 3 miles east of St. Thomas and 35 miles from St. Croix. Local transportation from St. Thomas is available by ferry. The island, 21 square miles, is 9 miles long and up to 4 miles wide.

Development, which is severely restricted, can be found in or near the lilliputian port of *Cruz Bay,* the island's only town, and the southwest corner where the island's largest resort, the modern *Hyatt Regency Virgin Grand Hotel,* is located. On the north side is the super deluxe *Caneel Bay.* Set in the magnificent gardens of an old sugar plantation, the latter resort fronts seven—yes, seven—of the prettiest beaches in the Caribbean. The tennis facilities are great, too.

The tranquility of St. John today belies its past as the scene of one of the bloodiest slave rebellions of the 18th century. In the early colonial period, the island seemed to have escaped most of the European escapades, except for occasional visits from pirates, castaways, or runaway slaves. After the island was taken over by Denmark in 1717, cultivation of sugar and cotton began in earnest. The plantations brought about a century of prosperity but not peace. In 1733 the slaves revolted and held St. John for six months. The Danes were able to end the insurrection only after the French sent reinforcements from Martinique.

Traditionally the slaves killed themselves either by jumping from a cliff or by shooting themselves rather than face the terrible punishment inflicted on those who revolted. After the 1733 revolt, about 300 are said to have jumped from a rock cliff on the northern shore of St. John.

Vestiges of several old plantations can be seen, as can petroglyphs of the Arawaks, the earliest known inhabitants of the island.

 ## IN BRIEF

TRANSPORTATION: Several ships call at St. John; those such as the *Sir Francis Drake* of Tallship Adventures sail around the U.S. and British Virgin Islands year-round, while others depart regularly from St. Thomas during the winter season only. But the great majority of people visit St. John on day trips from St. Thomas; this is one of the most delightful excursions available for cruise passengers, whether as an organized tour, a day sail, or on your own. (See the St. Thomas transportation and shore excursions sections for details.) Whether you arrive by ferry or sailboat from St. Thomas or by cruise ship, be sure to be on deck with your camera when you glide into this American Paradise.

FERRY SERVICE: Ferries depart Red Hook hourly from 6:30 A.M. to midnight for Cruz Bay and return from 6 A.M. to 11 P.M. Others depart from the Charlotte Amalie waterfront at 2-hour intervals from 7:15 A.M. to 3:45 P.M. There is also ferry service from St. John to Jost Van Dyke and Tortola.

SHORE EXCURSIONS: For ships that call at St. John, the most popular excursions include a two-hour island tour with a visit to the historic Annaberg Plantation, ($30 for one or two persons; $12 per person for three or more); a four-hour sailing excursion around the island with a stop at Honeymoon Beach for swimming and snorkeling, $48; and an hour's trip on a glass-bottom boat, $19. For those who like to hike, however, nothing beats the trails in the National Park—and they are free. They are described in more detail later in this chapter.

CRUZ BAY: Tiny Cruz Bay, almost always filled with yachts and other pleasure craft, hugs a narrow strip of land between the little harbor and the mountains. Most of the buildings and houses are West Indian–style in architecture and painted a medley of pastel colors. Until recently, the structures were small and blended into the landscape as naturally as the bougainvillea and hibiscus on the surrounding hillsides. Unfortunately, the character of the town is being drastically altered with the construction of hotels and shopping complexes. Although they are designed in "village" style, generally they are crowding the limited space around the harbor and turning the once-natural landscape into a tacky, T-shirt and fast-food mall.

Directly in front of the ferry pier is the town's little park and at the north end of the street are the St. John Taxi Association, Police Station, and Tourist Information Center where you can pick up maps and brochures of the island's shops and services.

PARK SERVICE VISITOR CENTER: On the north side of the harbor is the *Virgin Islands National Park Service Visitor Center,* which should be your top priority. It is open from 8 A.M. to 4:30 P.M. The center is well organized and offers a variety of activities which will introduce you to St. John in the most rewarding way. These include ranger-led tours, hikes, snorkeling trips, cultural and wildlife lectures, and film presentations. A schedule of activities is available in advance from the park service (Tel. 776–6201). Reservations during the winter season are strongly recommended. Write Virgin Islands National Park, Box 806, St. Thomas 00801 (Tel. 775–6238). The ranger-led hikes are highly recommended, as the rangers are very knowledgeable and provide valuable commentary on flora and history unavailable in general literature. The park also conducts a three-hour boat trip around St. John.

HIKES AND TOURS: Among its many facilities, the park has twenty-four hiking trails. A brochure, *Trail Guide for Safe Hiking,* outlining twenty-one trails with a map and tips on planning and preparations, is available from the park service. Most trails are designed in clusters of two or three contiguous paths to be taken in segments as short as 10 minutes, or, when strung together, as long as 2 to 4 hours. The most popular is *Reef Bay,* a 2.5-mile trail which takes 2 hours to cover downhill (in one direction). The trail begins 5 miles east of Cruz Bay on Centerline Road (the one road that traverses the island from Cruz Bay on the west to East End, the furthermost tip of the island). When the excursion is made with a park ranger, the return is made by boat from Reef Bay to the Visitor's Center in Cruz Bay. The downhill route extends through a variety of vegetation from a shady moist forest to an arid one. The remnants of four sugar estates and abandoned farming communities are visible. A small picnic site with toilet facilities is available near the beach at Reef Bay sugar mill.

Two self-guided trails leave from the entrance of the Cinnamon Bay campgrounds and provide an introduction to the park's vegetation and historic landmarks, all labeled. One is a loop trail of about an hour; the other starts from the camp and uses an old plantation road uphill through the forest to Centerline Road, terminating about a mile west of the Reef Bay trailhead. It takes about an hour.

Among the historic programs is the *Annaberg Cultural Demonstrations* (3 hours) which departs Tuesday, Wednesday, and Friday at 10 A.M. It visits the partially restored ruins of the *Annaberg Plantation*, where you can learn about tropical food, medicinal plants, weaving, baking, charcoal-making, and other skills islanders once needed to subsist. You can also tour the site on your own with a pamphlet available at the park entrance.

For those on organized tours, the main stop usually is *Trunk Bay*, a lovely beach and site of an underwater trail laid out by the park service for snorkelers. Snorkeling gear is available from the park service at the beach. The bay is located on the north shore, about 20 minutes from town.

Unfortunately, the reef is now badly deteriorated from overuse. But happily, snorkelers and divers have many other reefs around St. John to explore. Johnson Reef and Watermelon Cay on the north coast and Stevens Cay and Fishbowl at Cruz Bay are popular sites. At Honeymoon Beach, one of the sandy coves of Caneel Bay reached by a footpath, snorkelers can swim with spotted eagle ray.

For visitors on their own, taxis with driver/guides can be hired in Cruz Bay, 1 block from the pier. Or you can rent a car or jeep at several locations in the town; rates are about $50 per day. The day's target for most visitors is a circle route along North Shore Road (Route 20) and Centerline Road (Route 10), the island's two main roads, with stops for a swim, picnic, and short hikes. There are secondary roads and tracks which can be negotiated only by jeep; the park service strongly advises visitors not to strike off on their own without a briefing from a ranger at the Visitor Center first. That's my advice, too.

Coral Bay on the easternmost end of the island is the site of the first known Arawak settlement, about A.D. 200, and of Fort Frederick, built by the Danes in 1717. The fort fell to the rebels during the slave revolt of 1733. The island's highest peak, Bordeaux Mountain, 1,277 feet, is in the center of the island.

Before you leave St. John you will want to explore the little town of Cruz Bay, 3 streets wide and 4 streets deep; it is easy to do on foot. There are boutiques, open-air restaurants, and street vendors selling ice cream, cold drinks, and West Indian finger food.

Shopping and Dining in St. John

Understandably, St. John's beauty and tranquility have made it something of an artists' and artisans' community. Several local artists have stores in town, but with the new commercial development you will need to look hard to find them sandwiched between the T-shirt and junky merchandise shops.

The Pink Papaya (Lemon Tree Mall; Tel. 776–7266) is the attractive gallery and gift shop of Virgin Islands artist Lisa Etre, whose distinctive style reflects her West Indian environment in an imaginative, sophisticated way. In addition to original art and prints, elements from her paintings are used in designs on tableware, greeting cards, and other practical items that make lovely gifts.

Mongoose Junction, a 10-minute walk from the pier on the road leading to north-shore beaches, is an attractive shopping plaza designed as an artists' enclave, with rustic wooden buildings incorporating the trees in a natural setting. Among the group are boutique/studios belonging to local artists and transplanted mainlanders. *Donald Schnell Studio* (Tel. 800–253–7107) features ceramics by an American artist who comes originally from Michigan. Schnell uses natural materials—coral sand, woods, etc.—to create unusual but useful pieces such as lamps, dishes, candle holders, and planters. A recent expansion of Mongoose Junction has more than doubled its size and added more traditional shops—jewelry, sportswear, etc. *Batik Kitab* features St. John artist, Juliana Aradi, who works on silk, cotton, and linen. *Rusty Nail Originals* (Tel. 693–7740), one of the newest shops, has gifts, books, handcrafted jewelry, and island clothing. You will probably want to browse around all of the shops; each is different. At the center of the complex is a tree-shaded outdoor restaurant that provides an attractive setting for a light lunch or refreshment.

Asolare (Cruz Bay; Tel. 779–4747), reopened after extensive renovation, is an island favorite for Pacific Rim cuisine, which can be enjoyed along with spectacular views.

SPORTS IN ST. JOHN

Sailing, snorkeling, and diving in the waters of the National Park have long been at the top of the island's attraction. Two new ways to enjoy this paradise have recently been added: kayaking and snuba. Snuba is shallow-water diving that's something of a cross between snorkeling and diving without the serious gear. *Snuba of St. John* (Trunk Bay; Tel. 693–8063) has daily guided tours, starting at 9:30 A.M., for $45.

In recent years, kayaking has become very popular and is available in St. John from *Big Planet Sea Kayaking Center* (Mongoose Junction II; Tel. 776–6638), which offers a 4-hour guided tour of the beautiful coastal waters with time for swimming, snorkeling, and exploring isolated beaches accessible only by boat.

Low-key Water Sports (Cruz Bay; Tel. 693–8999; 800–835–7718) offers half-day kayak tours in the protected bays around St. John, departing at 10 A.M. Cost is $40. The company also rents scuba gear and has diving, snorkeling, and sportfishing excursions. A beginner's dive course is conducted daily at 1 P.M., $55.

Cruz Bay Watersports (Box 252, St. John 00830; Tel. 776–6234) has facilities for snorkeling and scuba with regularly scheduled dive trips daily. Beginners' scuba costs $55; a one-tank dive is $45; both depart at 2 P.M. A two-tank, two-location trip for certified divers is $65, and departs at 9 A.M. The company has day sails with snorkeling, drinks, and lunch for $60, departing at 10 A.M. and returning at 4 P.M.

FERRY SERVICE: Ferries depart Red Hook at the east end of St. Thomas every hour on the hour from 6:30 A.M. to midnight for Cruz Bay Dock and return hourly from 6 A.M. to 11 P.M. Cost: $3 adults, $1 children. Others depart from the downtown waterfront of Charlotte Amalie from 7:15

A.M. to 3:45 P.M. The ride costs $7 one way and takes 45 minutes.

ST. CROIX THE SLEEPING VIRGIN

Although St. Croix is the largest of the U.S. Virgin Islands and served as the capital for 200 years, it is less developed and generally less known to tourists and has long been overshadowed by St. Thomas as a port of call for cruise lines. But after the new $15 million pier in Frederiksted, located just north of the present one, is completed next year, it is expected that an increasing number of cruise lines will find St. Croix a happy alternative to overcrowded St. Thomas.

St. Croix has much to offer: Scenery, sight-seeing, sports, shopping, historic towns, pretty beaches, good restaurants, and some attractions that neither St. Thomas nor St. John can boast. A rain forest; botanic gardens; wildlife refuges for birds and leatherback turtles; three nature preserves and three parks, including both the newest park and the only underwater park run by the U.S. National Park Service; two 18-hole golf courses; and two towns on the National Historic Registry are some of its special features, and there are more.

St. Croix, located about 1,000 miles east-southeast of Miami, is the easternmost point of the United States. It also has the distinction of being the first place now under the American flag where Christopher Columbus is known to have been. He sighted the island on November 13, 1493, on his second voyage and claimed the land for Spain, naming it Santa Cruz or Holy Cross. Columbus sent his men ashore to replenish their ships' fresh water supplies, but when they were greeted by a hail of arrows from the native Carib Indians, the Spaniards did not linger. The island's Spanish name and flag didn't last long either. Indeed, by the time the Danish West India Company (which already owned St. Thomas and St. John) bought St. Croix in 1733, it had seen five flags—Spain, Holland, England, France, and the Knights of

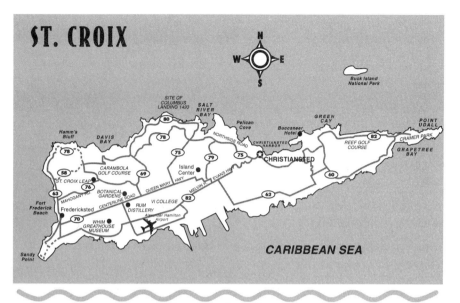

MAP OF ST. CROIX

Malta—fly over the land. The United States' purchase in 1917 brought the number to seven.

Today the Salt River estuary where Columbus is believed to have anchored has been designated as a national park; and the legacy of the French is retained in the name St. Croix (although the pronunciation, *St. Crow-e,* could set a Frenchman's teeth on edge). But it is the Danish heritage which is the most apparent and the source of island pride, particularly in its historic towns and monuments.

The 85-square-mile island is located 35 miles south of St. Thomas and St. John and is vastly different from its mountainous sisters. A low-lying island of gentle landscape and rolling hills, St, Croix was once covered with plantations and was one of the most prosperous sugar-producing centers of the New World. From this enterprise developed a plantation society of landed gentry that prevailed long after the abolition of slavery in 1848 and the death of the sugar mills.

Today many of the plantation homes and sugar mills have been restored as hotels and restaurants; and the central areas of *Christiansted,* the main town, and *Frederiksted,* the old capital, have been named to the National Historic Registry. Both towns are also ports of call. Frederiksted on the

west end of the island has a deep-water harbor, which can be used by all cruise lines. It is also convenient to several popular attractions included on most shore excursions.

On the other hand, Christiansted, located 17 miles from Frederiksted on the north shore, is a picture-perfect port with a small yacht-filled harbor trimmed by a historic waterfront of pastel-painted 17th- and 18th-century colonial buildings and anchored by a grand fort—all beautifully restored. Christiansted is the more developed of the two, particularly for shopping, restaurants, and water sports; and it conveniently faces 2 miles of coral reefs. But the relatively shallow water of the harbor limits Christiansted to receiving small ships—a condition some local people prefer. Small cruise ships such as the *Renaissance* arrive at Gallows Bay, a resort and residential area with a yacht basin, which is within walking distance (or a short taxi ride, $3 one way) from Christiansted. Passengers taking the excursion to Buck Island are picked up by boat directly from the ship.

Since the island has excellent roads, good transportation, and communications, travel is easy no matter which port is used. However, the port of call can influence your selection of activities because of its proximity and convenience to certain attractions.

A more serious limitation on seeing all of St. Croix is the length of time your ship is in port. Most ships calling at Frederiksted arrive about 7 or 8 A.M. and depart by 1 or 2 P.M. Such brief stopovers restrict the range of possibilities and limit tours to 3 or 3.5 hours. (A frequent comment by passengers concerns the need for more time in port in St. Croix. We agree.)

FREDERIKSTED

A WILLIAMSBURG IN THE MAKING

If your ship comes into Frederiksted, which will be the case for the majority of readers, you will need to make a choice of staying close to town to enjoy the beach and stroll through its historic center; taking an island tour; or singling out a specific sport that's high on your priority list—scuba diving, horseback riding, golf, or hiking.

At the Visitor's Bureau and Taxi Association kiosk at the pier, a list of taxi and tour prices is posted. For those who do not care to drive, the St. Croix Combined Taxi and Tour Association (P.O. Box 4490, Kingshill, St. Croix, USVI 00851; Tel. 772–2828) has more than one hundred members who act as driver/guides. Some sample taxi prices from Frederiksted: to Whim Greathouse, $4; to Sprat Hall, $6; to St. George Botanical Gardens, $3; to the airport, $4; to Christiansted, $20 (or $5 per person, minimum of 4); to Carambola Golf Club, $21 (round trip). For a different look *Crusian Helicopters* (Tel. 690–4356) takes you flight–seeing; *Classic Biplane Rides* (Tel. 690–7433), one of the newest attractions, offers tours from late November to late April. A 45-minute-long island tour costs $220 for two persons; a 20-minute tour costs two persons $130, and one-person $110.

BEACH/BOATING: For those who stay in town, Frederiksted has a pretty public beach, usually empty, only a few minutes' walk from the pier. And one of the most beautiful stretches of beach in the Caribbean lies south of town at Sandy Point,

a national wildlife refuge. You are allowed to swim there most of the year, although certain areas might be closed during the summer when the sea turtles come to lay their eggs.

HIKING AND BIKING: The northwest corner of St. Croix in the area known as the Rain Forest has winding roads with light traffic and paths in the woods that lead to small gulleys with streams and waterfalls, particularly after a heavy rain. The most scenic route is known as the *Western Scenic Road*, which begins (or ends) at Hams Bay on the northwest coast.

You can follow the coastal road (Route 63) north via Butler Bay, a private nature preserve of the St. Croix Landmarks Society, which is open to the public. The preserve is popular for birdwatching. A track along a gut with huge trees dangling with vines and festooned with bromeliads, leads inland to a pretty waterfall—after a rain.

Alternatively, you can reach Western Scenic Road by going east to the junction of Creque Dam Road and Scenic Road. There you should turn north and then west onto Western Scenic Road to ascend the ridge overlooking the north coast and Hams Bluff, where big waves break against the shore. The bluff is marked by a lighthouse.

The Caledonia Valley on the south side of the ridge is the island's only ravine with a year-round stream and is popular for birdwatching. The rock-strewn riverbed is dense with trees entwined with huge elephant ears and other vines. It has pools and a waterfall after a heavy rain. *St. Croix Bike and Tours* (Pier 69, Frederiksted, Tel. 772–2545) offers guided mountain bike and other excursions.

HORSEBACK RIDING: A member of the family that has owned Sprat Hall for more than 200 years also runs *Paul and Jill's Equestrian Stable* (Tel. 772–2880) adjacent to Sprat Hall Estate, where you can join trail rides that take you through the rain forest to some of the island's most scenic views. The cost is about $40. In addition, moonlight rides are made five nights prior to a full moon. *Buccaneer Hotel* (near Christiansted) has riding over trails on 300 acres of private land. Both facilities require advance reservations.

SCUBA DIVING: St. Croix, almost completely

surrounded by coral reefs, is heaven for divers and snorkelers. The most famous and popular site is *Buck Island Reef National Monument;* the greatest variety of coral and fish is found in the reefs of the north shore—both more accessible from Christiansted, where several dive operators are located, too. *Dive St. Croix* is the only operator authorized by the National Park Service to dive at Buck Island.

Frederiksted, however, is not without interest to divers and has been dubbed the "seahorse capital" of the region. The pilings of the old pier created a sort of underwater forest with depths of about 35 feet—a natural habitat for certain types of sealife. Sponges, plumeworms, and arrowcrabs cling to the pilings, and tiny yellow, orange, and red seahorse swim about. When the new pier is completed, the old pier will be removed. However, the Port Authority has been working with marine biologists to protect the marine life, particularly the famous seahorses, and transplant it to the new pier.

On the west coast 1 mile south of town, *King's Reef* has a 45-degree drop-off and diving from 40 to 100 feet on a slope rich with corals, seafans, sponges, gorgonians, and other sea life that includes spotted moray eels, sea turtles, lobsters, queen angels, and French angels.

GOLF: *Carambola Golf Club* (Tel. 778–5638; 6,856 yards, par 72) has a lovely 18-hole layout designed by Robert Trent Jones, situated about equidistant between Frederiksted and Christiansted on the north side of the island. It has a clubhouse with restaurant and bar overlooking the greens, a pro, and a well-equipped pro shop. While you may want to visit for a few practice swings, the chance of playing a round depends entirely on the length of time your ship is in port. Greens fees daily except Monday and Tuesday are $50 for 18 holes per person; cart for two, $25. On Monday and Tuesday the fees are $30 per person; cart, $16.

TENNIS: The Buccaneer Hotel has the island's largest complex, with eight tennis courts, including two lighted courts. (See the tennis section under Christiansted for details.) There are two public courts across from Fort Frederik.

HISTORIC WALKING TOUR: For history buffs, the old district of Frederiksted is directly in front of the pier. (You should stop at the *Visitors Bureau* by the pier to pick up a map which will help you identify the most significant places.) The old town is laid out in a grid running 7 blocks from Fort Frederik and the Customs House on the north to the Library and Queen Cross Street on the south, and 5 blocks deep from the waterfront (Strand Street) east to Prince Street.

Frederiksted was an almost deserted town in the 1970s, but federal legislation giving certain tax benefits to historic preservation incited community action. Now many old buildings have been renovated and more are being done all the time. City fathers dream of someday making it a Williamsburg of the Caribbean. Fortunately much of the old is still here to be saved.

Fort Frederik, which dates from 1752, has been restored in red and white brick as it was in 1820. The fort was the site of the emancipation of the slaves in 1848. Among the town's other important buildings are *Government House,* built in 1747; the *Customs House,* late 18th century; *St. Paul's Anglican Church,* 1817; and *St. Patrick's Roman Catholic Church,* 1848. There are also many historic residences and commercial buildings which you will be able to spot as you walk along the streets.

SHOPPING: While Christiansted offers more shops and greater variety, there has been a marked improvement in recent years in the quantity and quality of stores in Frederiksted as more renovated buildings become available and the number of cruise ships continues to grow.

If you want to stop for refreshment or a snack, *Le St. Tropez* (Limetree Court, 67 King Street; Tel. 772–3000) is an outdoor bistro on a treeshaded lane; its French owners offer reliable fare with a Mediterranean flavor. Moderate. Their evening restaurant, *Le Crocodile* (Royal Dane Hotel courtyard; Tel. 772–5700), is more elegant and pricey.

CHRISTIANSTED

THE PICTURE-PERFECT PORT

Christiansted is one of the Caribbean's prettiest, most charming little towns. In an area of about 5 square blocks you will find some of the best-preserved and most interesting landmarks in the Virgin Islands. Alongside them are shops, making it easy to combine a walking tour with a shopping excursion.

FORT CHRISTIAN A walking tour can start at the Christiansted National Historic Site at Fort Christian (open Monday through Friday, 8 A.M. to 5 P.M.; weekends and holidays, 9 A.M. to 5 P.M.) overlooking the harbor on the northeast end of King's Wharf. You may want to stop first at the Department of Tourism's *Visitors Bureau* (open Monday through Friday, 8 A.M. to 5 P.M.) by the harbor to pick up a map and other literature to aid you in locating the important buildings.

The fort, built in 1749, is the best preserved of the five Danish forts in the West Indies. It is under the supervision of the U.S. National Park Service. A brochure is available for a self-guided tour, and park rangers are on hand to answer questions. For real history buffs, it will be an hour well spent. The rangers know their history well and have fascinating tidbits about the fort not available in brochures. Among other things, they will show you the cell where Alexander Hamilton's mother was jailed for her "improprieties." Tut tut!

Between the fort and the parking lot (where tour buses wait for cruise passengers for the return to Frederiksted) is the *Old Danish Customs House and Post Office* built in 1751 and expanded several times. It is used as a library.

SCALEHOUSE Next to the parking lot at the foot of King Street is the building known as the Scalehouse, built in 1855. It was part of the Customs House where goods were weighed for tax purposes. Today, it houses the *Visitors Bureau* and a small museum.

GOVERNMENT HOUSE One block west on King Street is Government House, an imposing 18th-century townhouse built as a private home; it later served as the residence and offices of the royal Danish governor. The building's handsome outside staircase leads to a beautiful ballroom on the first floor. This wing was added in the 19th century after the house had become the governor's mansion. On the north side is a pretty inner courtyard with grand old trees. During the American Bicentennial

in 1976, when there was such feverish restoration here, the Danish government helped in the restoration and refurbishing of Government House as its contribution to the celebrations.

THE STEEPLE BUILDING At the corner of Church and Company streets stands the first church the Danes built after acquiring St. Croix in 1733. Completed in 1750, it was used as the Lutheran church, the state church of Denmark, until 1831. Afterward the building served many purposes—school, hospital, storehouse—and now contains a small museum of Arawak and Carib artifacts and displays on the workings of a sugar plantation. It is open Monday through Friday from 8 A.M. to 5 P.M.

KING'S WHARF A shopping expedition can start at the *Visitors Bureau* (open Monday through Friday, 8 A.M. to 5 P.M.) or King's Wharf where several rows of 18th- and 19th-century warehouses have been made into attractive, palm-shaded shopping plazas. The streets paralleling King Street—Company Street on the north, Strand Street on the south—also have attractive shops.

SHOPPING IN CHRISTIANSTED

Cruzans, as the people of St. Croix are called, maintain that their prices are better than those in St. Thomas because they do not have to pay the high rents required of St. Thomas stores nor the high commissions demanded by some cruise lines and cruise directors.

Christiansted's newest shopping plaza, King's Alley Walk, has a variety of stores, including *The White House*, which specializes in women's clothing in shades of white, off-white, ivory, and beige; the *Caribbean Bracelet Co.*, where you can buy bracelets made in the Dominican Republic; *Patrick's Watches* for repair or purchase; *Cruzan Cellars*, which stocks duty-free Caribbean rum; and a variety of other gift and clothing outlets. When you need a break, *Sippers Ice Cream* has ice cream and desserts; *St. Croix Chop House & Brew Pub* offers steaks, chops, and fish; and *A Taste of Asia* features Thai-Caribbean cuisine.

ART AND ARTISTS: St. Croix has an active art community of local artists and mainlanders who live there part of the year. *Gilliam-King Gallery*

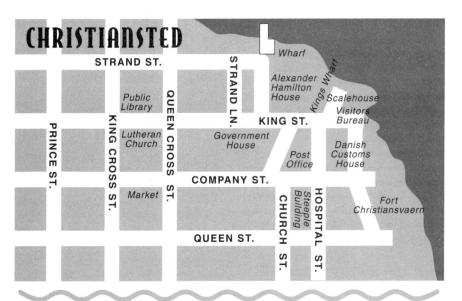

MAP OF CHRISTIANSTED

(Apothecary Hall, 2111 Company Street) features local artists Trudi Gilliam and Judith King. Gilliam specializes in metal sculpture with a distinctive style influenced by the sea and local environmental motifs; King works with oil and with silk screening. *The Gallery at the Pentheny* (1138 King Street; Tel. 773–2781) is a cooperative for local artists. Staffed by artists, it is on the ground floor of a historic building. Hours: Monday to Friday 10 A.M. to 5 P.M. *Folk Art Raders* (Strand and Queen Cross streets) stocks Caribbean art and artifacts, particularly iron sculpture, Haitian paintings, ceramics, carnival masks, and ethnic jewelry.

BOOKS/MAPS/POSTCARDS: *Jeltrups Books* (51 Company Street) and *The Bookie* (3 Strand Street) sell books and periodicals. *Church Street General Store* has cards and a bit of everything, including items by local artists. *Trader Bob's Dockside Bookshop and Gallery* (Anchor Way, Gallows Bay; Tel. 773–6001).

CHINA/CRYSTAL: *Little Switzerland* is known throughout the Caribbean for its stock of high-quality English bone china, French crystal, Swiss watches, Hummel figurines, and other gift items. You can request a catalogue in advance by calling 800–524–2010.

CLOTHING/SPORTSWEAR: *1870 Town Shoppes* (52 King Street) has attractive and fashionable sportswear at moderate prices, in a historic townhouse built in 1870. *Java Wraps* (Pan Am Pavilion), a long-established Caribbean chain, sells resortwear; its sister store on Company Street stocks antique furniture and household items. *PacifiCotton* (36 Strand Street) specializes in sportswear of 100 percent cotton for women and kids. *Courtship and Seduction* (Caravelle Arcade) has pretty, romantic lingerie and fun novelties.

CRAFTS: *Many Hands* (Pan Am Pavilion) displays handcrafts by 300 artisans living in the Virgin Islands. The products range from jewelry and ceramics to sculpture, paintings, and prints. *American West India Co.* (across from the Comanche Restaurant) specializes in products made in St. Croix and elsewhere in the West Indies, including gourmet foods, spices, herbal teas, and coffees, as well as clothing, Sea Island cotton, art, and jewelry. *St. Croix Leap* (Mahogany Road near Frederiksted; Route 76; Tel. 772–0421). If you are touring the eastern end of the island, stop here to watch craftsmen make bowls, vases, and other practical home products from native wood. The products are available for purchase. And remember, all crafts and original works of art are duty-free upon your return through U.S. Customs.

JEWELRY/WATCHES: *Colombian Emeralds* (43 Queen Cross Street), as the name implies, specializes in emeralds from Colombia, which produces about 90 percent of the world's supply. And remember, unmounted emeralds can be brought into the United States duty-free. *Little Switzerland* has the fullest collection of quality watches. *Sonya Ltd.* (Company and Church streets; Tel. 772–0421) specializes in hand-wrought gold and silver jewelry.

LEATHER/LUGGAGE: *Kicks* (57 Company Street) has footwear, handbags, luggage, and other accessories.

PERFUMES: *St. Croix Perfume Center* (53 King Street) has as complete a selection as any store in town, and at competitive prices.

If you want to stop for a snack or refreshment during your walking or shopping excursion through Christiansted, the landmark *Comanche* (Club Comanche Hotel, second floor) is an outdoor terrace with a varied menu of salads and snacks and a popular bar. Family-owned *Anabelle's Tea Room* (Company and King Cross streets), in the courtyard of a historic house, has an eclectic menu with some Cuban and West Indian dishes along with sandwiches. *The Chart House* (59 King's Wharf; Tel. 773–7718) has steaks, prime rib, fresh seafood, and their famous mud pie that's enough for three people. All three restaurants are moderately priced.

ST. CROIX JAZZ AND CARIBBEAN MUSIC AND ART FESTIVAL

This annual festival, usually in October, brings island artists and crafts people together to display their

work at the Island Center (Tel. 778–5272). The center is the venue for other events on the cultural calendar, which in the past has included dancers from the Alvin Ailey Dance Company, among others. The center also presents in-house productions.

EXCURSIONS AND SPORTS IN CHRISTIANSTED AND ENVIRONS

In the shopping plazas and at the *King Christian Hotel* facing the waterfront there are several car rental firms, travel agencies, and water-sports operators who make excursions to Buck Island, usually departing daily at 9 A.M. and returning at noon. The operators also offer scuba diving, sailing, windsurfing, and other water sports.

BUCK ISLAND The Buck Island Reef National Monument, 3.5 miles northeast of St. Croix, is a volcanic rock of about 300 acres surrounded by 550 acres of underwater coral gardens of unusual beauty and scientific interest. The island is a rookery for frigate birds and pelicans and a hatching area for the green turtle. The reef around Buck Island makes up the only underwater park in the U.S. National Park Service. A park service pamphlet explaining the reef and picturing some of the fish swimmers are likely to see is usually distributed to participants of snorkeling excursions.

The reef offers shallow-water snorkeling above the inner reef for beginners and deep-water diving along the outer barrier for experienced divers. The coral gardens of the inner reef have a trail with arrow markers and signs on the ocean floor to guide viewers along the reef. The trail is circular, 250 yards long, in water depths ranging from 12 to 15 feet. Different coral formations—staghorn, elkhorn, brain, and finger corals; seafans; feather dusters; and sea anemones—are seen. Specimens of elkhorn coral, the major builder of this reef, are some of the most massive in the world, according to marine biologists. More than 300 fish have been identified on the reef; among the most common are angelfish, blue tang, rock beauty, sergeant major, yellow tail snapper, and parrotfish. Hawksbill turtles may be seen in the seagrass on the southside. The trail takes about 45 minutes to swim. Inexperienced snorkelers are led by their guide along the reef.

Glass-bottom boats for nonswimmers and motorboats and catamarans with snorkeling equipment operate daily from King's Wharf in Christiansted to Buck Island. The ride to Buck Island takes about 30 minutes. The time spent at the reef is usually an hour, but can be longer, depending on one's interest and time schedule.

Buck Island has a sandy beach, picnic tables, and barbecue pits. One of the hiking trails leads to the top of the island, from which there is a lovely view of St. Croix. In order for the excursion not to be rushed, cruise ships that remain in port more than five hours sometimes include a picnic on Buck Island in the excursion sold on the ship.

Seven companies are authorized by the National Park Service to provide visitor services at Buck Island. Three of the operators offer excursions on sailing boats for up to six passengers; the others have larger or different types of craft. *Mile-Mark Watersports* (King Christian Hotel; Tel. 773–3434; 800–524–2012) has several excursions daily to Buck Island: A powerboat leaves at 9:30 A.M. and returns at 1 P.M.; cost is $35 per person; a catamaran or trimaran for twenty passengers runs from 10 A.M. to 4 P.M. and includes a beach barbecue, $60 per person; and on a smaller scale, a day sail for up to six people is $55 per person. Chances are it will be operating the excursion sold on your cruise ship.

SNORKELING AND SCUBA DIVING Buck Island is only one of 47 dive sites St. Croix claims. The most accessible in the immediate vicinity of Christiansted are in the harbor and along 6 miles of the north shore. There the reef is only 500 yards from the coast in water about 35 feet deep. The Cane Bay vicinity at the northwest end is particularly popular with experienced divers. *Pillar Coral*, an area beyond Buck Island, has columns of coral spiraling up 25 feet from a white sandy bottom. One of the tallest and largest coral pinnacles in the Caribbean stands at *North Cut*. In addition to *Miles-Mark Watersports*, there are other diver operators in Christiansted and Frederiksted. On the south coast of St. Croix, *Anchor Dive Center*, in the Salt River National Park, has daily dives to what it calls the "seven wonders of St. Croix."

GOLF AND TENNIS *Buccaneer Hotel* (Box 218, Christiansted; Tel. 773–2100), about a mile east of Christiansted, is a pink palace on 240 land-scaped acres with great views, beaches, and watersports facilities. Its eight Laykold courts make up the largest tennis complex on the island. Cost for nonguests is $10 per hour, $15 with lights. There are riding stables, a spa, and an 18-hole golf course where greens fees are $14 for 9 holes plus $8 per person for cart; $25 for 18 holes plus $18 for cart. There is, in addition, the fine *Carambola Golf Club* course (6,909 yards, par 72) located about 10 miles from Christiansted. Canegata Park, which is within walking distance from Christiansted, has four public courts; no fee.

HIKING AND BIKING: See information in this St. Croix section for hiking in the eastern area of the island near Frederiksted. *Take a Hike* (Tel. 778–6997) offers guided walking tours; advance arrangements are necessary. *St. Croix Bike and Tours* (Tel. 772–2545) offers guided mountain-bike excursions.

# A Drive around St. Croix

If this is your first visit to St. Croix, we recommend a tour of the island, either as a shore excursion or, if you have other people with whom to share costs, by taxi with a driver/guide. It is not worthwhile to rent a car unless your ship remains in port for the full day or overnight. Driver/guides can be arranged through the St. Croix Combined Taxi and Tour Association (Box 1514, Frederiksted, St. Croix, USVI 00841-1514; Tel. 778–1088).

Due to the brevity of the stopovers, ships calling at Frederiksted usually offer only one excursion: the St. Croix Island Tour (3.5 hours, $18 per person). If they have a second one it will most likely be a Buck Island Tour. Combined Taxi has a similar island tour from Gallows Bay/Christiansted for $18.

For ships calling at Christiansted, both the Island and Buck Island tours are likely to be available. If not, you can easily arrange to go to Buck Island with one of the water sports operators at King's Wharf.

A driving tour of St. Croix is usually made in a circular route from Frederiksted. (Bus tours follow the same route.) At the pier the street by the fort leads north to Route 63 along the coast for about 1 mile to Mahogany Road (Route 76), an east-west road that leads to the rain forest. Mahogany Road takes its name from the huge mahogany trees along the way; there are also turpentine and kapok trees.

RAIN FOREST Route 76 east and the intersecting Routes 763/765 pass through the rain forest, a stretch of lush tropical vegetation that is quite different from the rest of the island. The northwestern end is the most mountainous part of St. Croix. There is a secondary road known as the Scenic Road (Route 78), a narrow, winding road, not in the best condition. In the western sector, particularly after heavy rains, you may need a four-wheel-drive vehicle. It is also a popular stretch for hiking.

Along the way, you will encounter such charming names as Betsy's Jewel, Mary's Fancy, Judith's Fancy, Upper Love, and Jealousy. They are names of former sugar estates which have been kept by the heirs or present owners even though the estates have long since vanished. Route 76 continues east until it meets Route 69 and turns north to the Carambola Golf Course which spreads across one of the loveliest settings on St. Croix.

THE SALT RIVER NATIONAL PARK East of Carambola, Route 69 meets North Shore Road, Route 80, which continues east along the north coast to Salt River Bay, the site of Columbus's landing. The large bay at the mouth of the Salt River is an estuary and an important Arawak Indian site. The Salt River National Park—the newest park in the U.S. National Parks system—was signed into law in February 1992 to protect this area, which has historic and cultural as well as ecological significance.

Covering 912 acres, the site is the first place now under the U.S. flag where Christopher Columbus is known to have been and where some of his crew came ashore. The dedication of the new park in 1992 represented a commemoration of the 500th anniversary of Columbus's voyages to the New World. The Columbus stamp series issued by the U.S. Post Office in April 1992 includes a special cancellation depicting the

Caribs, who unleashed arrows at the Spanish intruders. The hostile encounter here was the first documented resistance to European encroachment in the Americas and resulted in fatalities on both sides. Among its other significant features, the site covers the Virgin Islands' largest remaining mangrove forests; hosts twenty-seven species of threatened or endangered plants and animals; and, at the mouth of the river, has a huge submarine canyon rich in marine life. A prehistoric complex at Salt River is one of the most important archaeological sites in the Virgin Islands. The area was inhabited as early as A.D. 50 and may have been a religious as well as permanent settlement. There is an Indian burial ground dating back to A.D. 1150.

Salt River was the base for several attempts to colonize St. Croix in the mid-17th century. The only surviving structure from the period is a triangular earthwork fortification begun by the English in 1641 and completed by the Dutch the following year. It is the only one of its type from this period to have survived in the West Indies. After the mid-1660s, the settlement at Salt River was relocated to the northeast coast at the present location of Christiansted. After Danish sovereignty was established in 1733, Salt River continued to play an important role in the island's economic development as a shipment point for sugar, rum, and molasses. In 1780, the Danish West Indian government built a customs house on the west shore of the bay to control smuggling.

The Salt River Dropoff at the mouth of the river is a prime scuba-diving location comprised of two sites: the east and west walls of a submerged canyon which shelve and plunge more than 1,000 feet. The walls are encrusted with corals, tub sponges, and forests of black coral and attract large schools of fish.

The creation of the park followed a long uphill struggle by St. Croix's local community to keep the area from being commercially developed. In future years the park will become a major attraction for St. Croix, just as the Virgin Islands National Park is to St. John. In the meantime, there's much work to be done: acquiring land now in private hands, establishing a joint territorial-federal commission to run the park, building a museum, and carving out nature trails.

Several north-south roads also lead to Queen Mary Highway, Route 70, better known as *Centerline Road*, one of two main arteries between Christiansted and Frederiksted. From Salt River Bay, Route 80 turns south to meet Northside Road (Route 75), which leads directly into town.

On organized excursions, the stop in Christiansted is only an hour (never enough time) to shop, tour, and browse. You will have to make a choice. You can take a 10-minute look at the fort, but if you do not take the time for a tour, it is hardly worth the visit, and you might better spend your time on a walking/shopping whirl around the town.

To conserve time, the return to Frederiksted can be made via the Melvin H. Evans Highway and the airport over land that is drier and flatter than on the north side. Or you can return on Centerline Road and stop at three of St. Croix's main attractions: St. George Botanical Garden, the Cruzan Rum Distillery, and Whim Greathouse.

ST. GEORGE VILLAGE BOTANICAL GARDEN

On the north side of Centerline Road, about 5 miles west of Frederiksted, are 16 acres of tropical garden landscaped around the ruins of a Danish sugar plantation workers' village dating from the 18th and 19th centuries. The gardens began in 1972 when the derelict site was chosen as a cleanup project of the local garden club. But as soon as the debris was cleared away, the members realized the site was a historic one. Then in 1976, the area was excavated by archaeologists who found an Arawak settlement dating from A.D. 100 to 900 beneath the colonial ruins. It is said to have been the largest of the 96 Indian villages that existed on St. Croix at the time of Columbus.

The gardens, designed to incorporate the colonial ruins, combine natural growth, landscaped plantings, and open land and are brightened with bougainvillea and other flowering bushes and trees. Approximately 500 species of trees and plants were found *in situ* and another 350 species have been added. The club's first priority is to display samples of the endangered native plants of St. Croix and the Virgin Islands. Two such plants to be seen are the St. Croix agave and a touch-me-not.

The standout is the cactus garden, which has a great variety of species. The gardens were badly damaged by Hurricane Hugo in 1989 but are on the way back to their former beautiful condition.

Among the restored ruins are the bake oven which is operating again and the blacksmith's shop where volunteer smiths using original tools produce items sold in the gift shop. Other restored buildings house the office and library. An excellent map is available at the entrance and walkways and paths are signposted for self-guided tours. Hours: Daily 9 A.M. to 4 P.M. Admission: $5 adults, $1 children.

The St. George Village Botanical Garden of St. Croix (P.O. Box 338, Frederiksted, 00840; Tel. 772–3874) is a privately supported and volunteer-managed garden. Contributions of money, plants, books, land, and labor come from people around the world.

CRUZAN RUM DISTILLERY

At the pavilion of the Virgin Islands' leading rum maker, visitors are offered a free tour, rum cocktails, and recipe booklets. Hours: Tours weekdays from 9 to 11:30 A.M. and 1 to 4 P.M.

WHIM GREATHOUSE AND MUSEUM

(Route 70) St. Croix's pride is Whim Greathouse, a restoration project of the St. Croix Landmarks Society begun in 1956. The beautifully restored plantation house, built in 1803, is furnished with lovely antiques; and the old kitchens, mill, and other buildings give visitors a good picture of life on a sugar plantation in the 18th and 19th centuries.

The Greathouse belonged to a Dane of Scots-French descent, Christopher MacEvoy, Jr., a member of a prominent island family. The house has several unusual features, including semicircular ends and only one bedroom. It is not built on a raised basement, as were most houses of its time, but was sunk and surrounded by a dry moat which provides both ventilation and light to the storerooms below. The walls, 3 feet thick, were built of cut stones and coral with lime and molasses used as mortar.

The furnishings date from before the early 19th century and have been acquired from Europe and the United States as well as locally. One of the oldest pieces is an oak wainscot chair dated from 1685 and found beneath the house. The estate was named "Whim" either after the type of machine known as a "whimmy" or, some say, on the whim of its owner.

In addition to the main house, you will see the cookhouse, bath house, museum, apothecary, water tower, bell tower, 1856 steam engines, animal mill, windmill, boiling shed, rum still, and sugar factory.

The complex has a museum, gift shop, and furniture showroom. Admission: $5 adults, $1 children. For information contact the Landmark Society (Tel. 772–0598). The Society offers tours of historic homes annually in February and March. Also in March, it stages an annual antiques auction.

SANDY POINT NATIONAL WILDLIFE REFUGE
On the southwestern tip of the island, 3 miles south of Frederiksted, is a protected area which is one of only two nesting grounds for the leatherback turtle in the United States. From March through June, the enormous leatherbacks— up to 6 feet in length and 1,000 pounds in weight—come ashore to dig their holes into which each lays as many as 80 eggs. Afterward, they cover the eggs with sand for protection and then lumber back to the sea, returning to repeat the ritual as many as six times during nesting season. After about two months, the hatchlings emerge from the hidden sandpits and in the evening or just before dawn dash to the sea. Hawksbill and green sea turtles also come here. Earthwatch, a United States-based, nonprofit research organization which monitors the turtles, allows visitors to participate in its programs. Inquiries should be made to the St. Croix Environmental Association (773–1989) or Earthwatch (617–926–8200). The group also conducts guided environmental tours.

PROJECT ANCHORS AWAY One of the newest conservation programs on the island, initiated after Hurricane Hugo in 1989 by the Island Conservation Effort, a nonprofit organization dedicated to the preservation of the island's natural resources, Project Anchors Away is designed to protect the coral reefs that surround St. Croix. A permanent mooring system for boats was put in place to mark thirteen of the most popular dive sites with twenty blue-and-white buoys. The buoys are tethered to eyebolts drilled into the coral sub-

base of the reefs. The aim is to eliminate the danger of a boat's anchor and chain accidentally damaging a reef. Dive boats moor on a first-come, first-serve basis. The system is similar to those in use off Bonaire, Tortola, and the Florida Keys.

St. Croix Aquarium (Caravelle Arcade, Christiansted; Tel. 773–8995), a visitor attraction and marine education center, offers guided tours by a marine biologist.

THE BRITISH VIRGIN ISLANDS

YACHTMAN'S HAVEN

The British Virgin Islands, an archipelago of about fifty green, mountainous islands, cays, and rocks, are spread over 59 square miles of sapphire waters along the Anegada Passage between the Caribbean Sea and the Atlantic. Mostly volcanic in origin and uninhabited, they have scalloped coastlines and idyllic little coves with white sand beaches.

In olden days their strategic location made them a favorite hiding place of pirates who plundered ships carrying treasures and cargo between the Old and New Worlds. Today, they are favorite hideaways of yachtsmen for their good anchorage, vacationers for their beaches, and a growing number of cruise ships determined to get away from the crowd.

The largest and most populated islands are *Tortola* (the capital), *Virgin Gorda*, and *Anegada*. Others, such as *Peter Island* or *Guana Island*, have become popular after being developed as private resorts; but for the most part the B.V.I., as the aficionados call them, are almost as virgin as the day Christopher Columbus discovered them.

The B.V.I. say frankly that they do not appeal to everyone. They have no golf courses or casinos and what little nighttime activity exists is very low-key. But what these islands lack in flashy entertainment is more than made up for in facilities for boating, scuba diving, deep-sea fishing, and windsurfing.

The British Virgin Islands are next-door neighbors of the U.S. group, and without a map it's hard to tell the difference. On the other hand, when you ask someone from the B.V.I. if there *is* a difference between their islands and ours, they will delight in answering, "Yes, the British Virgins are still virgin."

ARRIVING IN THE BRITISH VIRGIN ISLANDS

Most visitors arrive in the B.V.I. by water: on a cruise ship, by ferry boat, or in a private yacht—their own or one they have chartered. There are no direct flights from the United States; you must fly via San Juan, St. Thomas, or St. Croix to connect with American Eagle or another feeder line serving Tortola or Virgin Gorda. Scheduled air service to Tortola is also available from Anguilla, Antigua, St. Kitts, and St. Maarten.

Frequent ferry service connects Tortola with St. Thomas and St. John in about 1.5 hours. Less frequent service is available between either St. Thomas or Tortola and Virgin Gorda, between St. John and Jost Van Dyke and Tortola, and between Tortola and Anegada and Jost Van Dyke.

Tortola is the home of the largest yacht charter fleet in the Caribbean with many marinas where boats with or without crew can be chartered for a day or a year. Lying in close proximity astride Drake's Passage, the islands create a sheltered waterway that is one of the world's prime sailing locations. From their base in Tortola, boats criss-cross the passage to visit Peter and Norman islands directly across from Road Town; Virgin Gorda to the east/northeast; and Jost Van Dyke on the northwest. These are also the stops made most often by cruise ships, whether based in Tortola or St. Thomas or from more distant locations.

LOCAL TRANSPORTATION: Tortola's three entry points—Road Town, the main town on the south coast; the West End ferry landing; and the airport on Beef Island at the east end—are linked by paved roads. Beef Island is connected to Tortola by a bridge 300 feet long. Paved roads wind over the mountains to Brewers Bay, Cane Garden Bay, and other resort areas on the northwest coast. More remote areas are accessible by dirt roads, some requiring four-wheel drive. Taxis are plentiful in Tortola; they use fixed rates, based on distance.

SIGHT-SEEING: In Tortola and Virgin Gorda,

half-day tours by minivan are available from taxis and travel agencies. Virgin Gorda has an open-air jitney bus that shuttles between the airport, Spanish Town, the Baths, and some resort areas. It can be used to see most of the island on your own in less than three hours. Major car rental firms as well as independent ones have offices in Tortola, and there are several car rental companies on Virgin Gorda; no car hire service is available on the other islands. Remember, in this British colony driving is on the LEFT.

INFORMATION:

In the United States:
British Virgin Islands Tourist Board, 370 Lexington Ave., New York, N.Y. 10017; Tel. 212–696–0400; 800–835–8530; fax 212–949–8254.

In Tortola:
BVI Tourist Board, Box 134, Road Town, Tortola; Tel. 809–494–3134; fax 809–494–3860.
National Parks Trust, Fishlock Road, Road Town, Tortola; 809–494–3904.

TORTOLA AND ITS NEIGHBORS

Tortola is a sleepy little place with not a great deal of activity, but that's as it should be. Road Town is the only sizeable residential center in the B.V.I. It has shops and modest shopping plazas, hotels, restaurants, and bars with scratch bands and West Indian music. Most commercial activity is located along the south shore road and on Main Street, a picturesque street of small, pastel-painted shops. If you want to know more about the B.V.I., there's the *Virgin Islands Folk Museum,* operated by the Virgin Islands Historical Society.

BOTANIC GARDEN Road Town's prettiest attraction is the tropical Botanic Garden, created on a neglected site formerly occupied by the B.V.I. Agricultural Station. The 3-acre spread, opened in January 1987, is the work of the B.V.I. National Trust and volunteers from the Botanic Society and Garden Club. The Garden got its first professional curator/director in 1991.

The gardens are divided into about twenty collections of rare and indigenous tropical plants. Near the entrance, a three-tiered fountain serves as the central axis of the garden from which landscaped walks radiate in four directions, each leading to different sections. Generally, plants are grouped according to type of environmental habitat. The gardens are festooned with flowering shrubs and trees and contain an astonishing variety.

SAGE MOUNTAIN NATIONAL PARK In the 1960s Sage Mountain on Tortola and Spring Bay and Devil's Bay on Virgin Gorda were donated to the B.V.I. government by Laurance Rockefeller. The gift led to the creation of the B.V.I. National Parks Trust and the start of a land and sea conservation program with eleven of twenty-three proposed areas under management.

The 92-acre Sage Mountain National Park is situated on the peaks of the tall volcanic mountains that cross the center of Tortola and reach 1,780 feet, the highest elevation in either the U.S. or British Virgin Islands. Its vegetation, characteristic of a rain forest, is thought to be similar to that of the island's original growth. A road leads to the park entrance from which there are panoramic views. Two graveled, sign-posted trails, each about an hour's hike, wind through the forest, past huge elephant ears, hanging vines, lacey ferns, and a great variety of trees common to the Caribbean, such as kapok, mahogany, and white cedar, the B.V.I.'s national tree.

NORMAN ISLAND Across Drake's Passage from Tortola is uninhabited Norman Island, said to be the "Treasure Island" of Robert Louis Stevenson's novel. The island has old ruins, a salt pond with abundant birdlife, and footpaths. One path is a 30-minute hike up Spy Glass Hill from which you can get a fabulous 360-degree view. In olden days pirates used this vantage point to watch for Spanish treasure ships—hence its name. Apparently, the island is still a convenient base for illegal activity. B.V.I. authorities have seized boats smuggling drugs here. At Treasure Point there are partly submerged caves which can be enjoyed by snorkelers as well as divers.

RHONE NATIONAL MARINE PARK Southeast of Tortola at Salt Island lies the *Wreck of the Rhone,* the most famous—and favorite—shipwreck dive

in the Virgin Islands, if not the Caribbean, and the site where the movie *The Deep* was filmed. The wreck, lying at 20- to 80-foot depths west of Salt Island, has been made into a marine park covering 800 acres. Along with nearby reefs and caves, the park includes Dead Chest Island on the west, where seabirds nest on the tall cliffs.

The 310-foot Royal Mail Steamer *Rhone* sank in 1867 during a terrible hurricane. Anchored in calm seas off Peter Island, the ship was loading passengers and stores for its return trip to England when the sudden storm blew in. The ship lost its anchor when its cable broke, and, no longer safe at anchor, with her rigging torn by the winds, she steamed at top speed for open water to ride out the storm. But the hurricane struck again from another direction, forcing her onto the rocks at Salt Island. She split apart and sank with almost total loss of life. Parts of the ship can be seen by snorkelers as well as divers.

Salt Island has a few residents who still tend the salt ponds, a nice beach, and trails that lead up a hill to a wonderful view.

JOST VAN DYKE Off the northwest coast of Tortola and directly north of St. John, Jost Van Dyke's good anchorage and beautiful beaches make it a popular stop for yachts and small cruise ships that sail regularly through the Virgin Islands. Most anchor at yacht-filled Great Harbor, the main settlement surrounded by green peaks that rise up to 800 feet. The best-known bars in these parts are found by the beach: *The Soggy Dollar* at the Sand Castle and *Foxy's Tamarind Bay,* where a beach party with calypso music is the order of the day—any day.

 **VIRGIN GORDA**

Virgin Gorda is known for *The Baths,* an extraordinary grotto created by toppled gigantic rocks that have puzzled geologists for years. They are completely different from any other rock formation of the area. According to some geologists the rocks may have resulted from eruptions associated with the Ice Age. Worn smooth by wind and water over the millennia, the enormous rocks have fallen in such a way as to create labyrinths and caves that are fun to explore, although they are not real caves, of course. Where the sea rushes in and out, the formations near the shore catch the water, creating pools of crystal-clear water shimmering from the sunlight that filters between the rocks. They are delightful for a refreshing splash—hence their name. The area can be reached by land or sea, and the reefs fronting the Baths are popular for snorkeling.

Virgin Gorda rises from its boulder-strewn coast and sandy beaches on the south in a northerly direction to 1,370-foot Gorda Peak near the island's center. The top of the mountain is protected by the *Virgin Gorda Peak Park*, which covers 265 acres of forests. The park has a self-guided hiking trail leading to an observation point; it is actually the end of a paved road leading to Little Dix Bay—one of the Caribbean's famous resorts and the sister resort to Caneel Bay on St. John. Equally as expensive, exclusive, and low-keyed, the resorts were begun by Laurance Rockefeller as Rockresorts and were among the Caribbean's first ecologically designed resorts that related the hotel to its natural environment.

On the south end of the island is the *Devil's Bay National Park*, a secluded coral sand beach, which can be reached by a scenic trail in a 15-minute walk from the area of the Baths.

Virgin Gorda's other famous spots are *Bitter End,* a hotel/restaurant/bar that is probably the most popular watering hole in the Caribbean for the yachting crowd; and Necker Island, across the bay from Bitter End that belongs to English rock recording czar Richard Branson, who built his sumptuous nest on its summit. This ten-bedroom perch is available for rent at a mere $9,900 per day!

 ## Anegada

Unlike the other B.V.I. which are green and mountainous, Anegada is a flat, dry coral atoll

fringed by miles of sandy beaches and horseshoe-shaped reefs. The most northerly of the B.V.I., it was once a pirates' lair where the low-lying reefs caught pursuers unaware. An estimated 300 ships are thought to have gone down here. Today, those wrecks and the reefs attract divers, and the fish attracted to the reefs make the island's waters a prime fishing location.

Sports in the British Virgin Islands

In addition to sailing, the B.V.I.'s healthy and abundant reefs are popular for snorkeling and scuba diving. Most are found in water shallow enough for snorkelers to enjoy; the *Wreck of the Rhone* is one of the few deep dives available. Dive operators are based in Tortola and offer a full range of excursions. Glass-bottom boat tours are available, too.

The B.V.I. waters are also popular for live-aboard dive boats, the newest of which carry passengers in cruise ship–style comfort. Some are based in Tortola year-round; others visit from time to time. Since each day's dive destination depends on weather and sea conditions, these boats do not announce itineraries in advance, except in the most general way.

The B.V.I. waters teem with fish and the islands are adjacent to the 50-mile Puerto Rican Trench, yet deep-sea fishing is not fully developed here as it is in the neighboring U.S. Virgin Islands. Sport-fishing boats are available for charter in Tortola, Virgin Gorda, and Anegada; all three islands are a 30- to 45-minute boat ride from the trench.

Windsurfing equipment is available at most resorts. The northwest coast of Tortola, where the swells roll in from the Atlantic and break against the north end of Cane Garden Bay, is known to experienced surfers as the leading surfing location of the Virgin Islands.

St. Maarten/St. Martin

AND ITS NEIGHBORS

SABA, ST. EUSTATIUS, ANGUILLA, ST. BARTS

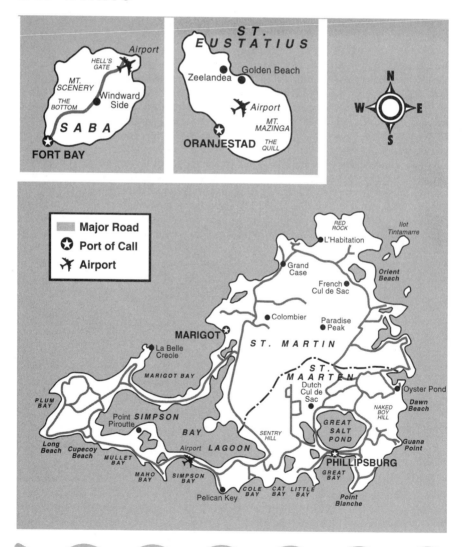

AT A GLANCE

CHAPTER CONTENTS

St. Maarten/St. Martin and Its Neighbors

THE DUTCH WINDWARD ISLANDS

AND THEIR NEIGHBORS

Centered at a cluster of lovely hideaways in the northeastern Caribbean are three of the most unusual and distinctive islands in the entire region. They share their seas with two neighbors that are the most talked-about gems in the ocean.

Sint Maarten (commonly written as St. Maarten) is the capital of the Dutch Windward Islands and the major cruise ship port of the group. It is an island of green mountain peaks that swoop down to scalloped bays and long stretches of powdery white sand beaches and the shimmering, turquoise sea. Situated on an island of only 37 square miles, St. Maarten shares more than half of the land with French St. Martin. Their split personality—Dutch on one side, French on the other—enables visitors to dine, swim, sun, sail, snorkel, scuba, ride horseback, and play tennis in two languages, under two flags, and never leave the island. The island is located 144 miles east of Puerto Rico, is a frequent port of call for cruise ships, and a home port for a few.

Saba, pronounced *Say*ba, the second member of the Dutch group, is unique. The 5-mile-square volcanic peak, 28 miles southwest of Sint Maarten, rises straight up from the sea. Its history reads like a fairy tale. It is an occasional port of call for small ships and is particularly popular for dive excursions from St. Maarten.

St. Eustatius, known as Statia, is the third of the Dutch Windwards and is 10 minutes by plane south of Saba. One needs some imagination to picture it today, but this island of only 8 square miles was once the richest free port in the Americas. It, too, is an occasional port of call.

Anguilla, a British colony located 5 miles north of St. Martin, was the best-kept secret in the Caribbean until the 1980s, when the addition of some highly publicized super-deluxe resorts brought trendsetters flocking to this spot of tranquility. You can easily discover Anguilla for yourself on a day trip from St. Maarten, and a few

small cruise ships have added Anguilla as a port of call.

St. Barts, a tiny Eden of 8 square miles, is a member of the French West Indies, complete with quality cuisine and topless beaches. Discovered by the Rockefellers and Rothschilds in the 1960s, it became the darling of show biz celebrities, and those who could afford to follow in their wake. St. Barts, too, is easy to visit on a day-sailing excursion or by air from St. Maarten, and its lilliputian capital—Gustavia—is a frequent port of call for cruise ships.

BEFORE CONCORDIA

Before Columbus got to St. Maarten in 1493 and claimed it for Spain, the island had been inhabited by the Carib Indians, the fierce tribes from whom the Caribbean takes its name. Columbus named the island San Martino in honor of St. Martin of Tours, on whose name day it was discovered.

More than a century later after the island had bounced back and forth among the Dutch, French, and Spanish, a young Dutchman of later New York fame, Peter Stuyvesant, tried to wrestle the island from Spain but lost a limb instead. He could have saved himself the ordeal because four years later, in 1648, the Spaniards abandoned their claim to the island to Holland.

When the Dutch sent their commander from St. Eustatius to take possession, they found the French waiting to do battle. But before much time had passed, the Dutch and the French agreed to stop fighting over the island and split the spoils instead. Legend has it that the accord has lasted more than three centuries, but in fact the island changed hands another 16 times before the Dutch were left unchallenged. Nonetheless, the place where the agreement was reached is known as Mt. Concordia, and the old accord is celebrated as an annual holiday, Concordia Day, on November 11.

Another local legend has it that the demarcation line between the Dutch and French sides was made by having a Dutchman and a Frenchman walk from a starting point in opposite directions around the island until they met. Either the Frenchman's wine helped him walk faster or the Dutchman was slowed down by his beer, because the French side of 21 square miles is slightly larger than the Dutch part of 16 square miles. (It's no longer merely a legend. In 1986, an enterprising New Yorker lent truth to the tale by walking around the entire island in 13 hours. Recently a hiking trail was created to enable anyone to replicate the walk.) What's really important today is that there are no border formalities and no real boundaries between the two. The only way you can tell you are crossing from one country to the other is by a welcome sign on the side of the road.

Yet the two sides of this island are different. Indeed, they are noticeably different beginning with the spelling of the names, *Sint Maarten* in Dutch and *Saint Martin* in French. Signs are in Dutch and French (they are also in English); the people speak Dutch or French (they also speak English). Two currencies, guilders and francs, circulate, but everyone takes dollars (even vending machines on the Dutch side take U.S. coins). There are two governments, two flags, and two sets of stamps—which your philatelic friends will love for their collections. But most important, the two sides of the island have distinctive personalities, each with its own unmistakable ambience.

The unusual combination, two islands for the price of one, has made St. Maarten one of the most popular vacation resorts in the Caribbean. Small as it is, St. Maarten has as many diversions as places ten times its size and in a wide range of prices and life-styles. The beaches are gorgeous, the water spectacular, and the sports facilities excellent. There's golf, scuba, tennis, windsurfing, fishing, riding, sailing, snorkeling, and biking.

St. Maarten has quiet corners in which to hide from the crowd and bouncing showplaces where you can be part of the action. You can be a barefoot beach bum, join a barbecue at a seaside resort, have cocktails at a glamorous perch, dine at a fancy gourmet restaurant, and top off the evening by whirling around the island's several casinos and discos.

You can shop for duty-free goods from around the world in trendy stores or air-conditioned malls on the main streets of Philipsburg and check out the French specialties in the boutiques of Marigot.

It is easy to rent a car or moped to tour the island. You might buy some Dutch cheese and French wine for a picnic by the shore or on a mountainside and enjoy the lovely scene with nearby islands in the distance.

It's probably no surprise that an island of two nationalities has a reputation as a gourmet's haven. What's particularly remarkable here is the variety: Italian, Mexican, Vietnamese, Indonesian, Chinese, French, Dutch, and West Indian.

Another reason for St. Maarten's popularity is its accessibility. Situated in the heart of the Caribbean between the Virgin Islands and the French West Indies, St. Maarten is a transportation hub for the northeastern Caribbean. It has long been a stop for cruise ships.

Note to Readers: *In presenting the material in this chapter, we have tried to be practical. A estimated 80 percent of all cruise ships arrive in Philipsburg. Therefore, the great majority of passengers need and want information on the facilities and services nearest and most convenient to that town. Hence, we have presented the material as a unit, making separate entries for French St. Martin when it seemed pertinent and clearer to do so.*

St. Maarten Fast Facts

POPULATION: Sint Maarten: 32,000; Saba: 1,090, St. Eustatius: 2,089.

MAIN TOWN: Philipsburg

GOVERNMENT: The three Dutch Windward Islands, together with Bonaire and Curaçao in the South Caribbean, make up the Netherlands Antilles. The government is a parliamentary democracy, headed by a governor who is appointed by and represents the queen of the Netherlands. The central government is in Curaçao; each island has its own representative body called the Island Council. The sixth member, Aruba, broke away from the group in 1986 to establish a separate government directly under the Crown.

CLIMATE: Average temperature is 80°F, cooled by trade winds year-round.

CLOTHING: Casual and comfortable summer sportswear for the day; casual and chic in the evening.

 CURRENCY: Netherlands Antilles guilder, written NAf. US $1 = NAf 1.77.

 CUSTOMS REGULATIONS: Cruise passengers who disembark in St. Maarten and return to the United States by plane must pay a departure tax of US $12. Those who are departing to other islands of the Netherlands Antilles pay US $6.

 ELECTRICITY: Sint Maarten and St. Martin have separate systems: the Dutch side uses 110–120 volts, 60 cycles, as in the United States.

 ENTRY FORMALITIES: Proof of citizenship for U.S. citizens, i.e., passport or birth certificate. A driver's license is suggested for car rental identification, but it cannot be used for proof of citizenship.

 LANGUAGE: Dutch is the official language of the Dutch Windwards; English is a common second language, but Papiamento is the local language of the Netherlands Antilles.

 PUBLIC HOLIDAYS: January 1, New Year's Day; Good Friday; Easter Monday; April 30, Coronation Day (Dutch); May 1, Labor Day; Whit Monday; Ascension Thursday; November 11, St. Maarten Day; December 25 and 26, Christmas. When cruise ships are in port on Sundays and holidays, some tourist shops open for a few hours.

 TELEPHONE AREA CODE: Sint Maarten and St. Martin have separate telephone systems, and that's where the island's two-country quaintness can lose some of its charm. A call between the two parts is an international phone call; sometimes it's easier to call New York from Philipsburg than to call Marigot, less than 8 miles away. So much for Concordia!

From the United States, the Sint Maarten code is 011 + 599 + 5 + the five-digit local number. To call from the Dutch side to the French side, dial 06 + the six-digit local number.

 TIME: One hour ahead of Eastern Standard Time; the same as Eastern Daylight Saving Time in summer.

 VACINNATION REQUIREMENTS: None

 AIRLINES:

From the United States, ALM, American, BWIA, and Continental; and American/American Eagle from San Juan to both St. Maarten and St. Martin.

Inter-Island, from Princess Juliana International Airport in Sint Maarten, Winair (Windward Islands Airways) has frequent daily service to Saba, St. Eustatius, Anguilla, St. Barts, St. Kitts, and St. Thomas; Air Guadeloupe flies daily to Guadeloupe. Air Aruba, Air Guadeloupe, Air Martinique, Air St. Barts, and LIAT also have service to neighboring islands.

 INFORMATION:

In the United States:
Sint Maarten Tourist Office, 675 Third Ave., No. 1806, New York, NY 10017; Tel. 212–953–2084; 800–STMAARTEN; fax 212–963–2145.

In Canada: Sint Maarten Tourist Board, 243 Ellerslie Ave., Willowdale, Toronto, Ontario M2N 1Y5; Tel. 416–223–3501; fax 416–223–6887.

In Port: Sint Maarten Tourist Bureau, Walter Nisbeth Road, No. 23, Imperial Bldg., Philipsburg; 22337; fax 22734.

 # ST. MARTIN FAST FACTS

 POPULATION: 28,524

 MAIN TOWNS: Marigot and Grand Case

GOVERNMENT: St. Martin is a subprefecture of Guadeloupe. Along with Guadeloupe, Martinique, and St. Barts, it is part of the French West Indies, whose nationals have French citizenship and the same rights and privileges as their countrymen in metropolitan France. St. Martin has a town council elected by the people and headed by a mayor; the subprefect is appointed by the French government.

 CLIMATE: Average temperature is 80°F, cooled by trade winds year-round.

 CLOTHING: Casual and comfortable summer sportswear for the day; casual and chic in the evening.

 CURRENCY: The French franc. Ff 5 = US $1.

 CUSTOMS REGULATIONS: Cruise passengers who disembark in St. Martin and return to the United States by plane must pay a departure tax of US $12. Those departing to another island of the Netherlands Antilles pay US $6.

 ELECTRICITY: St. Martin's electricity system is separate from the Dutch side and is the same as in France: 220 volts, 50 cycles.

 ENTRY FORMALITIES: Proof of citizenship for U.S. citizens, i.e., passport or birth certificate. A driver's license is suggested for car rental identification, but it cannot be used for proof of citizenship.

 LANGUAGE: French is the official language; English, although widely used, is not spoken by the local French people with the fluency of those with a Dutch language background.

 PUBLIC HOLIDAYS: January 1, New Year's Day; Good Friday; Easter Monday; May 1, Labor Day; Whit Monday; July 14, Bastille Day; Ascension Thursday; November 11, St. Maarten Day; December 25 and 26, Christmas. When cruise ships are in port on Sundays and holidays, tourist and other shops open for a few hours.

 TELEPHONE AREA CODE: St. Martin's telephone system is separate from Sint Maarten's. A call between the two parts is an international phone call. Sometimes it is easier to call New York from Marigot than to call Philipsburg, less than 8 miles away. From the United States, the Saint Martin code is 011 + 590 + the six-digit local number. To call from the French side to the Dutch side dial 19–599–5 + the five-digit local number.

 TIME: One hour ahead of Eastern Standard Time and the same as Eastern Daylight Saving Time in summer.

 VACCINATION REQUIREMENTS: None

 AIRLINES:

From the United States and intraisland service, see Sint Maarten Fast Facts.
From Esperance Airport, a small domestic airport in St. Martin, Air St. Barts flies daily to St. Barts. American Eagle now has service from San Juan to the French St. Martin as well as the Dutch side.

 INFORMATION:

In the United States: French West Indies Tourist Board
New York: 610 Fifth Ave.; NY 10020; Tel. 212–757–1125.
Beverly Hills: 9454 Wilshire Blvd.; Suite 715; CA 90212; Tel. 310–271–2661.
Chicago: 645 N. Michigan Ave.; IL 60611; Tel. 312–337–6301.
Dallas: 2305 Cedar Spring Rd. No. 205; TX 75201; Tel. 214–720–4010.

In Canada: Montreal: French Government Tourist Board, 1981 Avenue McGill College No. 490; Quebec H34 2W9; Tel. 514–288–4264; fax 514–844–8901.
Toronto: 30 St. Patrick St., Suite 900; Ontario M5T 3A3;
Tel. 416–593–6427; fax 416–979–7587.

In Port: St. Martin Tourist Office, Marigot (Tel. 87–57–21; fax 87–56–43).

Visitor's Bureau, City Hall, Rue Charles de Gaulle, Marigot. Monday through Friday, 8:30 A.M. to 1 P.M., and 2:30 to 5:30 P.M.; Saturday, 8 A.M. to noon.

Budget Planning

If you choose the beachcomber's St. Maarten, you will find that costs are reasonable. You can take advantage of the beaches near the pier, have a snack or light lunch at one of the modest places in town, and do your shopping on Frontstreet where there are ample bargains to be found.

However, if you choose the elegant side of the island for haute cuisine and shops with designer clothes you will find St. Maarten/St. Martin to be one of the most expensive islands in the Caribbean. Top French restaurants cost $200 or more for dinner for two persons; chic shops with fashions by Armani, Valentino, and other top designers may be 20 percent lower than U.S. prices, but they are still very expensive.

There isn't a great middle ground. So, it pays to look around, and do not be shy about asking the price. It will not endear you to the French to know that some restaurants have two sets of prices— one for their local clientele and one for tourists.

Interisland buses are inexpensive but not always convenient. Taxis, unless shared with others, are expensive. If you plan to tour on your own, a car rental is the best deal.

Drugs, Crime, and Today's Realities

St. Maarten/St. Martin, like other places, is not immune to today's social ills. Drugs and theft, particularly, are on the rise, and as a tourist you are an easy target. Rented cars, for example, have stickers and license plates that make them easy to identify. They are a favorite target of roadside bandits, who are sometimes staked out on less traveled roads.

You can reduce your vulnerability with prudence. Do not park in secluded or isolated areas unless you are with a group of people. Never leave valuables in your car or on the beach, including hotel beaches. Do not walk alone in remote or lightly trafficked areas, and most of all, do not give a ride to strangers or engage someone as a guide who approaches you on the street or beach.

The Dutch and French governments are aware of the problem, but in this writer's opinion, they have been slow to act. To some extent they must share the responsibility, because the island's unbridled growth has required the importation of many foreign workers who do not belong to the island's close-knit society and therefore lack a commitment to it. At the same time, the island's borders are so free and open that it is not easy to control them.

Author's Favorite Attractions

Self-Drive Excursion around St. Maarten/St. Martin
Day-Sail Picnic to Nearby Island
Horseback Riding Excursion
Snorkeling or Scuba Diving Excursion
America's Cup Regatta

Shore Excursions

Cruise lines usually offer several tours, but St. Maarten is an easy place to see and enjoy on your own. Further details on the places visited in these excursions are available elsewhere in this chapter.

Island Tour: 3 hours, $19. for first-time visitors who are reluctant to drive themselves, a bus tour offers a quick look at Philipsburg, Marigot, and parts in-between. It will not, however, be a satisfying excursion because the fun of St. Maarten/St. Martin is discovery—wandering about at your own pace, stopping for a swim here, a picnic there, sipping a drink or coffee at a sidewalk cafe, and as the local folks would say, "coolin' out." These are elements missing on a bus tour. A similar excursion by taxi for two hours will cost about $40 for two people plus $10 for each additional person.

Boat Excursions: 7–8 hours, $60–$70. A party cruise around Sint Maarten or to a deserted island for a picnic, swim, and snorkel are fun ways to spend the day and are recommended for those who do not want to rent a car. Boats leave from the marinas at the eastern bend of Great Bay in Philipsburg and at Simpson Bay Lagoon on the Dutch side and from Marigot Bay and Marina Port La Royale on the French side.

America's Cup Regatta: 3 hours, $55 to $70. Experience the fun and thrill of racing a yacht in an actual race. It's the most popular excursion in St. Maarten. You don't need experience, but you do need to be in good physical condition.

Scuba-Diving or Snorkeling Package: 3 hours, single tank, $56. Most cruise ships offer a variety of snorkeling and dive packages: some include an island tour; others include sailing around the island to the uninhabited islets off the northeast coast.

Underwater Adventures: 2.5 hours, $25 adults; $15 children. For a novel experience, Underwater Adventures at *Maho Water Sports* (Tel. 54387) will take you on a walk on the ocean floor to see the fish and coral even if you don't swim. Wearing headgear that completely covers your head (even your hair stays dry) and looks like an astronaut's helmet, you walk with an escort on the bottom of the sea to observe the fish and coral at close range. The excursion is designed for nonswimmers and folks of all ages.

PHILIPSBURG A NEAT DUTCH TREAT

As your ship approaches St. Maarten, the tall green mountains make the island seem much larger than it is; when you walk down the streets of Philipsburg, the capital of Dutch Sint Maarten, the crowds make it seem larger than it is too. But with only two downtown streets—Front and Back—its image as a bustling capital is relative.

The Dutch side, which saw its first hotel open in 1947, developed sooner and faster than its French counterpart, acquiring the majority of the island's hotels, banks, and stores. The site of the island's international airport, Philipsburg is also the major port of call for cruise ships.

Philipsburg, situated on a crest of land facing Great Bay, was founded in 1733 as a free port and named for John Philips, who served as commander of Sint Maarten from 1735 to 1746. It is still a free port. Frontstreet and the lanes leading to Backstreet are lined with trendy boutiques and air-conditioned malls selling duty-free goods from around the world at about 20 to 30 percent less than U.S. prices. Indeed, all of Sint Maarten is a free port, as in the U.S. Virgin Islands.

Sports facilities are excellent. Many hotels have tennis courts. Sint Maarten is a good place to learn to scuba dive because the reefs are accessible and situated in shallow, calm waters ideal for beginners. At the harbor you can arrange a fishing trip or day sail to a nearby island in a catamaran or ketch for a picnic; or you can tour the island by car, bicycle, or horseback.

PORT PROFILE: PHILIPSBURG

LOCATION/EMBARKATION: After you have visited large ports such as Nassau, San Juan, or St. Thomas, Philipsburg's little harbor on Great Bay will seem like a doll's town. Most ships anchor at sea and tender passengers to the pier located directly in front of the town center, or at the dock on the east side of town, or they pull dockside at *A.C. Wathey Pier* at Point Blanche, the easternmost tip of Great Bay, about a mile from Frontstreet.

Construction of a new $1.7 million pier in Philipsburg, scheduled for completion in 1997, will extend the smaller Captain Hodge's pier and have a tourist information office, telephone booths, restrooms, shopping kiosks, and taxi stand. The new wharf will accommodate up to seven tenders at one time. St. Maarten is also planning to build a new $30 million port.

At Wathey Pier, taxi and tour buses await arriving ships, or you can walk to the head of Frontstreet in about 5 minutes. Enroute you will pass *Bobby's Marina* where you can sign up for a picnic sail to a nearby secluded beach or deserted island or a day sail to a neighboring island. Most leave about 9 or 9:30 A.M.

LOCAL TRANSPORTATION: Whether your ship anchors at sea and you tender to the town pier or your ship docks at *Wathey Pier,* you will be near Frontstreet where it is easy to walk for shopping, hire a taxi for sight-seeing, or make your arrangements for a car rental.

TAXIS: No meters; rates are based on destination with two passengers per trip. A charge of US $2 is added for each additional person. You should always ask the fare in advance. Taxi drivers will most likely quote U.S. dollar prices, but be sure in advance to avoid a misunderstanding. Your driver will expect a tip of 10 to 15 percent. Taxi rates must have the approval of the government.

For a 2.5-hour island tour, the cost is $40, plus $10 per person. Other fares from Philipsburg are approximately:

West of Philipsburg: Little Bay, $7; Airport, Maho Bay, $10; Cupecoy Beach, Mullet Bay Resort and Casino, $12; La Samanna, $16.

East of Philipsburg: Dawn Beach and Oyster Pond, $16.

North of Philipsburg: Marigot, $16; Grande Case and Orient Beach, $20.

BUSES: For budget-minded travelers, public buses run between Philipsburg and Marigot from 6 A.M. to midnight. Fare is $1.50. Other buses run hourly between Mullet Bay, Simpson Bay, Cole Bay, and Grand Case. Busstops on the Dutch side are marked *Bushalte;* on the French side, *Arrêt.* If you cannot find either, buses will usually stop for you if you wave to them.

MOPEDS/MOTORBIKES: These are available from *Super Honda Bikes* (Tel. 25712), *Carter's Joy Rides* (Airport Road; Tel.44251), and at most hotels. *Rent-A-Scoot* (Tel. 87–20–59), on the French side, has scooters from $19, motorbikes from $32, and Harley's from $100. However, we do not recommend them unless you are a *very* experienced and careful driver. Sint Maarten's roads are narrow, hilly, replete with blind curves, and in bad condition. You are likely to hit potholes, and you most certainly will have to stop dead and without notice for a cow or goat that has strayed onto the road. Bikes are available for rent, but

parts of the island are too mountainous for pleasure biking for many people.

CAR RENTAL: Driving is on the right. Most companies have pickup and delivery service and offer unlimited mileage. You should book in advance, particularly in high season, and don't be surprised if your confirmed reservation is not filled. As we have noted many times in this book, intentions are good but execution often falls short of them. Expect to pay about US $40 for standard shift and US $50 for automatic with air-conditioning.

Avis, Tel. 42322, 800–331–1084
Budget, Tel. 800–527–0700
Cannegie, Tel. 54329 (cars and jeeps)
Hertz (Airport), Tel. 54314
National/Lucky, Tel. 42168; 800–328–4567

FERRY SERVICE: *From Philipsburg* to St. Barts, *White Octopus* and other catamarans depart from Bobby's Marina at 9 A.M. and return at 5 P.M. daily except Sunday. The trip is sold as a round-trip excursion for $50 and takes 1.5 hours. For reservations, call *Voyager* (Tel. 24096; 87–10–68) a high-speed ferry, departs from Marigot for St. Barts daily, except Thursday and Sunday, at 5:30 P.M. Cost is $56; on Thursday, it departs for Saba at 8:30 A.M. and returns at 5:30 P.M. Cost is $63. Ferry services have a start-and-stop history here.

EMERGENCY NUMBERS:
Medical Service/Philipsburg Hospital, Tel. 31111
Police/Sint Maarten, Tel. 22222
Ambulance, Tel. 22111
Alcoholics Anonymous, Monday, Wednesday, and Friday, 6 P.M., Catholic Rectory between Frontstreet and Backstreet

SERVICE CLUBS: *Kiwanis,* every Thursday, 12:30 P.M., Divi Little Bay Beach Hotel, Frontstreet; *Lions,* first and third Tuesday, 8 P.M., Holland House Hotel, Frontstreet; *Rotary,* noon, every Wednesday, Defiance Haven Hotel.

INFORMATION: *St. Maarten Tourist Board* has an information office on the main square in Philipsburg (Tel. 22337).

Marigot A French Delight

Marigot, the capital of French St. Martin, is about a 20-minute drive from Philipsburg. A decade ago, it was a village with a tiny port; now it has been transformed into a tourist mecca with as many hotels, shopping malls, marinas, and restaurants as the Dutch side.

St. Martin is unmistakably Gallic. You don't need the language, the signs, the food, the wine, or the khaki-clad gendarme to tell you so. The ambience is St. Tropez in the tropics—complete with sidewalk cafes, fishing boats, and topless beaches. In addition to the boutiques carrying fashionable French sportswear there are gourmet shops and grocery stores where you can stock up on familiar French products.

St. Martin is known for its large number of high-quality restaurants in so small a place, particularly in the tiny village of Grand Case a few miles beyond Marigot. But be prepared when the bill comes; the top French restaurants are as expensive as similar ones in New York.

Notes on Marigot

TAXIS: In Marigot, a taxi service is located at the port near the St. Martin Tourist Information Bureau. Sample fares from Marigot: to Grand Case Beach Club, $10; to Philipsburg, $10. An additional 25 percent is added after 9 P.M. and 50 percent after midnight.

FERRIES: From Marigot harbor, service to Anguilla leaves approximately every half hour, takes 15 minutes, and costs $20 round-trip, plus $4 departure taxes. Tickets may be purchased at a kiosk by the dock. The ferry dock in Anguilla is located on the south side of the island almost directly across from Grand Case, St. Martin. To St. Barts, *La Dame de Coeur* departs daily from Port la Royale for $50 round-trip, departing at 9 A.M. and returning at 4 P.M.; the *Voyager* ferry has frequent departures (see ferry information in St. Maarten section).

EMERGENCY NUMBERS:
Medical Service/Marigot Hospital,
Tel. 87–50–07
Police/St. Martin, Tel. 87–50–04
Ambulance, Tel. 87–86–25

INFORMATION: *St. Martin Tourist Information Bureau* is located on the waterfront in Marigot. Tel. 87–57–21.

St. Maarten & St. Martin On Your Own

A Walk through Philipsburg

Wathey Square in the heart of Philipsburg is a good place to start a stroll around town. The walk will take less than an hour unless you get sidetracked with shopping. The Sint Maarten Tourist Office on the east side of the square has free literature and maps.

COURTHOUSE Directly north of Wathey Square, the white clapboard building with green trim is the old Courthouse, built in 1793 and rebuilt in 1825. It originally was the house of the colony's commander and was used in subsequent years for the council chambers, courts, firehall, and jail. Today, the upper floor is still used by the courts; and the building also serves as the town hall. The post office, which used to be on the ground floor, has moved to a new building on Pondfill Road, two blocks to the northeast. A small outdoor market is in the block directly behind the Courthouse. On Fridays, there is music and other entertainment.

FRONTSTREET The street running east-west in front of the Courthouse is known as Frontstreet (*Vorstraat,* in Dutch); that behind it is Backstreet (*Achterstraat*). They are the two main streets of town. Frontstreet traffic runs one-way east; Backstreet, one-way west. The downtown is only 2 blocks deep as a result of the lay of the land. Philipsburg sits on a thin crest hemmed in by two bodies of water: Great Bay on the south and Salt Pond on the north; and it is anchored by high hills at both ends of the crest. In the early days, the pond provided the island with its major source of income, salt. Before refrigeration, salt was needed to preserve food and was one of the most important commodities in world trade.

Two new roads, Cannegieter Street and Walter Nisbet Road (better known as Pondfill Road and Ring Road) have been added through landfill of Salt Pond to relieve the downtown traffic congestion. They seem to have barely kept up with the growth.

On Frontstreet, you can turn left (west) and walk against the traffic to the "foot" of town, or turn right (east) and go in the direction of the traffic to the "head" of town. It does not matter which direction you choose since the entire length of the street—about 1 mile—and the little lanes, or *steegjes*, connecting Front and Back streets are lined with boutiques, restaurants, air-conditioned shopping malls, patio bars, and small hotels. (*When I do my walking, I try to pick the shady side of the street so as not to tire quickly from the Caribbean sun.*)

Along the way between the shopping arcades and modern buildings on Frontstreet, you will spot occasional old buildings of West Indian architecture with gingerbread or fretwork trim that have been renovated.

Guavaberry Tasting Shop St. Maarten liquor made from rum and a local fruit, guavaberry, can be purchased from a shop at the east end of Frontstreet housed in an historic building that dates from the late 18th century. The shop sells many flavors, any of which you can sample before you buy.

ROYAL GUEST HOUSE At the east end is the Pasanggrahan Hotel, once the Royal Guest House, which hosted Dutch Queen Juliana (she was Princess Juliana at the time) when she was en route to exile in Canada after the Nazi invasion of her country. The modest but charming inn, all but hidden behind its thick tropical gardens, was a favorite of those who discovered St. Maarten early on and is still popular with budget travelers. The hotel's front porch and restaurant are directly on Great Bay beach. Its moderately priced restaurant, facing the harbor, is a lovely place for lunch and a romantic setting for dinner. Happy hour in its Sidney Greenstreet Bar is especially popular with local dignitaries and the business community.

MUSEUM OF ST. MAARTEN At the east end of Frontstreet is the Museum of St. Maarten, which was created in 1989 by the St. Maarten Historic Foundation. It is located on the second floor of a small shopping complex. The modest museum has displays from excavations on the island and artifacts donated by long time residents. Hours: Monday through Friday 10 A.M. to 4 P.M.; Saturdays from 10 A.M. to noon; closed Sundays. Admission: US $1.

Next door to the museum is the gallery-museum of Mosera, one of St. Maarten's leading artists.

FORT AMSTERDAM Philipsburg does not have any "must-see" historic sites, but if you are interested, a pavement at the foot of Frontstreet goes over the hill to Little Bay and to the ruins of Fort Amsterdam at the end of the finger of land separating Great Bay and Little Bay. The fort, dating from the 17th century, was the first built by the Dutch and is on the foundation of an earlier Spanish fortification. From here you can spot the ruins of two other fortifications: Fort William on Fort Hill directly north; and Pointe Blanche at the eastern tip of Great Bay.

A DRIVE AROUND THE ISLAND

The best way to see and enjoy St. Maarten is to rent a car and drive around the island on your own, and when you find a pretty beach or a scenic view, stop for a swim, a photo, or a picnic. There is an easy circumferential route around the island with secondary roads for inland detours or to secluded beaches.

For a drive around the island, you should leave Philipsburg by the Ring Road which runs along Great Salt Pond and leads into Long Wall Road. At its western end it intersects with Bush Road and turns west (left) over Cole Bay Hill.

SINT MAARTEN ZOO AND BOTANIC GARDENS A short detour east on Arch Road will take you to the St. Maarten Zoological and Botanic Gardens. Situated on 3 acres in an area known as Madame Estate on the north side of Great Salt Road, the zoo and gardens feature animals and plants of the Caribbean region. The zoo's purpose is educational as well as recreational, but the Zoological Foundation, the non-profit organization that operates the zoo, hopes in time to make it an environmental "science center" for the island and to develop conservation and breeding programs. There are walk-through aviaries, a children's petting zoo, and a playground. Hours: Monday to Friday, 9 A.M. to 5 P.M.; Saturday and Sunday, 10 A.M. to 6 P.M. Admission: US $4 for adults; US $2 for senior citizens and children over two. For US $5, you can sponsor an animal for a week.

COLE BAY HILL CEMETERY Continuing west in the direction of the airport, you will pass the centuries-old cemetery where the Scottish adventurer John Philips lies buried on the hill overlooking the town he founded. The hill separates Philipsburg from the west end of the island where many of the best-known resorts and beaches are located. From an observation platform at the summit of the hill on a clear day you can see the neighboring islands of Saba, St. Eustatius, St. Barts, St. Kitts, and Nevis. The valley below overlooking Cay Bay is said to be the site where Peter Stuyvesant unsuccessfully battled the Spaniards in 1644.

SIMPSON BAY LAGOON After several winding miles, the road intersects with Welfare Road where you can turn right (north) to Marigot; or continue west along Simpson Bay Lagoon with many new condominiums, shopping plazas, and restaurants. The lagoon is the main setting for water sports.

MAHO BAY/MULLET BAY Continuing west, the road parallels the airport on the south, and at the end of the runway is Maho Bay. Here you should bear right up a hill where the road passes through the heart of the Maho Bay development and Mullet Bay Resort on the Dutch side. The area was changed extensively in the late 1980s with the addition of a large shopping center, several hotels and restaurants, and a casino complex and is now as much as the focal point of activity, day and night, as either Philipsburg or Marigot.

LONG BEACH The main road continues to Cupecoy and the French side where secondary roads lead to La Samanna, a very expensive luxury resort; Long Beach, one of the island's most magnificent stretches of sand; and Plum Beach. The western point is hilly and provides nice views of the island and coastline. West of Cupecoy is the dividing line between the two parts of the island. There is topless bathing on the French beaches.

BORDER MONUMENT Alternatively, on the north side of Cole Bay Hill, you can take the direct route to Marigot, passing the Border Monument that marks the boundary between the two countries. The monument was added in 1948 to commemorate the 300th anniversary of the Dutch and French accord.

ST. MARTIN MUSEUM At Sandy Ground on the south side of Marigot is the new *St. Martin Museum,* also called "On the trail of the Arawaks." Three permanent exhibits are on view: The first displays artifacts from archaeological excavations in St. Martin over the past decade, (some include artifacts dating back to 1800 B.C.); a second display covers early explorers and colonization; and the third presents the island from 1900 through the 1960s. The exhibits are labeled in French and English. There are also changing exhibits of works by local artists. Hours: 9 A.M. to 1 P.M.; 3 to 7 P.M. Historic tours of St. Martin can be reserved through the museum (Tel./fax 29–22–84); they depart at 9 A.M. and return at 11 A.M. Cost is US $30.

MARIGOT The little French capital, even with its modern incursions, is definitely worth a stroll. For the most part the town has retained its character, with many Creole or West Indian–style houses and colonial buildings. Most now house chic little boutiques, perfume shops, restaurants, or the occasional sidewalk cafe where the croissants are as tasty as in Paris.

At the harbor, filled with fishing and ferry boats, there is an outdoor fruit and vegetable market along with crafts and other stalls on Wednesdays, Fridays, and Saturdays. A landfill project expanded the waterfront area with a pretty promenade and parking area; the main shopping streets run east-west from the harbor. One of the main streets, Rue de la République, is lined with Marigot's smartest shops, in balconied creole buildings trimmed with filigree and gingerbread, reminiscent of New Orleans.

The town's most delightful spot is the yacht-filled Port de Royale marina, which you pass on your way into town. It is lined with seafood restaurants and sidewalk cafes—the best people-watching spots in town—where you really do feel you are in St. Tropez. Marigot has a supermarket where you can buy French cheese, wine, and other picnic supplies.

SAINT-LOUIS FORT Built in 1776 on a strategic hilltop above Marigot harbor, the fort is St. Martin's largest colonial fortification and at one time had fifteen cannons. Under the guidance of the St. Martin Historic and Cultural Foundation, the Fort has been made more accessible and is being restored. Steps from the car park of the Sous-Prefecture lead up the hill; from here there are grand views south, across the island to Simpson Lagoon and the leeward coast, and north, across the sea to Anguilla. The best time for a visit is early morning or late afternoon.

PARADISE PEAK After Marigot en route to Grand Case, country roads on the east lead to the village of Colombier and to Paradise Peak, the island's highest mountaintop. There is a short trail at the top from which there are panoramic views. On the south side of the road, just before Colombier, is La Rhumerie, the island's leading restaurant for creole cuisine; the name the French have given to West Indian cooking with a French touch.

GRAND CASE Five miles north of Marigot is Grand Case, a small town with an international reputation as a gourmet haven. The road through town passes at least a dozen restaurants that could command your attention. The town is also something of an artists' colony. Having had fewer modern intrusions than Marigot, Grand Case retains the charm that once characterized the island. At the north end of town, a dirt road on the west leads into Grand Case Beach, most of which is occupied by the Grand Case Beach Club, an American-operated beachfront hotel.

FRENCH CUL DE SAC At the north end of Grand Case, the road turns east and cuts across the north tip of the island, the most mountainous part, to French Cul de Sac and the eastern side of the island fronting the Atlantic Ocean. A very hilly road continues to *Le Meridian L'Habitation,* on one of St. Martin's prettiest beaches. Designed as a group of West Indian–inspired houses, it is

French St. Martin's largest resort, with a marina, water sports, horseback riding, and a spa.

ORIENT BEACH The main eastbound route continues along the coast where French St. Martin has seen its greatest development in recent years, with several large "village-style" hotels overlooking Cul de Sac and Orient Beach, one of the island's most beautiful beaches. The eastern end of Orient Beach is a nudist beach.

A group of islands facing the coast—Flat Island, Ilet Pinel, Green Key, and Petite Clef—is protected as a *Reserve Sous-Marine Regionale* (Underwater Nature Reserve). It is the island's most popular area for snorkeling; several day-sailing excursions from Philipsburg and Marigot come here daily.

ORLEANS Continuing south along the main road, you will pass through the most rural part of the island. A side road takes you into the interior to Orleans, the village of local artist Roland Richardson, who is also one of St. Martin's leading historians and conservationists. He welcomes visitors to his home on Thursdays (Tel. 87–32–24).

THE BUTTERFLY FARM On the Galion Beach Road at the foot of Paradise Peak's eastern skirt (about a 30-minute drive from Philipsburg) is the island's newest attraction, *La Ferme des Papillons* (87–31–21). In a 1,000-square meter of tropical gardens fenced with wire mesh like an aviary, you can see hundreds of rare and exotic butterflies flitting about freely.

A guide leads visitors through the exhibit area, identifying species, pointing out courtship and mating displays, and relating interesting facts and stories about these beautiful creatures. Visitors also see the various stages of the butterflies' life cycle, from egg laying to caterpillars hatching, growing and forming their chrysalis. The farm's gardens were created with a montage of blossoms to provide nectar for the butterflies and special plants to feed the caterpillars.

Visitors may wander through the gardens on their own to photograph and film or sit in the shaded areas to take in the tranquil atmosphere, watch the butterflies, and listen to the soothing pan music heard quietly in the background.

You are welcomed by the English owners, William and Karin Slayter, general manager John Coward, and a staff who will answer questions on all aspects of the butterflies. They can also provide tips for photographers and information on butterfly gardening and the farming techniques. Hours: 9 A.M. to 5 P.M. Admission: adults US $9.95; children US $4.50. A shop sells unusual butterfly gifts and T-shirts.

OYSTER POND/DAWN BEACH Immediately after crossing back over the Dutch/French border the road takes a sharp turn to the east and after another mile, you come to a fork. The eastern road leads to Dawn Beach and Oyster Pond resorts, another built-up area. Here, Captain Oliver's, a waterfront hotel, has one of the island's most popular restaurants and bars.

The return to Philipsburg can be made via Naked Boy Hill Road, a winding road that runs south along Salt Pond and into Philipsburg. This drive can easily be taken in the reverse direction. One advantage of the reverse route, particularly if it is an afternoon drive, would be to time your return to the western side for late afternoon. You have any number of places to watch a St. Martin sunset: La Belle Creole, Long Beach, Mullet Bay. Don't miss it!

 **SHOPPING**

On this half-Dutch, half-French island, with its duty-free goods and smart boutiques, shopping is as much an attraction as the restaurants and sports. Here you can buy blue-and-white Delft as easily as Limoges, Gouda, and Brie, not to mention Japanese cameras, Swiss watches, British woolens, Chinese linens, Colombian emeralds, and a host of other quality products from around the world.

Discounts might range from 20 to 40 percent off U.S. prices, but as we have noted many times before in this book, the best way to know if you are getting a good buy and measure the savings over stateside prices is to come prepared with prices from home. Local shopkeepers are very competitive, so it pays to shop around.

Also, do not be confused by U.S. customs regulations. Goods purchased in St. Maarten/St. Martin do not carry the same liberal privileges as

in the U.S. Virgin Islands, but rather fall under the normal allowance of $600.

Within the mile-long thoroughfare of Frontstreet and the small lanes leading to Backstreet in Philipsburg, there are as many as 500 shops! Yet even the most ardent shoppers will probably find they can check out the best in either Philipsburg or Marigot in an hour or 2.

Marigot is a shopper's delight; its attractive boutiques have a French touch. Cruise ships that call at Philipsburg often have transportation to Marigot or make a stop there on island tours. The main shopping streets of Marigot are Rue de la République, Liberté, and the Port La Royale Plaza at the marina. Many of the high-quality Philipsburg stores have branches here.

In recent years two areas west of Philipsburg—Simpson Bay and Maho Bay—have become shopping meccas, with attractive shopping complexes housing high-quality stores. Both have parking areas, which make them convenient for those driving cars.

Maho Bay shops are centered around Maho Bay Beach Hotel. The shops are upscale, and many are branches of popular Philipsburg and Marigot stores. Particularly attractive is the Cinnamon Grove Plaza, where boutiques are located in low-rise buildings of colorful West Indian–style architecture, designed around an outdoor courtyard and walkway.

The Plaza del Lago, the shopping arcade of the Simpson Bay Yacht Club, has such attractive stores as the Dutch Delft Shop, which carries the full line of Delft ware; Island Time, featuring Calvin Klein fashions for men and women; and stores for leather goods and home decorating. Stop & Shop is an outdoor deli/cafe which is a good place for a light lunch when you are shopping in the area.

All stores named below are on Frontstreet in Philipsburg unless indicated otherwise. Some stores close for lunch from noon to 1 P.M. When cruise ships are in port on Sundays and holidays, a few shops open for a few hours. Store hours on the French side are Monday to Saturday, 9 A.M. to noon and 2 to 6 P.M.

ART AND ARTISTS: In recent years, Sint Maarten/St. Martin has become something of an artists' colony for expatriates who live here all or part of the year. Some can be visited in their studio/galleries. There are also a few local artists of merit, and several galleries carry paintings of artists from around the Caribbean. And remember, you do not have to pay U.S. customs duty on original works of art.

In St. Maarten, *Art Gallery Mahoo* (36 Cinnamon Grove) features a wide selection of artists living in the Caribbean. *Greenwith Galleries* (Front Street; Tel. 23842) specializes in fine art of the Caribbean and represents 36 artists living on St. Maarten or nearby islands. It stocks original paintings in oil, watercolor, and acrylic; prints; sculpture; and ceramics in a wide range of prices. One of Greenwith's leading artists—Lucia Trifan, a political refugee from Romania who sailed into St. Maarten in the mid-1980s—is also exhibited at the *Paris Seven Art Gallery* (Port Royale, Marigot).

Katrina Art Gallery (Front Street) belongs to the ubiquitous French painter Alexandre Minguet, who has a studio/gallery at Rambaud Hill, a mountainside village between Marigot and Grand Case on the road to Paradise Peak and whose posters are everywhere. Another French artist, Carol Hine, whose watercolors evoke the lushness of the tropics but in soft colors, has her own gallery in St. Martin. In the New Amsterdam Shopping Center on the outskirts of Philipsburg is an art gallery and supply shop operated by Katy Roos, a talented surrealist and abstract artist from Budapest.

Simpson Bay Art Gallery (Airport Road; Tel. 43464), situated in a lovely stone and wood "dollhouse," features the fanciful and sometimes whimsical works of Mounette Radot, a French artist who has lived on St. Maarten for many years. She also designs fabrics and prints on silk and shows the work of local artists. Open daily, including Sunday. *Mosera Fine Arts Gallery* (Speetjens Arcade; Tel./fax 20702) is the gallery of Mosera Henry, one of St. Maarten's most talented artists who is originally from St. Lucia and has worked and exhibited in Guadeloupe. In addition to his works, the works of other artists are exhibited and poetry readings and plays are held on occasion. Hours: Monday through Friday,

10 A.M. to 2 P.M.; 3 to 5 P.M.

Among the island's other artists are Ria Zonneveld, who creates unusual clay busts with a touch of whimsy; Ruby Bute and Cyrnic Griffith, who are the best-known painters of local scenes; Harriet Sharkey; and Roland Richardson (87–32–24), the island's best known artist, who has a home studio in Orleans. The French side is particularly active with over a dozen galleries. Most are located in Marigot or Grand Case; many show the works of French and other Europeans and Americans who live in St. Martin part of the year.

In Grand Case, members of an artist family from New York include Gloria Lynn, a painter of local scenes; husband Martin Lynn, a sculptor; and sons Robert and Peter, who are also painters, each with a style of his own. The Lynns have a gallery in their home on the main street of town.

On the main road at Orient is *The Potters* where you can watch master potters and their apprentices at work and buy their products. (And remember, you do not have to pay U.S. customs duty on original works of art.)

BOOKS/MAPS/POSTCARDS: In Philipsburg, the *Shipwreck Shop* carries books, magazines, maps, postcards, and stamps, in addition to crafts. Postcard-sized reproductions of paintings and prints by island artists are sold here.

CAMERAS/ELECTRONICS: *Boolchand's* has three stores in the downtown area where you will find most of the leading names in Japanese cameras and electronic equipment. Be sure to bring prices from home for comparison. The shops also carry linens, jewelry, and Bally and Adidas shoes.

CHINA/CRYSTAL: *Little Switzerland,* familiar to those who have visited the Virgin Islands, carries only the highest quality English bone china, French crystal, Swiss watches, Hummel figurines, and other gift items. You can even request a catalogue in advance by calling 800–524–2010.

CRAFTS: *Impressions* (Promenade Arcade) specializes in authentic native arts and crafts from the Caribbean, folklore, occult artifacts, and herbs and spices. One of the shop's best artists is Moro from Haiti who makes carved and painted wood pieces that are very original and distinctive.

Another unusual craft, bread and fruit baskets made from fired coconut shells, comes from Nevis. *Seabreeze* (Promenade Arcade and Plaza del Lago, Simpson Bay) carries postcards and handpainted T-shirts by Ruby Bute. The *Shipwreck Shop* also specializes in handcrafts from throughout the Caribbean.

If you are a devotee of Haitian art, a small stall (next to Lily Dolls) on the waterfront in Marigot is operated by the wife of a Haitian artist who makes brightly painted houses and whimsical tap-tap buses out of iron. She also stocks a variety of works by yet-to-be-discovered Haitian painters.

CLOTHING: *Liz Claiborne, Ralph Lauren,* and *Tommy Hilfiger* are the most familiar labels with their own stores. *Bye-Bye* has sportswear; *Beach Stuff* carries bathing suits and resortwear. *Batik Caribe* (Promenade Arcade) and *Dalila* have hand-dyed batiks on 100 percent cotton. The stores have fabrics as well as beachwear. Swimwear by Gottex can be found at *Lil' Shoppe* (San Marco Arcade, Philipsburg; Tel. 22177).

La Romana is one of the top fashion stores and carries Armani and the other priests of Italian high fashion. But make no mistake, these are designer clothes at designer prices, and the unfriendly sales staff will do little to make you want to part with your money. *Leda of Venice* is another Italian specialist with Missoni, Valentino, and Carrano exclusives. Gucci and Fendi have their own boutiques. The *Ted Lapidus* store (La Residence Bldg., rue General de Gaulle, Marigot) is the designer's only boutique in the Caribbean and is a replica of the one in Paris. *Genesis* (Marigot) is the outlet for Kenzo.

If you haven't yet been introduced to *Base* (Old Street 113; Marigot on the harbor), you should go take a look at this madcap designer team, whose clothes are made in Antigua. Youthful, brilliant in design, amusing and sophisticated, Base has fast become one of the most popular shops for contemporary designs in the Caribbean.

FOOD SPECIALTIES: Dutch cheese and chocolates, as well as liquor, liqueurs, and wines are available at *Emile's Place* (Wathey Square and Mullet Bay Shopping Center).

JEWELRY: *H. Stern* stores are known from New York to Rio to Paris for jewelry of original design, using top quality precious and semiprecious stones. And their merchandise comes with an international one-year exchange guarantee. If emeralds are your passion, *Colombian Emeralds* has the largest collection, and they are quick to remind you that unmounted emeralds can be brought home to the United States free of customs duty. Their merchandise also carries a guarantee honored by the company's Miami office. *Artistic* carries Mikimoto pearls.

For more modest shoppers, *Treasure Cove,* situated in a restored West Indian house, has a wide selection of gold jewelry and semiprecious stones.

LEATHER/LUGGAGE: *Gucci* is the most familiar name, but there are several other stores, such as *Maximo Florence,* which carries high quality Italian leather handbags and accessories.

LINENS: *New Amsterdam* (you'll recognize it by the brightly painted tulips on the facade) specializes in hand-embroidered linens, as well as a variety of quality gifts and jewelry. There is a great selection of men's and women's sportswear, bathing suits, and shoes on the second floor.

LIQUOR: *Caribbean Liquors and Tobacco* (Emmaplein on the north-south street at the east end of Frontstreet, Tel. 22140) has a full line of liquors and wines.

PERFUMES: *The Yellow House, Lipstick,* and *Penha* have among the largest selections of cosmetics and French perfumes on the Dutch side. The latter store also carries sportswear and fashion jewelry. In Marigot, *Beauty and Scents* (rue General de Gaulle) and *Lipstick* (Rue de la République and Port La Royale Marina) are leading stores.

WATCHES: *Oro de Sol Jewelers* carries the top names such as Piaget, Concord, and Corum; *Spritzer & Fuhrmann* (Grand Casino Way, Mullet Bay Resort) is one of the most famous jewelers of the Caribbean. The store provides after-sales service in the United States at its New York outlet at 5 East 57th Street.

Dining and Restaurants

The number and variety of good restaurants on this small island are astonishing. At last count, there were 132 on the Dutch side alone. Yet it is the French side, with its gourmet selections, that has won the island international recognition, particularly in the tiny village of Grand Case.

All those listed below in Philipsburg are located on Frontstreet unless otherwise indicated and are convenient to the pier for lunch or dinner. Expensive means $70 or more for two persons; very expensive means $100 or more.

St. Maarten

Antoine's (at the water's edge; Tel.22964) is a seaside terrace popular as a stop for lunch or a more elegant candlelight dinner from a classic French menu. Open daily. Expensive.

Cheri's Cafe (Maho Shopping Center; Tel. 53361) is a lively open-air cafe and bar and the "in" spot, with music and dancing every night from 8 P.M. to 12:30 A.M. Food is served from 11 A.M. to midnight; the varied menu has salads, sandwiches, fresh fish, steaks, and great hamburgers. Moderate.

Saratoga (Simpson Bay; Tel. 42421) is one of the island's newest restaurants, created by two Culinary Institute of America graduates who trained under Alice Waters, the famous California chef. It specializes in New American cuisine with California and Southwest influences and has a delightful terrace setting overlooking the bay. Dinner only. Expensive.

Spartaco's (Cole Bay; Tel. 45379) offers classic northern Italian cuisine in an enchanting grotto ambience. Its owner was the maitre d'hotel at La Samanna for many years. Black pasta with squid is a specialty. Expensive.

Turtle Pier Bar and Restaurant (Simpson Bay; Tel. 52230) has a delightful setting on the lagoon with its own boat dock and sun deck where you can enjoy sandwiches and snacks. You enter the restaurant through a tropical "nature preserve" with parrots and other birds, monkeys, turtles

and other fauna that surrounds it and hides it from the road. Happy hour daily from 5 to 7 P.M. is one of the most popular spots on the island and every Friday evening, there is live calypso or jazz entertainment. Moderate.

St. Martin

Alabama (Grand Case) (87–81–66) is a local favorite for French cuisine, despite its unlikely name, since one owner, Karin, is from Austria and the other, Pascal, from France. They serve fish and steak with wonderful sauces and great dessert at reasonable prices. Closed Mondays.

Auberge Gourmande (Grand Case; Tel. 87–73–37), the best value of the town's leading dozen, offers superb food by the former chef of *Le Tastevin* (across the street). The decor has a fresh new look. Closed Wednesday. Moderately expensive.

Captain Oliver's Restaurant and Marina (Oyster Pond; Tel. 87–30–00) has a delightful waterfront setting where you can enjoy French and continental cuisine along with its loyal local following. Moderate.

Cha Cha Cha (Grand Case; Tel. 87–72–32) is situated in a beautiful building that once housed the gendarmerie. You may dine either inside, selecting from a varied menu with moderate prices, or in the garden, where tapas are served. Each of the dozen or so tapa selections costs $2.75. There's also an outdoor bar where a Spanish combo and singer are often featured. Moderately expensive.

Le Poisson d'Or (Marigot, Tel. 87–50–33) serves haute cuisine for only 15 tables in a beautiful setting of an old stone warehouse. Very expensive. The owners also have two Marigot favorites overlooking the harbor—*Messalina*, which specializes in Italian cuisine, and *La Vie en Rose*. Moderately expensive.

Le Tastevin (Grand Case; Tel. 87–55–45) has a delightful setting at the water's edge, where you can enjoy excellent cuisine from a contemporary French menu by the same owner as Auberge Gourmande across the road. Expensive.

Mini Club (Marigot; Tel. 87–50–69) is an old-time rustic favorite, especially on Wednesday and Saturday evenings for the large buffet ($35). Moderate.

La Rhumerie (on the road to Colombier; Tel.

87–56–98), situated in a private house in a small village between Marigot and Grand Case, is the island's top restaurant for Creole cuisine. Its setting is enhanced by a jungle of flowers and tropical greenery. Expensive.

SPORTS IN PHILIPSBURG AND ENVIRONS

In most cases you should contact the hotel or sports operator in advance to make arrangements, particularly during the peak season when demand is likely to be high.

BEACHES/SWIMMING: Sint Maarten is famous for its beaches—over three dozen lovely white sand stretches and coves where you might easily spend the day. Some are busy with people, facilities, and concessioners; others are quiet and secluded. Some of the beaches on French St. Martin are nude or topless; those on Sint Maarten are not. If you take a taxi to one of the more secluded beaches, be sure to arrange with the taxi a specific time to return, and agree in advance on the price of the round-trip fare.

For the reader's convenience, the beaches are listed by their proximity to the pier in Philipsburg. A taxi to west-side beaches costs about $8 to $10; those to the east side about $15. If you go as far north as Orient Bay, expect to pay about $20.

Great Bay, a mile-long strand directly in town on Great Bay, is obviously the most convenient, but with so much port and downtown activity, it is no longer as attractive as it once was. The water is clear, calm, and generally clean.

Little Bay, west of town within walking distance from the pier, is a smaller beach with lovely water, but it might be crowded as there are several hotels on the beach with water-sports concessioners.

Simpson Bay, immediately south of the airport, and *Maho Bay,* immediately west of the airport, are both within short cab rides from Philipsburg. Both have large hotels with water-sports concessioners.

Farther west, *Cupecoy Beach* is less accessible and has sandstone cliffs as its backdrop. A new parking lot next to the Ocean Club has made it much easier to reach. The far end of the beach is used for bathing in the buff. No facilities.

Long Beach at the far western end of the south shore is one of the most beautiful beaches in the Caribbean. At its eastern head is the posh resort of *La Samanna.* Rounding the westernmost point are *Plum Bay* and *Rouge Beach,* two secluded beaches more easily reached by boat than by car. They are popular with local residents and tourists in the know, and the latter is excellent for snorkeling. No facilities. They are topless beaches.

Oyster Pond and *Dawn Beach* are on the east side of Sint Maarten. The beach itself is beautiful and protected by a reef that stretches from Oyster Pond south to Guana Point, where Atlantic waves crash against the rocky shore. The south end is popular for surfing.

Orient Bay on the northeast side of French St. Martin is a rugged, magnificent beach sheltered by coral reefs, with an ever-changing sea that is sometimes calm and sometimes good for body-surfing. Ilet Pinel, a tiny island off the northeast coast at Orient Bay, is a favorite of day-boating excursions for its pristine beaches and reefs for snorkeling.

Orient Bay offers good swimming and water sports, such as windsurfing, parasailing, and sailing. As you walk along the long stretch of beach you pass some good seaside restaurants. The Orient Beach Club at the south end is a nudist beach. (A friend reports that a very dignified older couple from Texas raved about the food and the interesting people they met on the "Nude Cruise" day-sail they took at Orient Beach, and on their next visit to St. Martin, they took it for a second time.)

BOATING: St. Maarten offers excursions on two types of boats: large catamarans, holding up to twenty-five or more passengers, which sail to St. Barts for the day where passengers have two to three hours for sight-seeing, lunch, or the beach; and small sailboats for six to ten passengers which sail to a secluded beach or deserted island for a swim, snorkel, and picnic. Some boats sail to Tintamarre, an island off the northeast coast that is popular for snorkeling; others go to the islands off Anguilla. Boats leave from Bobby's Marina and Great Bay Marina on the east side of Philipsburg about 9 or 9:30 A.M. and return about 5 or 5:30 P.M. or leave at 11 A.M. and return at 2

P.M. Prices range from $60 to $70 per person, depending on services offered.

El Tigre at Great Bay Marina offers a daily catamaran party cruise with lunch and swim to St. Barts, departing at 9:30 A.M. and returning at 5:30 P.M. $45. Picnic/snorkeling cruises, $50.

Lagoon Cruises & Watersports at Simpson Bay Lagoon and Mullet Bay (Tel. 42801 ext. 337) has a variety of boats and offers daily cruises that are slightly different from the others.

Bluebeard I and *Bluebeard II* (9 Palapa Center; Tel. 52898) sail from Marigot at 9 A.M. for a swim and snorkel along Anguilla's coast or to tiny atolls with pristine beaches surrounded by fabulous reefs. A similar catamaran excursion offered by Seahawk Cruises (Tel. 87–59–49) departs from Marigot harbor at 9:15 A.M. and returns at 5 P.M.

Since some boats are chartered by cruise lines for their passengers when their ships are in port, you should inquire in advance if the boat will be available to take a cruise on your own or with your own party.

DEEP-SEA FISHING: Charters with tackle, bait, sandwiches, and drinks cost approximately $375 to $450 for a half day, $700 to $900 for a full day, and are available from all major marinas. The season for dolphin, kingfish, and barracuda is December to April; tuna is fished year-round. From time to time, or when there are not enough people to make up a full charter, there are boats that will take people on an individual basis. Inquire at Bobby's Marina (Great Bay; Tel. 22366).

GOLF: *Mullet Bay Resort* (Box 909; Tel. 52801) has the island's only golf course. The green fees for non-guests are $110 for 18 holes and $70 for 9 holes, Monday through Friday, and $120 and $80 on Saturday and Sunday. Many cruise ships that call at St. Maarten have golf packages with the hotel; they are sold by the shore excursion office on board.

HIKING: STINAPA, the local chapter of the National Parks Foundation of the Netherlands Antilles, has guided hikes once a month for a fee of $3. They are led by STINAPA director and environmentalist Francis van der Hoeven, a former teacher who is engaged in a study of the island's environment. Visitors can join the hike by contacting the chapter at Box 426, Philipsburg; Tel. 24454.

HORSEBACK RIDING: For equestrians, there is probably no better way to enjoy St. Maarten than on horseback. *Bayside Riding Club* (Orient; 87–80–93) takes small groups accompanied by experienced riders on trail rides twice daily. Reservations must be made in advance.

On the north side of the island at Anse Marcel, *Caid and Isa* (Tel. 87–45–70) offers similar excursions of 2.5 hours into the green hills and along the beach in French St. Martin. The rides depart at 9 A.M. and 3 P.M. daily. *OK Corral* (Coralita Beach, Tel. 87–31–81) offers two-hour rides for $40.

JOGGING: The *Road Runners Club* meets every Wednesday at 5:30 P.M. and Sunday at 6:30 A.M. at Pelican Resort & Casino parking lot. Contact Malcolm Maidwell of Tri-Sports (Tel. 43462).

SNORKELING/SCUBA: If you have never been snorkeling, St. Maarten is a good place to start because there are reefs near shore in shallow water so clear that visibility to 75 feet is normal and to 150 feet is not unusual. It is also a good place to try your first scuba dive. Scuba operators offer a one-day resort course which begins in a hotel pool with the basics about equipment and handling yourself underwater. You are then accompanied by a certified diver at a reef in calm and fairly shallow water for the real thing.

Among those offering the introductory course are *Ocean Explorers Dive Center* (Simpson Bay; Tel. 45252), $50. Daily excursions for certified divers depart at 9 A.M. and 1 P.M. and cost $45 for a single tank; lessons are held at 1:30 P.M.; snorkeling trip is $25. *Leeward Island Excursions* at Plaza del Lago also offers shallow- and deepwater dive trips daily. On the French side, *Pole-Sub* (Port la Royale Marine; Tel. 87–94–27) is a PADI operation and offers snorkeling and dive excursions for beginners as well as certified divers.

For experienced divers, St. Maarten offers a

variety of reefs and wrecks. Her seascape is characterized by coral reefs set in descending series of gentle hills and valleys associated with many small offshore islands. There are thick reefs of soft coral, sea whips and sea fans in shallow water, and a rich display of colorful fish.

Just off the entrance to Great Bay harbor lies the British man-of-war the *HMS Prostellyte*, sunk in 1801. The hull of the wooden ship is gone, but divers can see coral-encrusted anchors, cannons, and other of the ship's metal fittings.

Off the northeast coast on the French side, *Ilet Pinel* offers shallow diving; *Green Key* is a barrier reef rich with sea life; *Flat Island*, also known as *Tintamarre*, has sheltered coves and a sunken tugboat. Since 1988, the area comprising Flat Island, Ilet Pinel, Green Key, and Petite Clef has been protected as a *Reserve Sous-Marine Regionale* (Underwater Nature Reserve). *Orient Watersports* (Orient Bay, 97150 St. Martin; Tel. 87–33–85 ext. 42) offers snorkeling trips for $30 to Green Key, which is half a mile off the beach at Club Orient.

SAILBOARDING: Available at almost all beachside resorts and costs about $20 per hour for the use of equipment. The *St. Martin Windsurfing Association* (Tel. 87–93–24) arranges races and other activities. The best sailboarding is at Orient Bay, where water-sports operators rent boards and offer lessons.

Nightlife

St. Maarten's small-scale nightlife has music varying from piano bars and discos to steel bands and calypso several nights a week at large resorts and some restaurants specializing in Caribbean cuisine. On the Dutch side, the Maho area is the center of the action; on the French side, the Port Royal Marina draws the crowd. The *Turtle Pier* on Simpson Bay is one of the island's most popular spots for happy hour, and on Friday evenings there is live calypso or jazz entertainment.

Most cruise ships do not stay in port after sunset, but if your ship remains for the evening, check a newspaper and the booklet *St. Maarten Holiday* distributed free at the Tourist Office and hotels, for current information. *Discover Magazine*, published annually in November, has a wealth of knowledge on the history and culture of the island.

Small as it may be, the Dutch side of the island has ten casinos—probably more per visitor than any island in the Caribbean. All are located in or connected with a hotel and open at 1 P.M. Those closest to the Philipsburg pier are on Frontstreet: *Rouge et Noir* at Seaview Hotel (there's a disco adjacent) and the *Coliseum Casino*, with a gallery of slot machines surrounded by an upstairs shopping arcade. The decor, complete with Venus and Cupid statues, is so outrageous it's camp.

Cultural Events and Festivals

The highlight of the year in St. Maarten is *Carnival*, celebrated in mid- to late April with a specially constructed Carnival Village in Philipsburg. Colorful booths offering West Indian foods, games, and souvenirs line its perimeter, and a large stage is set up in the center for contests and shows. A beauty contest, parades, calypso and steel band competitions, and jump-ups are part of the two-week affair which culminates in a big parade on April 30, the anniversary of the coronation of Queen Beatrix of the Netherlands. On the French side, Carnival is celebrated during the traditional pre-Lenten period.

Another affair that is fast becoming a tradition is the *St. Martin Food Festival*, an all-day event held in late May in French Cul de Sac. Organized by the Historical and Cultural Foundation, it involves all segments of the society, but particularly the older citizens who dress in traditional costumes and contribute their own special dishes. There are demonstrations of traditional food preparation, such as cassava bread which the Europeans learned from the Arawak Indians, along with steel band and traditional music.

SABA THE STORYBOOK ISLE

Saba, pronounced *Sayba*, located 28 miles southwest of St. Maarten, is the most curious island in the Caribbean. It is a cone-shaped volcanic peak rising straight up from the sea to 3,000 feet. It has no flat land and no beaches.

In the 1930s when Dutch engineers surveyed the island's steep mountainous terrain, they concluded the construction of a road would be impossible. Undeterred, a local resident, Lambertus Hassell, decided to prove them wrong, even though he had no technical training. He sent away for an engineering correspondence course, studied, organized the island's citizens, and in 1943 completed the first three-quarters of a mile of road up the mountain face to the capital, The Bottom.

Twenty years later, in 1963, the last stretch was finished. It drops 1,312 feet in 20 hairpin turns and ends at the island's airport, which was cut out of the mountainside, too. It looks something like the deck of an aircraft carrier at sea. Landing here in one of Winair's STOL aircraft will be an experience you will never forget.

But then, everything about Saba is unusual and unforgettable. The population of about 1,200 is made up mostly of the descendants of Scottish, Irish, and Dutch settlers. And what a hardy bunch they must have been! Before the airport and road were built, people and goods were hoisted up the side of rock cliffs. The alternative was to climb the steep mountain paths to reach the island's several villages.

HELL'S GATE AND WINDWARDSIDE Today, the hand-laid road that zigs and zags up the mountain from the airport leads first to Hell's Gate and continues to Windwardside, a lilliputian village of gingerbread houses with white picket fences. If it were not for the tropical gardens that surround them, you could more easily imagine yourself on the set for *Hansel and Gretel* than on a Caribbean island. One of the homes, a sea captain's house built in the mid-19th century, is *The Saba Museum*, furnished with antiques. Hours:

Monday to Friday, 10 A.M. to noon and 1 to 3:30 P.M. There is a small donation admission.

MOUNT SCENERY From Windwardside, a series of 1,064 steps through the misty rain forest rich in flora and fauna leads to the summit of 2,855-foot Mount Scenery—well named for the magnificent panoramas of the Caribbean and neighboring islands which are there to reward hikers. Most trekkers take a picnic lunch and make a day of the climb to enjoy the views and vegetation along the way. Those with less time and energy can hike to one of several other locations on trails developed by the Saba Conservation Foundation (Box 18, Fort Bay, Saba, N.A.; Tel. 63295). They will be rewarded with lovely views as well.

The *Captain's Quarters* is the oldest of the island's tiny inns and guesthouses and has a lovely hillside setting with a swimming pool and open-air bar/restaurant that's the most popular stop for lunch. Another is *The Brigadoon* (Tel. 62380), operated by a delightful young couple, Penny and Greg Johnson (she's a New Yorker married to a Sabian), who serve some of the best food this writer has eaten in the Caribbean. Theirs is a winning combination because they grow all their own vegetables and serve fish fresh from the sea. *Scott's Place* is another favorite, known for its home cooking.

SABA ARTISANS' FOUNDATION At the Saba Artisans' Foundation you can find needlework, silk-screened fabrics, and beachwear—island specialties. And if your trip is in July, you might be on hand for Saba's Carnival.

THE BOTTOM From Windwardside, the road descends to The Bottom, another doll-like village of white clapboard houses with red gabled roofs and neat little gardens. The former *Government Guesthouse*, one of the town's most historic buildings, is now *Cranston's Antique Inn*.

SABA MARINE PARK Saba's steep volcanic cliffs drop beneath the sea where they are encrusted with a fantastic variety of reefs and marine life. To protect this treasure, the Saba Marine Park was developed in the 1980s with the help of the Netherlands Antilles National Park Foundation and the World Wildlife Fund of the Netherlands, among others. The park is comprised of the entire shoreline and seabed from the high-water mark to a depth of 200 feet and two offshore seamounts. It has twenty-six self-guided underwater trails and areas designated for recreation.

The main dive areas are on the west coast. Ladder Bay to Torrens Point is an all-purpose recreational zone and includes Saba's only "beach," a stretch of pebble shore with shallow water. Torrens Point has shallow and well-protected water and is suitable for snorkelers and novice divers. Its south side is particularly popular with photographers for its variety of corals and fish. For experienced divers, the most popular area is a seamount with three pinnacles, known as Third Encounter, Twilight Zone, and Outer Limits, that rise dramatically from the depths and are covered with brightly colored sponges and sea fans.

The most frequented sites are at Tent Bay to the southwest where the wall drops to 80 feet and is covered with colorful tube sponges and black coral. The reef is a long, shallow ledge at 50 feet with overhangs where snorkelers and divers can see huge barrel sponges, barracudas, hundreds of coneys, french angelfish, and more.

The Saba Conservation Foundation is responsible for the park. A guidebook of the park is available. *Saba Deep* (Tel. 63347; fax 63397) and *Sea Saba* (Tel. 62246) are the island's two fully equipped dive operators with their own dive boats. Each offers several dive trips daily and arranges fishing excursions. The Saba Bank, three miles southwest of Saba, is a 32-mile region of shallow water where fishing is terrific.

SIGHT-SEEING Taxis with driver/guides are available for tours of the island at the airport, or for those who arrive by boat, at Fort Bay, the port on the southwest corner of the island. Guided nature tours of Mt. Scenery and other locations can be arranged through the Saba Tourist Office.

AIR AND FERRY SERVICE/AIR EXCURSIONS
From St. Maarten, morning and afternoon flights on Winair are available daily, making it possible to visit Saba on a day trip ($86 round-trip) on your own. *The Edge,* a high-speed ferry, offers excursions to Saba from St. Maarten. Inquire at Pelican Marina in St. Maarten (Simpson Bay; Tel. 42640). Winair and local travel agencies also offer a variety of day packages to Saba. It is preferable to make advance arrangements because the tours depart early from the airport; if you wait until your boat docks to make arrangements, you might not have enough time.

The air tour—including round-trip airfare and transfers at both ends, a sight-seeing tour, lunch at Captain's Quarters and use of its pool and facilities, and a souvenir shirt—is about $95. It departs on Winair at 8:45 A.M. and returns at 5:15 P.M. You can ask your travel agent to make the arrangements when you purchase your cruise, or your cruise director or shipboard tour office should be able to make arrangements through their local agent. Similar air tours are available to Anguilla and St. Barts.

Alternatively, you can take potluck and buy a plane ticket at the airport and, when you arrive in Saba, pick up a taxi for touring. Or you can hire a taxi or rent a car in Anguilla or St. Barts. In the winter season, when demand is often greater than supply, you must have confirmed round-trip air transportation in advance; otherwise you run the risk of being stranded and missing your boat!

TELEPHONE AREA CODE: To phone Saba from the United States, dial 011–599–4 plus the local number.

 INFORMATION:

In the United States: Saba Tourist Information Office, c/o Classic Communications International, 10242 Northwest 47th St., No. 31, Ft. Lauderdale, FL, 33351; Tel. (954) 741–2681; 800–722–2394; fax (954) 741–1243.

In Saba: Saba Tourist Office, Windwardside, Saba, N.A.; Tel. 62231.

ST. EUSTATIUS

A CRUEL TWIST OF FATE

Statia, as St. Eustatius is known, is 10 minutes by plane south of Saba. You may need all the imagination you can summon to believe it today, but this island of only 8 square miles was once the richest free port in the Americas with a population of 8,000 (it has 1,700 today), where everything from cotton to contraband from around the world was traded. In the first 200 years after Columbus discovered it, the island changed hands twenty-two times!

FORT ORANJE During the American Revolution, the neutral position of Holland, which had claimed the island in 1640, was suspect to the British because St. Eustatius was used as a transit point for arms and goods destined for the rebels. On November 16, 1776, the island's garrison at Fort Oranje saluted the *Andrew Doria* flying the American flag—the first foreign port to do so after the United States declared its independence. The gesture enraged the British, and according to local lore, the British Navy sacked the town and destroyed the harbor, after having first flown the Dutch flag long enough to lure 150 merchant ships into the harbor and confiscate their cargo. (The late Barbara Tuchman's book *The First Salute*, published in 1988, derives from this incident.)

Over the centuries, this saga has been greatly embellished; some versions have the British burning the town to the ground and destroying the harbor's breakwater, causing the grand houses and warehouses to tumble into the sea. However, these tales are not substantiated by fact. For example, Rodney, the famous admiral who commanded the British fleet in the West Indies at the time, is known to have used the building which now houses the museum as his headquarters, and his report to the crown does not reflect any great destruction of the town; there are drawings of the town made at a later date which indicate that it was more or less intact; and maps of the time and later drawings show that the breakwater was not even built until about 1828. The island did suffer major damage from hurricanes over the centuries, and one might conclude that the events have become intertwined in the telling.

What is known, however, is that the island never recovered its wealth and high living. By the end of the 18th century, trade had given way to sugar production as the main source of income, and at one time there were seventy-six plantations—on an island only 8 miles square! After slavery was abolished, however, sugar was no longer the

lucrative crop it had been, and this entrepôt, which had been a major center of the slave trade, lost its economic base. The population of 15,000 dwindled to 1,500—about what it is today.

Under President Franklin D. Roosevelt, the United States expressed its belated thanks to Statia for being the first to recognize the fledging nation, and the fort and other buildings dating from the 18th century were restored with U.S. help. Although one may wonder why, Statia-America Day is celebrated on November 16.

ORANJESTAD The little town of Oranjestad is divided into two parts. Upper Town, a pretty little community of tree-shaded, cobblestone streets lined with West Indian gingerbread-trimmed houses and flowering gardens, grew up around the old fort atop a 150-foot cliff overlooking the sea. Lower Town, the site of the old harbor, is the docking area today and to the north is the island's main beach. Only a few feet beneath the sea rests centuries-old debris that has led researchers to call Statia "an archaeologist's nightmare and a scuba diver's dream."

The two parts of town are connected by the cobblestone pedestrian walk and a paved road. This central area has been declared a historic zone and the houses and buildings have been preserved. A great deal of restoration work has already been completed, and more is being done as funds—both government and private—become available. A brochure with a map for a self-guided tour of the fort and surrounding historic buildings is available from the Tourist Office. Number signs beginning in Lower Town mark the route to the fort, the museum, and other important structures. The road skirts a small beach at Smoke Alley (so named, it is said, because of the traders' heavy tobacco smoke in the old days) and bends to the Upper Town.

ST. EUSTATIUS HISTORICAL FOUNDATION MUSEUM In a colonial house across from the old fort is the town's museum, where artifacts from Indian settlements dating from 500 B.C., as well as 17- and 18th-century artifacts found in excavations on the island and the underwater ruins of warehouses, wharfs, and shipwrecks, are on display. The building, known as the Doncher

House, was the governor's home at the time the British captured the island following the *Andrew Doria* incident and was used for government offices over the years. Earlier in this century it was a private house and was expanded. Today, you enter the museum through the newer part, where the historical displays are arranged chronologically. The older section of the house has been furnished with antiques and period pieces to represent the home of an affluent merchant of the eighteenth century. The lower level is devoted to pre-Columbian artifacts found on the island. Among the exhibits are a copy of Rodney's orders of surrender to Johannes de Graaf, who was the governor of the island, and de Graaf's reply; and a diagram of a slave ship showing the space for each slave, as for a piece of cargo: a man, 6' x 1'; a woman, 5' x 1.4'; a girl, 4.6' x 1'.

In 1991, Doncher House won an American Express Preservation Award that recognizes excellence in the protection and enhancement of the Caribbean's cultural and architectural heritage. Scholars and students from the College of William and Mary in Williamsburg, Virginia, have been coming almost annually to excavate here and elsewhere on St. Eustatius: The college-accredited course runs six weeks and attracts students from all over the Hemisphere.

A group of buildings next to the museum includes the Guesthouse, a former inn, which was recently renovated and reopened by the Dutch queen on Statia Day in November 1992. The building now houses government offices, the courts, and the Tourist Bureau. An outside garden cafe has a lovely view overlooking the historic fort and the Caribbean Sea. A craft center is also being installed.

On the west side of the museum in a small West Indian house is *The Park Place*, the tiny gallery of artist Peggy McReynolds, formerly of Brooklyn Heights, New York. On display are the artist's lovely and very distinctive ceramic pieces and the paintings of other artists who live part of the year on Statia and nearby islands. The gallery is open from 9 A.M. to noon, Monday to Saturday. It holds exhibits from time to time and offers seminars with visiting artists and students.

DUTCH REFORM CHURCH A lane south of the Guesthouse passes by several typical old West Indian houses with gingerbread trim and leads to the restored ruins of an 18th-century church and graveyard filled with old tombstones. There are three flights of very steep steps leading to the top of the belltower, from where you can enjoy a wonderful view south, across the island to the Quill, and north, along the Caribbean coast. A few blocks away are the ruins of a synagogue that is thought to have been the second or third in the Western hemisphere.

THE QUILL Seen distinctively in the island's silhouette is the Quill, the crater of an extinct volcano which dominates the south end of the island. A series of eight signposted trails has been developed, enabling you to hike up to and around the crater's rim, down into the cone, and around the outside of the cone at about mid-girth. Designed as a series of contingent trails, the hikes can take from one hour to a full day.

The most popular trail leads from town up the western slope of the crater to the rim in about an hour. It meets another trail which is a steep path down to the floor of the crater, passing through steamy thick foliage where trees, protected from winds and hurricanes, grow tall, and their trunks and branches are entwined with enormous elephant ears, other vines, and sometimes tiny orchids. The crater's interior is planted with bananas, but over the years it has been cultivated with coffee, cacao, and cinnamon trees, which now grow wild.

Another trail at the rim is a hike of several hours to the crater's highest point, Mazinga Peak (1,980 feet), often concealed by clouds. It passes from dry woods through rain forest to the eerie world of elfin woodland at the top.

DIVING HAVEN Scuba divers have a heyday exploring the ruins of the old houses and warehouses in the old harbor which have lain undisturbed for 200 years. Farther out, the sea bottom is littered with hundreds of shipwrecks, some dating back 300 years. Atop this jumble grow corals that attract a great variety of fish and marine life. It is the combination of coral reefs, marine life, and historic shipwrecks, all untouched by commercial development, that makes Statia extraordinary and so exciting to divers. Most diving is in 20 to 80 feet of crystal-clear water, which makes it accessible to snorkelers, too.

At present, thirty sites have been charted. Among the most popular, a site dubbed the Supermarket is located about a half-mile off the coast from Lower Town at a 60-foot depth. It has two shipwrecks less than 50 yards apart with patches of beautiful coral and colorful sponges growing over them. There are rare fish to be seen here, but the most intriguing is the flying gurnards. These fish, about 12 inches long, are black with white spots and iridescent blue pectoral wings, and they move through the water like hovering birds. *Dive Statia* (Box 158; Tel. 82435), the island's one dive operator, is PADI and NAUI certified and has its own boats, which make two dives daily, at 9:30 A.M. and 2 P.M. An introductory course is US $45; single dive for certified divers, US $40.

AIR SERVICE: St. Eustatius is a 10-minute flight south of Saba or 17 minutes from St. Maarten. Winair has five flights daily; round-trip airfare is $86. The airport is located mid-island, about 1.5 miles from town. A tour can be arranged with a taxi at the airport, and cars are available to rent. An island tour of about 3 hours costs $40 for up to four people.

TELEPHONE AREA CODE: To phone St. Eustatius from the U.S., dial 011–599–3 plus local number.

 **INFORMATION:**

In St. Eustatius: St. Eustatius Tourist Bureau, Fort Oranjestraat 3, Oranjestad, St. Eustatius, N.A.; Tel. 82209 or 82213. There are tourist information centers at the pier in Lower Town and at the airport.

 **ANGUILLA**

TRANQUILITY WRAPPED IN BLUE

Anguilla is a British colony which has the distinction of rebelling to *remain* a colony. Until its super-deluxe resorts were spread across the pages of slick travel and fashion magazines, Anguilla was the best-kept secret in the Caribbean. The small coral island 5 miles north of St. Martin is especially noted for its three dozen gleaming white sand beaches—which you can have practically to yourself—and the clear, blue-green waters which surround it.

Even with all the attention, the island's unspoiled quality remains. But then, the Anguillans are as unspoiled and appealing as their island. Until the tourism boom began, most were fishermen supplying the restaurants in St. Martin. The 16-mile-long island still has no golf courses or casinos; there are as many goats and sheep as people; and *The Valley,* the administrative center, is its one and only town.

Known to its original Arawak Indian inhabitants as Malliouhana, the island takes its name from the French word for eel, *anguille,* or the Spanish, *anguilla*—they were both here—because of its shape. In the past when it had only a few tiny hotels and guest houses, the tranquil island appealed to true beachcombers who cared little for social conveniences. Yachtsmen, too, have long been attracted to the spectacular waters around Anguilla, as have snorkelers and scuba divers from neighboring islands. Two large reefs with huge coral formations growing to the surface of the sea lie off the island's coast. The reefs and the gorgeous beaches are some of the reasons Anguilla is such a popular destination for day-sailing excursions from St. Martin.

NATIONAL TRUST In 1990, concerned about its phenomenal growth, Anguilla created a National Trust with a permanent staff to oversee the preservation of the island's cultural and national heritage and direct the volunteer organizations which were already active. These include the Archaeological and Historical Society, which organized the 1979 survey—the first scientific survey of the island—that unearthed 33 sites of antiquity; the Horticultural Society, which organizes periodic clean-up and beautification drives; the Marine Heritage Society, the driving force behind the creation of marine parks; and various cultural groups working to preserve Anguilla's folklore, music, and other traditions.

In 1990, the Anguillan government took its first

major step to improve the management of its marine resources. Six wrecks resting near Anguilla's shores were towed to sea and sunk to create artificial reefs, which have become nurseries for fish and new sites for divers. Their removal also eliminated a potential boating and marine hazard in Road Bay, the island's main harbor.

More recently, Anguilla has taken measures to institute its new Marine Park, developing permanent moorings for boats to protect the reefs from anchors and implementing a ban on the importation or use of such equipment as jet skis.

ANGUILLA MUSEUM Another ongoing project is a national museum to be situated in the Old Customs House in The Valley; the museum will house some of the artifacts that have been uncovered in the excavation of the pre-Columbian settlements identified on the island, along with other historical exhibits. The building has been undergoing renovation for five years. Funds for the project have been supplied in part by the Canadian International Development Agency (CIDA), the Anguillan government, and the Anguilla Social Security Board, but there is not enough to finish the job.

SIGHT-SEEING There are no "must-see" attractions in Anguilla. The pleasures here are the island's nature and the people's naturalness. Both are best discovered by renting a car and driving the length of the island, stopping for a swim here, lunch there, and a look where any side road leads you. You are likely to get lost several times, but not to worry. The local people are approachable, very friendly, and hospitable. Simply by your asking, they will be happy to direct you back to the main road.

One of the super-deluxe hotels which has received so much attention is *Malliouhana*, situated on the island's northwest coast overlooking two spectacular beaches. It is Mediterranean in design with graceful interiors by Larry Peabody, known for his stylish decor in other Caribbean resorts. The indulgent cuisine is directed by chefs of La Bonne Auberge on the French Riviera. The resort has three terraced swimming pools, tennis courts, and water sports; but if you want to do any more than look, you will need to make arrangements in advance and be prepared to spend $100 for lunch. The other posh resort is *Cap Juluca*, a sybaritic fantasy in Moorish design on one of the

most magnificent powdery white sand beaches in the Caribbean. Its terrace restaurant, *Eclipse,* overlooking the sea with St. Martin in the distance, has an imaginative selection of light cuisine with a French flair designed for warm Caribbean days.

For such a small island, Anguilla has an extraordinary number of good restaurants; fifty at last count.

Overlooking Sandy Ground, the main port and yacht harbor at the west end of the island, is the *Riviera,* a delightful terrace restaurant and bar in a West Indian–style cottage at the water's edge. Owner Didier Van is as French as his name, and so is his food. The *soupe de poisson* is delicious. It's an ideal place to have a long, lazy lunch, maybe with a swim between courses.

Hibernia (Island Harbour; Tel. 497–4290) is not only the best restaurant on Anguilla but easily one of the best in the Caribbean. The French owner is a serious chef who smokes his own fish and knows how to combine creole flavors with fine French cuisine. He has also spent time in the Orient and gives some of his dishes a dash of Asia. All of it can be enjoyed on a terrace overlooking the Caribbean and the tiny settlement of Island Harbour, the main fishing center on the eastern end of Anguilla.

Koal Keel (Tel. 497–2930), in one of the oldest houses on the island, should be at the top of your list for its setting as much as its cuisine. The eclectic menu includes some French, some Caribbean, and some of the chef's creations. The ancient stone-lined cistern of the house is now a wine and brandy cellar where tastings are held. Other parts of the house house a rum and cigar store and a bakery.

One of Anguilla's most popular outings is a day on Scilly Cay, a minuscule, beach-encircled island facing Island Harbour. Only a few minutes away by boat the island is an ideal place to swim, cool out, and feast on lobster.

WATERSPORTS The island now has two dive operators, both of which are PADI training facilities. *The Dive Shop,* on the beach at Sandy Ground (Tel. 497–2020), is open daily and has a full range of water-sports equipment and a regularly scheduled picnic excursion by sail or motorboat several days a week. Similar trips can be arranged on request. A one-tank dive is $35; two-tank, $60.

The second operator, *Anguillan Divers Ltd.,* is at Island Harbour on the east end of the island.

SHOPPING Anguilla is slowly acquiring shops, particularly in hotels, and there are several artists and sculptors on the island.

TRANSPORTATION American Airlines/American Eagle has daily service from San Juan to Anguilla, and Winair makes the five-minute trip from St. Maarten to Anguilla several times daily for a round-trip fare of $50. Ferries from St. Martin take 15 minutes and cost $10 one-way plus US $2 port tax. They leave from Marigot harbor almost every 30 minutes during the day. The ferry dock in Anguilla is located on the south side of the island, where you can hire a taxi for an island tour or rent a car (essential for touring the island because there is no regular bus service).

Connors Car Rental (Tel. 497–2433) has reasonable rates and is conveniently located in the center of the island; it has new small vans as well as cars. A standard small car costs about $35 per day. They will deliver the car upon request and will arrange your Anguilla driver's license (US $6.25) on the spot. Driving is on the LEFT.

TELEPHONE AREA CODE: 809; 264 (the latter number is the new area code but a specific start date has not been designated)

INFORMATION:

In the United States:
   Anguilla Tourist Information Office,
   c/o Medhurst & Associates,
   1208 Washington Dr., Centerport, NY 11721;
   Tel. 516–425–0900; fax: 516–425–0903.
In Anguilla:
   Anguilla Tourist Board, P.O. Box 1388, The
   Valley, Anguilla, B.W.I.; Tel. 800–553–4939;
   497–2759; fax 497–2710.
Anguilla Life, a quarterly published by veteran
   Caribbean writer Claire Devener, is a
   valuable source. Contact East Caribbean
   Publishing Co., Box 109, Anguilla, B.W.I.;
   Tel. 497–3080.

ST. BARTS

THE DARLING OF THE JET SET

Serendipitous is one way St. Barts, or St. Barthélemy, has been described. Simply gorgeous is another. Located 10 minutes by air from St. Maarten, it's a long way from Mother France or the surrogate cousins of the French West Indies to which it belongs.

St. Barts's air terminal has car rental facilities, a restaurant, and shops, but none of them make the landing of Winair's STOL planes any easier. They put down on a runway between two mountain peaks that catches a crosswind just as the plane is about to hit the ground. If you still have your heart when your feet hit the ground, it will be stolen by the sight of this tiny Eden—8 square miles of green mountains and three dozen gorgeous beaches.

You can join the celebrities and others on the trail of the Rockefellers and Rothschilds who discovered this delightful hideaway two decades ago, but all of you are Johnny-come-latelies. First there were the Arawaks and the Caribs. Then came Christopher Columbus who named it for his brother's patron saint. He was followed by French colonists from St. Kitts, the Knights of Malta, French settlers from Normandy and Brittany, the British, Frenchmen again, the Swedes, and finally the French for a fourth and last time.

In addition to being the only Caribbean island the Swedes ever possessed, St. Barts has a number of features that make it different, if not unique, among the islands of the Caribbean. Although pirates liked the island for its deeply indented bays, where they could hide, and merchant ships used the sheltered harbors for protection during hurricanes, the little island was too dry and rocky to be coveted for agriculture. It attracted only small farmers who had to scratch for a living; it was never converted to a sugar economy like most other Caribbean islands. Slaves were never imported, so the plantation society typical of the colonial Caribbean, and the melange of European, African, and Asian cultures which it spawned, never developed.

Rather, St. Barts is a minuscule remnant of ancient France, with fair-skinned farmers and blue-eyed fishermen who speak a dialect passed down by their 17th-century ancestors from Normandy and Brittany—a dialect even Frenchmen cannot understand. In their neat little villages surrounded by meadows marked with ancient stone fences, the older women still wear the starched bonnets seen in the French provinces of their ancestors and spend their days weaving distinctive straw hats and baskets with designs that resemble old lace.

Against this background of a conservative, closely knit society with Old World traditions, St. Barts has become a modern playground of worldly French sophistication for the rich and famous from both sides of the Atlantic. The tourist boom is slowly changing the island's character, but the paradox remains. While the Frenchmen from Normandy left the most enduring mark, the Swedes also left their legacy: a bit of architecture, some street signs in Swedish, a cemetery, and, of course, Gustavia, the capital, which was named for their monarch, King Gustav III. Today the small port is visited regularly by ships on Eastern Caribbean cruises during the winter season; and it is a popular destination for catamaran cruises that sail daily from Philipsburg.

St. Barts offers the best that money can buy—and you will need plenty of it. Around the port, you will find fashionable boutiques with famous French designer clothes and accessories, attractive restaurants with some of the best cuisine in the Caribbean, and bistros and outdoor cafes with an unmistakable French ambience.

A WALK AROUND GUSTAVIA

The delightful little town of Gustavia, with its lilliputian port, has a pretty setting: yachts bob in the harbor and red-roofed houses climb the surrounding green hills. Only 3 blocks deep, the town has no must-see historic sites and can be explored on foot in an hour, even if you stop now and then to check out the boutiques and enjoy a refreshment at a sidewalk cafe that lends a French air to the setting.

The Mairie de St. Barth, or Town Hall, and some restaurants are housed in old buildings dating from the 18th century. St. Barts Municipal Museum (Musée Municipal de St. Barthelemy) on the south side of the harbor depicts the island's history through photographs, documents, costumes, and antiques. It is open Monday to Thursday from 8 A.M. to noon and 1:30 to 5:30 P.M. and Friday afternoon and Saturday morning. Admission is 10Ff.

Old fortifications are located on both sides of the harbor. On the south side of town, a 5-minute walk past Fort Karl leads to Petite Anse de Galet, also known as Shell Beach, where there is good shelling. On the north, Fort Gustav offers a pretty view of the harbor.

A steep road by the landmark clock tower on the east side of town leads 1 mile to Morne Lurin with a fabulous panoramic view that stretches from Gustavia on the south to the airport and St. Jean Bay on the north. Since the road up is very steep, you might prefer to take a taxi there and walk back. The steep, rough road continues over the hill to Anse du Gouverneur, a cove with one of the island's most beautiful, secluded beaches, bracketed by jagged cliffs.

A DRIVE AROUND THE ISLAND

The quickest way to get into the St. Barts mode is to rent a jeep and wander about, following your whim. You might stop at a beach for a swim or in a village to sip an aperitif; ramble down a county lane or turn up a hillside road for a view. St. Barts is only about 10 square miles and can easily be toured by car in half a day. The narrow roads, which were yesterday's donkey tracks, twist and turn their way to secluded beaches through tiny hillside villages and along rocky shores.

West of Gustavia the road forks northeast to the airport and northwest to Corossol, the most traditional of the island's tiny fishing villages, where the old Norman dialect can be heard. Some elderly women here still wear long blue-and-white checked dresses and the *calèche*, a stiff-brimmed bonnet derived from a Breton style of the 17th century. The women are very shy and disappear at the first sight of strangers who might be trying to take their pictures. Put away your camera and take an interest in the straw hats they want to sell you, and you will find the reception quite different. The straw they use is handwoven from the fan-shaped fronds of latania palms. It is the finest, most supple straw in the Caribbean. Corossol also has the Inter Oceans Museum, a private collection of shells, open daily from 10 A.M. to 4 P.M. Admission: 20Ff.

Farther along, the road winds its way to Anse des Flamands, where you will see another of the island's beautiful coves with a wide, half-mile stretch of knee-deep, blinding white sand fringed by latania palms and framed by weather-worn rock washed by intensely turquoise seas. There are several resorts here.

Anse de Colombier on the northwest end of the island is a pretty cove accessible only by foot or boat. En route to Colombier, the road passes the boutique and workshop of St. Barts's best-known fabric designer, Jean-Yves Froment, who specializes in beachwear and casual attire. At the

end of the main road a path leads down the wooded slopes to the secluded beach. The cove is a favorite destination for day-charter boats from Gustavia; sunsets here are splendid. From April through August, sea turtles come to lay their eggs.

Northeast from Gustavia, the hilly, twisting road passes the airport and skirts St. Jean Bay on its way to the eastern end of the island. The bay, rimmed by white sand beaches and bathed by calm, reef-protected turquoise waters, is divided about mid-point by a small promontory topped by tiny Eden Rock, the island's first hotel. It has recently been renovated by its new owners. You'll want to stop here for a meal or drink and enjoy the great view across St. Barts.

St. Jean Bay is the hub of St. Barts's resort and water sports activity. Its quiet waters are ideal for snorkelers. The hill behind Eden Rock has wonderful views of the bay. Just beyond Eden Rock, a road inland crosses the island to Grande Saline, where a footpath leads to Anse de Grande Saline, a secluded cove with a half-mile beach of alabaster sand and beautiful clear waters. Although topless bathing is the norm—this is as

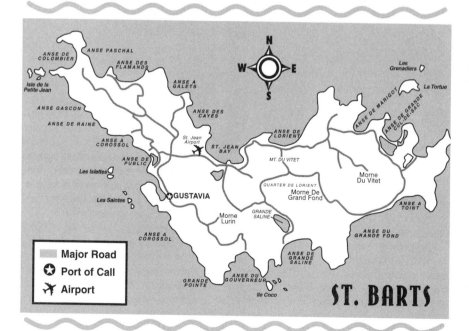

much France as the Riviera is—nude bathing is prohibited.

At the eastern end of St. Jean Bay lies Lorient, a palm-fringed beach used by local families but seldom noticed by tourists. Its long rolling waves make it popular with surfers and windsurfers. Jutting out to sea between Lorient Bay and Marigot Bay on the east are the jagged cliffs of Milou and Mangin, where Atlantic waves crash against rock. Pointe Milou is a fashionable residential area of elegant homes and resorts.

Rising behind Lorient are the island's highest peaks—898-foot Morne de Grand Fond on the west and 938-foot Morne du Vitet on the east. One road passes between the mountains to the south coast; another loops around Morne du Vitet via Grand Cul de Sac; and a third winds up Morne du Vitet. All three pass centuries-old rural landscapes of farmhouses, grazing cattle, and patchwork fields outlined by low stone fences on the green hillsides overlooking the coast.

Grand Cul de Sac, a large bay on the northeast, is another resort center where shallow, reef-protected waters are ideal for novice windsurfers and snorkelers. From Grand Cul de Sac, a less-traveled road passes over the mountain to Anse de Toiny through wild landscapes that remind people of the Normandy coast.

SHOPPING St. Barts is a duty-free port where French perfumes and famous brand-name products are sold for about 20 percent less than prices in the U.S. Occasionally you might find great savings, particularly if you hit a sale, but as we have indicated previously, St. Barts is not a place for bargains. As in most of France, stores close for lunch.

For French china, crystal, and silver, *Carat* (Quai de la République) has Baccarat, Lalique, Christofle, and other famous high-quality brands. Boutiques of Hermes, Gucci, and other famous designers are found in Gustavia, St. Jean, and the La Savane Commercial Center opposite the airport. Fine French vintages stored in temperature-controlled rooms are sold at *La Cave du Port Franc,* along with paintings and antique objets d'art. All the well-known French labels are available, but more unusual are the items made locally from natural products. Some perfumes, colognes, lotions,

and suntan oils are sold under the trademark "M," and others under the mark "P."

The women of Corossol and Colombier are famous for their handwoven straw products—baskets, handbags, and broadbrimmed hats for men and women—whose delicate, supple quality is superior to others found in the Caribbean. Other locally crafted products include sandals and shell jewelry sold in Gustavia. Fashionable mementos such as T-shirts with the logo "St. Barth/D'Abord" are available at *Parfums de France,* and a canvas tote bag stamped "Loulou's Marine" is sold at the well-known nautical supply shop in Gustavia.

Le 'Ti Marche in Gustavia is a little market devoted to the arts and artisans of the island. Set up in stalls on rue du Roi Oscar II near the City Hall, the market is open every morning except Sunday. In addition to the exquisite straw work by the women of Corossol, you will find a line of fragrant body oils, toilet waters, and rum punches under the label *Belou's "P",* created and bottled by hand by Helene Muntal and Franck Garcia, a duo from Paris who now live on St. Barts. Other products include jewelry by Annelisa Gee who also sells it at her boutique, *Made in St. Barth,* in St. Jean's; and paintings by artists living in St. Barts.

DINING By some accounts St. Barts is the gastronomic capital of the Caribbean. Renowned chefs from France frequently visit the island, and some teach classes during the winter season. Young chefs who have trained in France's best restaurants have been coming to work on St. Barts over the past decade and have brought with them high standards and creativity. By combining local ingredients, Gallic traditions, and modern trends, they have created a new French Caribbean cuisine. Most restaurants are small, but each has something special, either in food, setting, or atmosphere.

About half of the sixty or so restaurants are only open for dinner; most close on Sunday and some open only during the winter season. Three courses without wine will cost about $30 per person for a modest meal, $60 or more per person for an expensive one. Most restaurants accept major credit cards, but some do not; inquire in advance.

In Gustavia on or near the harbor, the dining room of the Hotel Carl Gustaf, has a stunning view from high above the harbor; some established favorites open for lunch are the moderately priced *L'Escale;* and *La Marine,* with picnic-style tables and benches on a waterside terrace. One of the most popular restaurants for creole cuisine—and moderately priced by St. Barts' standards—is *New Born* (en route to Manapany Hotel at Anse des Cayes; Tel. 27–67–07). Here, authentic creole dishes such as *accras* (codfish fritters), *boudin* (sausage), *blaff* (poached fish), and *calalou* are served a stone's throw from the beach in a simple pleasant setting.

The open porch at *Bar de l'Oubli,* across the street from Loulou's Marine, is a great people-watching spot reminiscent of Saint-Tropez. *Le Select,* diagonally across from Loulou's, is a long-standing local hangout for snacks, drinks, and people-watching. *Eddy's Ghetto* (off rue du General de Gaulle) is the second generation of Le Select.

NIGHTLIFE St. Barts has no movie houses or casinos. Leisurely dining is the main pastime. Young locals and visitors gather at such popular hangouts as Le Select or Bar de l'Oubli or at a disco or places featuring jazz. *St. Barth Magazine,* a free lively French/English publication, is the best source of information on current attractions.

SPORTS St. Barts has good facilities for water sports. In most cases you should contact the hotel or sports operator in advance to make arrangements, particularly during the peak season. There are about a dozen tennis courts, but there is no golf course. St. Barts is scalloped with more than two dozen pearly beaches bathed by calm turquoise waters, and few are ever crowded, even in peak season. All beaches are public and free.

Anse du Gouveneur, near the port, and Anse de Grande Saline, also on the south coast, are the most secluded beaches; St. Jean on the north coast and Grand Cul de Sac on the northeast are the most developed ones and have hotels, restaurants, and water sports. Anse des Flamands on the northwest, a fabulous crest of deep white sand fringed with lantana palms, has hotels and restaurants.

St. Barts's popularity for yachting is due in part to its location midway between Antigua and Virgin Gorda, two major sailing centers. Annually, the island hosts the colorful Route du Rose, a regatta that leaves St. Tropez in early November and arrives in Gustavia in early December. It is accompanied by a Salon du Rose—a week of festivities sponsored by the producers of Provence rose wine—and ends with a regatta around the island.

St. Barts's pretty landscapes and country roads with light traffic make walking, hiking, and horseback riding popular pastimes. The island's small size means that almost any location is within easy reach, although the hilly terrain and hot sun can cause distances to be deceiving. *Ranch des Flamands* (Tel. 27–80–72) at Anse des Flamands has excursions daily.

St. Barts is almost completely surrounded by shallow-water reefs, better suited for snorkeling than diving and often within swimming distance of shore. At St. Jean Bay, the most accessible reefs with a great variety of fish lie northwest of Eden Rock. The best dive locations are on the west coast, within easy reach of Gustavia, at about 50- to 60-foot depths.

Dive operators run several boat trips daily in the winter season; groups are limited to six people. *La Marine Service* (Tel. 27–70–34) offers PADI and French certification. Dive trips cost about 250 Ff per person, gear included.

ENTERTAINMENT The annual St. Barts Music Festival in late January/early February features classical music and dance programs, including artists from the U.S. and Europe. Concerts are held in the church of Lorient; dance programs are staged at the wharf in Gustavia. The Festival of St. Barthelemy (August 24), a colorful event in Gustavia, celebrates the feast day of the island's patron saint with a regatta, fireworks, a public ball, and much wining and dining. The Feast of St. Louis (August 25) is celebrated in Corossol with a fishing festival, election of king and queen, a windsurfing regatta, and a public ball.

LOCAL TRANSPORTATION Cars can be rented for about $60 per day with unlimited mileage. Gas is extra and costs about $3.25 per gallon. Advance reservations are necessary, especially during the winter season. Most car rental firms are located at the airport. Most but not all take major credit cards. Employees at *Soleil Caraibe* (Tel. 27–67–18) are nice people to deal with.

Driving is on the right side of the road. The speed limit is 28 mph, which suits the roads and terrain but not the French drivers from the mainland. As veterans of the death-defying roads of France, they will not be denied the challenge of St. Barts's roller-coaster, corkscrew roads and race around St. Barts as though they were practicing for the Grand Prix.

TELEPHONE AREA CODE: 590. To call St. Barts from the U.S., dial 011–590 + the St. Barts number. To call the U.S. from St. Barts, dial 19, wait for a second dial tone, then dial 1 + area code + the number. To call Dutch St. Maarten from St. Barts, dial 3 + the St. Maarten number.

AIR SERVICE: There are no direct flights between the U.S. or Canada and St. Barts. The main gateway is St. Maarten, where frequent flights are available via Winair at $58 round-trip, and from French St. Martin via Air St. Barts or Air St. Thomas. The flight takes 10 minutes. St. Barts's small airport and short landing strip can handle nothing larger than twenty-seat STOL aircraft. It is not equipped for night landing.

INFORMATION:

In the United States:
French West Indies Tourist Board,
444 Madison Ave., New York, NY 10022;
Tel. 212–757–1125.
Tourists may also dial "France on Call,"
1–900–990–0040, for 95 cents per minute.

In Canada:
French Government Tourist Board,
1918 Ave. McGill College No. 490,
Montreal, P.Q. H34 2W9;
Tel. 514–288–4264; fax 514–844–8901;
and 30 Patrick St., Suite 700,
Toronto, Ont., M5T 3A3;
Tel. 416–593–6427; fax 416–979–7587.

In St. Barts:
Office du Tourisme,
Quai General de Gaulle, Gustavia;
Tel. 27–87–27; fax 27–74–47.
Mailing address: St. Barts Tourist Office,
B.P. 113, Gustavia, 97098 Cedex, St.
Barthelemy, F.W.I.
Hours: 8:30 A.M. to 6 P.M., Monday to Friday and until noon on Saturday.

Appendix

CHART OF CRUISE SHIPS SAILING THE NORTHERN/NORTHEASTERN CARIBBEAN

*E*very effort has been made to ensure the accuracy of the information regarding the ships' ports of call and prices, but keep in mind that cruise lines often change itineraries for a variety of reasons. Before you make plans, you should obtain the most current information from the cruise line or your travel agent.

Prices are for ``cruise only'' unless indicated otherwise and are based on per person, double occupancy rates, ranging from the least expensive cabin in low season to the best cabin in high season. Rates for holiday and special cruises and owners, president's and other top suites are not included (unless all the ship's accommodations are suites).

Itinerary codes are given in parentheses: (A) alternating itineraries (not all ports are included in every cruise, nor are they necessarily visited in the order listed); (B) same itinerary except for holidays; (C) same itinerary year-round or during season or months indicated.

Ship (Cruise Line)	Ports of Call*	Price Range	Duration/ Season
Amazing Grace (Windjammer Barefoot Cruises)	Bahamas or Trinidad to Freeport, Grenada, Antigua, St. Lucia, St. Vincent, Dominica. (A)	$1,075 to $2,900	13 days June–Oct/ Nov.–May
Carnival Destiny (Carnival Cruise Line)	Miami to San Juan, St. Croix, and St. Thomas; or Playa del Carmen, Cozumel, Grand Cayman, Ocho Rios. (C)	$1,309 to $2,059*	7 days Year-round
Century (Celebrity Cruises)	Ft. Lauderdale to San Juan, St. Thomas, St. Maarten, Nassau; or, Playa del Carmen/Calica, Grand Cayman, Cozumel, Key West. (C)	$975 to $1,125*	7 days Year-round
Club Med 1 & 2 (Club Med)	Martinique to St. Lucia, Tobago Cays, Bequia, Mayreau, Barbados, Carriacou; or Los Roques, Blanquilla, Carriacou, Barbados, Mayreau; or Les Saintes, St. Barts, Virgin Gorda, Jost Van Dyke, St. Thomas, St. Kitts; or St. Lucia, Union, Grenada, Blanquilla, Trinidad, Mayreau; or Les Saintes, St. Martin, Tintamarre, San Juan, Virgin Gorda, St. Kitts. (C)	$2,128 to $3,384 w/air	7 days Nov. '97- March '98
CostaRomantica (Costa Cruises)	Ft. Lauderdale to San Juan, St. Thomas/St. John, Serena Cay/Casa de Campo, Nassau; or Key West, Playadel Carmen/Cozumel, Ocho Rios, Grand Cayman.	$849 to $2,449	7 days Dec.–Apr.

Ship (Cruise Line)	Ports of Call*	Price Range	Duration/ Season
CostaVictoria (Costa)	Ft. Lauderdale to San Juan, St. Thomas/St. John, Serena Cay/Casa de Campo, Nassau; or to Key West, Playa del Carmen, Cozumel, Ocho Rios, Grand Cayman.	$849 to $2,449	7 days Nov.–April
Disney Magic (Disney Cruise Line)	Port Canaveral to Nassau, Gorda Cay. Three to four days with Disney World Packages. (C)	$769–$2,289 $1,229–$3,439	3–4 days 7 days Year-round
Disney Wonder	tba	tba	tba
Dolphin IV	Port Canaveral to Freeport. (C)	$129–$229	2 days Year-round
Ecstasy (Carnival)	Miami to Nassau; or to Key West, Playa del Carmen, and Cozumel. (C)	$559–$1,239	3, 4 days Year-round
Enchantment of the Seas (Royal Caribbean International)	Miami to St. Maarten, St. Thomas/St. John, CocoCay; or Key West, Playa del Carmen/ Cozumel, Ocho Rios, Grand Cayman. (B)	$1,199 to $2,299*	7 days Year-round
Fantasy (Carnival)	Port Canaveral to Nassau; or Nassau and Freeport. (C)	$559–$1,239	3, 4 days Year-round
Fascination (Carnival)	San Juan to St. Thomas, St. Maarten, Dominica, Barbados, and Martinique. (C)	$1,109 to $2,009*	7 days Year-round
Flying Cloud (Windjammer)	Tortola to Salt Island, Virgin Gorda, Beef Island, GreenCay, Sandy Cay, Norman Island, Deadman's Bay, Cooper Island, Jost Van Dyke, Peter Island. (A)	$650 to $975	6 days June-Oct./ Nov.-May
Galaxy (Celebrity)	San Juan to Catalina Island (Dominican Republic), Barbados, Martinique, Antigua, St. Thomas. (C)	$1,075 to $1,175*	7 days Winter
Grand Princess (Princess)	Ft. Lauderdale to (San Juan, St. Thomas, St. Maarten) Princess Cays, Montego Bay, Grand Cayman, Playa del Carmen/Cozumel. (B)	$1,349–$3,339 Winter	7 days
Grandeur of the Seas (Royal Caribbean)	Miami to Labadee, San Juan, St. Thomas, CocoCay. (B)	$1,199 to $2,299*	7 days Year-round
Horizon (Celebrity)	Ft. Lauderdale to St. Maarten, St. Lucia, Barbados, Antigua, St. Thomas; or, to Curacao, La Guaira, Grenada, Barbados, Martinique, St. Thomas. (C)	$1,294 to $1,504*	10, 11 days Winter

Ship (Cruise Line)	Ports of Call*	Price Range	Duration/ Season
Inspiration (Carnival)	San Juan to St. Thomas, Guadeloupe, Grenada, St. Lucia and Santo Domingo.(C)	$1,109 to $2,009*	7 days Year-round
IslandBreeze (Dolphin)	Santo Domingo to Barbados, St. Lucia, Guadeloupe, St. Maarten, St. Thomas; or to Curacao, Caracas,Grenada, Martinique and St. Croix. (C)	$895 to $2,095*	7 days Dec.-Apr.
Leeward	Miami to Nassau and Great Stirrup Cay-Private Island; or Key West and Great Stirrup Cay-Private Island; or to Playa del Carmen, Cozumel, and Key West. (C)	$609–$1,299 with air	3, 4 days Year-round
Mayan Prince (American Canadian Caribbean Line)	Virgin Islands; or St. Maarten to Antigua; or Antigua to Grenada; or Trinidad/Orinoco/ Tobago; or Venezuela Islands, Bonaire, Curaçao; or Turks & Caicos to Nassau. (A)	$1,405 to $2,499	12 days Winter
Monarch of the Seas	San Juan to St. Thomas, Martinique, Barbados, Antigua, St. Maarten. (B) to $2,599* (Royal Caribbean)	$1,099	7 days Year-round
Nantucket Clipper (Clipper)	St. Thomas to St. John, Jost Van Dyke, Tortola, Virgin Gorda, Salt and Norman islands in U.S. and British Virgin Islands. (A)	$1,950 to $3,050	7 nights Winter
Nordic Empress (Royal Caribbean)	San Juan to St. Thomas and St. Maarten, St. Croix. (C)	$499 to $1,399*	3, 4 days Sept–March
Nordic Express (Royal Caribbean)	Port Canaveral to Nassau and CocoCay. (B)	$699–$2,399 with air	3, 4 days Summer
Norway (Norwegian Cruise Line)	Miami to St. Maarten, St. John/St. Thomas, Great Stirrup Cay; or, occasional cruises to Ochos Rios, Grand Cayman, Playa del Carmen/ Cozumel,Great Stirrup Cay. (C)	$499 to $3,549**	7 days Winter
Norwegian Majesty (NCL)	Miami to Playa del Carmen, Cozumel; or Key West, Nassau, Royal Isle. (C)	$369–$2,099	3–7 days Winter, Spring
Norwegian Sea (NCL)	San Juan to Santo Domingo, Barbados, Dominica, Antigua, St. Thomas; or Santo Domingo, St. Lucia, St. Kitts, St. Maarten, St. Thomas. (B)	$549 to $2,499	7 days

Ship (Cruise Line)	Ports of Call*	Price Range	Duration/ Season
Norwegian Wind (NCL)	San Juan to Barbados, St. Lucia, St. Barts, or Tortola optional ferry to Virgin Gorda), St. Thomas. (A)	$699 to $2,799*	7 days to Dec. 1997
Ryndam (Holland America Line)	Ft. Lauderdale to St. Kitts, Martinique, Trinidad, Roseau/Cabrits (Dominica), St. Thomas, Half MoonCay (Bahamas); or, St. Maarten, Castries/ Soufriere (St. Lucia), Barbados, Basse-Terre/ Pointe-a-Pitre (Guadeloupe), St. John/St. Thomas, Nassau; or, Nassau, St. Thomas, St. Maarten, Castries/Soufriere,Barbados, Half Moon Cay. (C)	$2,048 to $3,808	10 days Oct.-April
Seabreeze (Dolphin)	Miami to Nassau, San Juan, St. Thomas/St. John; or Playa del Carmen/Cozumel, Montego Bay, Grand Cayman. (C)	$795 to $1,745*	7 days Year-round
Seabourn Pride (Seabourn Cruise Line)	Ft. Lauderdale to St. John, St. Barts, St. Thomas, St. Martin, Virgin Gorda. (B) Ft. Lauderdale to St. John, St. Barts, St. Thomas, Virgin Gorda, St. Martin. (B)	$1,995 to $7,600+ $2,990 to $9,780	5, 10 days Nov.–Dec. '97 5, 10 days Nov.–Dec. '98
Sea Goddess I (Cunard)	St. Thomas to St. Barts and Jost Van Dyke; or, St. Barts, St. Martin and Virgin Gorda. (C) St. Thomas to St. John, St. Martin, St. Barts, Antigua, Virgin Gorda, Jost Van Dyke	$1,900 to $3,500 $4,700 to $7,100	3, 4 days November 7 days Nov.–March
Sensation (Carnival)	San Juan to St. Thomas, St. Maarten. (C)	$1,109 to $2,009 *	7 days Year-round
Silver Cloud (Silversea Cruise Line)	Nassau to Grand Cayman, Aruba, Guadeloupe, Iles des Saintes, Virgin Gorda, and Ft. Lauderdale or Barbados to Antiqua, Virgin Gorda, and Ft. Lauderdale. (A)	$2,645–$8,395 Fall	6–10 days
Sovereign of the Seas (Royal Caribbean)	Miami to Nassau, CocoBay. (C)	$599–$2,149 with air	3–7 days Year-round
Splendour of the Seas (Royal Caribbean)	Miami to Playa del Carmen/Cozumel, Grand Cayman, Ocho Rios, St. Thomas, San Juan, Labadee. Or, Key West, Curacao, Aruba, Ocho Rios, Grand Cayman, Playa del Carmen/Cozumel. (B)	$1,899 to $3,399*	10,11 days Nov.–Apr.

Ship (Cruise Line)	Ports of Call*	Price Range	Duration/ Season
Star/Ship Oceanic (Premier Cruise Line)	Port Canaveral to Nassau, Lucaya. (C)	$699–$1,789 with three- to four-day Disney package	3,4 days Year-round
Star Clipper (Star Clippers)	Barbados Carriacou, Grenada, Union Island, St. Vincent, St. Lucia; or Martinique, Dominica, St. Lucia, Tobago Cays, Bequia. (C)	$1,095 to $2,595	7 days Nov.–Jan.
Statendam (HAL)	Ft. Lauderdale to Curacao, Bonaire, Grenada, Roseau/Cabrits (Dominica), St. John/St. Thomas, Nassau; or, St. Kitts, Martinique, Trinidad, Roseau/Cabrits, St. Thomas, Half Moon Cay, Bahamas. (C)	$2,048 to $3,808	10 days Nov.–March
Veendam (HAL)	Ft. Lauderdale to St. Kitts, St. John/St. Thomas, Nassau (1997)/ Half Moon Cay (1998), Bahamas; or, Key West, Playa del Carmen/Cozumel, Ocho Rios, Grand Cayman. (C)	$1,248 to $2,568	7 days Year-round
Westerdam (HAL)	1997-Ft. Lauderdale to St. Maarten, St. John/ St. Thomas, Nassau 1998-Nassau, San Juan, St. John/St. Thomas, Half Moon Cay, Bahamas. (C)	$1,248 to $2,178	7 days Year-round
Wind Spirit (Windstar)	St. Thomas, Saba, St. Martin, Iles des Saintes, St. Barts, Virgin Gorda, Jost Van Dyke. Or, to Iles des Saintes, Vieux Fort (St. Lucia), Bonaire, Aruba, Curacao, Santo Domingo, St. Croix, St. Barts. (C)	$2,495 to $3,395	5, 7, 14 days Nov.– Dec. '97
	St. Thomas, St. John, St. Martin, St. Barts, Tortola, Virgin Gorda, Jost Van Dyke. (C)	$3,495 to $3,895	7 days Jan.–Mar./ Nov.–Dec. '98

* Prices include port charges
+10th Anniversary Cruise Only Tariffs (1997 only)

Index

A

Abaco Islands, 72
Activities. *See individual activity.*
Air travel, free, 13
Air/sea packages, 13–14
Alcaldia (City Hall) (Ponce), 145
Alcazar (Santo Domingo), 95
Alice Town (Bimini Islands), 73
All Saints Church (Charlotte Amalie), 163
Altos de Chavon (Santo Domingo), 108
Amber Museum (Puerto Plata), 109
American Canadian Caribbean Line, 21
Andros Island (Out Islands), 73
Anegada (B.V.I.), 191
Anguilla
  car rental, 218
  location of, 216
Anguilla Museum, 216
Antigua, location of, 4
Antiques. *See* Art/Antiques.
Aquarium (Santo Domingo), 101
Architecture, general notes on, 6
Ardastra Gardens and Zoo (Nassau), 57
Arecibo Observatory (Puerto Rico), 142
Arsenal (San Juan), 125
Art Alive Festival (St. Thomas), 168
Art/Antiques
  in Casa de Campo, 107, 108
  in Haiti, 82
  in Christiansted, 182
  in Nassau, 61
  in San Juan, 131
  in Santo Domingo, 102–3
  in St. Maarten/St. Martin, 205
  in St. Thomas, 168
Arts Festival of San Sebastian (Puerto Rico), 138
Aruba, location of, 4
Atlantis Resort and Casino, 60

B

Bacardi Rum Distillery (San Juan), 122
Bahamas, The

entertainment in, 65
fast facts, 46
festivals/celebrations, 65
general location of, 44
at a glance, 43
history, 44
map, 42
ports of call in, x
Bahamas Historical Society Museum (Nassau), 54
Balcony House (Nassau), 57
Ballaja Barrio (San Juan), 127
Barbados, location of, 4
Barbuda, location of, 4
Baseball
  in San Juan, 137
  in Santo Domingo, 106
Baths, The (Virgin Gorda), 190
Beaches/Swimming
  in Cap Haitien, 85
  in Freeport, 68
  general notes on, 7
  in Nassau, 63
  in Puerto Plata, 111
  in San Juan, 135
  in Santo Domingo, 106
  in St. Croix, 180
  in St. Maarten/St. Martin, 209
  in St. Thomas, 170
Benitez Fishing Charters (San Juan), 135
Beracha Veshalom Vegmiluth Hasidim
  Synagogue (Charlotte Amalie), 163
Berry Islands (Out Islands), 73
Bimini Islands (Out Islands), 73
Biking in Nassau, 63
  in Freeport, 68
  in Santo Domingo, 106
  on St. Croix, 180, 185
Birdwatching, in Freeport, 70
Bluebeard's Tower (Charlotte Amalie), 165
Boating/Sailing
  in Freeport, 70
  general notes on, 67
  in Nassau, 63

ABOUT THE AUTHOR

Kay Showker is a veteran writer, photographer, and lecturer on travel. Her assignments have taken her to more than a hundred countries—in the Caribbean and around the world. She is the author of *The 100 Best Resorts of the Caribbean* (Globe Pequot Press, 1995); *Caribbean Ports of Call, A Guide for Today's Cruise Passengers: Western Region and Central America from the Bahamas to the Panama Canal* (Globe Pequot Press, 1996); *Eastern Caribbean Ports of Call* (Globe Pequot Press, 1991), which was honored in the Benjamin Franklin Awards of 1991; *The Outdoor Traveler's Guide to the Caribbean* (Stewart, Tabori & Chang, 1989), which was named first-runner-up as "Travel Guidebook of the Year" in 1990; two Fodor guides—*Egypt* and *Jordan and the Holy Land;* and *The Unofficial Guide to Cruises* (Macmillan, 1997), which won the Society of American Writers Foundation's 1996 Lowell Thomas award for "Best Travel Guidebook of the Year."

Ms. Showker's articles appear in *Travel and Leisure, Travel Holiday, National Geographic Traveler, Caribbean Travel and Life, Cruise Views and Leisure Travel,* and other magazines and newspapers across the country, and she has appeared as a travel expert on network and cable television. She served as senior editor of *Travel Weekly,* the industry's major trade publication, with which she was associated for 11 years.

A native of Kingsport, Tennessee, Ms. Showker received a Master's degree in international affairs from the School of Advanced International Studies of Johns Hopkins University in Washington, D.C. In 1996, she was the first travel journalist to receive the *Sucrier d'Or* Award given by the government of Martinique. She was the first recipient of the Caribbean Tourism Association Award for excellence in journalism; she was named "Travel Writer of the Year" by the Bahamas Hotel Association in 1990; and she received the 1989 *Marcia Vickery Wallace Memorial Award for Travel Journalism* given by the Jamaica Tourist Board in conjunction with the Caribbean Tourism Organization. She has served as a consultant to government and private organizations on travel and tourism.